Exploring the
JDS LINUX
DESKTOP

Other Linux resources from O'Reilly

Related titles

Linux in a Nutshell
Linux Network
   Administrator's Guide
Running Linux
Linux Server Hacks

Linux Security Cookbook™
Linux Web Server CD
   Bookshelf
Learning the bash Shell

Linux Books Resource Center

linux.oreilly.com is a complete catalog of O'Reilly's books on Linux and Unix and related technologies, including sample chapters and code examples.

ONLamp.com is the premier site for the open source web platform: Linux, Apache, MySQL and either Perl, Python, or PHP.

Conferences

O'Reilly brings diverse innovators together to nurture the ideas that spark revolutionary industries. We specialize in documenting the latest tools and systems, translating the innovator's knowledge into useful skills for those in the trenches. Visit *conferences.oreilly.com* for our upcoming events.

The O'Reilly Network Safari® Bookshelf™ (*safari.oreilly.com*) is the premier online reference library for programmers and IT professionals. Search across thousands of electronic books simultaneously and zero in on the information you need in seconds. Read the books on your Bookshelf from cover to cover or simply flip to the page you need. You can even cut and paste code and download chapters for offline viewing. Try it today for free.

Exploring the
JDS LINUX DESKTOP

Tom Adelstein and Sam Hiser

O'REILLY®

Beijing · Cambridge · Farnham · Köln · Paris · Sebastopol · Taipei · Tokyo

Exploring the JDS Linux Desktop

by Tom Adelstein and Sam Hiser

Published by O'Reilly Media, Inc., 1005 Gravenstein Highway North, Sebastopol, CA 95472.

O'Reilly books may be purchased for educational, business, or sales promotional use. Online editions are also available for most titles (*safari.oreilly.com*). For more information, contact our corporate/institutional sales department: (800) 998-9938 or *corporate@oreilly.com*.

Editor:	Andy Oram
Production Editor:	Matt Hutchinson
Production Services:	GEX, Inc.
Cover Designer:	Emma Colby
Interior Designer:	David Futato

Printing History:

September 2004:	First Edition.

RepKover™ This book uses RepKover,™ a durable and flexible lay-flat binding.

ISBN: 0-596-00752-3

[M]

Table of Contents

Foreword

Students, software developers, and computer experts from around the world have used Linux and open source software for years. Finally, Tom Adelstein and Sam Hiser have written a book to help the rest of us get started with Linux and open source applications. In *Exploring the JDS Linux Desktop*, Adelstein and Hiser take you on a step-by-step tour of Sun Microsystems' Java Desktop System. Beginning with instructions for installing JDS using the included CD-ROM, through the use of all the JDS tools and applications, they share their insight, tips for new Linux users, and enough shortcuts that even experienced Linux users are likely to learn new tricks.

As any Linux user will tell you, there isn't anything particularly challenging about using individual Linux applications. Anyone who can use a web browser can use Mozilla. If you have ever used a word processor or spreadsheet, you should feel right at home with Sun's Star Office suite of applications. Previously, what made Linux difficult was that to get started, you usually needed to download, install, and configure the operating system and your favorite applications from a dozen or more different web sites or CDs. It's no wonder that getting the correct versions of the correct Linux and open source applications to work together was regarded by many as a black art best left to computer geeks.

As Adelstein and Hiser show, if you are technically savvy enough to update your anti-virus software or install a new version of your favorite PC music player, you can quickly be up and running Linux with the JDS CD included with this book. To Linux newbies, the biggest surprise might be that with JDS's built-in security you won't need any additional anti-virus software, while at the same time you can use JDS to play all your favorite CDs just like on your old system. The JDS email client can be configured to connect to almost any standard email server, and StarOffice does a great job reading and writing competing productivity tool file formats.

If you're not quite sure you're ready to jump head-first into the Java Desktop System, don't fear. The included demo CD installs a full copy of JDS into your PC's memory, typically in under 10 minutes, without touching the current operating system installed on your hard drive. In less time than the average laptop battery lasts, you can use *Exploring the JDS Linux Desktop* to learn Linux basics, ranging from housekeeping chores such as networking setup to JDS's key productivity tools: email, web browsing, word processing, instant messaging, and others. When you're ready to return to your original OS, simply reboot your computer, and you're back to where you were before you installed the JDS demo CD.

Thanks to the near infinite flexibility of Linux software, JDS's desktop, menus, icons, file folders, and other user interface features are so intuitively familiar to other window system users that you might not notice the next time you reboot your desktop that it has returned to its disk-resident operating system. At the same time, this should give readers confidence to experiment with JDS at their own pace, working through the chapters knowing they can return to their regular OS to update their anti-virus software whenever they need to. Soon, however, I expect many readers will be visiting their favorite online store to purchase a full copy of Java Desktop System, installing a permanent copy and saying goodbye forever to the trials and tribulations of proprietary operating systems.

So don't just read this book—try out the included CD as you read each chapter, and start enjoying the benefits of Linux and open source that Adelstein, Hiser, and a growing number of mainstream PC users running Java Desktop System are experiencing every day.

—Marc Hamilton
Director of Client Services
Sun Microsystems Inc.

Preface

Sun Microsystems' Java™ Desktop System (JDS) offers a comfortable and exciting way to use your personal computer. People who use a PC at work and/or at home will find JDS pleasantly surprising. Sun has produced an intuitive desktop that allows you not only to use what you already know about a computer but also to do more than you thought you could.

This book focuses on the basics of using the JDS and its applications, so you can begin using JDS immediately. We help you quickly set up your operating system, connect to the Internet, and work with many kinds of documents. We offer you a way to learn while you're getting things done on your computer.

You will like JDS. Although other user-friendly operating systems for personal computers exist, they do not combine the polish, the wealth of software, the security, and the support from a trusted company that you get with JDS.

The authors of this book specialize in Linux and do consulting in the open source software space. From a business perspective, JDS provides a promising way forward. When people ask us to help them find opportunities in their organizations to use open source software, we look for ways to reduce costs, better use their resources, and improve security. The Java Desktop offers individuals and organizations a safe, manageable, and secure desktop operating system at a very competitive price.

Look and Feel

In creating JDS, Sun took the well known and robust GNU/Linux system as a starting point, but they added a higher level of quality to put JDS on par with Windows XP and Mac OS X when it comes to usability, for a fraction of the cost. Sun added sophisticated, but unobtrusive, components to the desktop to provide a consistent look and feel across all desktop software. Unlike desktops from other distributions, Sun has added enhancements so that every folder, application, and interface provides the same quality of presentation.

Aside from adding to the visual appeal of the desktop, Sun's improvements increase the utility of software applications on JDS. One of the programs included allows you to work with photographs and other graphic images in the same way as a professional does. Similarly, Sun's word processor and spreadsheet programs provide equivalent functionality to the best Microsoft Office programs.

Audience

We wrote this book for people who want to use and to learn JDS quickly. We aim to provide you with an immediate understanding of the computer, while you become familiar with the simplest ways to get things done. You will learn to navigate the desktop and Internet, and to use applications such as the StarWriter word processor.

Whether you have just begun using personal computers or you're a veteran, you will find this book helpful, as it contains plenty of examples and information on how to make the most of a desktop computer environment. Regardless of your sophistication with computers, there's plenty of material between these covers for you to learn.

You will also discover that this book works as a reference guide. At times we encounter tasks that we rarely use in everyday life. You may do something once on the JDS system and then forget about it. You may want to keep this book handy so that you can quickly find how to do those things which you only use occasionally.

This book contains things many people find central to their computing experience at work and at play. Yet the system is so powerful that people could study it for years. Our intention is to help new, everyday users become highly productive using JDS. We're not trying to develop Unix system administrators, as there are already many books available for that purpose. However, many system administrators can find much useful information here.

Conventions Used in This Book

This book uses some typographic conventions that can help you navigate through the text easily. When you see certain kinds of typefaces, you'll know they have special meanings:

Italic
> Used to show arguments and variables that should be replaced with user-supplied values. Italic is also used to indicate filenames and directories and to highlight comments in examples.

`Constant Width`
> Used to show the contents of files or the output from commands.

Constant Width Bold

Used in examples to show commands or other text that should be typed literally by the user.

Constant Width Italic

Used in examples to show text that should be replaced with user-supplied values.

 This icon signifies a tip, suggestion, or general note.

 This icon indicates a warning or caution.

Using Code Examples

This book is here to help you get your job done. In general, you may use the code in this book in your programs and documentation. You do not need to contact us for permission unless you're reproducing a significant portion of the code. For example, writing a program that uses several chunks of code from this book does not require permission. Selling or distributing a CD-ROM of examples from O'Reilly books *does* require permission. Answering a question by citing this book and quoting example code does not require permission. Incorporating a significant amount of example code from this book into your product's documentation *does* require permission.

We appreciate, but do not require, attribution. An attribution usually includes the title, author, publisher, and ISBN. For example: *Exploring the JDS Linux Desktop*, by Tom Adelstein and Sam Hiser. Copyright 2004 O'Reilly Media, Inc., 0-596-00752-3.

If you feel your use of code examples falls outside fair use or the permission given above, feel free to contact us at *permissions@oreilly.com*.

We'd Like to Hear from You

We have tested and verified all the information in this book to the best of our abilities, but you may find that features have changed (or even that we have made mistakes!). Please let us know about any errors you find, as well as your suggestions for future editions, by writing:

O'Reilly Media, Inc.
1005 Gravenstein Highway North
Sebastopol, CA 95472
(800) 998-9938 (in the United States or Canada)

(707) 829-0515 (international or local)
(707) 829-0104 (fax)

We have a web page for this book, where we list errata, examples, and any additional information. You can access this page at:

http://www.oreily.com/catalog/jds/

To comment or ask technical questions about this book, send email to:

bookquestions@oreilly.com

For more information about books, conferences, resource centers, and the O'Reilly Network, see the O'Reilly web site at:

http://www.oreilly.com

Acknowledgments

We realize the production of a book like JDS requires the cooperative efforts of many people. We wonder how we could have completed this work without our editor, Andy Oram. From inception to completion, Andy demonstrated how important great editing is to the success of any book. He operated much like a producer, director, casting department, and fight manager. In all our years of writing, we have never experienced a more committed person. Thank you, Andy!

Yvonne Adelstein, Tom's wife, helped us from the start by taking the point of view of the many nontechnical users who will experience JDS. In progressing from a computer newbie to a capable Linux user over the course of this project, Yvonne provided valuable insights, as well as hands-on editing, to help us better address the needs of readers coming fresh to Linux and to keep us from straying too far into technical jargon.

The chapters on StarOffice are animated by the dedication of the developers, marketers and users of OpenOffice.org around the world, including the Sun team in Europe.

Several reviewers, some from O'Reilly, and some working elsewhere, dedicated themselves to the success of this book. In particular, we want to thank Bruce Bell, Keith Burgess, Brian Goodyear, Nigel Horne, Rick Rezinas, and Andreas Strid.

CHAPTER 1

Introducing the JDS Linux Desktop

Welcome to Sun's Java™ Desktop System. JDS helps you unleash the power of Linux without much of a learning curve. You get the convenience of a familiar and friendly desktop screen along with the secure, stable, and extensible Linux operating system.

In this chapter, you become familiar with the JDS desktop and quickly learn how to be productive. In later chapters, you will discover many useful and exciting features of Linux and Sun's productivity tools.

JDS combines many advances in personal computer technology. Sun engineers blended those advances into a progressive and secure system. While you enjoy email, web browsing, and editing documents, you can stop worrying about email viruses. From the ground up, Sun built JDS with security in mind.

As you begin to use JDS, you can sense the power and stability of Linux under the hood. But you do not really have to deal with the engine. You just see a user-friendly and attractive desktop that helps you surf the Internet, send email, keep track of your activities, look at your family pictures, watch videos, listen to music, and use your word processor. You can still create and read PDF files and work with graphics in the same way as you do with Photoshop. You can also use your flatbed scanner to send faxes and copy documents the way you have in the past. You can continue utilizing Instant Messaging and chat.

Sun Microsystems has created the first viable alternative to a Microsoft desktop in 15 years. They offer you the opportunity to use the same computer hardware with which you're already acquainted. If you've been running Windows 98 and don't want to spring the cash for an expensive new computer and the latest Windows upgrade, you can get a feature-full and secure operating system in JDS. JDS works with the newest hardware, so you can continue to use your flat screen monitor, your DVD drive, and your digital camera. When you balance the checkbook, you'll notice that, instead of spending $1,200 on software upgrades alone, you'll spend only around $100 for everything that you're likely to need.

If you want to use Windows sometimes, you have several options. Chapter 9 shows you how to run Windows applications or the entire Windows operating system together with JDS. You can also set up your computer to offer you a choice when you power it on: you can work on JDS for a while and then reboot into Windows.

JDS runs very fast. As you go about your familiar emailing and document editing, you will notice an overall performance increase on your existing hardware.

Sun conceived JDS as a solution that enables you to work at home or at the office. Even with the low cost, when you start up, you will find more applications loaded on your system than you get on a Microsoft system. You'll also notice that you have the tools on the system that you need for programming, for running a web server, or for trying out powerful Internet services.

So What Do You Get?

Good question! JDS comes with software applications that differ, but function as well or better, than those distributed by Microsoft. Let's do a fast recap:

- JDS provides an intuitive user interface that enables you to locate documents, access menus, launch applications, and personalize your work environment. JDS comes with a set of development tools and utilities. The desktop has a unified look and feel.

- JDS includes a personal information-management tool that combines email, calendaring, scheduling, contact management, and task lists. This personal organizer works much like a Day-Timer. But it also has workgroup capabilities and can synchronize and manage information, using the included connector to the Sun ONE Calendar and Messaging servers.

- JDS is compatible with many PDAs (personal digital assistants), as well, and offers several tools for keeping your information up to date.

- JDS has an Instant Messaging client that supports the Sun ONE Instant Messaging server and other instant messaging clients such as AOL Instant Messenger and Yahoo.

- Sun has taken the flexible Mozilla browser and bumped up its capabilities in JDS, adding commercial plug-ins, network security services, and personal security management. You can use the Mozilla web browser suite to communicate with people over the Internet, participate in discussion groups, and create web pages, in addition to surfing the Web.

- In addition to replacing the Windows operating system, you now have an alternative to Microsoft Office. The JDS comes with the full-function office productivity suite, StarOffice 7.

StarOffice 7 provides you with applications for word processing, developing spreadsheets, making presentations, creating graphics, editing photos, publishing to the Web, and connecting to relational databases.

StarOffice 7 gives you the same features you've found in Microsoft Office. You'll also find that you can save and open your documents in Microsoft formats such as Word, Excel, and PowerPoint. You will find StarOffice to be both user-friendly and compatible with other software.

- JDS provides multimedia applications such as CD and media players, sound recording, a movie player called Totem, Real Networks media player, and Macromedia Shockwave Flash. JDS comes with CD-burning software and supports XCDROAST, one of the better CD/DVD-burning applications.

- JDS comes with the Java Runtime Environment (JRE) for the Java Programming Language. This allows applications to work in JDS, as well as other operating systems, without having to rewrite the software for each one.

Table 1-1 summarizes the features and benefits of JDS.

Table 1-1. Key features and benefits of JDS

Feature	Benefits
Simple, complete, and open	• Integrated desktop environment
	• Simplified user interface, with familiar desktop themes and file manager views
	• Runs on a broad range of desktop and laptop computers
	• Full support of open source components and standards
Secure	• Linux/Unix strict security system prevents viruses and worms from modifying system files
	• Utilizes Java sandbox security infrastructure that prevents viruses from infecting the system environment
Interoperable	• Leverages common file formats: use/read/edit your Microsoft Office documents
	• Windows, Macintosh, Unix file and printer sharing
	• Communicates with standard communications servers: IMAP, POP, SMTP, Sun Java Enterprise System servers (formerly Sun ONE), etc.
Cost-effective	• Price is approximately 20 percent of the price of a Windows XP/Pro and Office 2003 upgrade, and even lower with special promotions
	• Includes the premium StarOffice 7 productivity suite, at no additional cost
	• Less-demanding hardware requirements that often allow you to extend the life of older existing systems
	• Compatible with hundreds of free open source applications

If you are a Windows or Macintosh user, many things you do now may seem both familiar and logical as you begin to use JDS. But don't forget that you are using an entirely new operating system. Some things require a few repetitions before you feel comfortable with them.

While putting JDS together, Sun Microsystems ran a usability study with people of many skill sets. Sun engaged people in a series of tasks on both JDS and Windows XP. Sun discovered that moving from Windows 9x to JDS required minimal learning, not much different from moving to Windows XP. This means anyone can easily migrate to JDS.

How to Use This Book

This book targets new users of Linux and those having to migrate from existing Windows operating systems. Linux has spread to new parts of the world and to places where personal computers have not been available historically. If you fit into any of these groups, this book can help you become productive quickly. Novices can benefit by reading the chapters in sequence.

General Linux users, small- and medium-sized businesses, early adopter enterprises, and government offices can also find this book helpful. We have provided a detailed table of contents, appendixes, and an index for finding information you may need if you encounter unfamiliar territory while attempting to use JDS.

Experienced users may want to browse through the book instead of trying to read it from cover to cover. You can use it as a reference, as well as a user's guide. We also provide annotated links to help you find information available in the Linux and Java communities.

System Requirements

JDS requires modest hardware resources. Sun Microsystems provides for both a minimum supported configuration and a recommended one. The minimum supported configuration uses an Intel Pentium II 266 MHz–compatible processor and a 4 GB hard disk, and 128 MB RAM and a color monitor with at least an 800 × 600 screen resolution.

Sun recommends a Pentium III compatible processor, 600 MHz or faster, at least a 4 GB hard disk, at least 256 MB RAM, and a 1,024 × 768 screen resolution, or better. More details on system requirements appear in Appendix F.

Installing JDS

Installation of JDS is explained at length in Appendix F. Sun also provides complete installation instructions on the Documentation CD that comes with JDS.

You can try out all the features of JDS, without actually installing it on your system. A demo version is provided on the JDS Demonstration CD, included with this book.

Simply insert the CD into your CD-ROM drive, power off (shut down) your computer, and restart it.

 Make sure you can boot from the CD-ROM drive if you wish to install JDS from either the full installation package or the demonstration CD. See Appendix F if you have trouble.

The JDS Demonstration CD takes about three minutes to start up on a system with an 800 MHz processor. When you are running JDS from the CD, you cannot save documents or settings, or do anything else that affects your hard disk. However, you can try out all the applications and configuration tools. If you reboot with the CD, all your settings will revert to what you started with. When you reboot your computer without the CD, you will be back in your old operating system as if nothing happened.

What's on Your JDS Screen

When you start a session for the first time, you will see a startup screen, as in Figure 1-1, with a strip at the bottom of the screen called a *panel* and various *icons*, which are small pictures related to particular files or functions of the system.

When you double-click on an icon, it opens a window that appears to float above the desktop screen. After you open a window, you can usually open items within the window, such as folders, programs, and documents.

In JDS, you can open, close, size, reduce, enlarge, and position windows on the desktop. You can open multiple windows simultaneously and maneuver them. Whether you open a window to run a program, or display the contents of a file or the elements of your computer, some window frame characteristics remain constant. These include the Window menu on the top panel or the scroll bars on the right side and bottom of the pane. If you have used either Mac OS or Microsoft Windows, the JDS desktop should feel comfortable.

Icons on the Desktop

JDS always starts with at least five icons on the desktop. In this section, we summarize what each one does. You may be able to explore parts of the system right now, but many features may seem confusing until we explain them in later chapters.

Most of the icons run a general-purpose system browser called *Nautilus*, which we describe in detail in Chapter 3. For now, all you need to know is that you can double-click on anything that appears in the window to work with it. You can also drag objects around the screen and use the drop-down menus at the top of the Nautilus screen. The Go menu has a number of interesting features, some of which we describe in upcoming chapters.

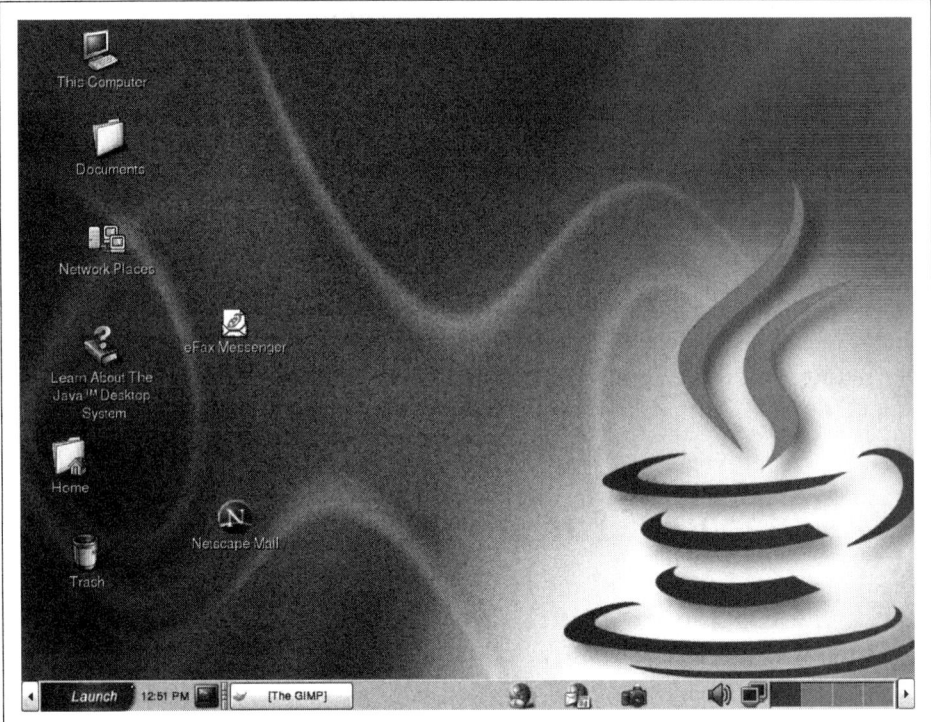

Figure 1-1. A sample startup screen

This Computer

Figure 1-2 shows the icon for the This Computer feature.

Figure 1-2. This Computer icon

When clicked, this icon displays the hard drive icons, the floppy disk and CD icons, a folder for preferences, network places, and documents.

Preferences allow you to manage your environment. For instance, you can change how your display looks, configure devices (such as the keyboard, mouse, printers, PDAs, and sounds), change your password, and determine how you connect to the Internet.

The Display selection allows you to set your desktop's background or wallpaper. You can also change your default fonts (styles in which text appears), menus, and tool bars. You can alter the themes (aesthetic aspects of how the desktop appears), the screen resolution, the screen saver, and window behavior.

The System icon also serves an important role on JDS. If you have little or no experience using Linux, you may want to peek at the items here but not try to change anything yet. If you have a working knowledge of Linux, you'll find several administrative tools you can use under this icon.

Documents

Figure 1-3 shows the icon for the Documents feature.

Figure 1-3. Documents icon

This folder gives you quick access to files stored in the default directory used by the main tools that are utilized on JDS for document manipulation: the StarOffice tools described in Chapters 6–8.

Network Places

Figure 1-4 shows the icon for the Network Places feature.

Figure 1-4. Network Places icon

Most people's computers are on a network, whether it is their company's campus or their own home. This icon provides access to the computers on the network, organized into a hierarchical tree of folders, just as documents are on a local system. As you click on each icon, you see smaller subsets of the network, individual systems within the network, and folders on the systems. Details on setting up a network are given in Chapter 4.

Some systems require you to provide a password before accessing resources. If you are supposed to have access, the system administrator will have told you what password to use. Sometimes you can gain access just by virtue of logging in to JDS, because the remote system can learn from your system who you are.

Trash

Figure 1-5 shows the icon for the Trash feature.

Figure 1-5. Trash icon

When you select documents or other objects and delete them, they go into your Trash and can be viewed using this icon. If you regret deleting them and want them back, you can simply drag them from the Trash into the folder where you want them. If you get low on disk space, you can permanently delete objects from this window.

Learn About the Java Desktop System

Figure 1-6 shows the icon for the Learn About the Java Desktop System feature.

Figure 1-6. Learn About The Java Desktop System icon

This icon launches a browser from which you can access help to learn about JDS and its applications.

Bottom panel

Across the bottom of your screen is a gray strip, or *panel*, that provides both valuable information and powerful access to features on your system. Figure 1-7 shows this panel.

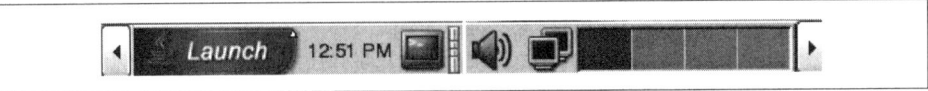

Figure 1-7. The GNOME panel

The following items appear in the panel by default:

Main menu launch icon
Contains applications and tools to help you configure JDS for your hardware and preferences.

Clock
Displays the current time.

Network monitor
Looks like two small monitors and flashes to show when network activity is going on.

Window list
Displays a button for each window that is open on this workspace. You can click on a window list button to minimize and to restore windows.

Workspace Switcher
Displays a visual representation of your workspaces, which are discussed in the following section. You can use Workspace Switcher to switch between workspaces.

Workspaces

The JDS workspaces feature allows you to create multiple, personalized workspaces for different projects or purposes and place them on different virtual desktops. For instance, suppose you are working on project X and have a few documents on the desktop for easy referral. You also have project Y for which you need other documents and a multi-tabbed browser. By placing each project on a separate desktop in the workspaces switcher, you can quickly switch between the two projects at a moments notice. Workspaces also allow better organization of work and prevent pieces from being buried.

As another example of the use of workspaces, you may find that placing email and the browser on a separate desktop increases your work efficiency. Or perhaps you want to keep one workspace for business and one for family or fun. JDS takes multi-tasking to new levels with this Workspaces feature. As you learn more programs on JDS and increase your workload, you'll discover the value of separating your tasks on multiple workspaces.

The Workspace Switcher is a separate program, known as an *applet*, and is located on the bottom right bar of the JDS desktop. The Workspace Switcher is a rectangle, divided into four boxes. Each box represents a workspace, or desktop, miniaturized into a small icon within the box. This miniaturized depiction helps you recognize what you placed in each workspace for easy switching between workspaces. Each workspace contains the same desktop background and menus that you are used to seeing. You may run different applications and open different windows in each workspace.

Figure 1-8 shows the Workspace Switcher applet when the user has started up a separate application in each of the four workspaces. The first workspace, on the left, is running the StarWriter word processor. The second is running email, the third has a folder window (Nautilus), and the fourth contains a web browser. The currently open workspace, the fourth window with the browser occupies your screen, is highlighted with a darker color, as shown in Figure 1-8.

Figure 1-8. The JDS Workspace Switcher applet

Instead of displaying a pictorial representation of the workspaces on the JDS desktop, you can change the Workspace Switcher to display the numbers of the workspaces. This is available if you right-click on the Workspace Switcher and choose Preferences from the menu that pops up. In general, objects displayed by JDS provide a menu when you right-click them, and you can often customize them in radical ways by choosing Preferences.

To switch among workspaces, click on the box that represents the workspace you're interested in. The associated workspace is maximized and occupies your screen. You can start a new window in that workspace simply by clicking on the document or program you want to open. You can move something from the current workspace to another workspace in two ways. The first is to drag the tiny depiction of the window from one box in the Workspace Switcher to another. The second is to go to the top frame of the window you want to move and right-click on the top strip. Select "Move to another workspace" and select the workspace into which you want to move the window.

If you'd like to change the number of workspaces, right-click on the workspaces applet, select Preferences, then choose the number of workspaces desired. You may also add additional rows in the same way.

Where to Find the Information You Need

Newcomers may feel a bit overwhelmed at the breadth of new options and features upon venturing into JDS. Consider those feelings natural. This book puts the most important tools for being productive in your hands. Sun also provides documentation, some on its web site and some right on the system you are using.

Once you are familiar with JDS, you can benefit from the Help application. Start help simply by clicking on the "Learn About the Java Desktop System" icon, discussed earlier in this chapter, or hold down your mouse on the Launch menu at the bottom left of the panel and select Help. The second method is shown in Figure 1-9.

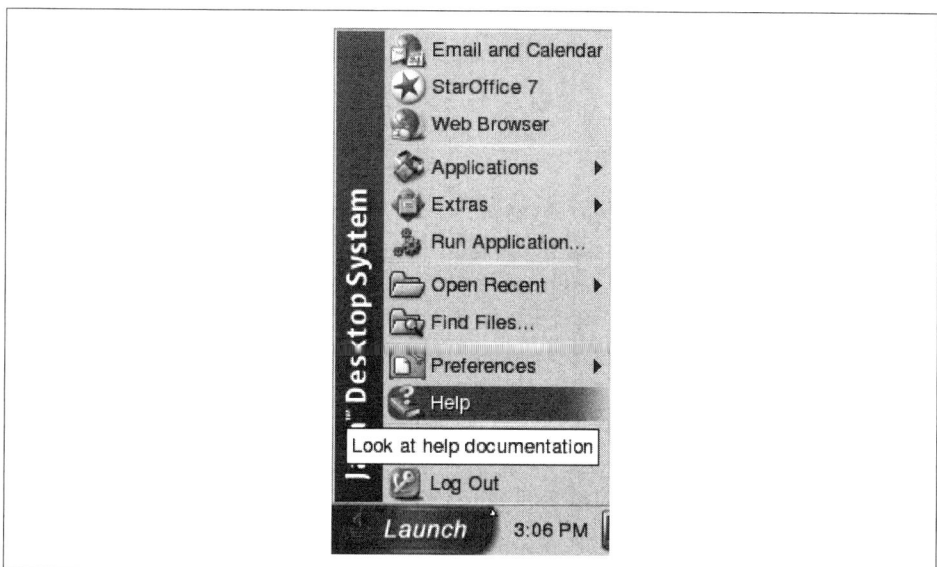

Figure 1-9. Click Launch and then Help

The initial window shown in Help lists three main topics. The document provided under "Java Desktop System" summarizes some of the same, basic tasks that we discuss in this book. The "GNOME – Desktop" documents describe how to deal with windows, icons, the mouse, and other features of your desktop. (The desktop's name is GNOME.) Finally, "Additional documents" contains standard documentation for many Linux-related tools; this is valuable for experienced Linux users.

You can jump to a particular topic as long as you know the name of the application. For instance, when you read the section on email in Chapter 6, you learn that the email program on JDS is called Evolution. To get detailed documentation on Evolution, press the Index icon at the top of the Help window and enter "evolution" into the "Search for" box near the top left. The result is Figure 1-10. In this window, you can scroll down the lefthand pane to view a table of contents and select topics, and scroll down the righthand pane to read the documentation.

Besides the Help window on the desktop, many applications contain their own context-sensitive help menus.

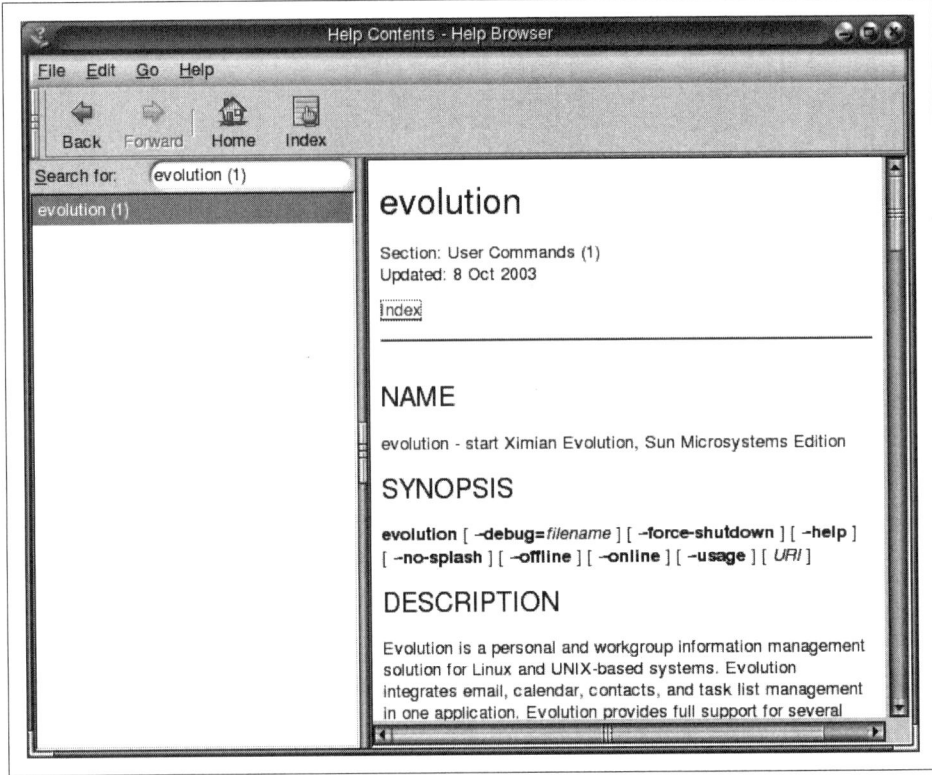

Figure 1-10. JDS Help browser

Other Sources of Information You May Need to Run JDS

In the JDS set of CD-ROMs, Sun has included a documentation CD. Here you can find PDF and HTML versions of the documentation for JDS. You can find the same documentation online at *http://docs.sun.com*.

There is also an online support site at *http://supportforum.sun.com/*. The initial screen for this site is shown in Figure 1-11.

The forums, Frequently Asked Questions (FAQs), and knowledge base at this site are aimed toward more seasoned veterans of Linux. However, we strongly suggest that newbies join the Support Forum at *http://supportforum.sun.com/sjds/* and pose questions as they encounter problems. The community usually answers questions quickly; the authors have found it to be a valuable resource.

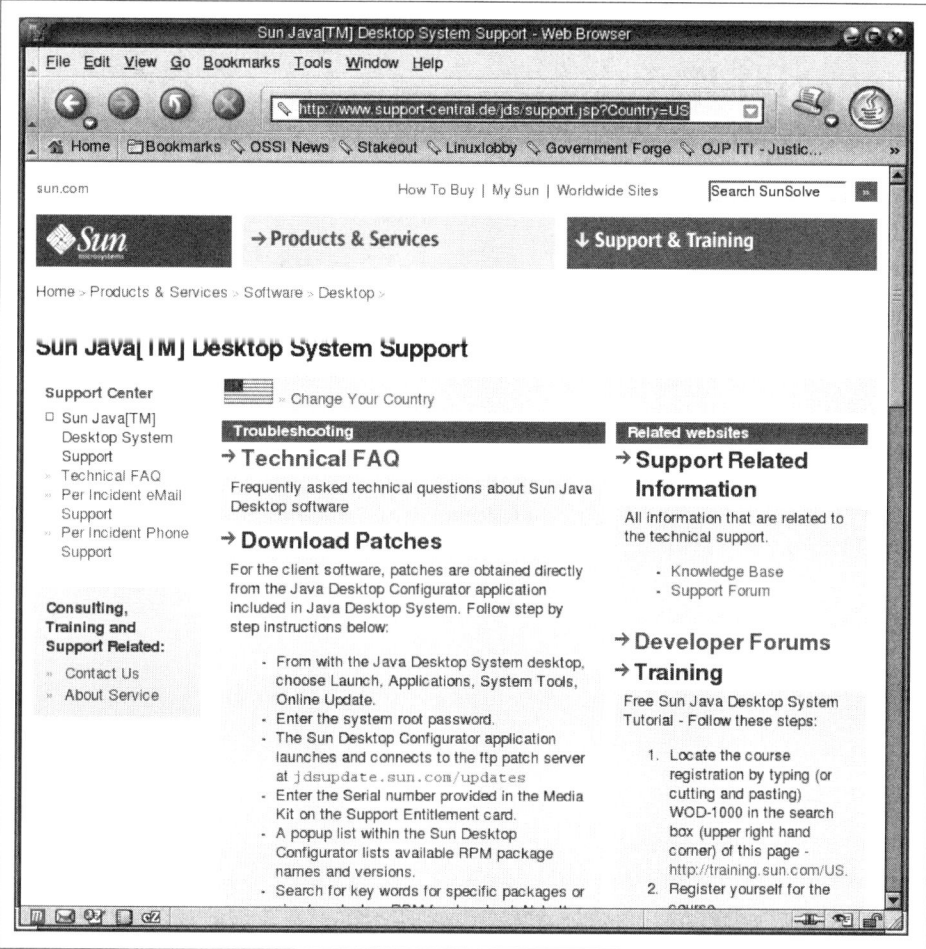

Figure 1-11. Sun's JDS online help portal

What's Next?

Now that we have introduced you to JDS, we can start getting some work done. In the next chapter, we cover basic tasks such as accessing CD-ROMs and working with documents. You can also learn how to find files on your computer and change some system settings to suit your preferences.

CHAPTER 2
Essential JDS

Most people can quickly get going with the Java Desktop System, knowing intuitively how to navigate the system and handle its windows. The habits you learned on other computers can usually guide you. But it helps to know the details of window, file, and application handling on JDS, so you can use the system more efficiently when performing complex tasks.

The basics of using a personal computer at home and at work include knowing how to:

- Start and stop your system correctly
- Initiate and terminate programs
- Manage windows
- Access system settings and preferences
- Manage different users
- Recognize and access files and folders

Starting JDS

Let's begin by getting acquainted with some terms you will use on a regular basis:

Boot
Computer start-up, during which time the computer loads the operating system and the configuration files into memory.

Authenticate
Prove your identity through your user name and password so that your computer or network can give you access to files and services.

Log on
Enter your system or attach to a network.

Ending a session
Closing a desktop session, without turning off the computer.

Shutting down
> Ending the operating system's active state in such a way that all background programs close cleanly and data is saved prior to powering down the hardware.

Terminal
> A text window which allows one to communicate with the computer through simple commands.

Directories
> Collections of files. The terms *folder* and *directory* can be used interchangeably.

Booting and Logging In

To start JDS, simply turn on your computer and monitor. If you use a dual-boot environment (See Appendix F.), select the JDS System from the Start menu. As your computer boots, JDS loads the files which it needs to run. Notice the JDS splash screen as the Linux kernel boots.

The information you can see during the boot process includes initializing and testing the hardware on your computer, and starting or stopping software that runs in the background. Few people care about the boot process. You can liken it to an automobile: you do not need to know what goes on under the hood to drive the car. Using your computer doesn't require knowledge of what runs in the background. However, if you notice an error during boot, it can sometimes alert you to a problem you can fix: for instance, you may have forgotten to plug in your network cable if you notice error messages related to networking or remote file sharing.

After the operating system loads, you see a password dialog box asking for your user name and your password (see Figure 2-1). At this point, you are about to put JDS into gear. Once you enter your user name and password, the Java desktop appears, and it's time to start working or playing.

With JDS you must enter your user name and password using the exact combination of upper- and lowercase letters that you specified during setup, or that your administrator provided.

Automatic Login

Sometimes people do not want to bother entering a user name and password every time they start their computer. If you want to start your computer and have it log you in without the login screen, you can set up JDS in that manner.

However, you should usually keep the login screen for the sake of security. Automatic login presents risks, especially in a work environment, because anyone who has physical access to your computer (a member of the nighttime cleaning crew, for instance) can procure all your files. But if you work at home or are setting up a multiple-user

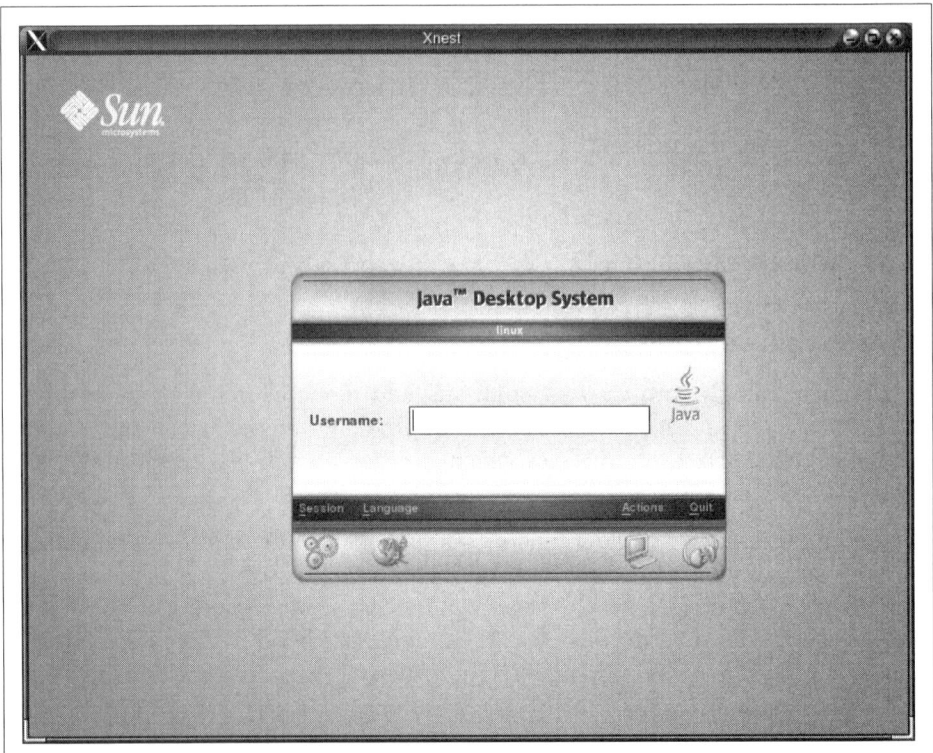

Figure 2-1. The JDS Logon screen

kiosk setting, with only a temporary guest user account, you may want to use this option.

To start the computer without having to enter your user name and password upon bootup, click on the Launch menu at the bottom left of the JDS panel and follow the menu items Applications → System Tools → Administration → Login Screen Setup to reach the configuration screen, shown in Figure 2-2. (In the previous JDS Release I, the menu items are Applications → System Tools → Login Screen Setup.) Under the General tab in the center of the window appears the term Automatic Login. Click the checkbox next to the term "Login a user automatically on first bootup." Finally, choose your user name from the drop-down box next to the term "Automatic login username" and close the box.

Ending a Session or Shutting Down JDS

When you finish using your computer and leave the area, you should probably *log out* so that no one can wander in and gain access to your files, email account, etc. If you have a user name on a network, everything done on the computer with this identifier is considered your work. Imagine if someone were to enter incorrect data or to

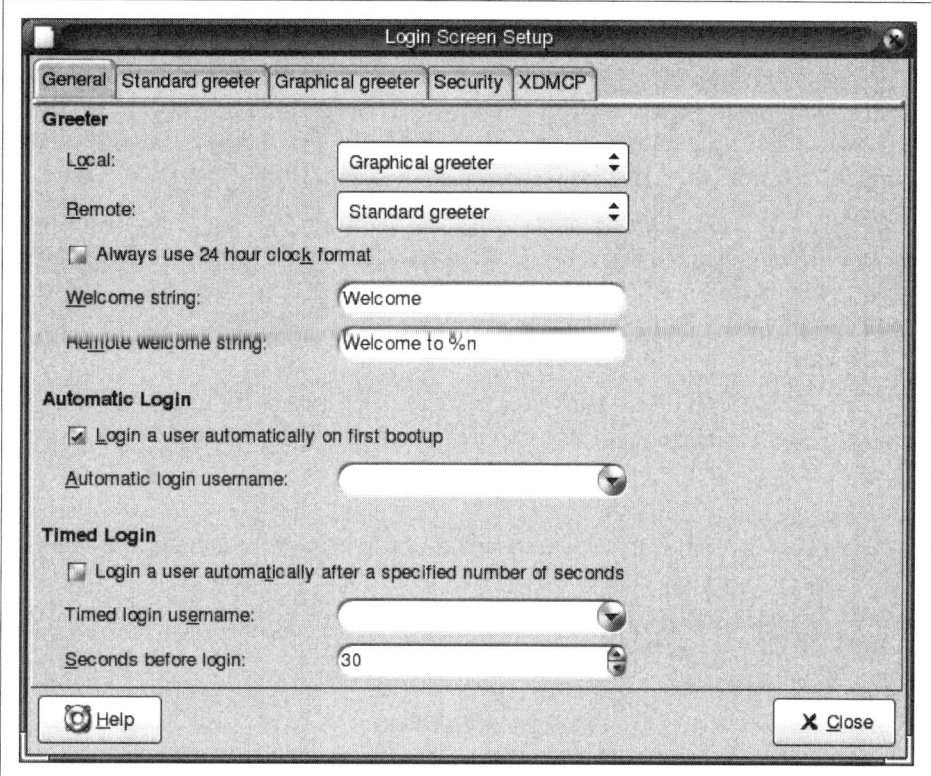

Figure 2-2. Using an Automatic Login

conduct improper behavior on your account, and it was traced back to you. Logging out helps keep the system secure.

An alternative to logging out is to lock the screen, as described in the next section, and unlock it when you come back. But logging out gives other people a chance to use your system.

Whereas logging out leaves your computer running, *shutting down* terminates all processing so that the hardware can be powered off. Many people let their Linux workstations run day and night, without shutting them down. In some organizations, your idle workstation joins in as part of a supercomputing grid during the evening hours. Since Linux computers can run months and even years without having to restart, you may not have to shut down your JDS system.

However, if you want to turn off your computer, you must first shut down JDS to ensure that you don't lose any data or corrupt any files. Some computers automatically turn off the power at the end of the shutdown sequence. (Usually, the monitor is still running, though, and needs to be turned off by hand.) Other computers require that you manually turn off the power switch on the computer box.

If you switch off your computer before JDS has shut down—or if a power failure interrupts your work unexpectedly—you can lose data. In fact, even if you carefully save your documents, the data may not be safely stored to disk if your system powers down without shutting down JDS first. Many applications remember what you did between saves, and the next time you run the application they ask you whether you'd like to restore the data that you failed to save. But a clean shutdown is safer.

Both logging out and shutting down can be started through the same menu item: click on the Launch menu at the bottom left of the JDS panel and choose Log Out, as shown in Figure 2-3. This will bring you to the same JDS dialog box that is shown in Figure 2-4. It offers the following choices.

Log Out
> Choose this option to take you back to the Logon Screen, as shown in Figure 2-1. From there, you can choose to shut down the operating system or log on as another user (explained later in the chapter).

Shut Down
> Choose this option when you are ready to finish using your computer for the day and want to switch off the power. If your computer does not have the auto-power control enabled, JDS displays a message telling you to shut off your computer when it is safe to do so.

Restart the Computer
> Choose this option to restart the computer. In JDS, you usually need this option only after you make updates to the operating system. After completion of the update installation, the On-Line Update dialog may suggest you use this option.

Cancel
> Choose this option if you change your mind and do not want to restart the computer.

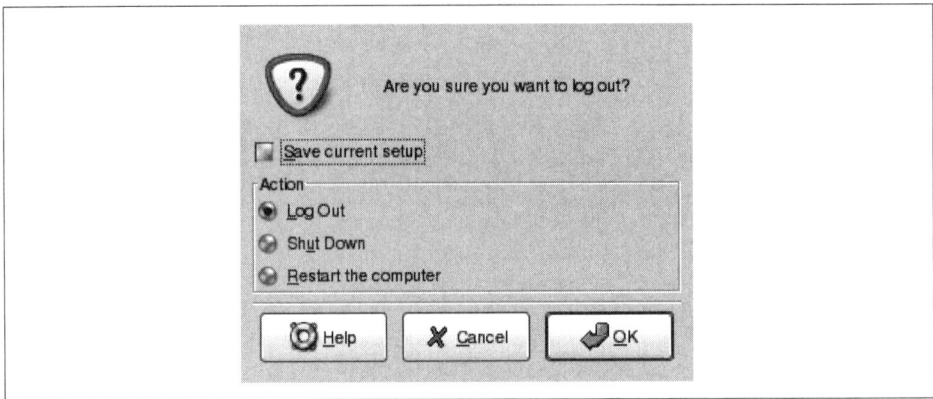

Figure 2-3. Choosing Log Out from the Launch menu

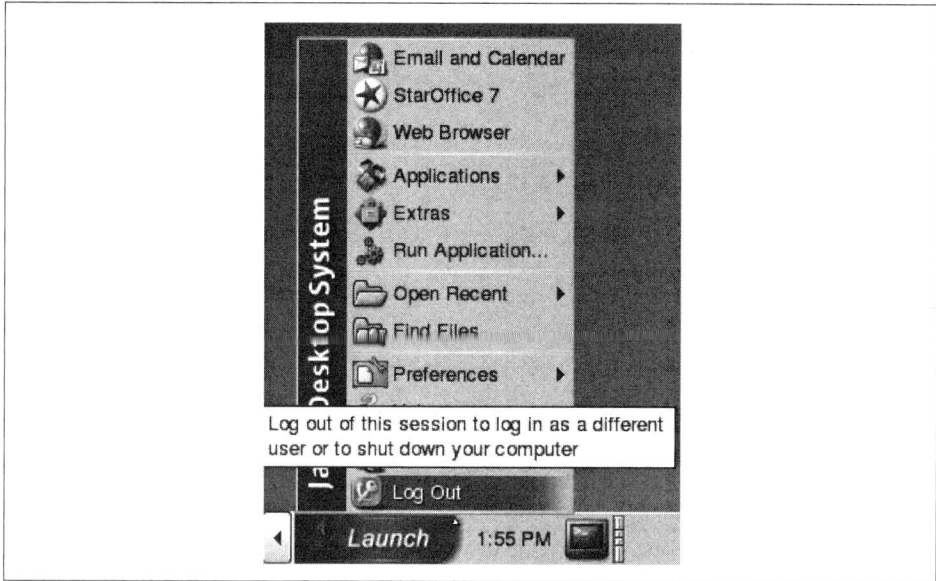

Figure 2-4. Log Out screen

If you would like your applications to restart each time you log in, as you left them when you last logged out, you can set this up from the Launch menu. Select Preferences → Advanced → Sessions. In the resulting dialog box, click on the "Session options" tab in the upper-left corner. Click on the box "Automatically save changes to session" and close the box to save the setting.

Locking the Screen

An alternative to logging out is to lock the screen. This choice is usually taken by users when they plan to leave the computer briefly and need a convenient way to secure the screen. Sometimes JDS even locks the screen automatically when the computer has been idle for a long time; we show you how to control this behavior later in this section.

Locking the screen allows you to keep your session going, while preventing someone else from accessing your desktop. As discussed earlier, when you are in a work environment, you should leave your desktop protected while you are away.

To lock your screen, choose Launch → Lock Screen. Alternatively, if a Lock button exists on your panel, click on the "Lock this computer" button. To add the Lock button to the panel for this convenience, right-click on the panel and choose Add to Panel → Actions → Lock. When you lock your screen, the screen saver starts.

To unlock the screen, move your mouse over the screen saver to display the locked screen login window, shown in Figure 2-5. Enter your user name and password in the locked screen dialog, then press Return. Your desktop reappears.

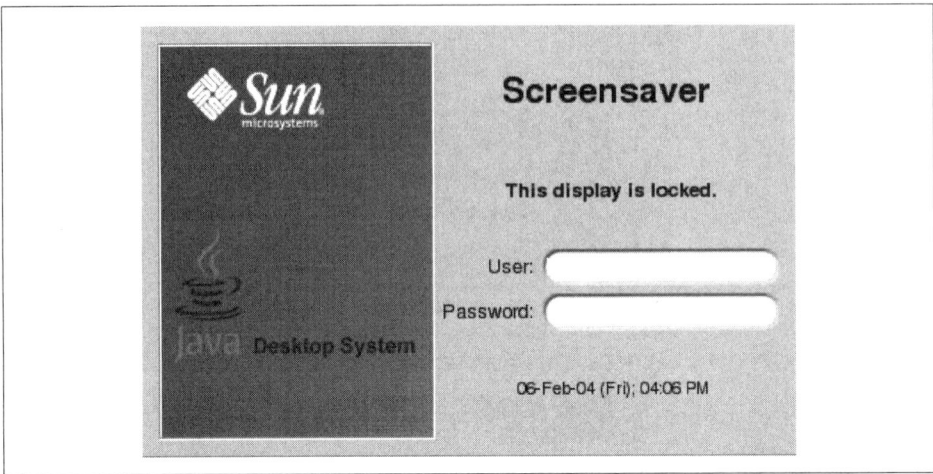

Figure 2-5. Login screen used when you lock the screen

To add additional security, some systems lock the screen after the system has been idle for a long time. Therefore, if you forget to lock your screen, while taking a break, helping a coworker, or leaving for any other reason, intruders are shut out.

If it is not already enabled, you can set up automatic locking by choosing Launch → Preferences → Display → Screensaver. Check the Lock Screen box and choose the number of minutes for the system to wait before the screen saver automatically starts on an idle desktop.

Running Programs

The JDS provides three ways to start programs:

- Click on the Launch menu and follow the menu selections to the desired program. Many JDS users choose this method because it provides an intuitive interface for the large number of JDS programs.
- Select icons, called *launchers,* from the desktop or from the lower bar panel. Those who prefer pictures or symbols like this option; it's also the quickest way to start an application and allows for fewer hand movements.
- Enter a command on the command line from a window called a Terminal. This is necessary for applications that are not available through the other two methods.

Typical Program Behavior

We start by using the Launch menu, which holds most of the common applications you want to use, such as your word processor, email and calendar, and web browser. Let's take a quick look at the menu, shown in Figure 2-6, which appears when you click on the Launch button.

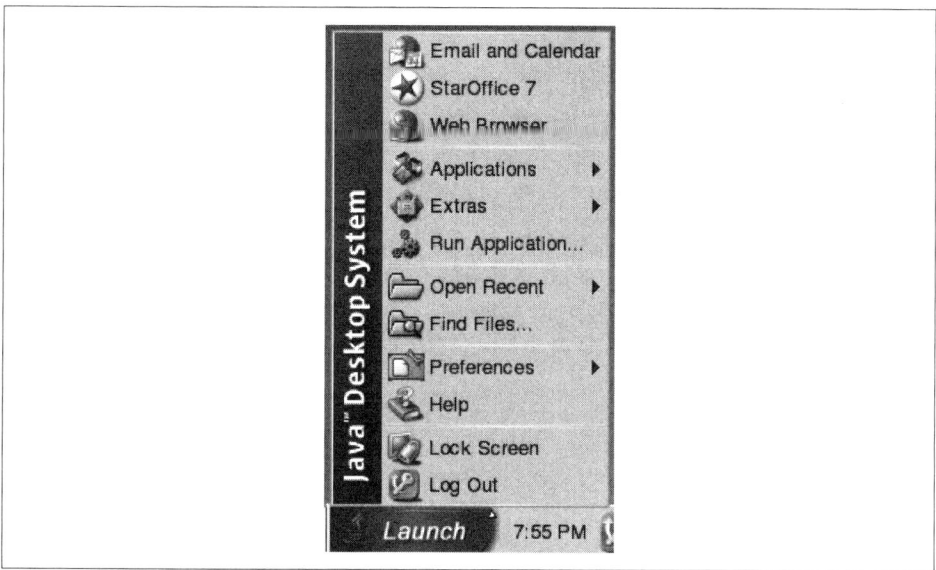

Figure 2-6. Launch menu

In Figure 2-6, we can see the selections from which to start a program. Beginning at the top, three of the most commonly used programs are listed. Below these is an icon for Applications, which you will use frequently. Figure 2-7 shows some of the JDS applications listed here. (Please note that the applications listed may differ on your system, depending on the options chosen during installation.) For instance, if you want to use the JDS word processor, select Launch → Applications → Office → StarOffice 7 → Text Document and just start typing your text into the window that appears.

Further down the Launch menu is a Folder icon labeled Open Recent. Most JDS users find this an easy way to start documents on which they have recently been working, as illustrated in Figure 2-8. Place the mouse pointer over the icon next to the document you want to open, click once, and the document opens in the appropriate application.

When you open an application on the JDS desktop, it has several buttons in an outer frame around the edges. These buttons, along with scrollbars for windows displaying large amounts of data, are the same for every application. In addition, inside this outer frame, each application displays a variety of buttons that are specific to that

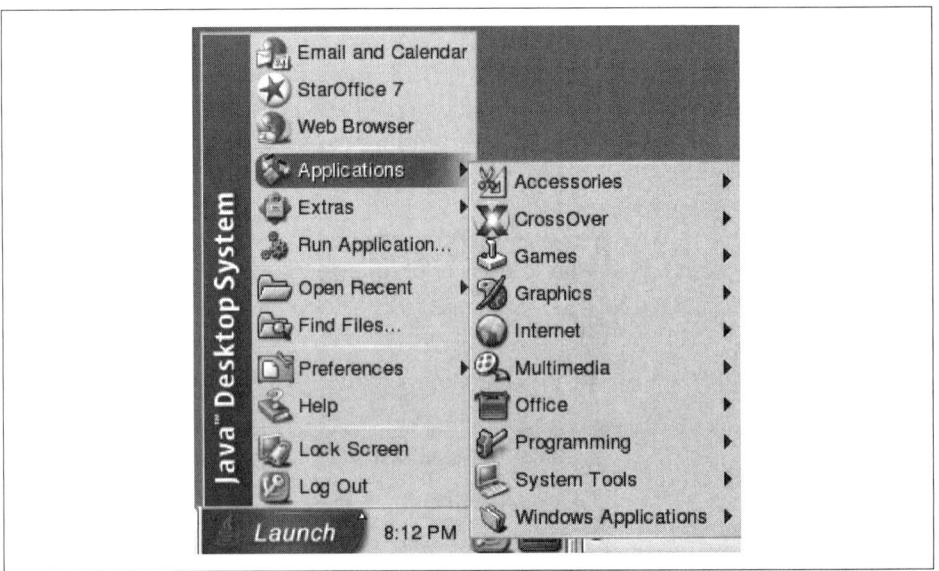

Figure 2-7. The Applications menu

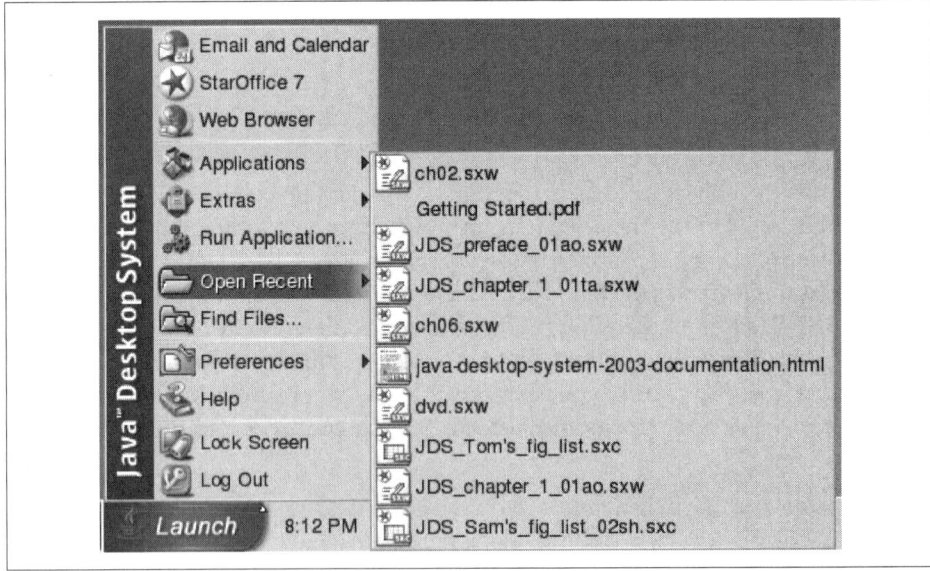

Figure 2-8. The Recent Documents menu

application. In this section, we look at a simple application to give you a feel for how to manipulate applications on the JDS desktop.

This application, called *gedit*, may also be useful to you if you have to edit plain text files. For instance, suppose you want to compose a long email message in plain text. The word processor saves its text with extra formatting, so it's better as an email attachment than as a source of plain text for email. The *gedit* utility lacks the formatting that a word processor provides but offers powerful features and convenient keystrokes for editing plain text. Another use of *gedit* is to edit configuration files (software settings), in the rare cases when your desktop does not let you configure something through dialog boxes.

Start the editor with Launch → Applications → Accessories → Text Editor, as shown in Figure 2-9. The window, shown in Figure 2-10, is the result. We've typed some text into the window to show what it looks like while you're working.

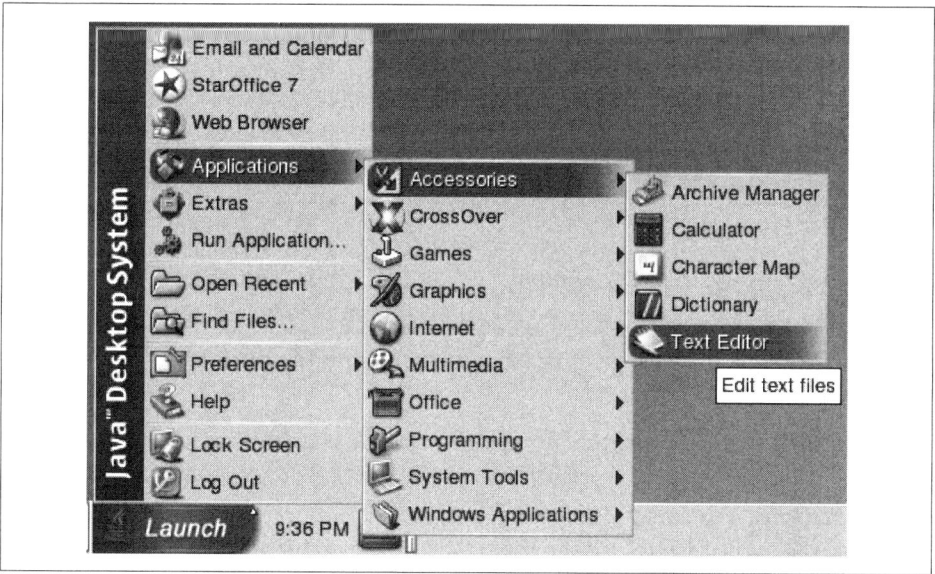

Figure 2-9. Starting the Text Editor

Once the Text Editor window opens on the desktop, the Launch menus close. There are several things you can do on the outer frame, which, as we've said, is the same for every application. These functions are familiar to most users of a desktop system, but we focus on some details in the following section.

General Window Tips

A *window* is any box on the desktop that shows a running program, a file, an icon, a dialog box, or some other graphical element. Windows can move around the desktop, so you can manage your space. Many of the window components and commands are the same in all the most popular JDS programs, which makes it easy for you to manage your work. Yet keep in mind that, although most windows appear similar, some of the menu bars may vary, depending on what tasks need to be done in that window.

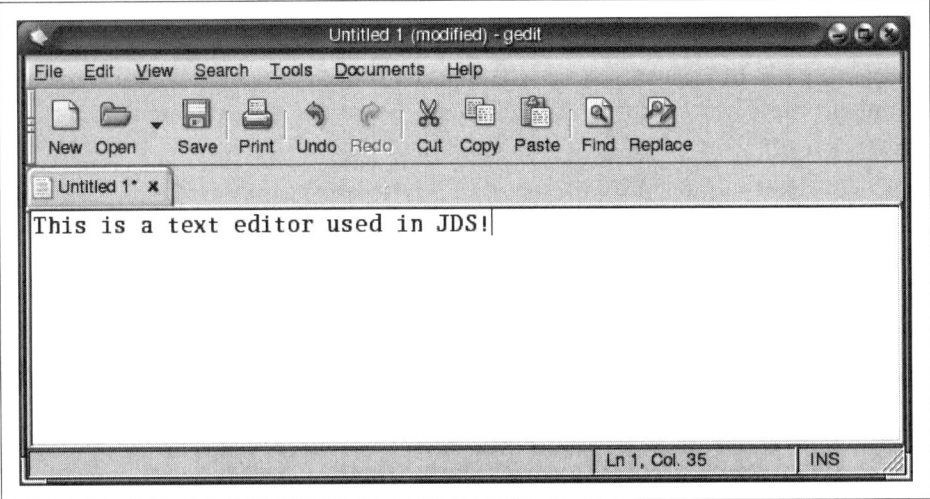

Figure 2-10. Using the JDS Text Editor

As we have already demonstrated in this chapter, you can open, close, reduce, enlarge, and move most windows on the desktop. Let's practice these.

With the window open for *gedit* or any other program of your choice, you can perform the following operations:

- To move the window, press the mouse over the top bar that contains the window's title and move it. If necessary, first reduce the window from full screen size.

- To *maximize* the window (to make it take up the entire screen of your monitor), press the middle button of the three that appear at the top right. Press this button again to return the window to its previous size.

- Press the button to the immediate left to *minimize* the window. It disappears from the screen, and the title of the window is placed in a box on the lowest panel of the desktop. Click on this small box to bring the window back on to the desktop to its original size.

  Minimizing allows you to essentially clean off your desktop so that you can work on one window at a time. With more of your desktop screen open, you can see the icons on your desktop that were hidden by the larger windows. For beginners, it is easy to confuse the two concepts of minimize and unmaximize. Just practice it a bit, and the two become familiar to you.

- If you want to view a window that is partially covered by another, click anywhere within the bottom window, and it will move to the top, possibly covering other windows.

- All the windows open in the current workspace have icons that appear on the panel on the bottom of the screen. You can bring any window to the forefront by clicking on its icon.

- All these functions are also accessible by right-clicking on a window or icon. The menu that comes up contains some other functions that you may also find useful, such as menu items that move the window or icon to a different workspace.

- If you open a number of windows, notice that their identifying boxes fill up the bottom panel; the boxes get smaller and smaller, and the titles are harder to see. This is one of the many reasons to use the Workspace Switcher, located on the bottom right panel. This feature is described in Chapter 1. It lets you place your windows in a more organized fashion for retrieval.

- Most windows have scrollbars and arrows on one or two sides of the frame. These allow you to roll up and down the screen or pane, as needed, when the full page within the window is not visible. Place your mouse pointer over arrows and click them to move the window's content in the directions they indicate (up and down, or side to side). Or drag the scrollbar in the same manner. But sometimes resizing or maximizing a window is better than using scrollbars to see all the content.

- To resize a window, place the mouse pointer anywhere on the edge or corner of the window. You know that your mouse pointer is in the right position when the pointer arrow changes into an arrow pointing in both directions. You may want to practice sizing a number of windows to fit on the desktop.

Applications offer toolbars just below the title bar. Some toolbars have menu items such as File and Window, while others show the same features as icons. The main toolbars' contents vary from window to window, so it is a good idea to click on the toolbars and explore your options as you begin to use the various applications. Some windows have only one toolbar, whereas others have two or three rows, and even a side toolbar. The toolbars for the main programs are discussed at greater length in following chapters.

The major operations provided by *gedit*, like most applications, are available from a menu bar at the top. For example, choose Edit → Preferences to see some of this program's options. The result is Figure 2-11. Feel free to explore the various options available in *gedit* through the drop-down menus.

Closing an Application

Like other applications and windows in JDS, you can close *gedit* in several ways. We illustrate three of these methods in Figures 2-12 and 2-13.

- Click on the close button at the top, righthand corner of the window.
- Click on File → Quit, shown in Figure 2-13.
- Press CTRL-Q. This is not available in all applications. If you look closely at the drop-down menu in Figure 2-13, you notice that it mentions Ctrl-Q as a keystroke equivalent, or shortcut, for File → Quit. Such key combinations for performing tasks are called *shortcuts*.

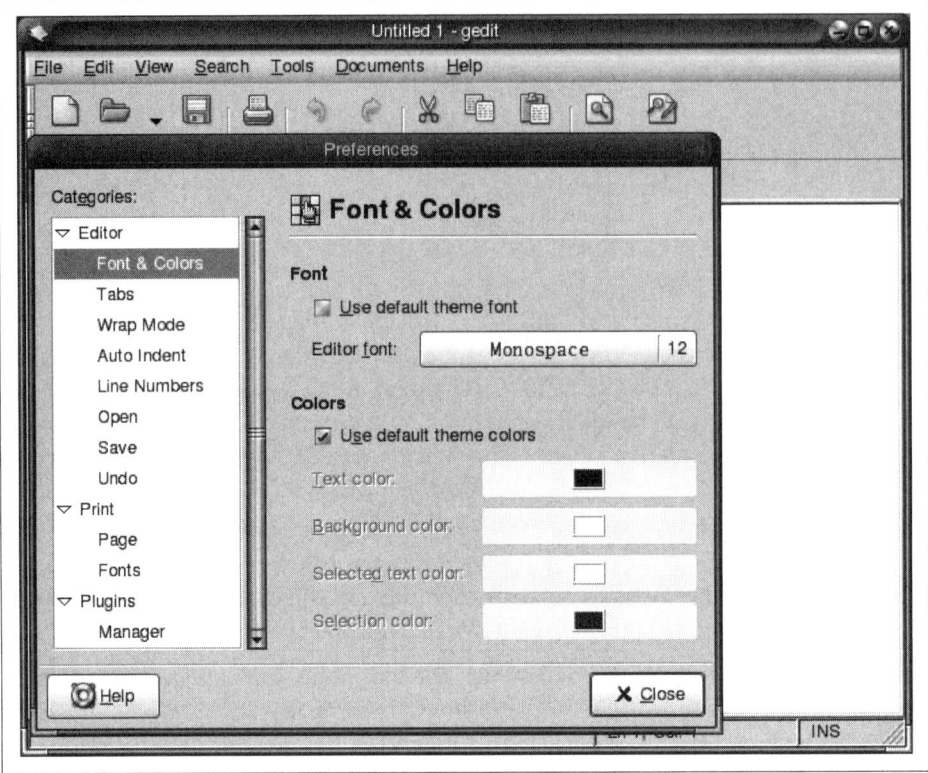

Figure 2-11. gedit preferences

If you entered any text into *gedit* before closing it and failed to save the text in a file, you see the dialog box shown in Figure 2-14. Many (but not all) applications under JDS protect you from losing data by reminding you that you haven't saved your changes.

Starting a Program with the Terminal

JDS provides an excellent graphical user interface (GUI). In most cases, you can perform any task you need by simply using the keyboard, mouse, and icons. But you shouldn't ignore the features made available by JDS's underlying Linux operating system, which you can access through a terminal.

The JDS Terminal is an application that allows you to type commands to the system. As many Apple Macintosh OS X users have discovered, the Terminal can provide you with many powerful functions. Linux commands are beyond the scope of this book, but if you know what you want to do, we can show you how to access the Terminal and use it as another alternative to starting and terminating a program. A selection of useful commands is in Appendix A.

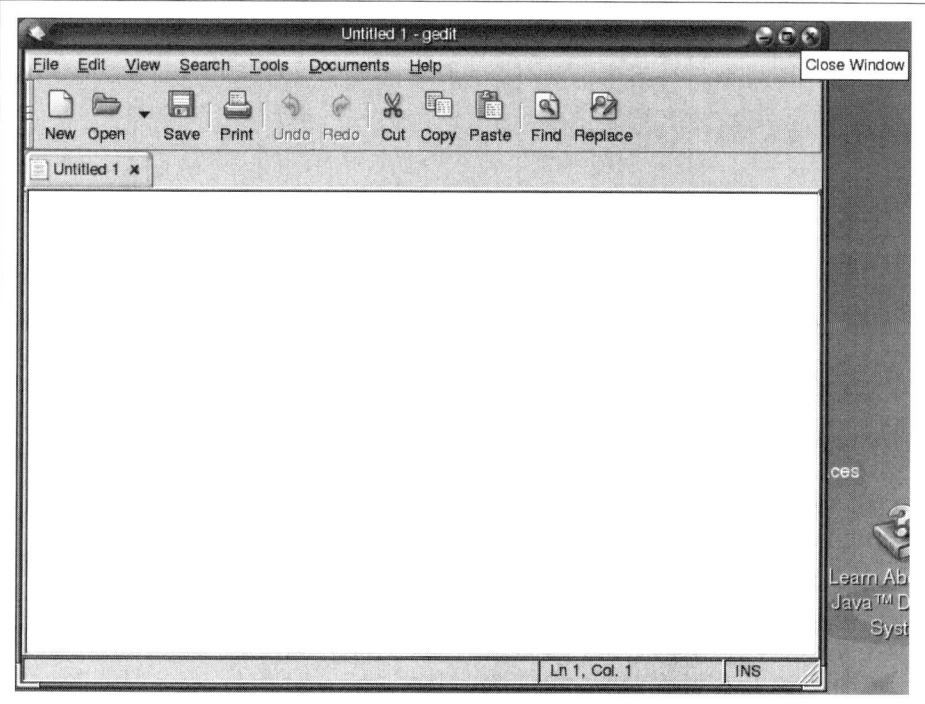

Figure 2-12. Terminating an application with the close button

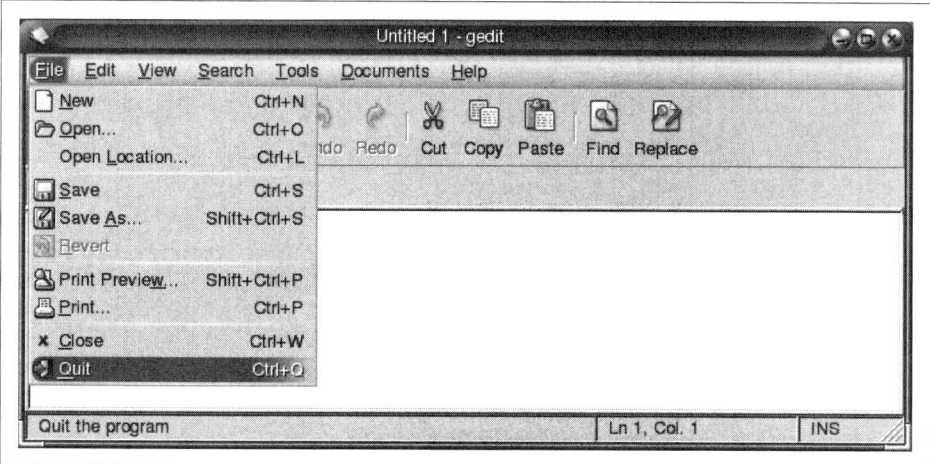

Figure 2-13. Terminating an application with the drop-down menu

You can access the Terminal through a series of menus, shown in Figure 2-15. Figure 2-16 shows the terminal itself. The window doesn't have many interesting features because it exists merely as a place to type in your commands.

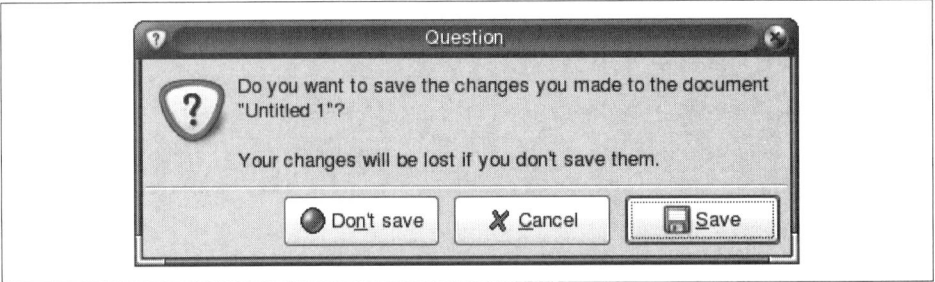

Figure 2-14. Fail Safe dialog box

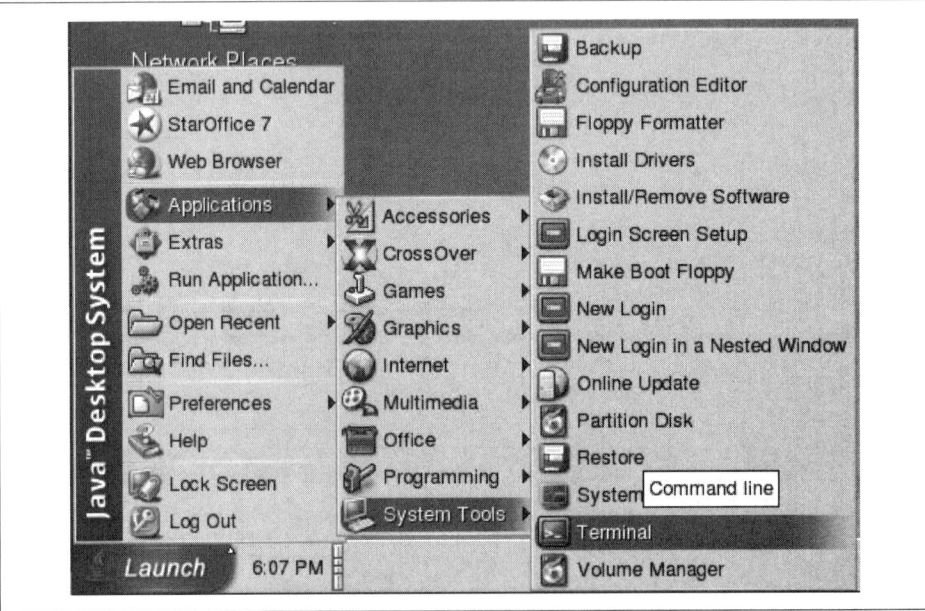

Figure 2-15. Initiating the Terminal

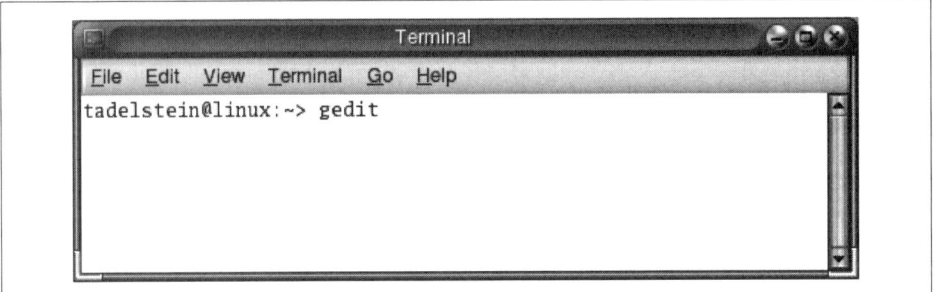

Figure 2-16. The Linux Terminal

In Figure 2-16, we have opened a Linux terminal, which placed us in our home directory, typed the command *gedit*, and pressed the return key. This starts a new window (not shown here) exactly as if we had chosen the text editor from the Launch menu, as in the previous section.

At this point, you do not need to have much understanding of the Linux Terminal other than to know that it exists and that you can start a program using it. If you learn more about Linux, you can learn to do many exciting things you didn't know existed with your personal computer.

What Windowing System Does JDS Use?

The X Window System, developed by Digital Equipment Corporation and MIT in the mid-to-late 1980s, provided the first graphical environment for Unix computer systems. This system, often just called X, allowed users to open multiple windows to perform various tasks simultaneously. For instance, you could send a large file across the network in one window, while editing a document in another and answering your mail in a third.

Most of the features we discuss in this chapter are provided by another layer on top of X, called the window manager. This window manager is responsible for recognizing launchers, moving and closing windows, and so on.

Accessing System Settings and Preferences

The icon on the desktop labeled This Computer provides access to disks, files, and folders throughout your computer. For instance, if you want to open files on a floppy disk or CD-ROM, you can find them on the appropriate icon under This Computer. It also contains tools needed to set up, manage, and control your user settings. So let's take a look at this folder by clicking on the This Computer icon, located on the desktop. It typically looks like Figure 2-17.

If you have used Microsoft Windows, notice that JDS's This Computer somewhat differs in its look and feel from Microsoft's My Computer, but the functions are similar. The icons in JDS look different, which you can see by comparing Figures 2-17 and 2-18.

Another difference between the two systems is in the names of the items used to configure systems elements. JDS's Preferences, shown in Figure 2-19, behave similarly to the Control Panel found in Windows's My Computer. Figure 2-20 shows a Windows XP Control Panel.

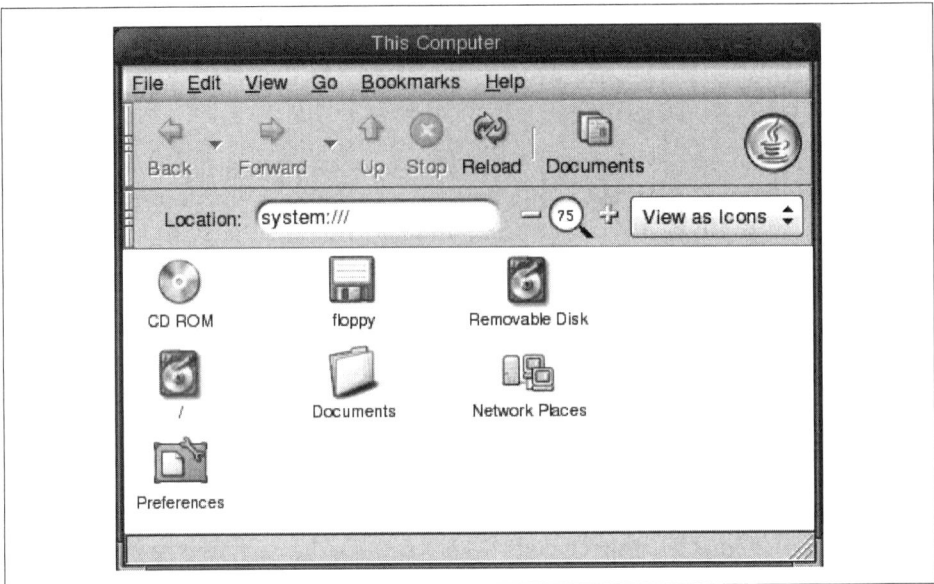

Figure 2-17. This Computer

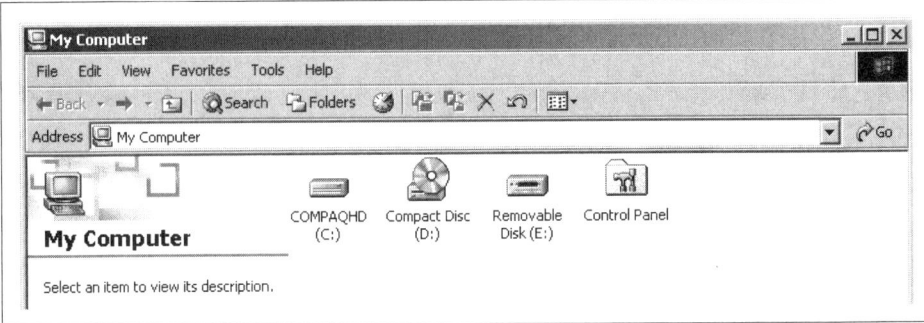

Figure 2-18. The My Computer Folder from Windows 2000

Managing Users

JDS allows many users to share a computer, keeping their files separate and making sure nobody can step on anybody else's files or activities.

On your system, one user, called *root*, always exists. The root user has administrative rights to all the resources on a computer system. In Linux, we also refer to root as superuser.

You can always log on to your computer as root if you have the password. When you perform certain advanced tasks affecting the functioning of the computer system, such as adding a user, you are prompted for a root password. In addition, knowledgeable

Figure 2-19. The Preferences window

users of Linux and JDS can run programs as root from the Terminal window that was discussed earlier. We cover this subject in greater detail later in another chapter. For now, do not access the root account unless you have extensive experience using Linux. The root user can alter critical system resources, and you could accidently make your system unusable.

To manage users, navigate to the Systems-settings window by selecting Launch → Preferences → System. You see an icon called Users and Groups. Double-click on the icon and you are prompted for the root password.

Once you enter the root password and click OK, you see a Java Desktop Configuration Screen that allows you to add, edit, and delete users.

Depending on the action you select, the Java Desktop System Configurator guides you through the process. Each step has detailed instructions on the left side of the configuration window.

Accessing Directories (Folders)

The final topic in our discussion of the basics of the JDS deals with accessing directories, which many people also call folders.

JDS runs on top of Linux and uses the conventions of the Linux Operating System. As with most operating systems, all files and directories are arranged in a hierarchy. Forward slashes are used to separate names as you go down the treelike hierarchy.

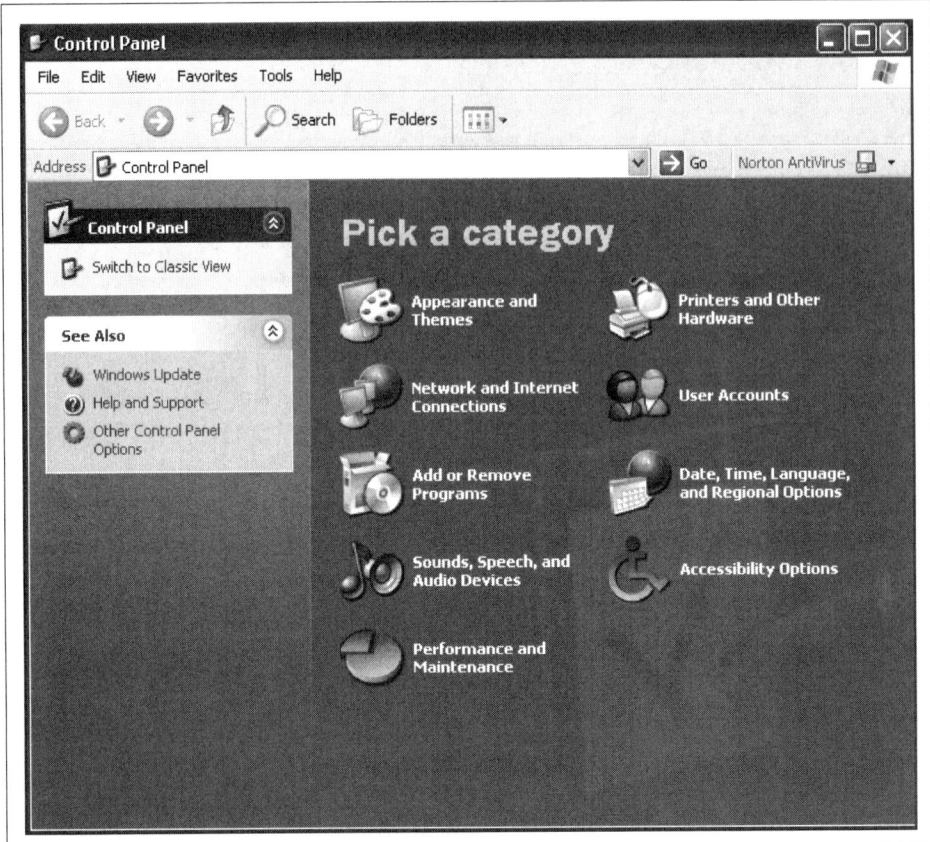

Figure 2-20. Microsoft Windows Control Panel

Thus, the name */home/tom/documents* means "the directory documents under the directory tom under the directory home."

Unlike other systems, which provide a separate hierarchy for each disk drive (hard drive), Linux provides a single hierarchy that includes every drive and partition. We call the topmost directory of the directory tree the *root directory*, which is written as just a forward slash (/). All directories and files are below this root directory.

When you log in to Linux, the system places you in a special directory, known as your *home directory*. Each user has a distinct home directory, where the user creates personal files. This makes it simple for the user to find files previously created, because they are isolated from the files of other users.

Figure 2-21 shows a typical portion of a JDS file hierarchy. Notice the box called "home." This box represents the area within the Linux directory structure in which a user's home directory exists. So the home directory for user tom is */home/tom*. If the user has a file in his Documents directory, in the subdirectory text, we can refer to it as */home/tom/Documents/text/filename*.

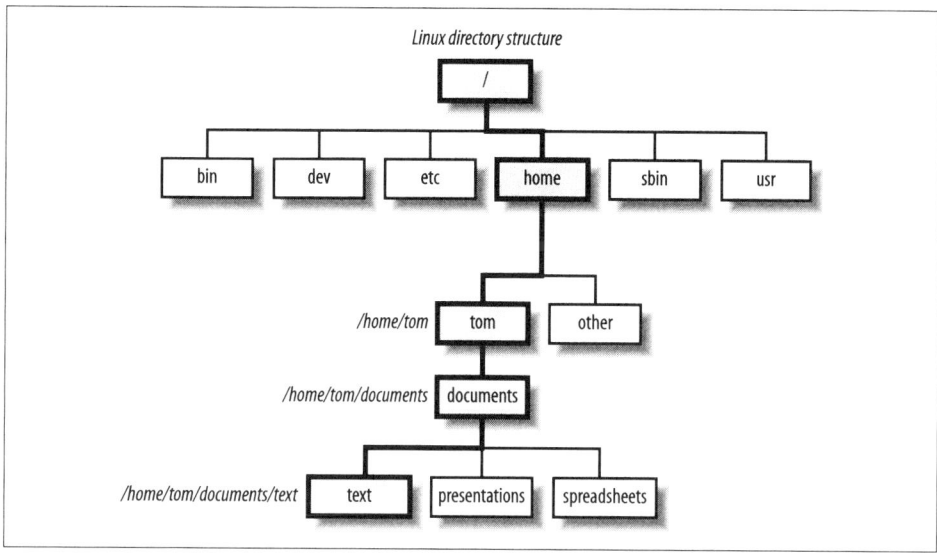

Figure 2-21. Linux directory structure

Common Linux Directories

If you have to poke around the Linux directory structure to carry out some administrative task that was not done through dialog boxes, you may find the information in Table 2-1 helpful.

Table 2-1. Linux directories

Directory	Contents
bin	This directory contains most of the executable files of applications. The name is short for "binary," which describes most executable files. An executable file in Linux does not necessarily have an extension by which you can identify it. In Nautilus, you can often find out what the file is by right-clicking on the file and selecting Properties.
boot	This directory contains the Linux kernel and the files used by the bootloader to start Linux.
dev	This directory contains files representing devices such as hard disks and floppies.
etc	This directory houses the configuration files for various applications and system daemons. Traditionally, to configure the applications or services in Linux, you had to manually edit these configuration files (usually plain text files).
home	This directory contains the home directories of the users. Note that the root (administrator) home directory does not exist within home. The root's home directory is /root.
lib	This directory contains libraries used by numerous programs and applications.
mnt	This directory commonly contains the mount points. A mount point is the place where you can access other data devices such as CDs and floppies.

Table 2-1. Linux directories (continued)

Directory	Contents
opt	This directory can be used by third-party applications (those that come from outside JDS) as their installation directory.
proc	This directory contains information about the Linux kernel and files and sometimes permits system administrators to dynamically change kernel behavior.
sbin	This directory is where JDS places applications or commands used by the system administrator.
tmp	This directory is used by applications for storing their temporary files.
usr	This directory is where most Linux applications usually get installed.
var	This directory is used for storing material headed for the printer, log files, cache files, etc.

Table 2-1 contains the names of the Linux directory tree. People new to Linux or Unix may find the naming conventions of the directory to be strange. If you do, please do not feel concerned; we have all struggled with these conventions.

Linux inherited the operating system concepts of Unix, and when the original Unix developers named things, they used abbreviations and acronyms. Over time, you may value having the directory information on the tip of your tongue. Until then, just having some recognition of the information in Table 2-1 can help you get around or recognize where you end up by accident. That may also help you find your way home.

So What Have We Learned?

Navigating around JDS can have a similar look and feel to systems you may have used in the past, like Windows 98 or XP. However, a big difference lies underneath the user interface where you find Linux: a powerful, stable and secure operating system.

Knowing the JDS system of files and their associated directories (folders) allows you to proceed with more confidence. The Linux directory structure differs from other operating systems, by using a hierachical structure, regardless of what partitions or disk drive it covers. As a user, you have complete control over your home directory and can create other directories within your home directory.

From this point forward, we discover additional powerful features included in JDS that provide a robust and exciting user experience.

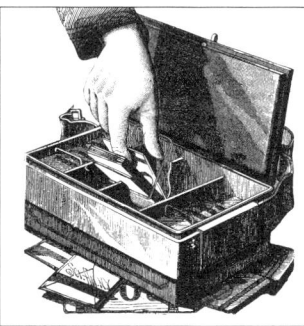

CHAPTER 3

Toward JDS Proficiency

In this chapter, you learn how to:

- Master the Nautilus browser, which provides convenient access to files and applications
- Do some customizations that can put some conveniences at your fingertips
- Set up printers, if they are not recognized automatically by JDS when it is installed

The first section of this chapter, "Role of the Operating System," offers you some background that can help you handle situations that are just a bit out of the ordinary, such as when you've forgotten where some application placed a file, or when someone sends you a file that you don't know how to handle. The material we present in this section is not critical for your immediate use. If something confuses you later, the background in the section may help.

Role of the Operating System

Regardless of the operating system you use, you need to know where things exist in the system, what they mean, and how to use them. If you switch to JDS from another desktop system, you won't find everything in the same place. For example, Games has its own extended menu, unlike Windows, where it is often placed under Accessories. When you look for the Word Count in the Word Processor, you can find it under File → Properties, instead of Tools → Word Count.

But different systems have much deeper differences that can puzzle you until you are aware of them. For example, consider how different systems handle characters in filenames and folders:

- On Windows and the Macintosh, the case of letters does not matter. *Mydoc* and *MYDOC* refer to the same file. But on Linux, and therefore JDS, the names refer to two different files. If you save a file under one name and try to open it using the other, you find yourself with a new, empty file.

- Windows separates the names of directories with backslashes, as in *Documents\ Mydoc*, whereas Linux uses forward slashes, as in *Documents/Mydoc*.

- Spaces are common in Windows and Macintosh names, such as My Documents, whereas they are rarely used and hard to include in Linux names.

As you are learning JDS, you can expect other differences in both appearance and behavior to crop up. These differences are caused by profound choices made in the parts of the operating system that underlie the desktop.

Under the Desktop

In Chapter 1, we said that JDS is based on Linux, which provides key system functions such as handling users, files, memory, and networking. We also mentioned that the desktop (the graphical user interface) was GNOME, heavily customized by Sun Microsystems to provide its own branded look. GNOME, in turn, is built on more basic GUI functions provided by the X Window System.

Separating critical system functions from the desktop is not unusual. Mac OS X offers a GUI called Aqua and an underlying operating system called Darwin that is very similar to Linux. Microsoft Windows used to have the same structure: the graphical interface was layered on top of an operating system called MS-DOS. While Microsoft gradually brought all the functions into an integrated graphical operating system, it still provides a command-line interface, known as the MS-DOS prompt.

 When we speak about a computer interface, we mean the layer between the language that the machine understands and human language. Some researchers call a computer interface a *human-computer interface*, or HCI. In particular, a graphical user interface employs pictures to represent text commands to the operating system. When you click on an icon to open a folder or application, this executes a text command. In turn, the computer interprets the text command and changes it to computer code or machine language. This chain of events, starting with the mouse click, takes little time and is invisible to the user. But if you are curious to see what command is run by an icon, right-click on the icon and choose Properties; the window that pops up shows the associated command along with other information.

Some reasons for the separation of desktop and underlying functions is historical. Operating systems were accessible at first only to batch jobs written in programming languages. Then command-line interfaces were added. Desktops came even later.

But there are other reasons for the separation. One is to facilitate the development of new and better desktops. Another is to allow access by the command line, which is a very powerful and efficient interface for advanced users. (Users with even more training can write scripts or programs that manipulate the operating system functions very efficiently.)

The Nautilus File Manager

The Nautilus file manager works a lot like a web browser. But Nautilus lets you see your operating system and other computers on your network, while your web browser finds web pages.

Nautilus makes it easy to manage files and the rest of your system. Figure 3-1 presents an example of a window displayed by Nautilus.

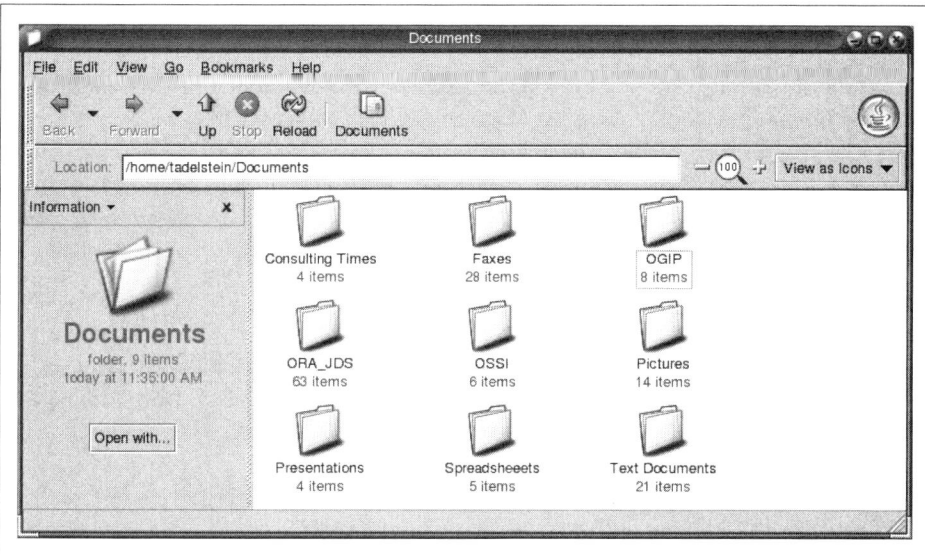

Figure 3-1. The Nautilus browser

Files reside on your hard drive or on the drive of a remote system you have rights to. Think of your computer and operating system as a downtown office building and think of Nautilus as an elevator with a full view of each floor. With the elevator's monitor, you can see thumbnails of everything on each floor as you reach it and therefore everything in the building.

For example, if you work in a forty-story office building, your company may be on the twentieth floor, and your office may be in suite 2050. Your desk sits in corridor D, in the third cubicle from door 2 on the right. Your project files reside in your lower-righthand desk drawer, in alphabetical order. This is an example of a hierarchy, an inverted tree structure describing everything in the building.

Now think of the JDS files and folders as your office building. The contractors created a hierarchical addressing scheme, with the penthouse at the top. The penthouse is the root of the tree, represented by / (a slash). Figure 2-21 in Chapter 2 showed a part of the hierarchy.

On several of the floors of your office building, activities occur which do not require your attention. You do not need to know much about the shipping docks, maintenance areas, security, air-conditioning, etc. Even on your company's floor, you may not need to know what goes on in the executive offices, in recruiting, or in the conference rooms. And you may not be given access to these areas.

Similarly, with JDS, you know that other things occur in the operating system that don't concern you. You probably do not need to know the hard drive locations of the files that connect you to the Internet. But Nautilus is there to take you throughout the hierarchy where you do want to go, if you have access rights (permissions).

To explore Nautilus, double-click on the icon called Documents on your desktop. A window opens and you can see the contents of this folder. It may be empty if you have not yet used StarOffice to create any documents. In that case, you can find another folder that has something in it. Click your mouse in the Location box, erase the word Documents, and press the Enter key. Nautilus will display your home directory with all its contents.

The window contains icons that represent the files and folders under the current location. For example, if you created a folder called *work* and saved a file in it, you can find the file by clicking on the *work* icon. You can then click on the icon for the file, and JDS opens it, using an application that it chooses based on the filename's suffix.

The Nautilus file manager helps you:

- Find files and folders quickly
- Add and delete files and folders
- Customize your files and folders by adding information to them
- Write data from your hard drive to CD or DVD recorders

Let's add something to your open Documents folder. Select File → New Folder from the drop-down menu at the top. You see a folder icon with the text "untitled folder" beneath it. Type **My Novel** and press Enter. You have a subfolder under the Documents folder, in which you can save files from the StarOffice tools described in Chapters 7 and 8, or from other applications.

If you don't actually want to write a novel, right-click on the folder you just created and choose the "Move to Trash" option from the resulting menu. The folder disappears, but JDS keeps it around in case you change your mind.

Select Go → Trash from the drop-down menu, and your missing folder appears. To get rid of this folder permanently and free up the disk space it uses, right-click on it and select "Delete from Trash" from the menu that appears.

Nautilus also has the hidden task of managing the files that control how your desktop looks and feels. You shouldn't have to deal with these files. They simply record what you do through JDS's graphical interface.

Icons and Thumbnails

Icons of various types let you know what the items are in Nautilus and on the desktop. Some of the icons you encounter on a regular basis are shown in Table 3-1.

Table 3-1. Common icons

Icon	Represents
	A folder icon, representing a Linux directory. Each folder can contain files and other folders. Double-click on a folder to see the contents.
	Indicates you chose the Information button. When you press that button, this icon appears on the side pane of your file browser.
	An associated file, meaning that the file identified by this icon has an application associated with it. When you click on the icon, the application is invoked to open the file. In this case, the file has an *.sxw* extension and can be opened by StarOffice Writer.
	Another associated file. In this case, the file has a *.doc* extension. It can also be opened by StarOffice Writer.
	A nonassociated file. The system does not know which application to use to open this file.
	A spin box, which lets you increase or decrease a numerical value by typing in a new value or by clicking on the arrows at the right.

Some icons reveal the contents of the files with which they are associated. For instance, if you store a photograph in a JPEG file, its icon actually shows a tiny image of the photograph; this type of icon is called a thumbnail. Examples are shown in the file manager window in Figure 3-2.

What You Can Do in the File Manager

Let's look at few of the things you can do in the file manager. First, here are the main parts of the window and what they do:

Menu bar
> Contains the File, Edit, View, Go, Bookmarks, and Help drop-down menus that offer most of the things you can do with the file manager.

Toolbar
> Contains the Back, Forward, Up, Stop, Reload, and Documents buttons that let you move around the file manager.

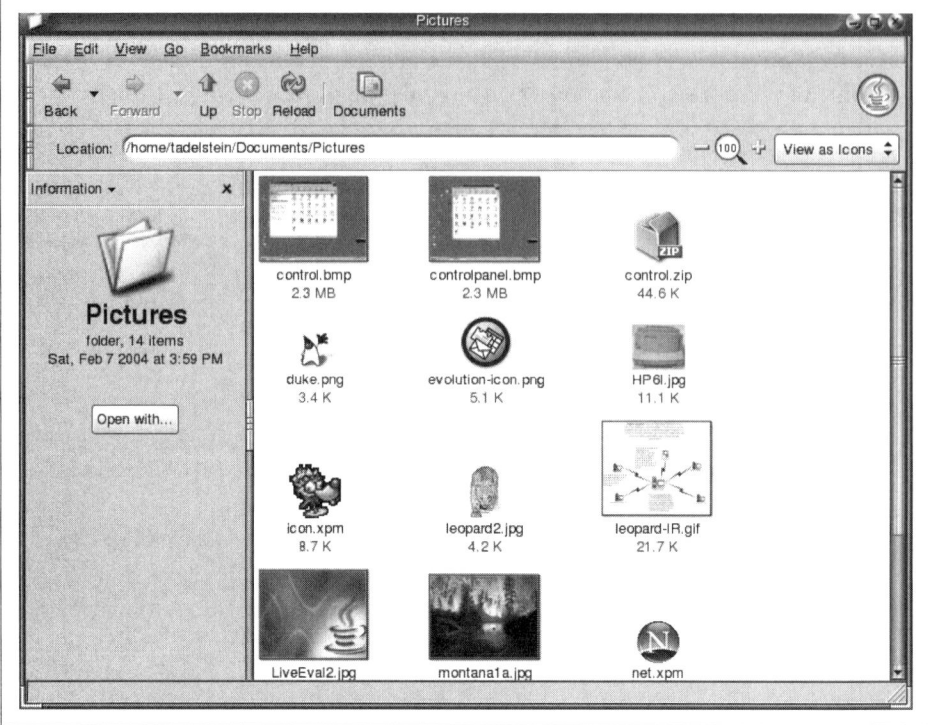

Figure 3-2. Thumbnails in the Pictures folder

Go menu

Lets you move to places on your desktop. For instance, you can view your Trash folder from here and retrieve documents you deleted. The CD Creator item is particularly useful for copying files to a blank CD (if your computer contains a CD burner). This feature is discussed in an upcoming chapter.

Location (address) bar

This is similar to the address bar of a web browser, but it doubles as a window on system files and applications. The contents are:

Location

Shows where you are on the system as you browse. You can also enter locations directly.

Zoom button

Lets you increase or decrease the size of items in the window pane. You can increase the size to see more details of small images or decrease the size to see more contents without scrolling.

"View as button"

A drop-down list to the right of the zoom icon. Choose "View as list" in order to see more details about files, particularly the date when they were last changed.

View pane

The main window of the Nautilus browser. It shows the various files, folders, and other items in the current folder or location.

Side pane

A bar to the left of the view pane. If it is not visible, you can bring it up by choosing the View drop-down menu and clicking on "Side pane." It shows a variety of information, depending on how you set the button at the top:

Information

Shows details about the current location in the view pane.

Emblems

Provides a number of icons you can use to mark files with practical information (such as whether it's a presentation) or not so practical information (such as whether it's cool).

History

Shows the locations you visited, from the most recent to the least recent. You can easily move forward and backward from this view.

Notes

Allows you to type a reminder to yourself, regarding the current location. For example, if you create a directory called Downloads, you can write a note about it to describe what the folder does.

Tree

Shows the hierarchy of folders and files, so you can quickly move to the one you want.

The Nautilus file manager window also provides pop-up menus for fast and convenient access to specific tools. To open a pop-up menu, right-click in a file manager window. The choices listed in this menu depend on where you right-click. For example, when you right-click on a file or folder, you can choose things to do with the file or folder. When you right-click on the background of a view pane, you can choose the way things look in the view pane.

Looking through the hierarchy of folders

As you use JDS, you soon build up so many files that you want to organize them by task or topic. It's a good idea to think right from the start about how to break up files into different folders.

The Tree view of the file manager's side pane, discussed in the previous section, can be very useful to help you navigate among different directories. For instance, if you type a slash (/) into the Location window and press Enter, you see a tree in the side panel, similar to the one shown in Figure 3-3. Most of these files are infrastructure to keep the system working and should not be changed by users, but browsing the hierarchy can get you used to using the file manager. Click on the triangle to the left of any folder. This expands the list of folders to show the contents of the folder you clicked on and turns the arrow into a triangle pointing down. Click on this triangle, and the list of folders contracts again.

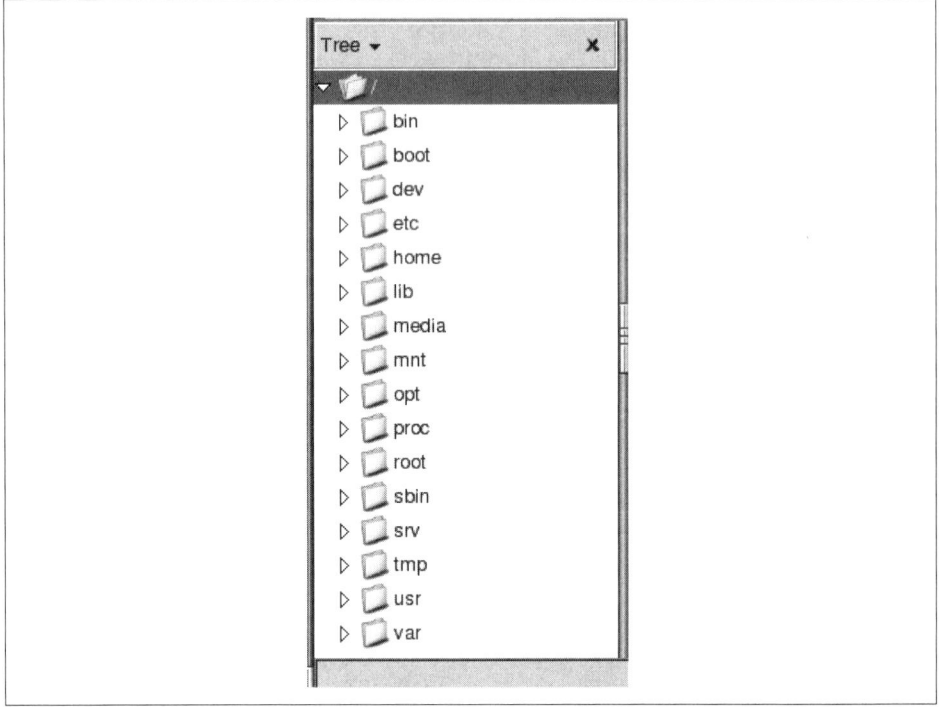

Figure 3-3. The JDS directory

Computer Resources and the This Computer Window

In JDS, the This Computer icon, shown in Figure 3-4, lets you access all the drives on your computer (such as the CD reader), open documents, launch programs, and customize your system. It's the JDS equivalent to My Computer in Microsoft Windows. We looked briefly at This Computer in the previous chapters, and now we can explore it in detail.

Figure 3-4. This Computer icon

This Computer is a Nautilus window, like the Documents window. When you double-click on the icon, it opens a window, with the location called *system:///*. We can see this in the Location area of the window, shown in Figure 3-5. A recap of the items in the This Computer folder is shown in Table 3-2.

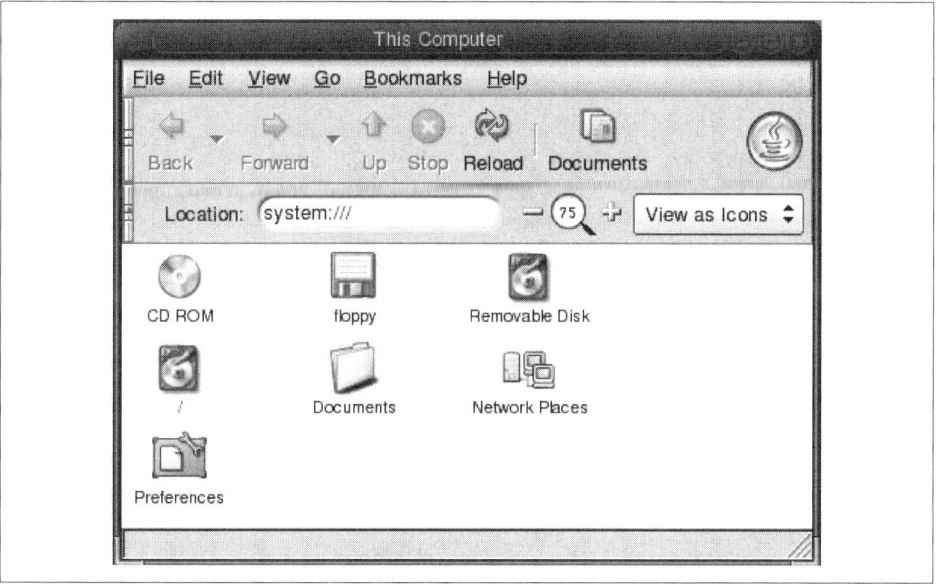

Figure 3-5. This Computer window, or System Folder

Table 3-2. This Computer contents

Icon	Represents
CD ROM	Your CD-ROM drive. If a CD-ROM is inserted, double-click on the icon to show the files on the drive.
Floppy	Your floppy drive. If a floppy disk is inserted, double-click on the icon to show the files on the drive.
Removable Disk	Shows Iomega Zip Disks and other media attached to your computer.
File System	This is simply a slash (/) in JDS . Clicking on this icon shows you the contents of all your disks. For thin clients and network computers, the Root Disk icon opens your home directory.
Documents	Opens the same Nautilus window as the Documents icon on the desktop. This shows the folders in which most users store the majority of their documents.
Network Places	You can browse other systems on your network and their shared directories, using this icon. We cover Network Places extensively in the next chapter.
Preferences	Lets you make changes in JDS. Options include changing the *themes* that control the look of your desktop, setting the resolution of your monitor, specifying your Internet connection, changing your password, and so on.

File Types and Their Associated Applications

Any time you manipulate and save data or some other setting on your computer, you are interacting with a file. The file extension or suffix (the final part of the filename, following a period) are the way in which most desktop systems know how to handle files—that is, which files go with which applications. In Table 3-3, we list some common extensions for files and what they mean, to give you an idea how this works.

Table 3-3. File extensions

File extension	Format description and type
.doc .dot	A document in Microsoft Word format. Regular Word documents use the .doc extension, while Microsoft Word Templates use the .dot extension.
.gif	GIF (Graphical Interchange Format), the most common graphics format found on the Internet.
.html .htm	HTML (Hypertext Markup Language), the code of simple web pages.
.pdf	Adobe Acrobat's Portable Document Format.

Adding a Home Directory to Your Desktop

If you have used Windows or Mac OS, you may want something similar to Windows Explorer or the Finder Icon on JDS. You can do this in a few steps. Although many JDS applications offer basic file management, a home directory accessible through the file manager can provide the most powerful tool for organizing your files. This window allows you to create new folders, copy and move files between folders, delete files, and rename files.

First, place your cursor on some empty space on your JDS desktop area. Then right-click your mouse. You notice a small window called a Context menu. From the Context menu, choose New Launcher. (See Figure 3-6.)

Next, you see another window titled Create Launcher. Type:

Home

in the Name and "Generic name" input areas (Figure 3-7). Next, go to the Type area and click on the right side of the bar with the two small arrows pointed up and down. Chose Link from that menu.

Next, type the path of your home directory, */home/your-directory_name*. You can browse to it (using the button to the right of the URL) if you don't know the name of your home directory.

After you fill in the text fields, press the icon button and choose one that suits you. In our example, we selected the yellow folder with the little house next to it, titled *Blueprint-gnome-fs-home.png*, in Figure 3-8.

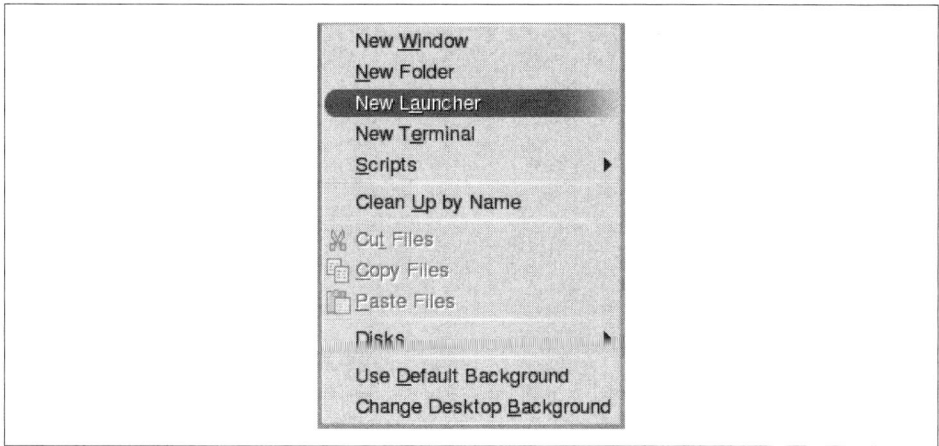

Figure 3-6. Context menu: choose New Launcher

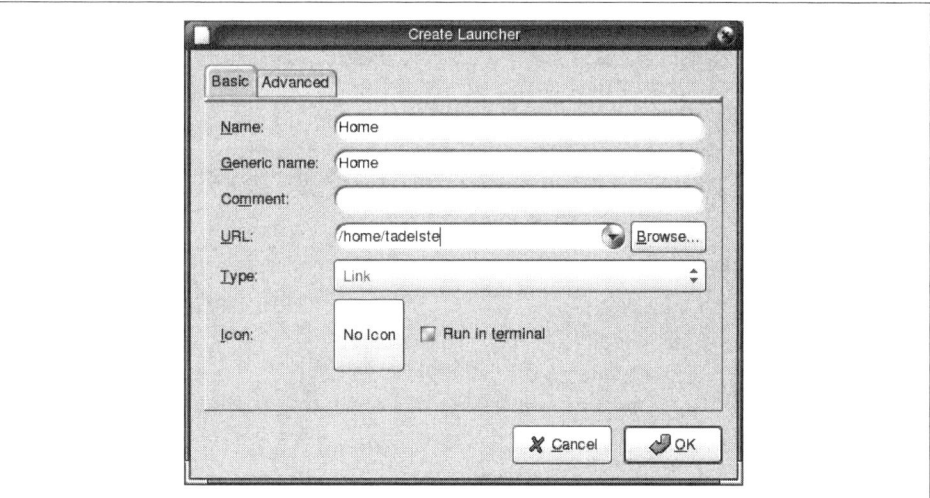

Figure 3-7. Create Launcher window

After you click OK, your Create Launcher window should look similar to the one in Figure 3-9. If everything looks correct, click OK, and you should have an icon on your desktop that resembles the icon you selected. When you click on it, you see a window with your directories in it, similar to Figure 3-10.

You now have a shortcut to your Home Directory, similar to that in Windows Explorer.

Adding applications to the Panel and Launch menu

Let's look at a useful customization you can make to your desktop. The second item from the bottom of the System Tools menu, the Terminal, represents a tool many

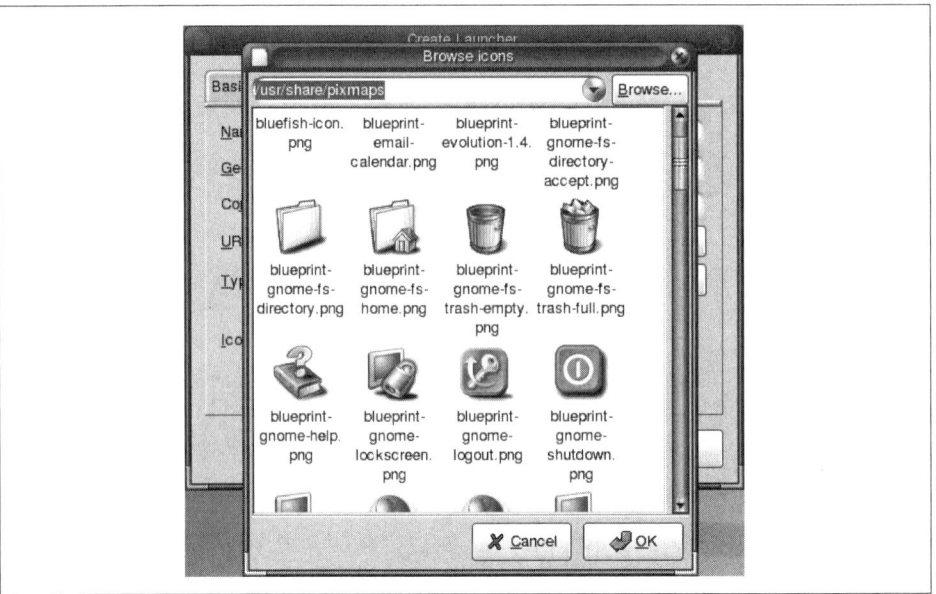

Figure 3-8. Choose an icon

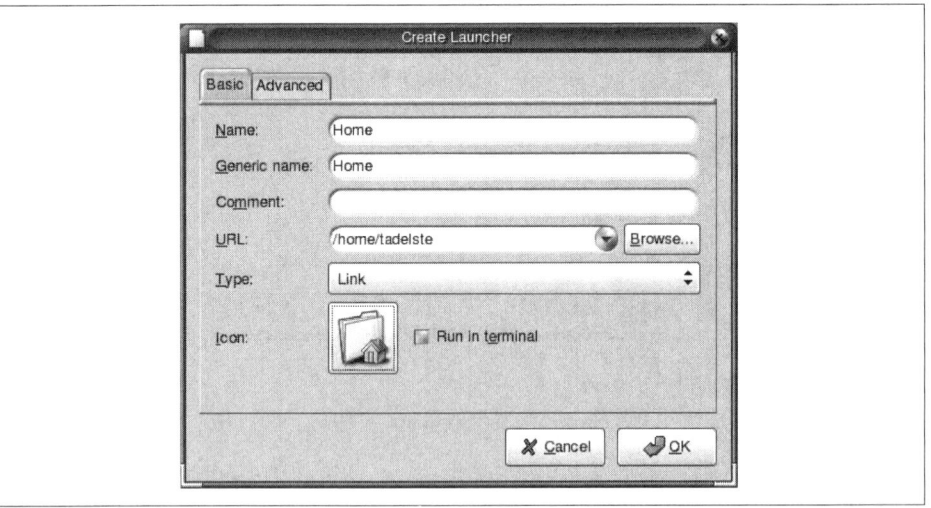

Figure 3-9. Completed Launcher window

people use regularly. If you find a need to go beyond the menus and icons on your desktop and enter some Linux commands by hand, the Terminal may prove important to you. So here we show how to add a launcher for the Terminal to make it easier to start up.

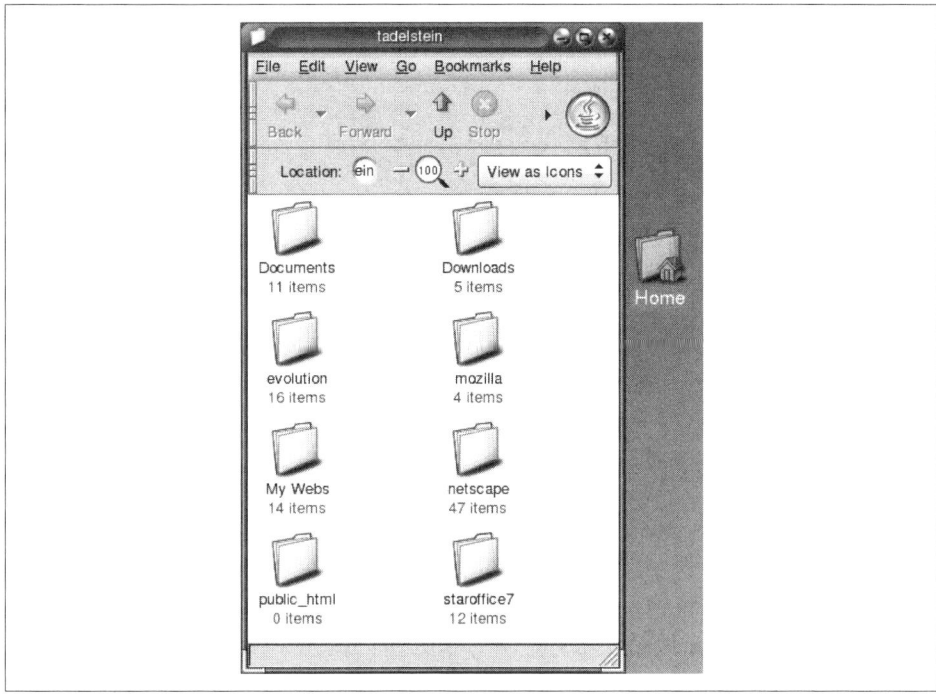

Figure 3-10. Home Directory window and Launcher icon

You can see in Figure 3-11 that a Terminal launcher was added to the panel on the bottom of the screen: it appears as an icon, near the center of the bottom of the figure. Clicking this icon has exactly the same effect as choosing Launch → Applications → Systems Tools → Terminal.

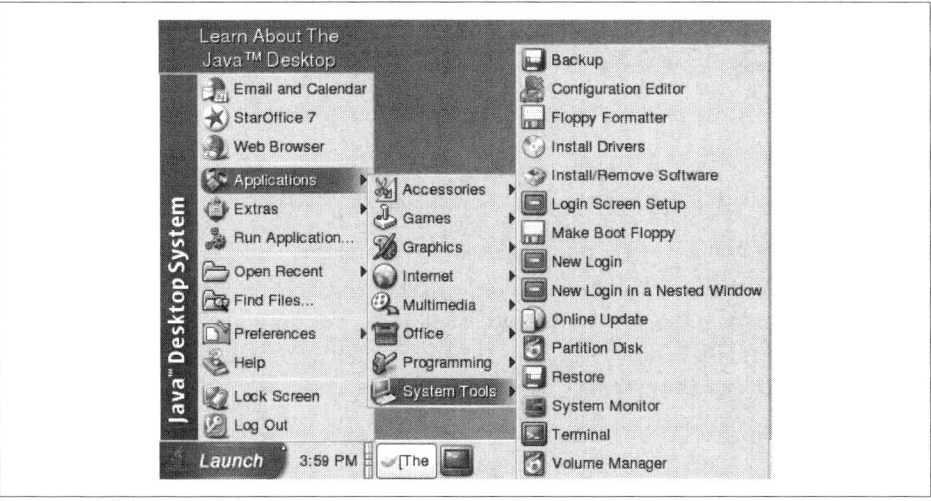

Figure 3-11. Terminal Launcher on panel

Figure 3-12 summarizes the menus you have to pull up to add the Terminal icon to the panel.

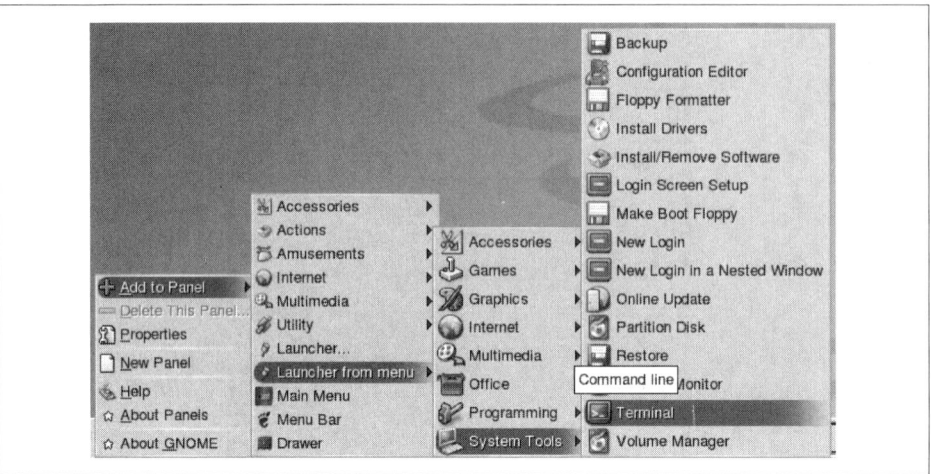

Figure 3-12. Adding Terminal to the Gnome panel

Start by finding an open spot on the Gnome panel and right-click your mouse. The menu in Figure 3-13 appears. We refer to this menu as the Panel menu.

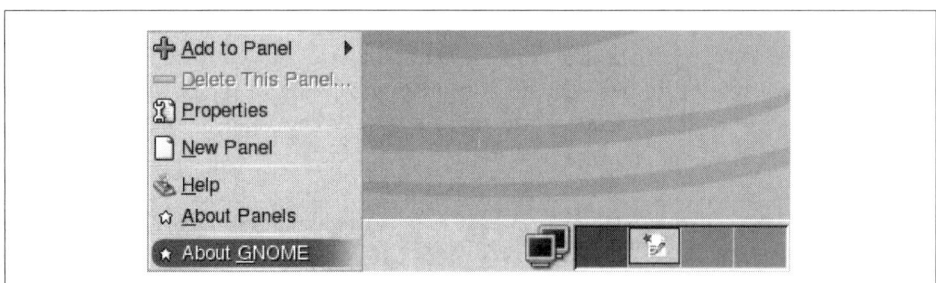

Figure 3-13. Panel Menu

At this point, you can select the menu entry Add to Panel. This puts up a menu that gives you a large selection of tools, many of which you cannot find in the Launch menus.

Figure 3-14 shows the Add to Panel selections. Notice the menu item that says Launcher from menu. That selection allows you to add anything you want from the main Launcher menu. You can see the available options by selecting the Panel menu and exploring the applications.

Let's go ahead and add the Terminal to the Panel and move it into position. Right-click on the Panel and the Context menu appears. Use your mouse to reach the Terminal by selecting Add to Panel → Launcher from menu → System Tools → Terminal. Release your mouse button to select the Terminal.

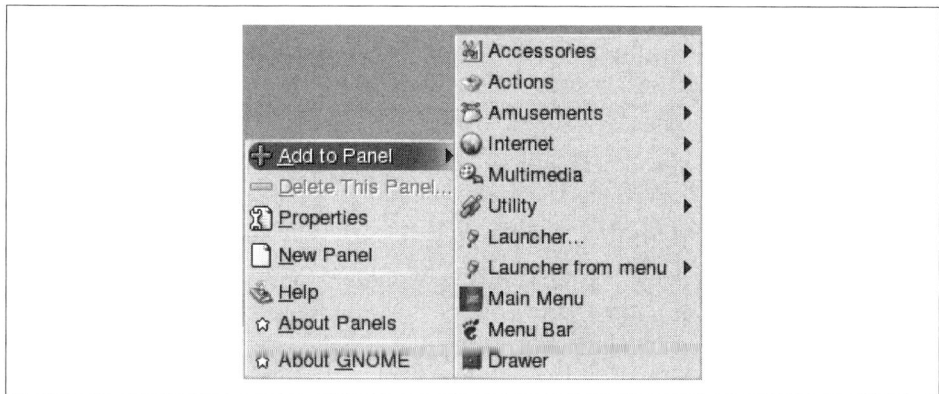

Figure 3-14. Add to Panel selections

Another way to achieve the same effect is to follow the cascading menus as if you were selecting Terminal from the Launch menu. Then right-click on Terminal and select "Add this launcher to panel."

As you can see in Figure 3-15, the Terminal icon appears to the left of the Add to Panel menu. You can similarly add any item in the main menu or any of the applications on the Add to Panel menu.

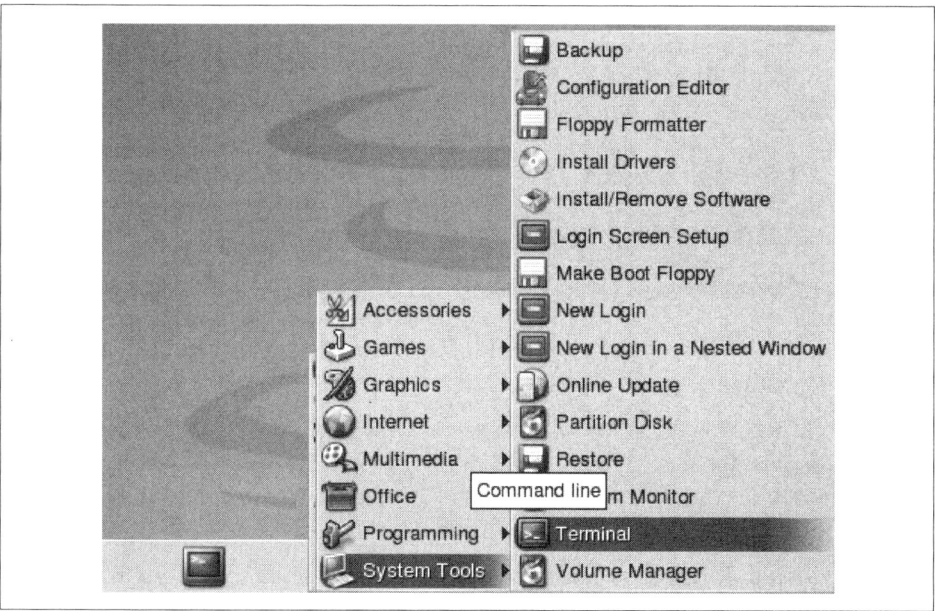

Figure 3-15. Terminal icon added to the Gnome panel

If you want to move a panel icon into another position, place your mouse pointer over the icon, such as the Terminal, right-click it, and select Move. The icon will float along the panel, following your mouse (note that the cursor changes its shape into a cross). Click when you have finished moving it to anchor the icon, then right-click the icon again and select "lock." Your icon now appears in the same location any time you log in to JDS.

Adding items to the Launch menu

The Launch menu is not fixed for all time; you can edit it in a couple of ways.

The first way is to open the Documents window on your desktop and type **applications:///** in the address area. This shows the icons representing the major subjects on the menu bar. Click any of them and you see the submenus. Add or delete launcher icons as you please, or copy icons from one folder to the next. All your changes show up in the Launch menu.

You can also edit the menu bar by clicking through to the submenus, finding the item you want to change, and right-clicking the menu bar. You then see a menu that lets you make various changes.

Utilities you can add to the Gnome JDS panel

Let's look at some popular utilities that you may use every day and may want to add to your panel. The first set comes from the Accessories menu. See Figure 3-16.

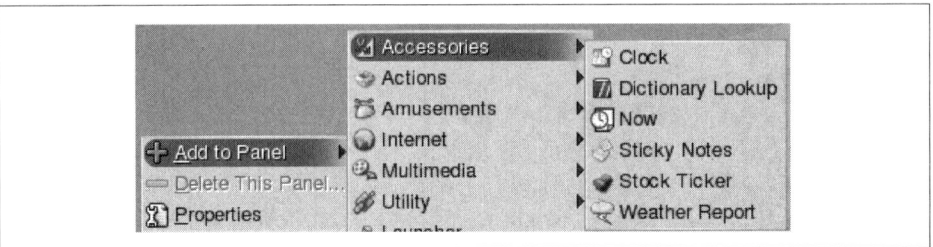

Figure 3-16. Accessories you can add to your Gnome panel

If you do not have a clock on your panel, select the Clock icon, and it immediately appears on your panel.

The Clock icon on your panel has options you can select by right-clicking the icon and selecting Preferences. You can have the icon show seconds, the date, UTC (Greenwich) time, and/or the city. When the date and time appear on the panel, you can drag them and paste them into a document.

Now let's look at Figure 3-17 and consider some actions you may want available on your desktop.

As you can see, you have some interesting choices. Force Quit uses the Unix command *xkill*. When you use this, it ends a process that is running on the desktop. This is normally not a good way to close a window; usually you should click on the button

Figure 3-17. Actions you can add to your Gnome panel

with the cross at the top of the window, or close it using the File menu. But once in a while you find a window that's hung and won't respond to anything you ask it to do; Force Quit is valuable for these extreme situations.

For example, suppose you encounter a spike in your Internet connection when you are receiving mail. This can cause the screen to freeze until the Internet connection recycles. If you do not want to wait for the connection to recycle, you can clear the desktop by pressing the Force Quit icon and by placing the cursor over the application. When you click your mouse, a small dialog box will appear and ask if you want to force the application to quit. Press OK to terminate the application.

The Screenshot icon has many uses, especially for writers or people who want to do art work from images off the Web. If you come across an image on your desktop you want to capture, select the Screenshot icon, and it lets you save a screenshot in the directory *html* under your home directory.

If you try out an icon and decide you no longer want it, right-click on it and select Remove From Panel.

Let's look at one more menu of items you can add to your panel; you can try out the remainder on your own. Just remember that whatever you add, you can also remove with a right-click of your mouse.

You may find the Utility menu in your Add to Panel selections valuable for two reasons. First, you may delete an icon by mistake, such as your Window List. Second, depending on the kind of work you do, items from the Utility menu can increase your productivity.

Let's look at the Window List icon, which reserves space on your panel to show what open applications exist on your desktop. For example, you may have Mozilla, StarOffice Writer, and Email open but minimized. If so, you can see that they are active and minimized. Without the Window List, all you can see is which applications are minimized in one particular virtual workspace.

 Even experienced Linux users accidently delete icons from their panels. Rest assured that you can replace them by going to the Utility menu to add them back. (See Figure 3-18.)

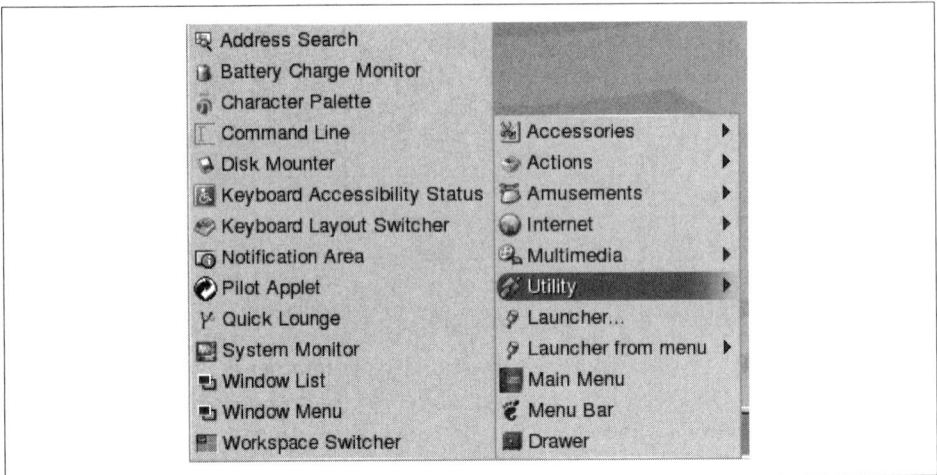

Figure 3-18. Utilities you can add to your Gnome panel on the left side

If you use a laptop, you may want the Battery Charge Monitor on your panel. Palm Pilots users can syncronize their PDAs by adding the Pilot Applet. Most of the remaining icons are self-explanatory.

JDS Printing System

Now that you have familiarity with some of the essential JDS desktop tools, we can begin using them. In this section, we want to set up our printer or printers. JDS supports the majority of printers available on the market, in addition to older model legacy printers. During installation, JDS will have searched your system and allowed you to set up any attached printers. However, some people wait until after installation to configure their printers or need to use printers connected to a network.

A post installation utility exists for setting up printers in the Preference menu. In Figure 3-19, you can see what happens when you select Launch → Preferences → Printers. In the screenshot, you can also see the context-sensitive help dialog that says "Manage Printers."

When you select Printers from the Preference menu, JDS launches a console, as seen in Figure 3-20, with the location *printers:///*. Notice that two printers show up; JDS has scanned the network and located two shared printers. One is an Epson 777i on a Macintosh OS X system, and the other runs a shared HP-6L on a Windows 98 workstation. Note that it may take JDS some time to browse the network looking for printers, during which time a busy cursor appears.

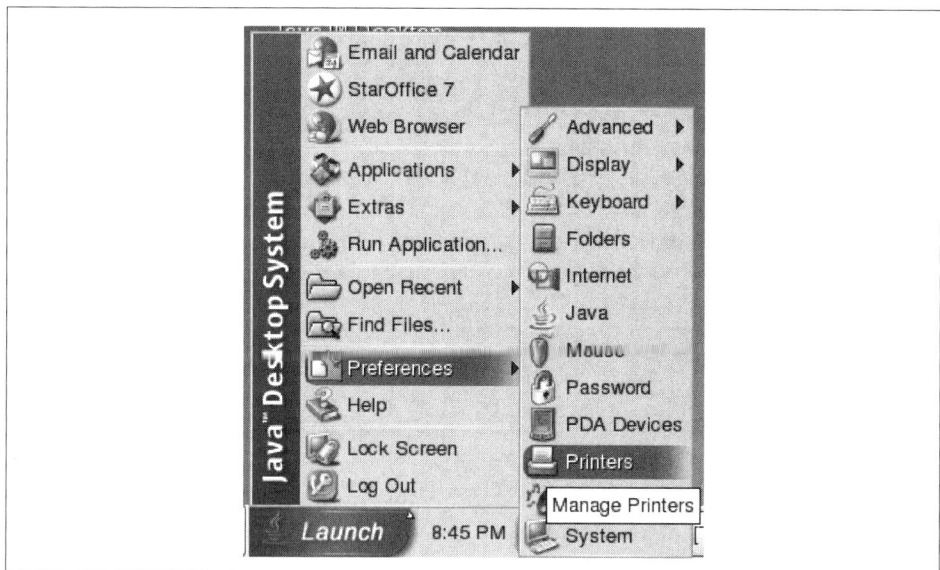

Figure 3-19. Launching the printer console

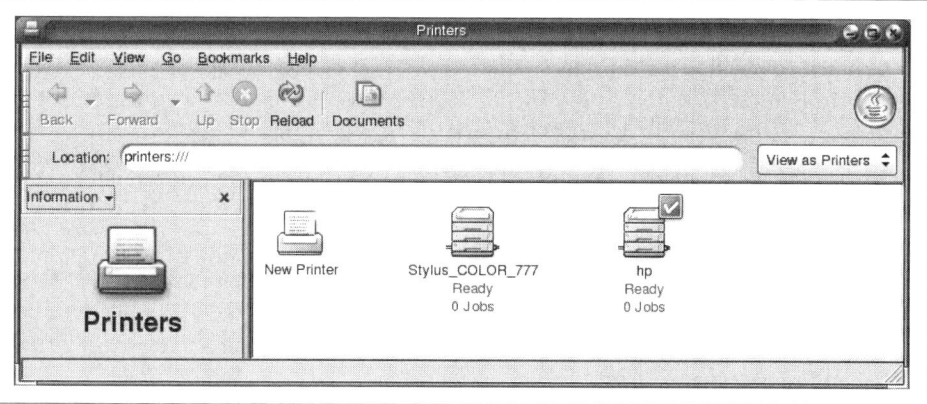

Figure 3-20. The printer console

Even though these printers show up as if you're directly connected to them, they are on other systems. Therefore, each time you try to print something, JDS needs to create a local queue, feed the printer code to that queue, and transmit the data to the remote printer. So let's see how to set up the local queue and establish a relationship with the remote printer.

Start by selecting New Printer. You are prompted to enter the root password. The dialog box says you are modifying a printer, but don't be confused—this process ends in adding a new printer. Next, the New Printer assistant appears, as shown in Figure 3-21.

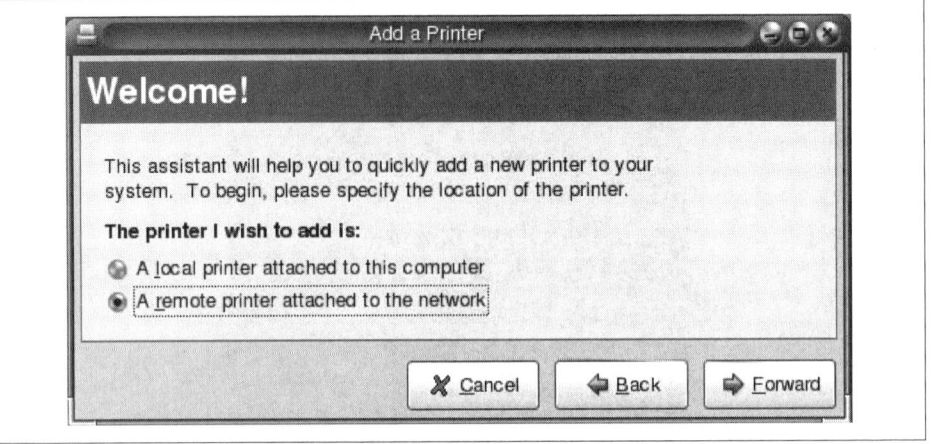

Figure 3-21. Start of the Printer Setup Assistant

If you choose to set up a local printer—one directly connected to your computer—JDS scans the various ports where a printer could be installed and reports back. For example, if you connected your printer to a USB port, JDS finds the printer connected to the port and tells you that it found a USB printer. JDS then configures your printer with the appropriate driver.

If you need to use a remote printer attached to the network, that choice is available, as well. In Figure 3-21, you can see where a user selected the Remote Printer option. Pressing the Forward button leads to the dialog box in Figure 3-22.

In this box, you can see that the user selected a remote Windows printer. The remote printer could also exist on a Linux or Unix box if set up using Samba. (Samba is a set of programs that allows file and printer sharing between Windows and Linux file systems.) When setting up a remote printer, you have four choices of printer types: Unix Printer (LPD), Windows Printer (SMB), CUPS Printer (IPP), or HP JetDirect Printer. The type of printer you choose depends on the machine and how the printer is attached on the remote box.

In Figure 3-22, we connected to an Epson 777, shared through Samba. This particular computer that is sharing its color inkjet printer uses OS X Panther and exists on a Windows network.

To set JDS to use this printer, you need to know some information about the printer's host computer. Notice that Figure 3-22 specifies the Host as an IP address, the name of the printer used by that computer, the name of the domain or workgroup that both your computer and the printer's computer share, and a place for a user name and password. In this situation, a user account exists on the Mac OS X computer for the JDS user, so we can leave the user name and password blank.

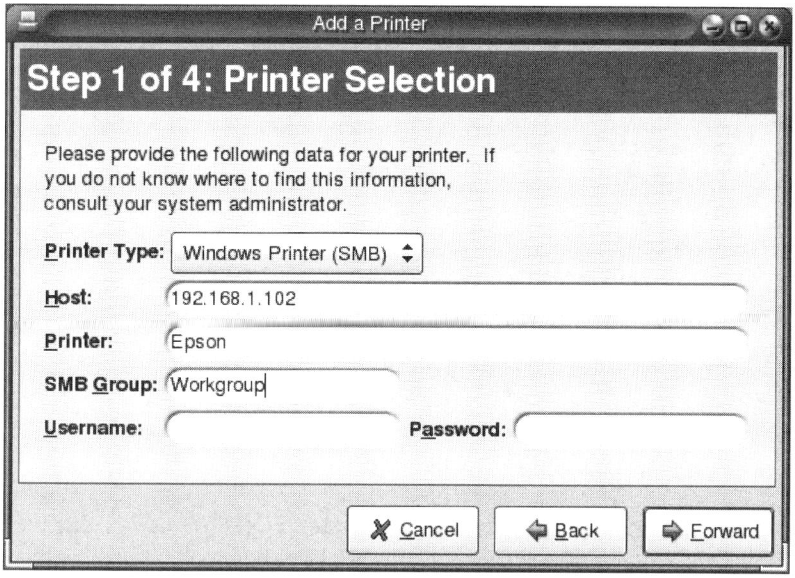

Figure 3-22. Selecting the priner type

In Figures 3-23 and 3-24, you can see how we configure the printer queues. Figure 3-23 shows the screen titled Step 2 of 4, where the New Printer assistant allows you to select a printer brand (Manufacturer) and below that to select a model.

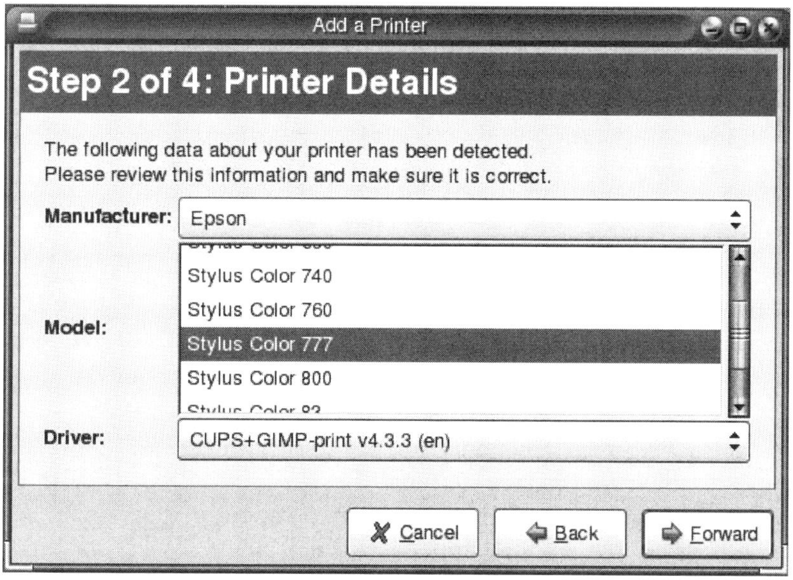

Figure 3-23. Selecting the printer model

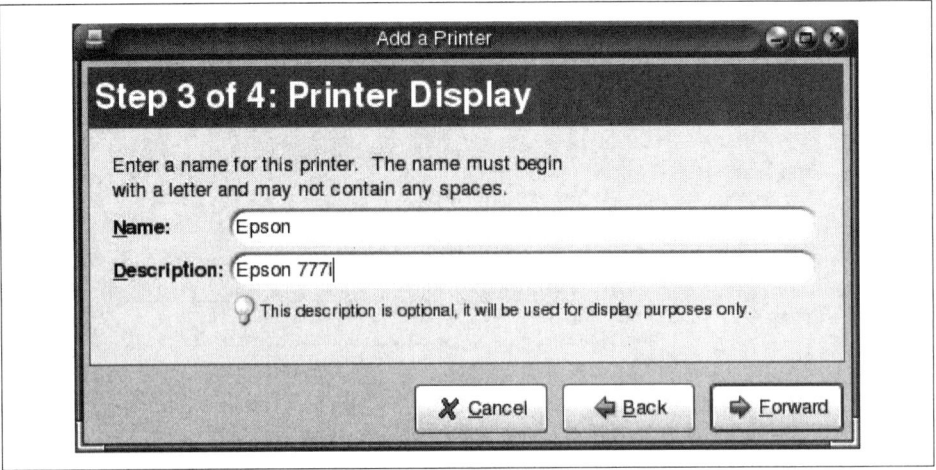

Figure 3-24. Naming the printer queue

In Figure 3-25, which shows the screen labeled Step 3 of 4, we named our printer display Epson, which mirrors the printer name used by the machine physically attached to the printer. Next, we used the description to indicate the model of the Epson printer.

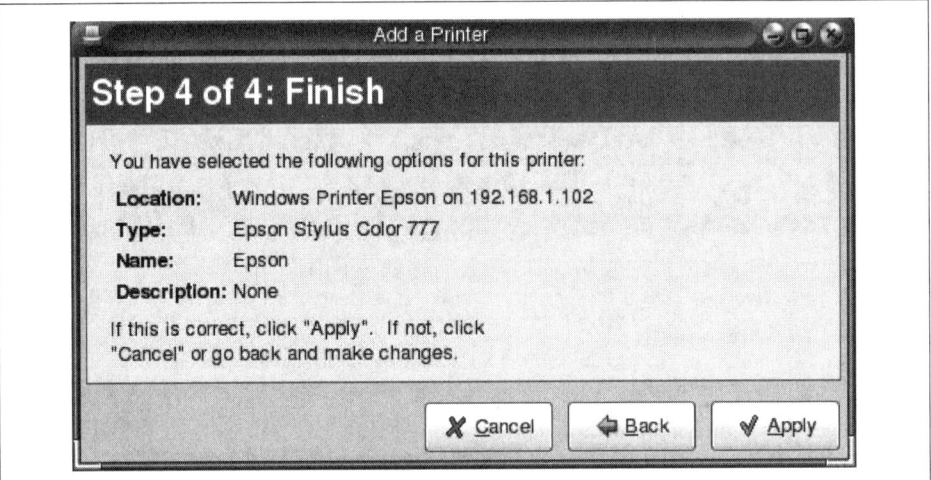

Figure 3-25. Last step verifying the setup

As we complete the final step of adding the Network Printer, the assistant presents Step 4 of 4, shown in Figure 3-25. Here the new printer assistant provides the options associated with the printer, including the location, type of printer, name, and description. Notice that the description field in Figure 3-25 did not pick up the description.

You can now select the Back button to see if you successfully added the description and if not, complete Step 3. Once you select Apply in Step 4, you have completed your printer installation.

Gaining JDS Proficiency

In this chapter, we addressed several issues related to files, directories, and file management. As you begin using Linux and JDS you'll find this information extremely valuable. Your knowledge of the Nautilus file manager will have a direct bearing on your productivity.

We have also learned about tools to manage files and directories, customize your desktop, set up printers, and enhance your computing experience in various ways. In the next chapter, we address issues related to networking, such as getting connected to the Internet and using networking services. We show you how to add software to your system in Chapter 5, and to update it when security fixes and other improvements are released.

Chapters 6 and 7 have the information that makes you truly productive. There we introduce applications that people use in their everyday work lives, including Mozilla web browser, Email and personal information management, Word Processing, and the use of Instant Messaging. As you progress into those chapters, you will find that the basics learned in this chapter make a difference in your effectiveness.

CHAPTER 4

JDS Networking

You've already learned enough to start doing productive work with JDS. If you are in a work environment, the JDS installation probably connected you to your organization's network, and through this internal network to the larger Internet. If so, you can jump right to Chapter 6 to try out email, web browsing, and instant messaging.

If you are at home or in a small office and have a connection through an Internet service provider, you may need to perform a few more steps to use your Internet connection. You may also need to do more work to use a wireless connection or share resources on your system with others. JDS comes with a Configuration Assistant that can have you up and running with an Internet connection in just a few minutes. You need a Linux compliant modem and/or network card for this to work. Some of the questions this chapter can answer include:

- How do I set up an Internet connection?
- How do I share documents, resources, and/or my Internet connection?
- What if I have different operating systems running on my network; how do I make them work together?

Looking at the Internet

JDS and Linux exist as children of the Internet. Unlike other operating systems, Linux developers built Linux from the ground up as an Internet OS. All a computer needs to work in almost any Internet capacity comes with Linux.

Built for Broadband

JDS works well with DSL or cable. If you have a high-speed connection, you belong to a group of millions of people who will not need a conventional dial-up modem. Instead, your computer needs a network card. Most newer computers have network facilities and dial-up modems built into the main circuit board or motherboard. JDS can recognize the chipmaker of the cards and pre-configure its network connection.

The network card of the PC needs to communicate with your DSL or cable modem. If you have a broadband connection, your provider probably furnished you with a modem. Your provider also gave you an Internet identification number. Every computer on the Internet requires a unique ID number that we commonly call an IP address. Your provider set your system to get one automatically each time you connect to the provider.

Figure 4-1 shows that two options are available when you use a network card. The first option, called automatic address setup, uses a method known as Dynamic Host Configuration Protocol (DHCP). It's extremely simple for you to configure and works well for nearly all home and small office users. The ISP's DHCP server provides you an IP address and other networking information without your intervention.

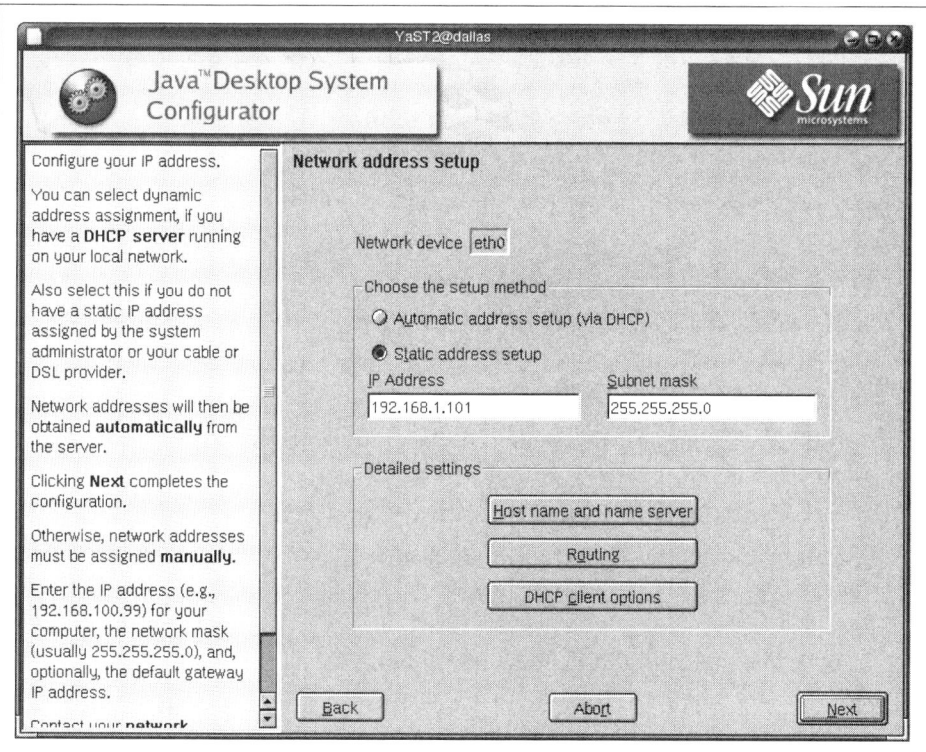

Figure 4-1. Network address setup

The second configuration method allows for static addresses. This is for more advanced users who want to run servers on their systems, and requires you to do more work. (The sidebar "Configuring a Static Address" summarizes what an advanced user needs for this type of configuration.)

Configuring a Static Address

If your ISP provides you with a static IP address, you can set up an Internet connection through your network configuration tool.

You need the following information to set up this kind of connection:

- ISP access phone number.
- Your username and password.
- ISP's DNS servers.
- Information for the ISP's services:
    — The incoming mail server address, such as *pop3.isp.net or mail.isp.net*.
    — The outgoing SMTP mail server address. It might have the same address as the incoming mail server. However it is often called *smtp.isp.net*.
    — The Usenet or newsgroup server address, which usually looks something like *news.isp.com or nntp.isp.net*.
    — Any proxy servers the ISP may have established.

Your Internet provider will furnish you with the information you need to set up your connection. You do not need to become a networking guru to use JDS.

To configure the network card of your PC or laptop, follow these steps:

1. Select Launch → Preferences → System, which opens a Nautilus browser window showing the location *system-settings:///*.
2. In this window, double-click the Hardware icon.
3. In the Hardware window, double click the Network Card icon and provide the password of the root user if prompted for it.
4. Now you're in the Yast2 configuration window. Select the Change buttons below the "Already configured devices" section.
5. In the Network cards configuration overview window, select the Edit button.
6. Select the "Static address setup" option and fill out the IP address in the IP Address text field. In the "Subnet mask" field, fill out the value (usually 255.255.255.0).
7. Click the Next button and then the Finish button.
8. Completely log out from the Sun Java Desktop System and then log back in. If your network does not appear to be active, you can reboot your PC to make the changes effective.

To set up the Sun Java Desktop System with a broadband Internet connection, follow these steps:

1. Select Launch → Preferences → System to open the system-settings:// window.
2. In this window, double-click Network Settings.
3. In the Network Settings window select DSL Network.
4. Provide the root password, if asked.
5. In the DSL configuration screen, perform the following actions:
   a. Enter the user name and password for the broadband account.
   b. Make sure the PPP mode is set to PPP over Ethernet, or PPP over ATM, depending on your country of residence.
   c. Choose the appropriate setting for the Ethernet card or VPI/VCI field. If the PC has only one Ethernet card, eth0 is the correct value.
   d. If the Internet connection needs to start automatically when browsing begins, enable the Dial on demand setting.
   e. Click the Finish button after entering the settings.

Dial-up Connections to the Internet

A dial-up connection using a dial-up PC modem is not only much slower than a DSL or cable connection, but more complex to set up. If you have access to DSL or cable Internet service, we recommend that you use it. This section is for JDS users who need to set up the slower dial-up access.

A large number of different PC modems exists, and JDS does not recognize all of them. Usually, however, it will work out of the box with your modem unless you have a WinModem.

WinModems and Linux

A WinModem lacks parts found in regular modems—these parts are "emulated" by software. This lowers the unit cost to manufacture them. These modems work primarily with Microsoft Windows, thus the name. A WinModem requires software to emulate the hardware missing from the modem card.

The Linmodem.org project provides extensive materials to assist you in adding the drivers to your JDS system. You can find the project at *http://linmodems.org*, and we will not attempt to duplicate their materials here.

If you have a regular modem, setting up your dial-up connection should go smoothly.

Connecting by Dial-up Modem

To use your dial-up modem, you must first tell JDS that you have a PC modem. Click Launch → Preferences → System → Hardware, and you will see a screen similar to Figure 4-2.

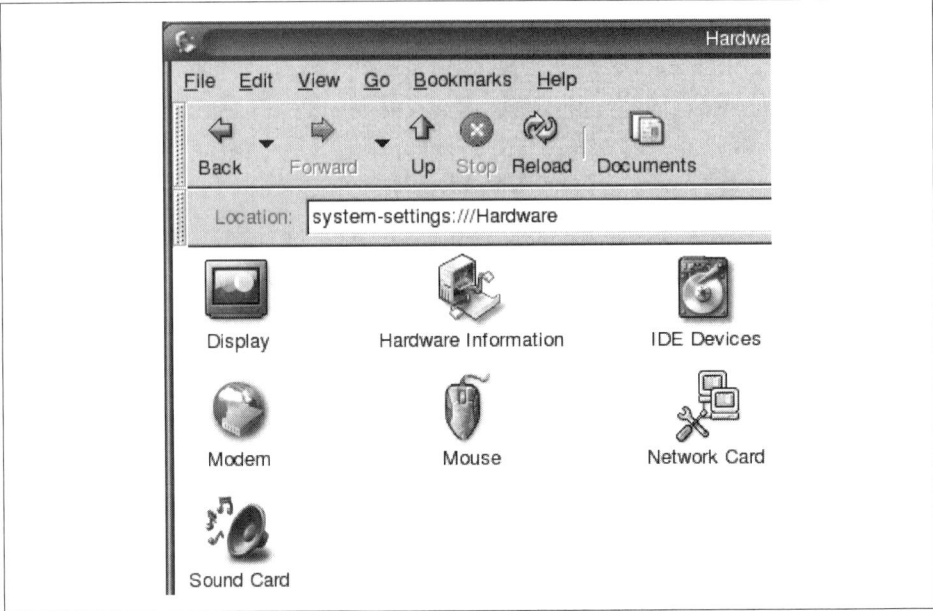

Figure 4-2. Step 1 in configuring your modem

When you select the Modem icon, you may see a prompt for the root password. If so, enter it as root. The Java Desktop System Configuration Assistant will begin a process to detect your modem. After the detection process, you'll see a screen similar to Figure 4-3, which shows the name of the name and make of the modem. In this example, the system found a U.S. Robotics modem compatible with Linux.

If you select the Configure button, you will see a screen similar to Figure 4-4. You will need to open this screen if you require a prefix such as 1 or 0 to get an outside line. Only facilities with PBX phone systems require you to use this option.

Adding Your ISP Information

Figure 4-3 shows an area titled Already Configured Devices. If you select the Change button, you have the opportunity to enter your information from your Internet Service Provider.

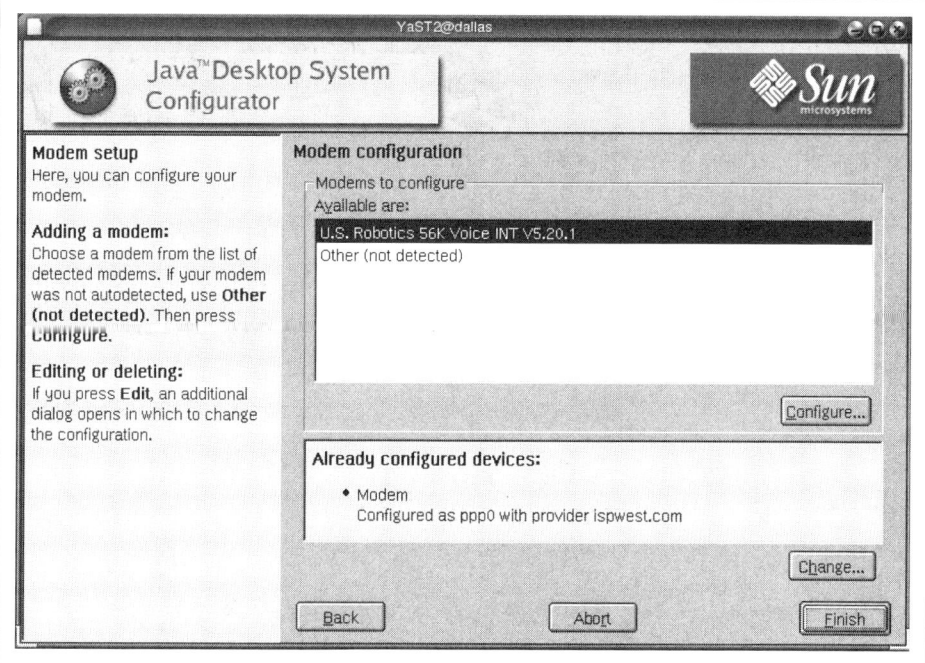

Figure 4-3. Modem autodetected

JDS provides you with a list of service providers, which may include one to which you already subscribe. Figure 4-5 illustrates the screen you will see after pressing the Change button.

To find your ISP on the list of providers, or if you wish to choose one with whom to sign up, select Next, and a screen like the one in Figure 4-6 assists you in gaining access to an ISP.

To configure your dial-up account, you will need the information in the sidebar "Configuring a Static Address." In the screen shown in Figure 4-7, enter:

- Your ISP's local access phone number
- Your Username and Password

Select the Next button on the lower right. This shows the screen in Figure 4-8, where you need to enter your ISP's DNS servers.

Next, you will need to complete the screen for your ISP mail services. The Information you need includes:

- The incoming mail server address, such as *pop3.isp.net* or *mail.isp.net*.
- The outgoing SMTP mail server address. That might have the same address as the incoming mail server, or something such as *smtp.isp.com*.

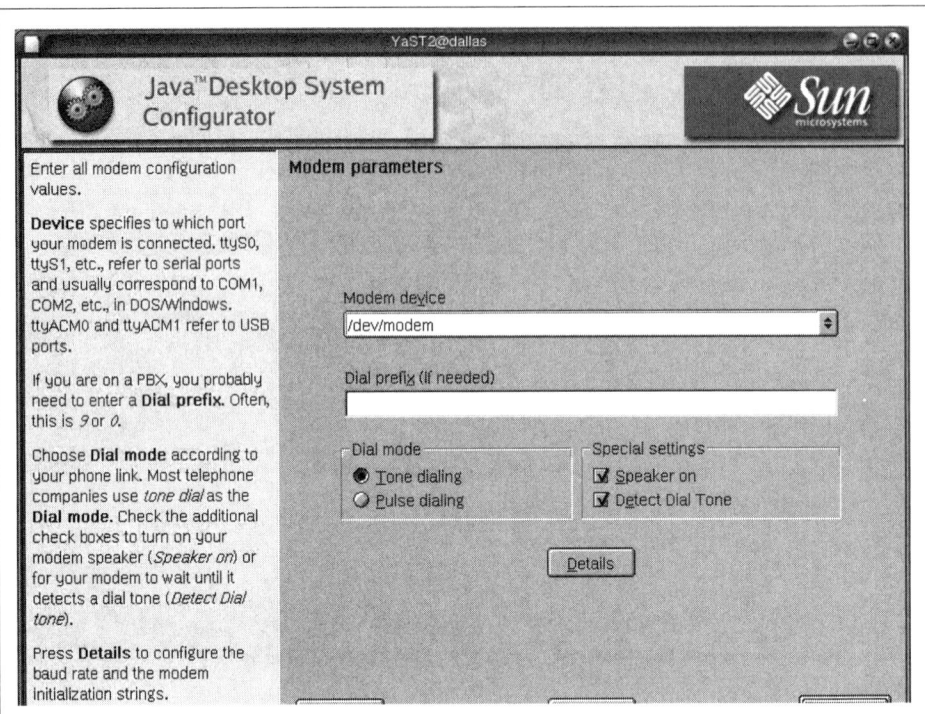

Figure 4-4. Adding a dial prefix

Once you have completed setting up your modem and ISP connectivity, you will see the Java Desktop Configurator saving the modem configuration. Figure 4-9 provides a screenshot of what you will see as JDS completes this task.

Modem sessions

JDS uses a program called WvDial to reach the Internet. If you activate the Dial on demand feature as shown in Figure 4-8, your Internet connection starts automatically. For example, when you enter a web address in Mozilla or start email, your system will dial up your Internet provider.

Once you dial up, you remain connected to the Internet. If you do not have unlimited access and need to manage your hours, you may not want to dial in automatically. In that event, you can use WvDial through a terminal.

To initiate a terminal session, select Launch → Applications → System Tools → Terminal, type the command:

```
wvdial
```

and press Enter. You should see a dialog similar to the one shown in Figure 4-10.

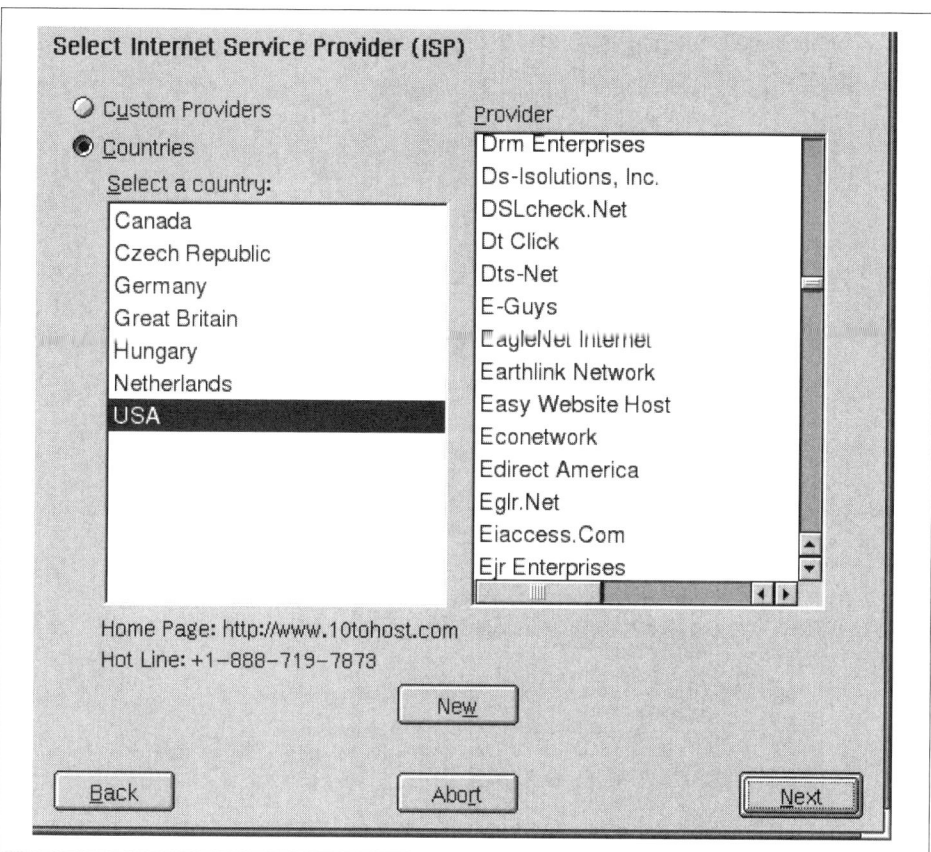

Figure 4-5. List of Internet Service Providers

After connecting to the Internet successfully, you can start using your browser, email, instant messaging, and other Internet utilities.

If you wish to end your connection to the Internet, type:

```
kill wvdial
```

in another terminal and your session will end.

JDS in a Local Network

If you use JDS at work, system administrators are usually responsible for setting up your network connections. JDS functions as a network client and your responsibilities for setting up and maintaining the network become minor, if any at all.

You may use JDS at home with other Linux computers. In that situation, JDS requires you to perform some setup. You can use either NFS connectivity between Linux computers or implement the Windows filesystem sharing utility: Samba.

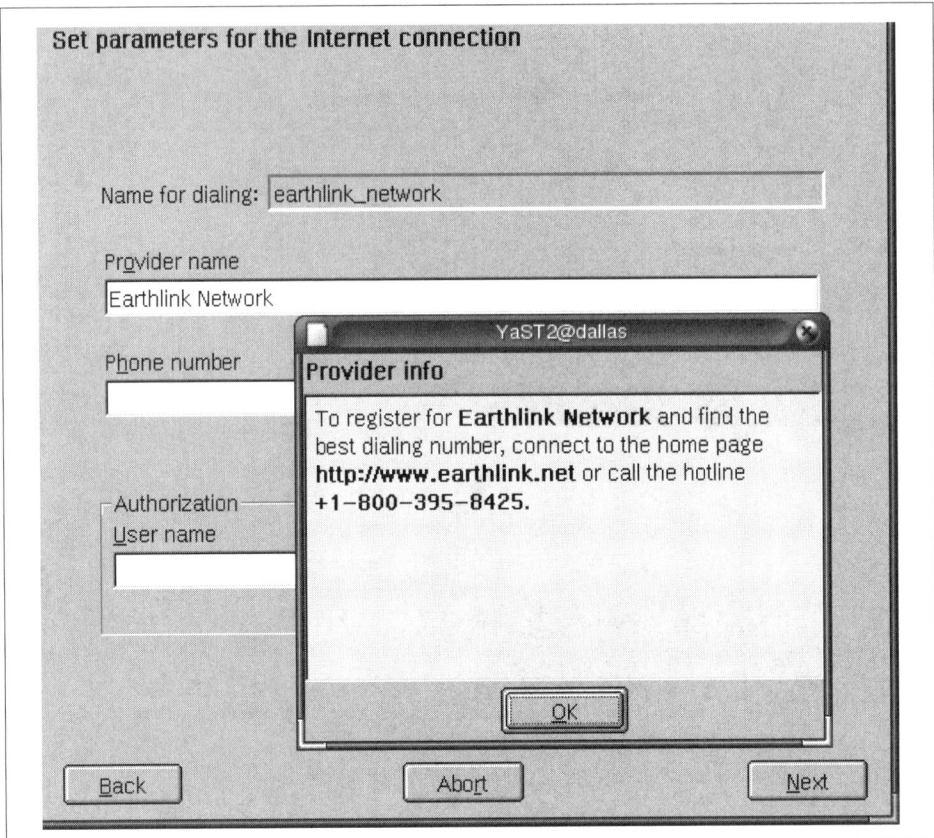

Figure 4-6. Selecting a Service Provider

JDS integrates well with Windows, Unix, and Apple Macintosh OS X computers in a network. Multi-computer households often utilize networking equipment found in a typical business environment.

Proponents often say Linux provides glue to disparate operating systems. JDS connects easily and gracefully to other Linux systems, MacOS, Microsoft Windows, UNIX, Novell NetWare, and a variety of other systems.

With your computers connected, you can:

- Share printers among computers
- Use a single Internet connection
- Share files such as images, spreadsheets, and documents
- Play networked games that allow multiple players at different computers
- Send the output of a device like a DVD Player or a Webcam to your other computers

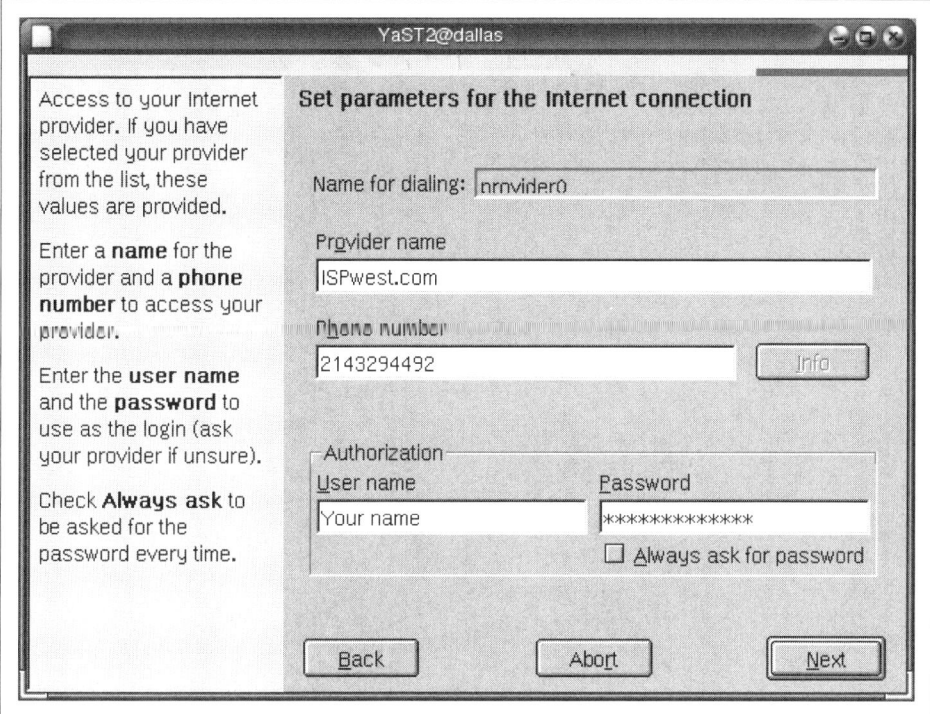

Access to your Internet provider. If you have selected your provider from the list, these values are provided.

Enter a **name** for the provider and a **phone number** to access your provider.

Enter the **user name** and the **password** to use as the login (ask your provider if unsure).

Check **Always ask** to be asked for the password every time.

Set parameters for the Internet connection

Name for dialing: providerO

Provider name

ISPwest.com

Phone number

2143294492   [Info]

Authorization

User name   Password

Your name   ************

☐ Always ask for password

[Back]   [Abort]   [Next]

Figure 4-7. Entering your personal information

You can configure JDS for a homogeneous network, or one that is a network of different computer operating systems. Let's look at each.

If you add your JDS computer to an existing network, it will automatically detect the presence of the other systems. The Network Places icon on your desktop will help you graphically see the other computers.

Let's look at an example. In Figure 4-11, we selected the Network Places icon on the JDS desktop and opened the Nautilus browser. As you can see, JDS comes pre-configured and ready to work with Unix and Linux systems, as well as Windows.

In Figure 4-12, we selected the Windows Network and found a domain called WORKGROUP. In Figure 4-13, having double-clicked on the WORKGROUP icon, we located the computers existing on that network. Each computer is called a *host* when we talk about networking. (And yes, people who get resources from hosts are sometimes called *guests*, but more often *clients*.)

In a larger Windows network, we could see numerous domains and workgroups such as Sales, Accounting, Human Resources, etc. In a small network, you often just see a single domain.

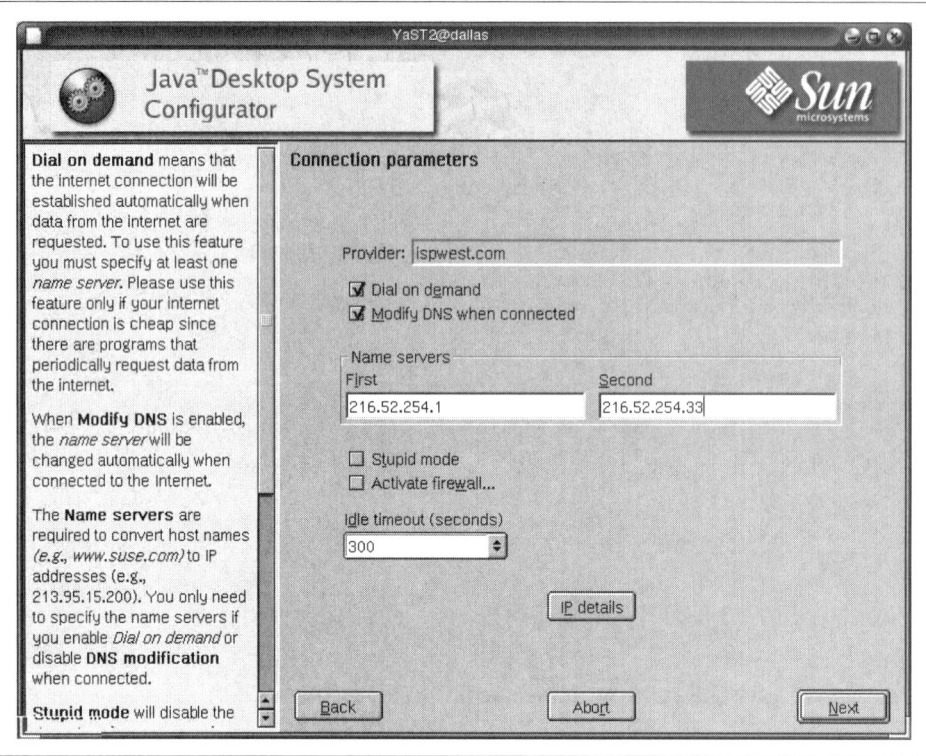

Figure 4-8. Adding your ISP's DNS information

Back to our example. The computers in the WORKGROUP are all Windows systems (or use software to mimic Windows). The abbreviation smb represents these computers, which use the Microsoft's Server Message Block filesystem. Just remember that if you see computers under the *smb://location*, you have found a Microsoft network, or one like it being served with the Unix software Samba.

When you select a computer in the smb://workgroup, you actually have made a call to that computer saying you want to access it. If you select any of the computers, the Network Places screen will let you know if resources exist for your use. So, if you selected the computer Dallas, it would respond with a logon screen, such as the one in Figure 4-14.

The resources on Dallas are private, which is why you need to submit a Username and Password. These are the user names given to you to access the remote machine, not your JDS name and password.

In Figure 4-15, you can see that when we selected the computer Dell from Figure 4-13, the system provided a folder called *winshare*.

The *winshare* folder on the Dell host can contain any type of file.

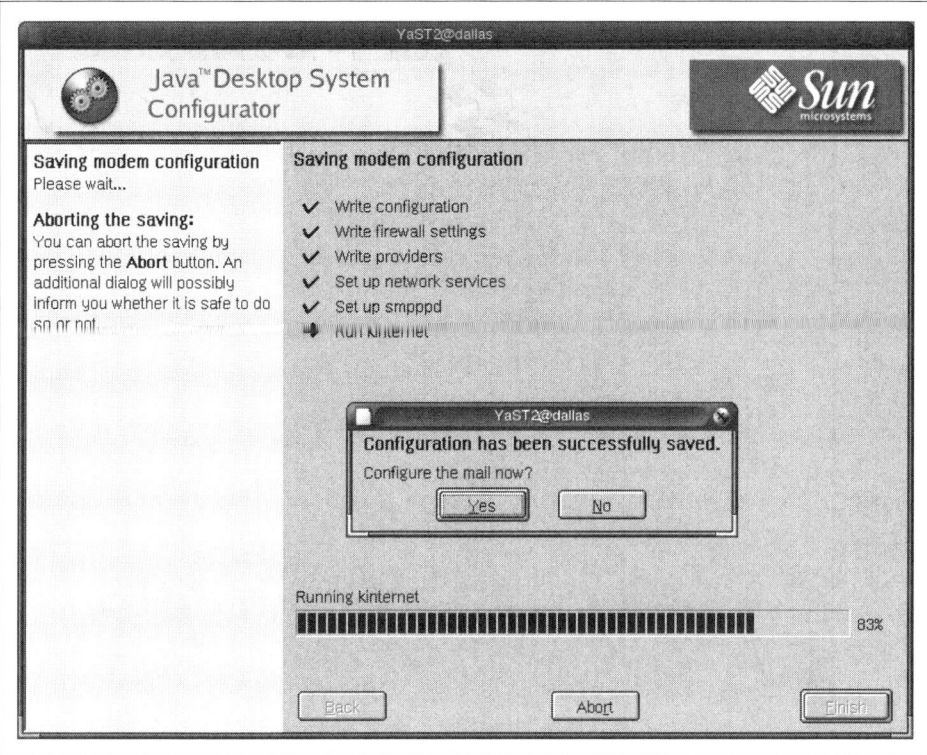

Figure 4-9. Configuring mail services

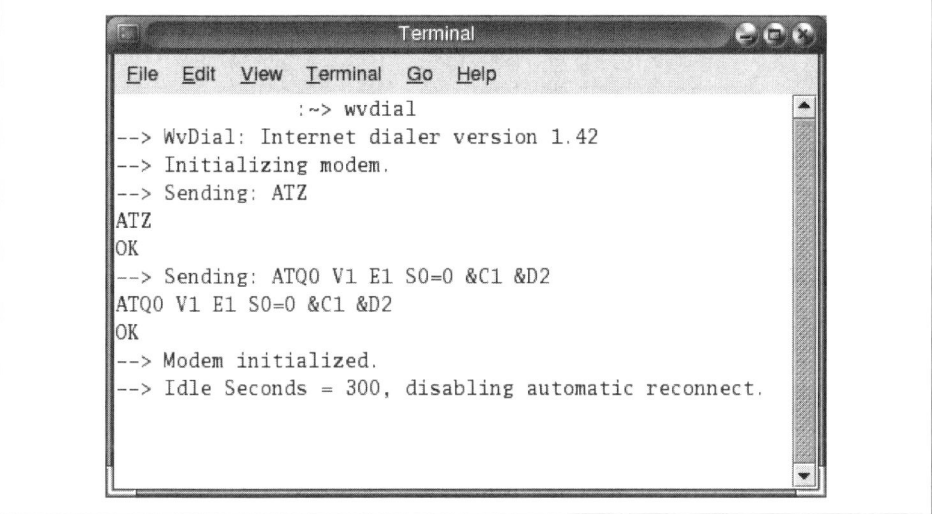

Figure 4-10. Running WvDialer in terminal mode

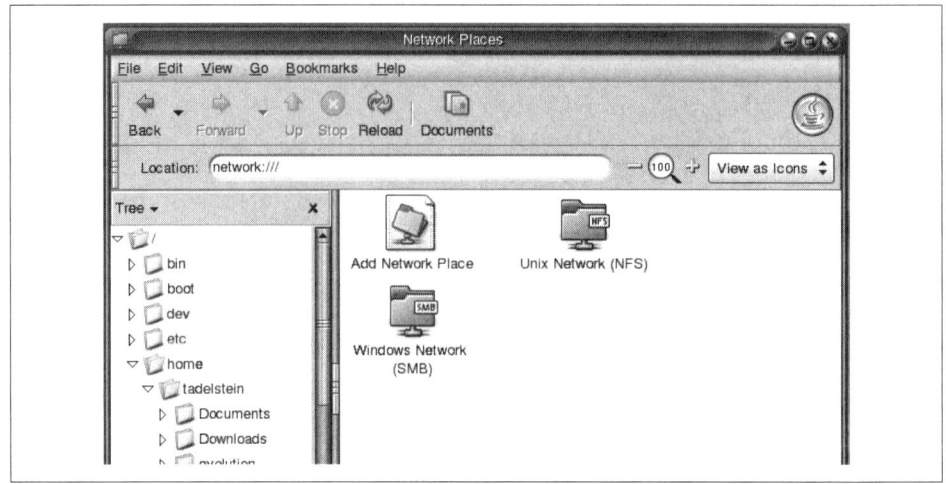

Figure 4-11. The Nautilus browser view of networking types

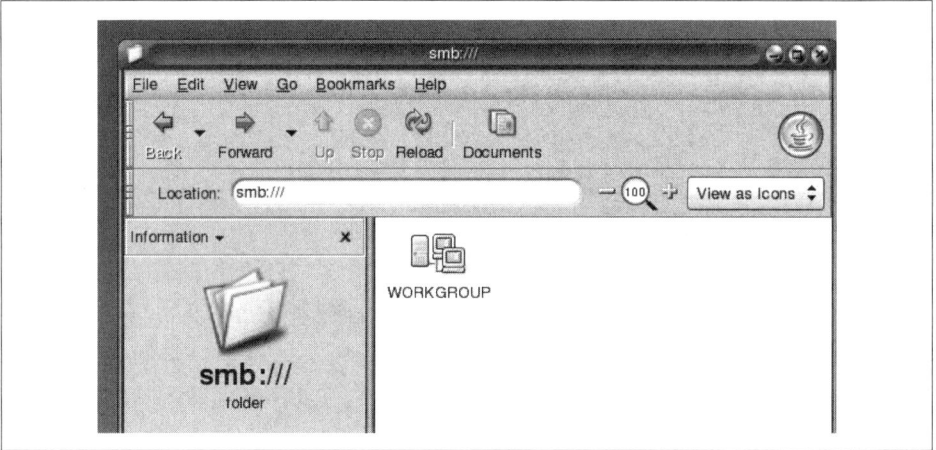

Figure 4-12. A Windows domain on the network

In Figure 4-13, you will also notice that the icon for Windows network bears the abbreviation smb, whose meaning you now understand. The Unix network, however, bears the abbreviation NFS, which stands for Network File System. Linux, Solaris, and Apple Mac OS X use the NFS sharing protocols.

When we select the NFS option in Figure 4-11, we can see the NFS servers (that is any computers that offer files to share over the NFS protocols) on the network. In our example, the server shows up in Figure 4-16 with the IP address 192.168.1.102.

Figure 4-13. A Windows network

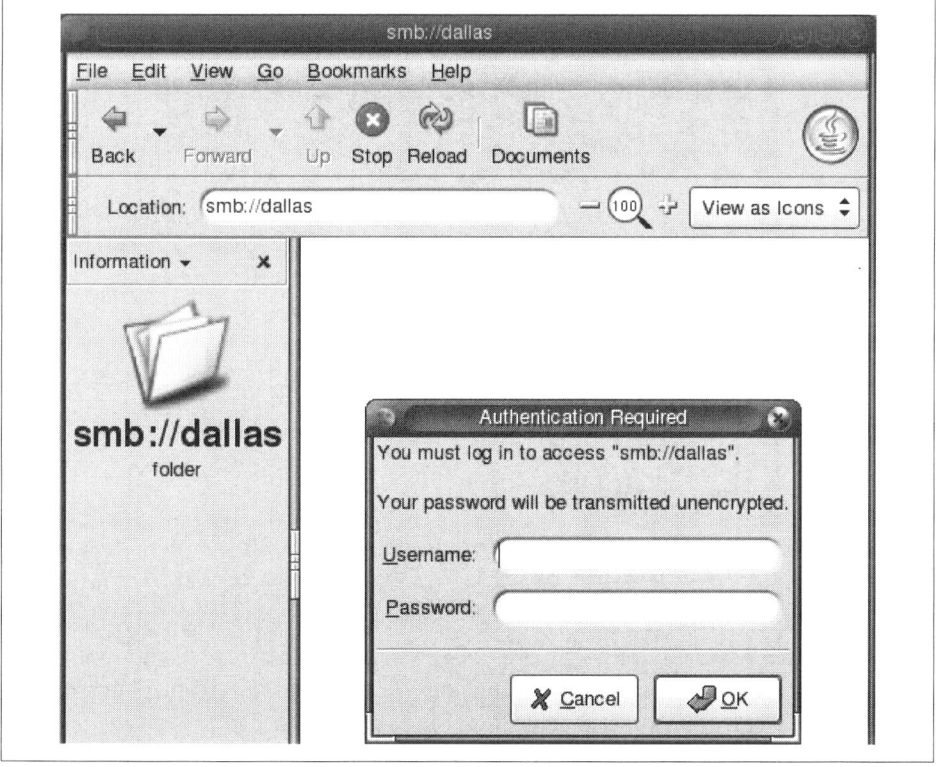

Figure 4-14. Authentication request from computer Dallas

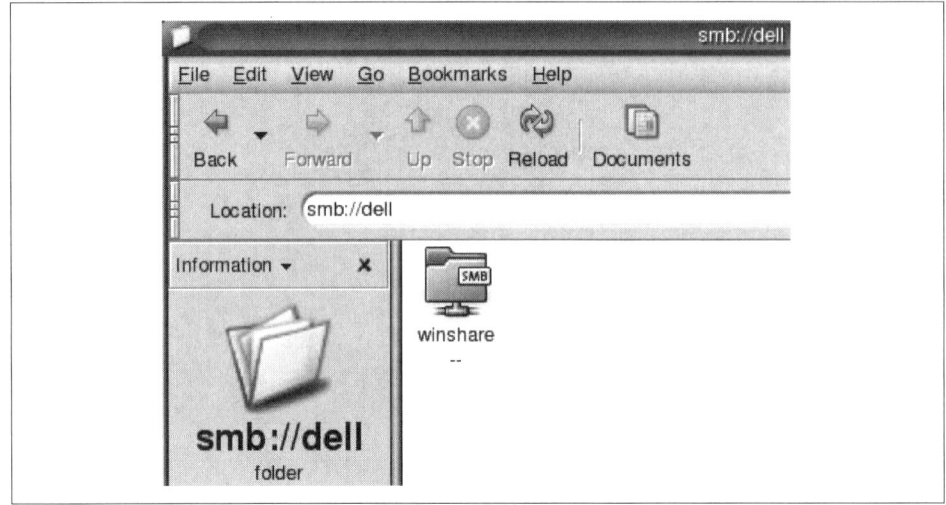

Figure 4-15. A shared folder on the computer Dell in a Windows workgroup

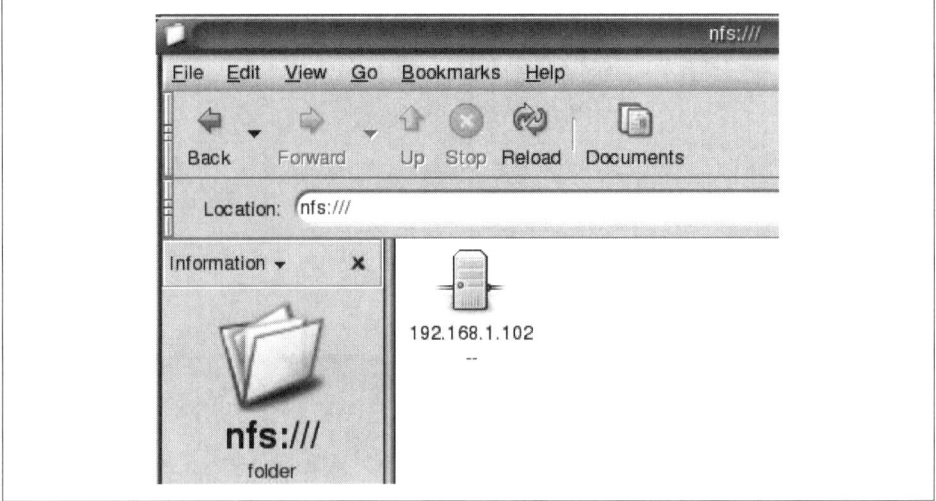

Figure 4-16. An NFS server in the JDS domain

You can identify an NFS server by its IP address. In our smb example, this same server had the name of Dell, in Figure 4-13, and provided the Windows folder, *winshare*, in Figure 4-15. This IP address can be reached only from your internal, local network. The system is not usually visible to the Internet.

The computer in the smb example uses the Linux operating system and functions as both an NFS server (Unix file sharing) and a Windows Workgroup member. You can see here the flexibility of Linux and JDS in a networked environment.

When you select the NFS computer icon, shown in Figure 4-16, you will see that the server opens its home directory, as shown in Figure 4-17. The icon indicates that you cannot write to this folder because of the W symbol. However, if you select this folder, it will take you to your home directory, and you can access it in the read-write mode.

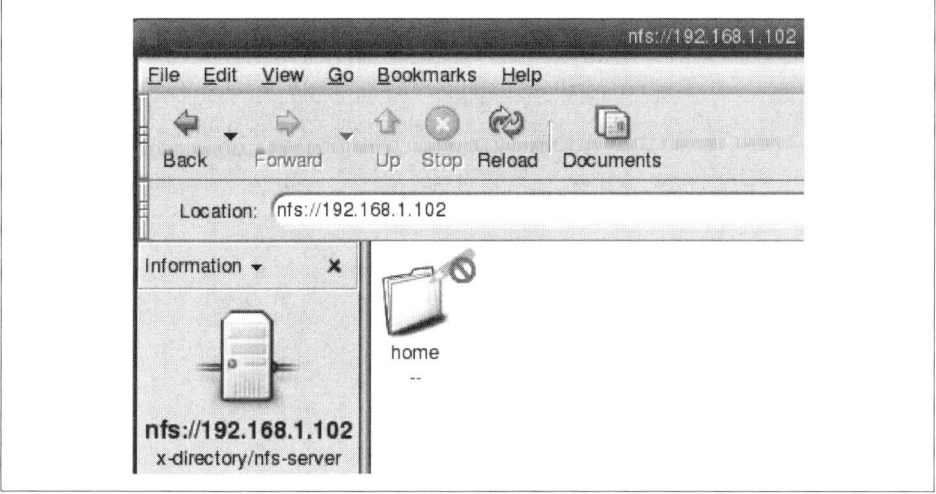

Figure 4-17. The shared NFS folder for server 192.168.1.102

In this example, our JDS actually stores its users' home directories on an NFS server and lets users access their directories over the network. In large Unix environments, client machines often maintain their home directories on an NFS server in this manner. This facilitates file sharing among users, robust backups, and other benefits.

Going Wireless

JDS supports wireless networking. Large enterprises, colleges and universities, and mobile organizations have found that wireless networking offers:

- Freedom—work anywhere
- Quick, effortless installation
- Elimination of the cost, time, and hassle of cabling
- Ease of expansion

Since wireless networking devices do not require cables, you can use your JDS computer anywhere in an office or home, even out on the patio. Outside of the home, you can find wireless networking in hotspots at coffee shops, businesses, airports, etc.—they are great when you're on the road and need to get some work done.

In Figure 4-18, you can get an idea of how people configure wireless networks. In place of the traditional Ethernet cable, a wireless network card, bridge and/or hub uses radio frequencies to transmit signals amongst devices on the network. JDS recognizes wireless network cards, which in turn communicate with the facilities on a network.

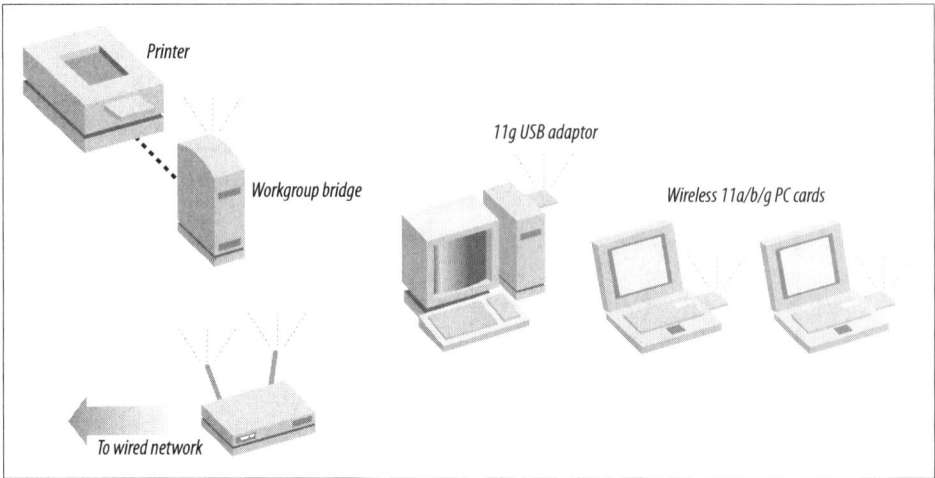

Figure 4-18. Sample wireless network

Public and Private Hotspots

Outside of the office or home, many stores, restaurants, and other sites now offer wireless access. Some do it free of cost, some (such as hotels) require you to register and pay a daily fee, and some offer a subscription that lets you use their facilities in many different places as you travel. Regardless of the business aspects of wireless networking, all these sites are called *hotspots*.

What Kinds of Hotspots Exist?

Two basic kinds of hotspots exist: public and private. You can see the growth of public hotspots allowing wireless connectivity in many airports, hotels, college campuses, public areas, coffee shops, and restaurants. Public hotspots can be free or commercial.

Private hotspots can be located in the workplace, or you may have a private group of users who choose to create and share a hotspot.

Community hotspots fall somewhere between the spectrum of public and private. They offer free access, yet use privately owned access points. Public organizations create community hotspots and can be independent or affiliated with a nonprofit organization.

What Do You Need to Join a Hotspot?

As a JDS user, you will need a wireless network card, which can either be a PCMCIA device or a chip set built into a laptop. If you don't have wireless connectivity built into your computer, you could consider buying a Wireless-G card, which can attach to both Wireless-B and Wireless-G hotspots.

How Do You Find a Public or Community Hotspot?

Wireless service providers, colleges, airports, hotels, restaurants, and coffee shops publicize their public hotspots. You can also go online to find directories and web sites of public and community hotspots. The wireless compatibility organization, the Wi-Fi Alliance, hosts a "Wi-Fi ZONE"™ listing service at *www.wi-fizone.org*.

Joining Wireless Hotspots

Your JDS computer broadcasts a request and hooks up with whatever hotspot responds. In other words, joining happens automatically.

Login procedures for public hotspots vary. At free hotspots, such as those in restaurants that want to attract more people, you survey the local area for access points, and then log onto the restaurant's access point using the network's name. At commercial hotspots, before you log in for the first time, you have to set up an account that is usually billed monthly, similar to a cell phone account. Once you have an account, you log in each time you connect.

Independent commercial hotspots exist, as do wireless Internet service providers (WISP). WISPs offer accounts that can be used at their affiliated hotspots. Pricing plans vary.

Private Hotspots

For hotspots at work or shared by a closed group of individuals, you should get the appropriate SSID and security settings from a network administrator. SSID is short for *service set identifier* (similar to an encrypted password). The SSID contains a 32-bit character-sized key attached to the header of packets on a Wireless LAN. A wireless connection cannot join the network unless it can provide the unique SSID.

How Secure Is the Hotspot?

Private hotspots implement security measures to stay closed to the public. Public and community hotspots tend to have few security measures. If you want a secure connection, see whether the hotspot offers an encrypted Virtual Private Network (VPN) pass-through capability.

Different Networking Protocols Available in JDS

Suppose you edited a chapter in a book and wanted to transfer the file from one computer to another. You look at the file and see that it takes up 15 megabytes. You can't put the file on a floppy disk and walk it over to the other computer. The file is too big. You can't email the file because your Internet Service Provider only lets you send files up to 10 megabytes. What do you do?

The first researchers on the Internet asked similar questions as the one above. Linux, the underlying operating system for the Java Desktop System, embodies some of the best and most advanced solutions to these questions. You will find numerous tools in JDS to accomplish tasks associated with network protocols.

Let's examine the situation of transferring the file from your computer to another. People have used File Transfer Protocol (FTP) to move documents from one computer to another for years. JDS provides Secure FTP (SFTP) in the event you want to move a file from one computer on your network to another.

In Figure 4-19, one person uses SFTP to transfer a file from a Mac OS X to a home directory on JDS.

JDS Networking Recap

In this chapter, we covered how to set up your Internet connectivity, locate systems on local area networks, and interoperate with remote machines. The material in this chapter prepares you for the next sections of the book, which covers the rich environment available under JDS.

In Chapter 6, we explain the primary user Internet tasks of email, web browsing and instant messaging. We also provide information in Appendix A, which covers networking commands. Appendix C provides information you can use to access remote systems to retrieve and edit files or set up applications on hosted servers.

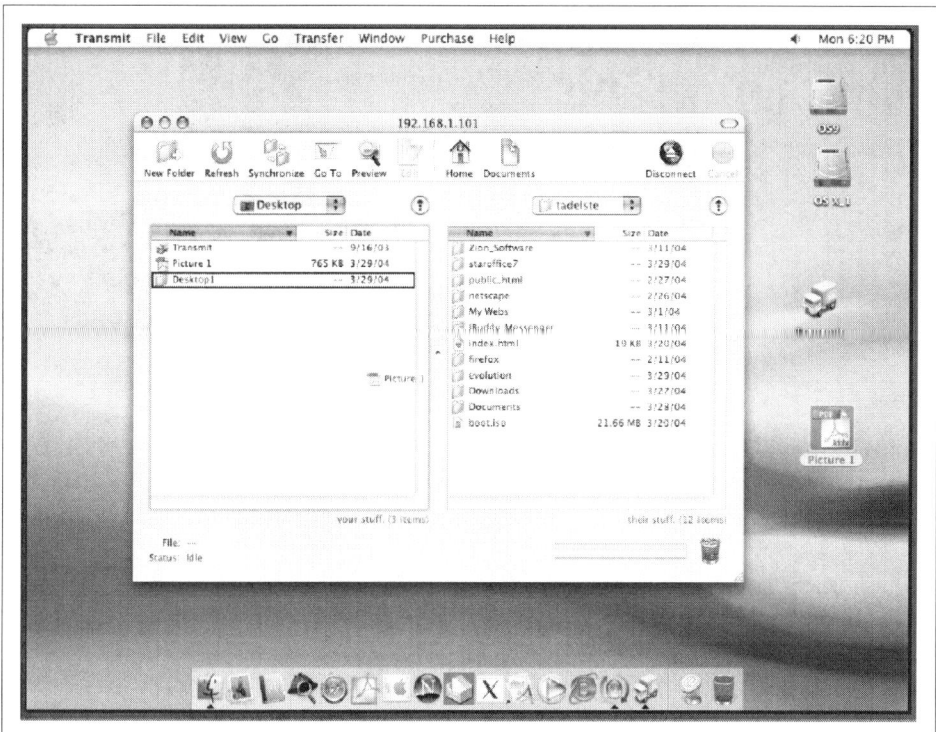

Figure 4-19. Using SFTP to transfer a file

CHAPTER 5
Maintaining and Supporting JDS

You have now become familiar with many important features of the Java Desktop System. Your next step is to explore JDS maintenance and support. In this chapter, you will learn how to:

- Update your operating system software using the the Sun Java Update Service
- Add or Remove software using either Sun's Desktop Configurator or the Linux text-based package management system
- Back up your important files and folders

While JDS is quite powerful out of the box, you may run into the need for software that is not loaded by default. You should know how to upgrade software when security fixes are announced or when new software features and improvements are available.

A Word About Packages

Linux software usually comes in something called a package. If you needed a software program, you would normally find it on a download site on the Internet. You would download the software, install it, and find it afterward in your menu. When you click on the icon in the menu, it would starts the program.

Inside a JDS package, a programmer places a spec file, which tells the operating system how to install the software, what shared libraries it needs, where the program should go on the menu, and other information vital to installing the software.

So when you see the term package, just remember it contains software, which you want to install, and information on how to install it.

Using Online Update

Constant improvement is a basic feature of the computer field. Sun Microsystems provides, after extensive testing, easy online updates to software that runs on JDS. New software performance features, enhanced security, and ease of use are a few of the reasons for these periodic updates. While it's unnecessary to upgrade a piece of software every time a new release appears, consider particularly installing security fixes, because publicly known security problems could render your system vulnerable without the update.

Using System Tools

The Launch → Applications → Systems Tools menu shows a number of important applications you may need to support JDS. Figure 5-1 shows the menu items on the System Tools Menu in JDS Release II. Although the menu differs slightly from JDS Release I, Figure 5-1 provides you with an inclusive view.

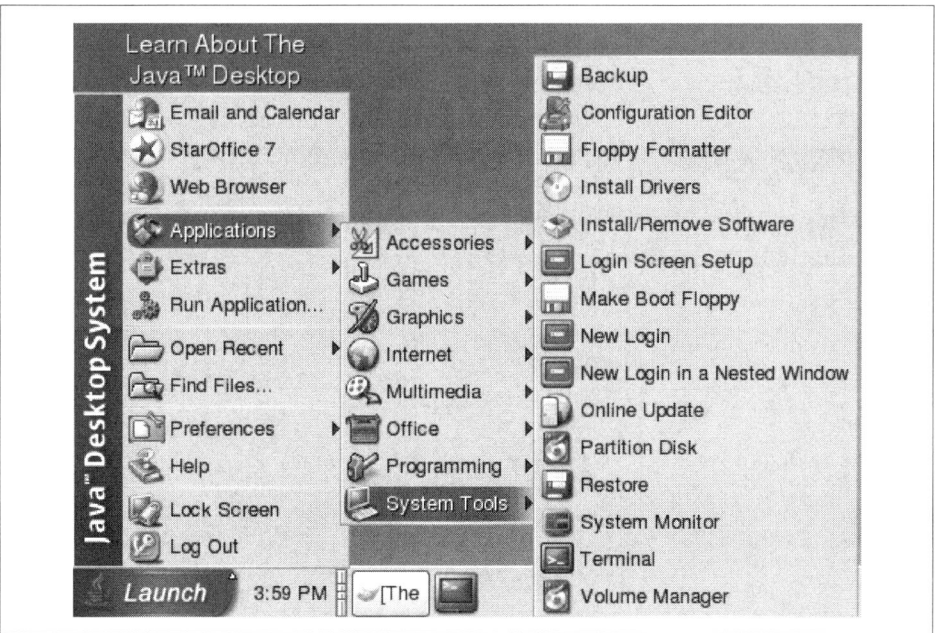

Figure 5-1. System Tools menu from JDS 2003

Most of these tools have names that describe what they do. Earlier, we discussed the terminal tool and how it is used to deliver text-based commands to the system. This chapter focuses on the following items from the menu:

- Online Update
- Install/Remove Software
- File Backups and File Restores (in Release I this is a single item called Backup)

 We have found that the first version of JDS's Online Update (Yast Online Update) appeared to work better than the Sun Online Update Service available from the menu in Release II. Both versions come in JDS Release II, so we're using the Yast Online Update to demonstrate this important function.

In JDS Release I, selecting Online Update brought up a window similar to the screen-shot in Figure 5-2. In JDS Release II, you'll see instead the Sun Java System Update screen in Figure 5-3. The tool that came with the first release of JDS is still available in Release II; you have to use your terminal to reach it. We're going to demonstrate the use of the earlier tool for the reason noted above, and because it provides a richer set of options. Both tools, however, have identical functionality.

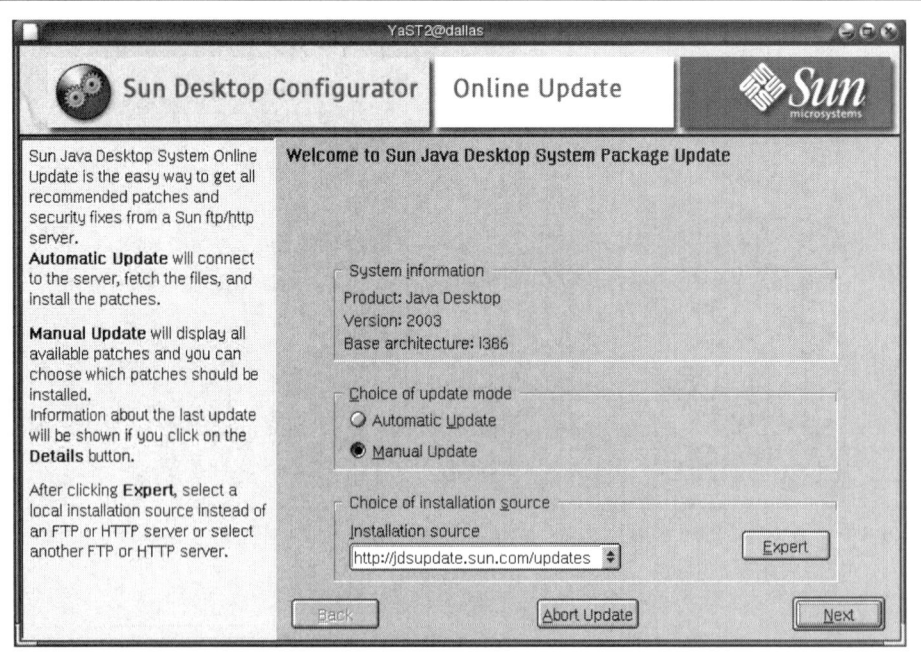

Figure 5-2. Sun Java System Update Service

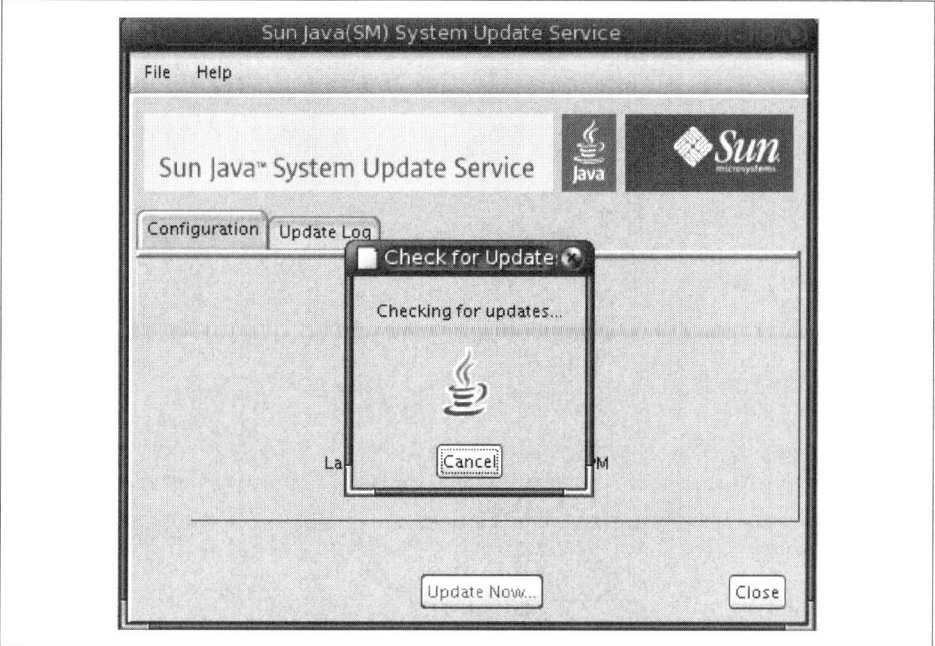

Figure 5-3. Sun Desktop Configurator: Online Update

Open a terminal by selecting Launch → Applicatons → System Tools → Terminal.

In the terminal, enter *su*, provide the system administrator's (root) password, and enter yast2. Then from the Yast2 console, select Online Update.

Online Update calls up the Sun Desktop Configurator utility, which helps you install patches and security fixes online from a Sun server. Sun tends to use patches to upgrade the Linux kernel and applications rather than replace the entire package. This increases the speed of installing upgrades, especially if you have a slow Internet connection.

Notice in Figure 5-2 that you have two options under the heading "Choice of update mode." You can have JDS install the most recent patches automatically or you can choose the Manual Update option. You can choose manual or automatic each time you launch OnLine Update to check for patches.

The manual option allows you to determine which patches you want installed on your JDS, in case you have a reason to be selective. In the example shown in Figure 5-2, Manual Update was the chosen update mode.

The installation source dialog box is preset to the JDS update site by default. To begin the Update process, push the Next button at the bottom right of the screen.

Notice in Figure 5-4 that a pop-up screen requests your Registation data. The Code refers to your JDS serial number.

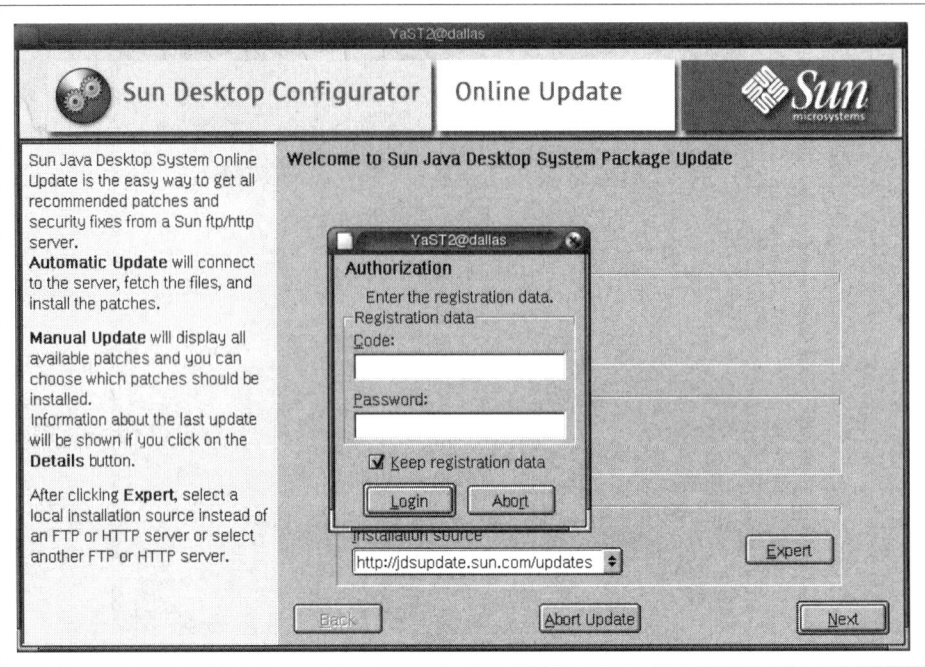

Figure 5-4. Authorization to access the JDS Update site

Your JDS came with a media kit, in which you received a colorful document called the Sun Java Desktop System Support Entitlement Certificate. In the upper-lefthand column, you will find a Serial Number that has 16 digits divided into blocks of four, such as 2149 8716 9973 1040.

Online Update may want you to place dashes between the blocks of four digits when you enter it as the Code, such as 2149-8716-9973-1040. Enter your serial number and choose a password. Make sure to remember or record this password for future use. If desired, check the box "Keep registration data." to save the Code and password for use of Online Updates.

Once you select Login, you will receive a message saying "Initializing for FTP/HTTP Update. One Moment Please...".

This opens a new screen, as depicted in Figure 5-5. On the top left corner is a drop-down menu called Filter. From there, you can select one of the following:

- YOU (Yast2 Online Update)
- Package Groups
- Search

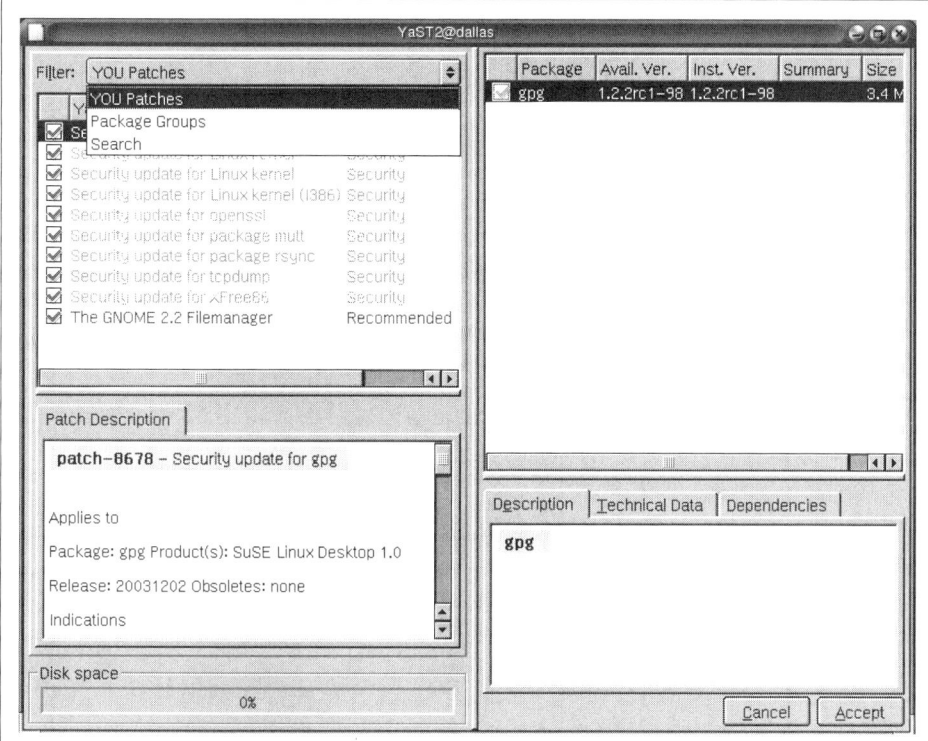

Figure 5-5. Yast Online Update

Online Update opens in the YOU view. If you want to see which packages the patches affect, you can choose Package Groups. Finally, you can use the Search option if the list of patches is lengthy, and you wish to find out if you have applied specific patches previously.

In Figure 5-5, the list of patches previously applied contains check marks in the boxes to the left of their descriptions. Security patches have red lettering, and Recommended patches contain blue lettering.

To help you decide if you want to download any uninstalled patches, highlight the line containing the patch, and a description will appear in the window pane below the patch list. To the right are two panes with additional patch information. (Technical data and dependencies are described in the next section.) To apply the patch, if you consider it appropriate, check the box to its left and push the Accept button on the bottom-right of the screen.

The patches will begin downloading. As each download completes, a check mark in the right window pane will appear. Next, the Sun Configurator will begin installing the other selected patches. Once the installation completes, a check mark will appear to the left of the patch description again. When all patches have check marks, the process is completed, and a dialog box will say "Installation successful."

Press the Next button at the bottom of the screen, and a list of activities being performed by the installation procedure will appear under the "Writing the system configuration" window, similar to that shown in Figure 5-6. Select Finish to save the system configuration.

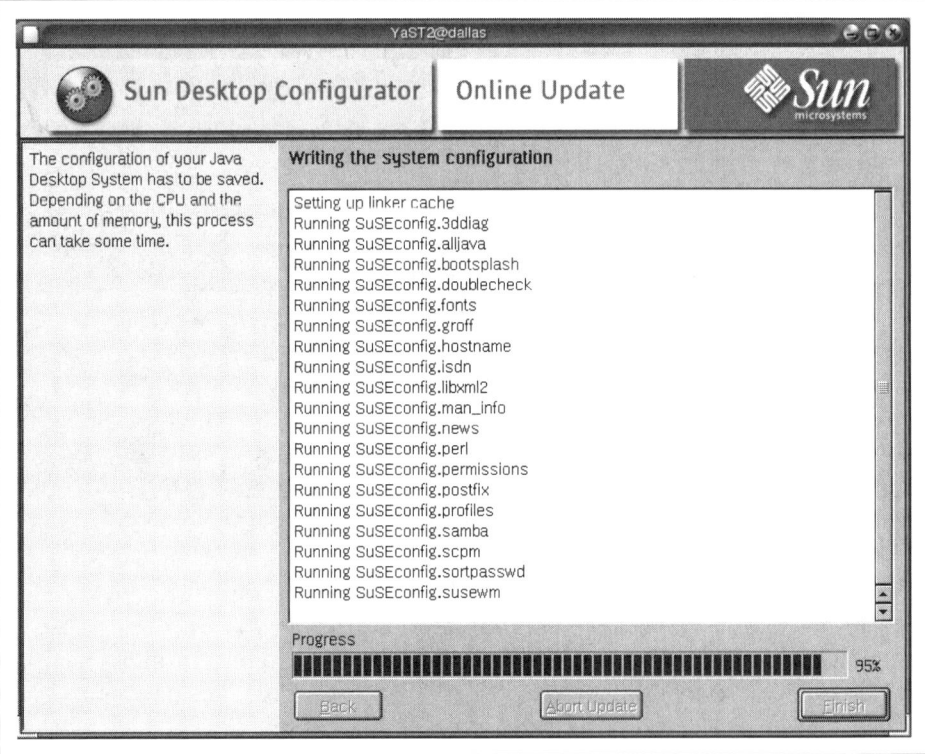

Figure 5-6. Writing the System Configurator

The Online Update window closes automatically.

After an online update, some users should log out of JDS, while others should reboot. If you do not receive a message to reboot, your system will not require you to. You might find rebooting a good practice if Online Update made any patches to the Linux kernel. The Online Update will tell you if a kernel patch needs to be installed. (If something interrupts the installation, your system software will not be affected and you can restart at another time.)

Install/Remove Software

To put a new application on your system, or remove one you don't want to keep, select the Install/Remove Software utility from the System Tools menu with Launch → Applications → Systems Tools → Install/Remove Software. You are prompted to enter the root password, which you or your system administrator chose when installing JDS. Next you see a window showing the installed software on your JDS. A screen-shot of the window appears in Figure 5-7.

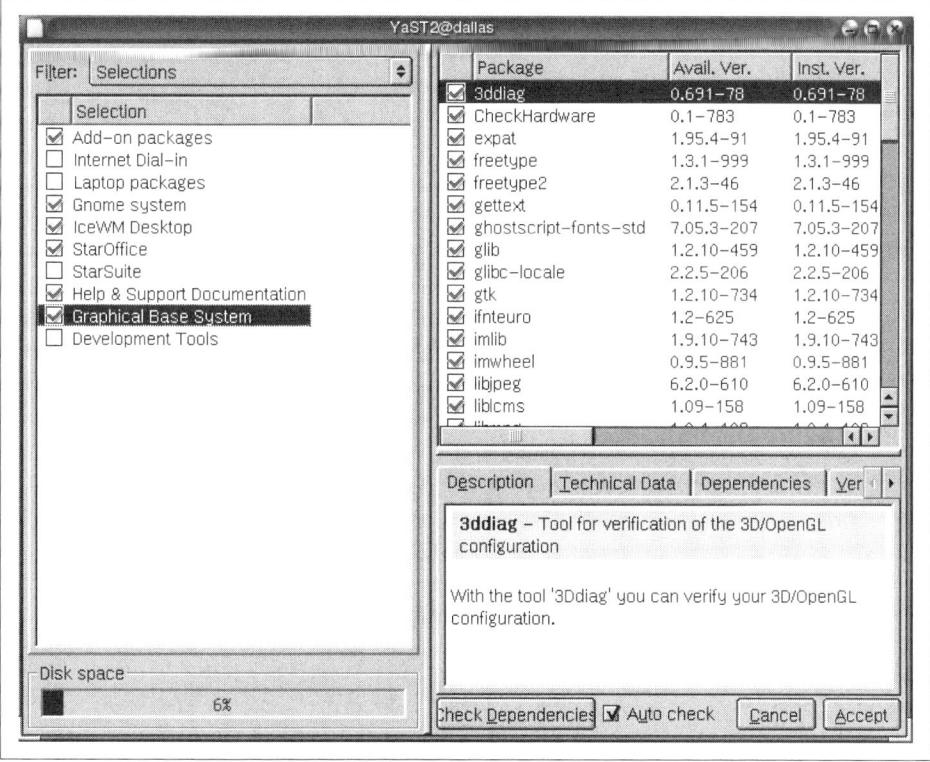

Figure 5-7. JDS Software Installation Tool

This tool looks similar to the one used in the Java Desktop System Online Update. The selections on the top-left pane allow you to present different views of the system packages, as discussed earlier. The choices include:

- Selections
- Package Groups
- Search

The JDS Software Installation tool opens in the Selections view; however, if you want to see which packages fall under categories such as "Development Tools," you can choose the Package Groups view, shown in Figure 5-8.

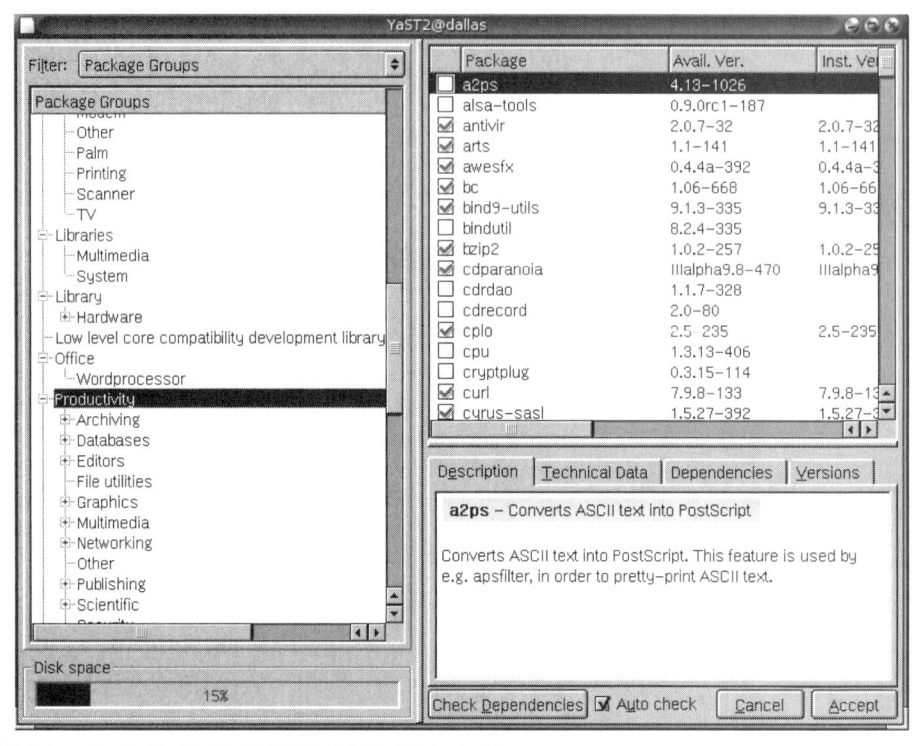

Figure 5-8. Software installation in Package Groups view

Finally, you can choose Search to search the list of packages and find out whether you have installed specific ones. For example, in Figure 5-9, we did a search on "mc" and found the packages we had installed.

Use Figures 5-7 and 5-8 to acquaint yourself with this important utility. For example, notice the package selections and categories in the left window. As you change from one to another, notice which versions are available and installed in the upper-right window pane. The lower-right pane contains a description of the package you select with additional tabs such as Technical Data and Dependencies.

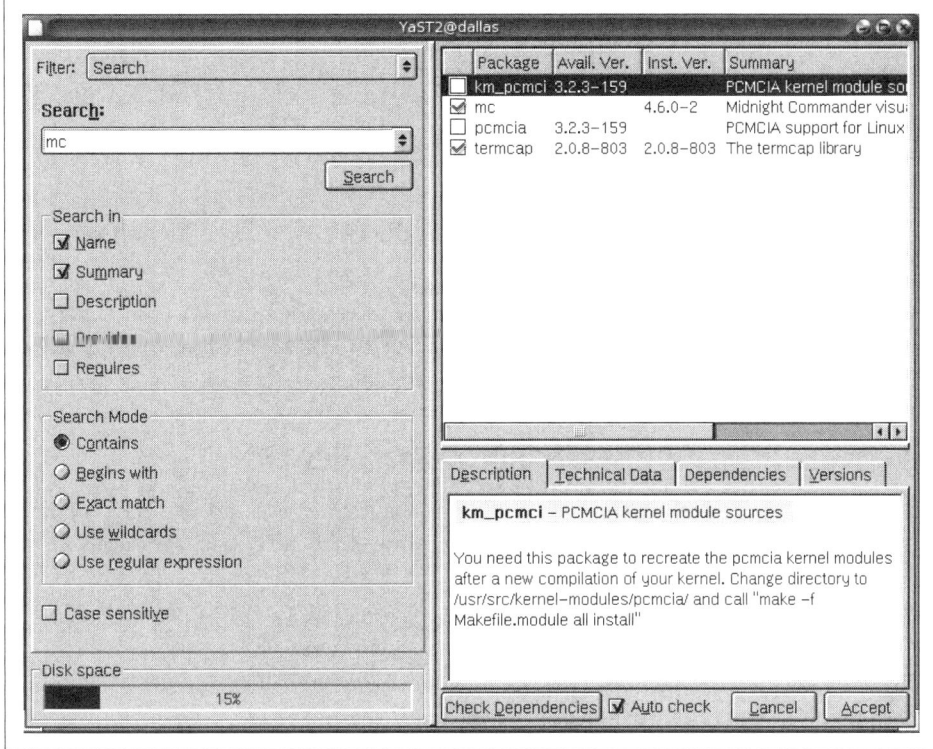

Figure 5-9. The Software Installation Tool in the search mode

 Linux programs rely on static and dynamic libraries of software routines, some of which come preinstalled with the base Linux system and others of which have to be installed independently. The term *dependencies* refers to these requirements that exist between packages. For example, package gaim may require files that are installed by package gtk-2. gtk-2 must be installed, or else gaim will have this unresolved dependency. Normally, the JDS installation manager will disallow the installation of packages with unresolved dependencies.

In Figure 5-7, notice in the left window that four package selections remain unchecked:

- Internet Dial-in
- Laptop Packages
- StarSuite
- Development Tools

These selections are useful to specific types of users, and can be left unchecked by others. For example, systems without a dial-up modem don't need the first unselected package set. Additionally, unless you use a laptop you do not require the Laptop

Packages. StarSuite 7 software supports some Asian languages, including Simplified Chinese, Traditional Chinese, Japanese and Korean.

The last package, Development Tools, is often important when you do upgrades and add software tools. The Development Tools packages contain software and shared libraries, which allow you to build and modify programs.

Suppose you decide you need one or more of the unchecked packages. Just check the boxes beside the packages in the left window and then push the Accept button in the lower-righthand corner.

The Sun Desktop Configurator tool will scan your package database and then ask you to insert the necessary CD-ROMs from your media kit. Follow the CD-ROM instructions and the requested packages will install.

Maintenance Mode: Install/Remove Packages

A time could come when you want a new package that you did not have or need when JDS was installed. In fact, there is a wealth of third-party packages that are not supported by Sun but run very nicely on JDS. In this section, we explain how to find and install new packages.

Updated and Sun Support

Sun supports only packages that come on its CD-ROMs or from its Online Updates. Therefore, one could theoretically invalidate the Sun support agreement by adding software from other sources such as the Internet. The local RPM Package manager does not know if its database contains RPMs provided by Sun or other sources. Packages not provided by Sun are considered unsupported. You should keep track of packages not provided by Sun. In the event you have a maintenance problem, you might need to uninstall them.

In Figure 5-10, you can see the view of JDS's package database, which includes all RPMs installed on your system. In the Package Groups view, Sun shows the database hierarchically. It breaks packages into categories such as Productivity, Libraries, Office, System, etc.

The hierarchical view helps you locate dependencies or applications you may need in order to accomplish tasks that a default installation doesn't cover. Also, if you install a package from an open source project not included with JDS, you can access it from this view.

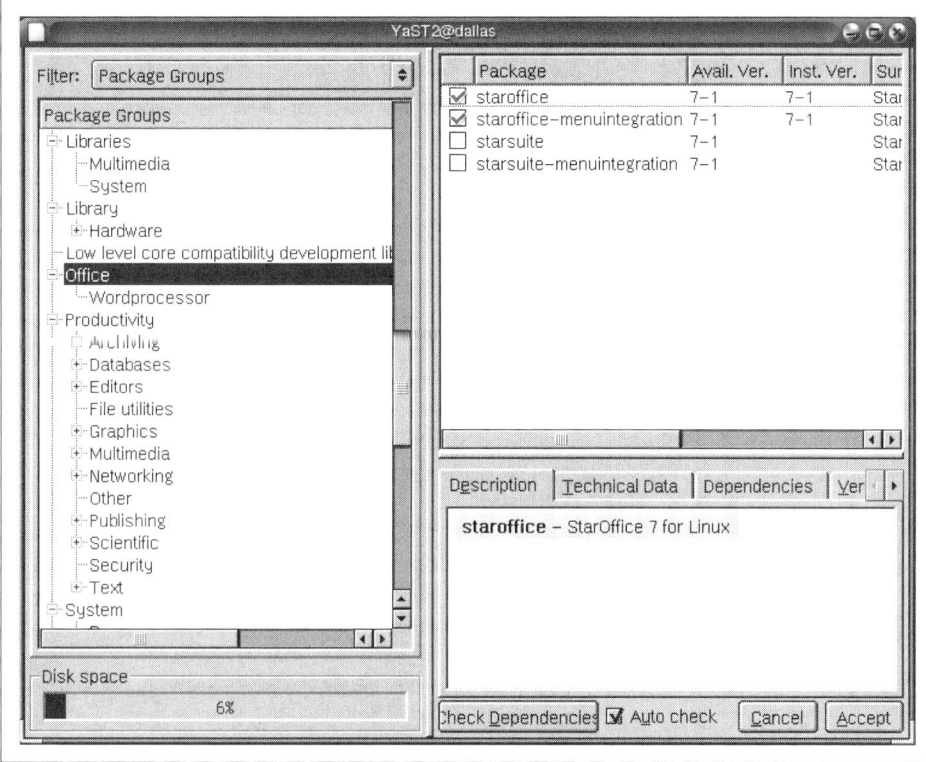

Figure 5-10. Package Group ViewJDS Software Installation Tool

In the JDS native state, the JDS Package Groups list in the left pane has a multitude of supported software available from which to choose. You can find other download-able software at the website *http://jdshelp.org*.

We will demonstrate how to use the Package Search tool to examine Midnight Com-mander, an open source file management tool similar to an older program called Norton Commander that used to be extremely popular on Windows systems. (Infor-mation about this program is available at *http://www.ibiblio.org/mc/*.) Figure 5-11 shows the Search view of the Software Installation tool; notice that in the upper-left dialog box we entered "mc," the abbreviation for Midnight Commander. The right window pane has a check next to "mc," indicating that it has been installed.

The search mode buttons to the left of the sceen give you choices in how to set up the search. For example, if you can remember only part of the software name, make the appropriate selection.

Though "mc" did not come with the out-of-the-box JDS distribution, the JDS's RPM system included it in its database and displayed in this utility after it was installed by the user. Midnight Commander is an example of software you can build to install on JDS. You will see how later in this chapter.

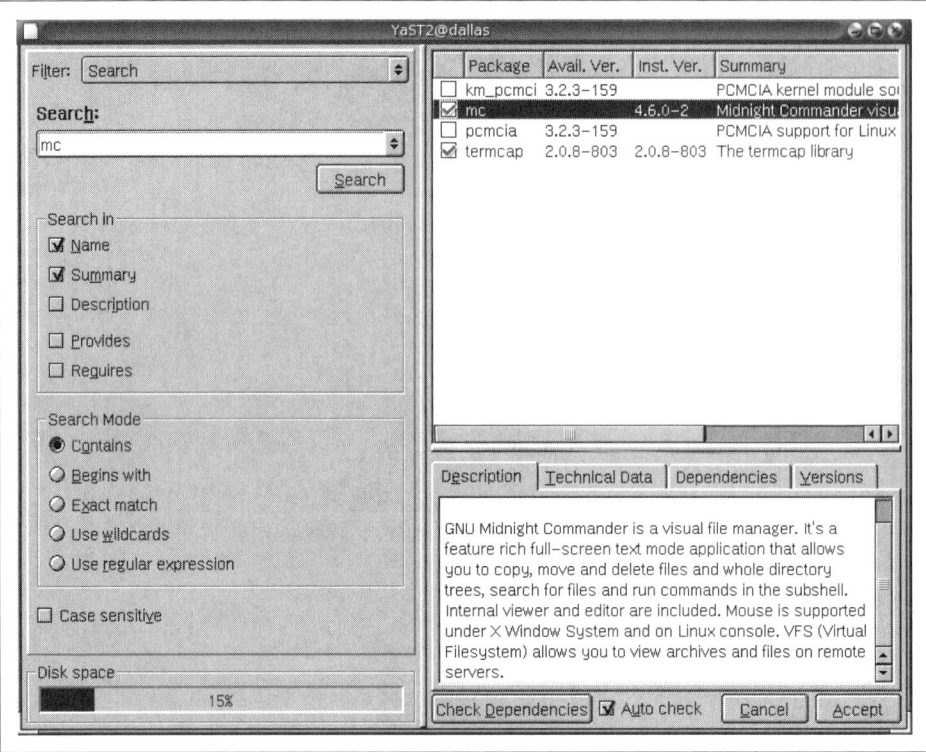

Figure 5-11. Search ViewJDS Software Installation Tool

We installed "mc" manually using the text method, but we could uninstall it with the Add/Remove packages utility in the same manner as all other software. To remove "mc," uncheck the box to the left of the package and press the Accept button. You may remove software in any of the three views of this utility.

Adding New Software

You may want to add software that Sun does not support to your distribution of JDS. Advanced users of Linux would have little problem doing this. Novices will need a little background.

JDS began life as a custom build of several components, including the SUSE Linux Professional distribution reengineered by Sun Microsystems. Sun also custom-built the Gnome desktop, added proprietary third party software, and added their own Java Runtime Environment and Java programs. To control the applications they would support, Sun compiled the entire Linux distribution with glibc 2.25, a slightly different version of the Linux core development library, from the version in current use by most distributions.

Different versions of a library usually provide the same functionality, but because of tiny differences in data layout, a program compiled with one version of the library fails to run with an operating system compiled with a different version. For this reason, to run new applications on JDS, you have to build them using the same glibc library, 2.25. This is not hard; we'll show you how to do that here.

The last time SUSE used version 2.25 of the glibc library to build their Linux distribution was Version 8.1 of the distribution. As of this writing, SUSE's lastest distribution uses glibc 2.3; it was used in SUSE Versions 8.2, 9.0, and 9.1. So, if you look for SUSE applications on the Internet or from a newer SUSE distribution, they will not install on JDS. On the other hand, if you attempt to use a package from SUSE 8.1, you will be using versions two years old that could contain bugs or be out of date. In this chapter, we present a better solution.

Understanding the JDS Text-Based Package Management System

JDS uses the popular RPM system for installation, updates, removal, and maintenace of software. Both the Online Update and Install/Remove utilities described above depend on the text-based RPM system to function. By learning the text-based interface to the RPM management system, you can extend the capabilities of your system by adding software from projects not included in the JDS packages.

 We cover the RPM package management system in Appendix D. You can find further information about this system at *http://www.rpm.org/*.

RPM originally stood for Red Hat Package Manager, because it was developed by the Linux distributor Red Hat. Now, its maintainers just refer to the system as the RPM Package Manager.

The majority of Linux distributions, as well as a few other operating systems, use the RPM system. It has many features similar to installation programs found on Microsoft Windows. Developers have even ported converted RPM to Microsoft Windows and Mac OS X.

Let's look at an example of RPM in use.

To demonstrate use of the RPM system for an installaton on JDS, we chose the application AOL Instant Messenger (AIM). You would start by downloading *aim-1.5.286-1.i386.rpm* from their web site at *http://www.aim.com* and carry out the following instructions:

1. Download AIM onto your system.
2. Log in as root.

3. On the command line, type the rpm command as shown in the example:

```
rpm -i aim-1.5.286-1.i386.rpm
```

in which 1.5.286-1 represents the AIM version and release numbers. On the other hand, if you already have an older version of the package installed and want to install a higher version of AIM, use the rpm upgrade option. For example:

```
rpm -U aim-1.5.286-1.i386.rpm
```

4. To run AIM, open a terminal and type:

```
/usr/bin/aim
```

on the command line.

In the next section, we'll explain the process step by step.

The central task in installing unsupported software on JDS is to use source RPMs. Other RPMs will not install; attempts to do so will give you error messages saying that you are trying to use the wrong version of glibc. After reading the previous section, you understand why. Source RPMs take more effort but should install successfully.

The typical sequence in adding software not included with JDS is:

1. Locate the web site of the desired software package.

2. Read the documentation about the software package—i.e. dependencies, version number, other required software.

3. Query the RPM database on your JDS to find out if the packages already exist and in what version. They may need to be updated.

4. Choose the RPMs to download from the web site. The RPMs have to be compatible or written for JDS.

5. Build the source RPMs, which yield binary RPMs (those ready to install, as demonstrated below).

6. Upgrade the packages on your JDS from the binary RPMs built from the source files.

7. Install the binary RPMs you downloaded.

Example: Installing XCDROAST

Here is another example, in greater detail, of adding software to JDS. We'll use XCDROAST, CD burning software, in this demonstration. XCDROAST performs many functions not found in the Nautilus Browser's CD-Burn that is included with JDS. The most important of those involves creating bootable CD-ROM disks, which you may need to upgrade JDS.

To add XCDROAST we had to upgrade the underlying software called cdrtools. We learned this from the requirements specified by the web page.

We found the source RPMs for cdrtools at the download site for the project: *http://xcdroast.sourceforge.net/RPMS/a15/src.rpm/*. We also noticed that a current version of the program existed at *http://xcdroast.sourceforge.net/RPMS/a15/suse-8.1/*. We decided to use the version for SUSE 8.1 because, as discussed, the project team built it for glibc 2.25.

 The XCDROAST Project currently provides binary RPMs for JDS at the following URL:

> *http://xcdroast.sourceforge.net/RPMS/a15/sun_jds/*

As this shows, the instructions in this section may become increasingly unncessary as JDS becomes more popular and software developers create packages for it.

We had to compile the source RPMs (*rpm --rebuild filename.src.rpm*) and add the packages from Development Tools, using the Install/Remove Software tool mentioned earlier in this chapter. We then built the cdrtools with the command:

```
su
Password: (fill in your password)

rpm --rebuild cdrtools-2.00.3-1.src.rpm.
```

Once the build process completed, we found our new RPMs in the directory usr/src/packages/RPMS/i386. We installed the cdrtools with the command:

```
rpm -U cdrtools*.rpm
```

Then we downloaded and installed the binary RPMs for XCDROAST:

```
rpm -i xcdroast*.rpm
```

In Figure 5-12, you can see that after installation, the JDS menu system found XCDROAST in the local RPM database and added an icon to launch the program under Launch → Applications → Other.

Backing Up and Restoring Files and Folders

Some work environments provide robust and carefully tested procedures for backing up data on users' systems, so that a failed disk or a slip of the hand on the mouse will not result in irretrievably lost data. But a surprising number of organizations do not provide adequate backups. Some back up their servers but not desktops. So you may be responsible for taking care of any data that's important to you. And if you are using a computer system at home, you definitely need to perform your own backups.

JDS provides for data protection with a backup and restore facility. JDS File Backups and File Restores work in tandem to:

- Create a compressed archive of files and folders.
- Write the archive to one of several removable media types.
- Restore them later if necessary.

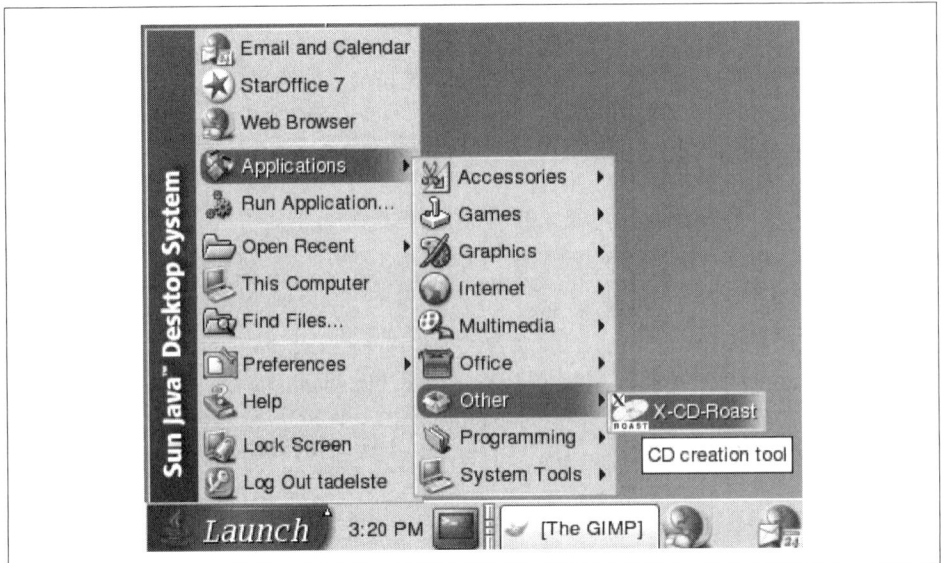

Figure 5-12. XCDROAST automatically added to the JDS launch menus

A compressed archive can be stored on your choice of:

- Floppies
- Zip disks
- CD-ROM disks

The compressed archive takes up less room than the original data does on your hard drive. For instance, if you put all your files in a single directory, it may take up 800 million bytes of data, or 800 megabytes. By using a program to compress them, they could be reduced to a size of only 80 megabytes.

We call the collection of those compressed files an archive. Archives take a collection of files and put them into a single file. So if you had 100 files in your documents directory and you compressed them into an archive, we could call that archive *documents.tar.gz*. We could then transfer the archive to off-line storage as a single file rather than 100 files.

Archives serve as an important service in data management. If your machine fails, you could lose all the files you created. Before that happens, you want to save them so your work won't be lost forever. If you back up your data frequently, you'll have more recent data to restart from after disaster strikes.

JDS Backup Module

The JDS backup module helps you generate a system-wide backup. It will also break up the archive into multiple volumes to allow you to fit the entire archive on several disks, if necessary. For example, if you are using CD-ROM disks to store your backups and you have an archive too large for a single CD-ROM, JDS backup module will break the archive into a set of files to fit on the CD-ROMs. The filenames created from the archive would be listed as *01_archive.tar.gz, 02_archive.tar.gz*, etc. This will let you copy each on a recordable CD-ROM.

Unlike enterprise backup programs, the JDS archive saves information only about changed packages, storage areas for system and user files, and configuration files. The JDS developers saw little reason to backup the RPMs that already existed on your installation CD-ROM. This allows you to create a smaller image. Backups made in this manner take less time and allow for an efficient way to reconstitute the system.

Before starting your backup, make sure you have enough space in the partition containing the */tmp* directory to store all the files being backed up. As the name suggests, */tmp* provides temporary storage during backup. You can find how much free space exists in your partitions by running the *df* command. If */tmp* is larger than */home* (which contains the bulk of the data you are backing up), you probably have enough temporary space.

Unmodified, the JDS backup files include information about packages changed since the original installation and your home directory files, which includes patches installed with Online Update and software added by the methods we discussed in the two earlier sections of this chapter.

You should restore from the Backup Files modules only if your system goes down completely. For saving data files from your home directory, use the GNOME CD Burn available in the Nautilus File Manager discussed in Chapter 3 or use another removable media system such as Iomega Zip Disks.

The backup procedures grab information not related to packages themselves, including configuration files and folders in your home directory. The backup will include storage areas on the hard disk crucial to system restoration including the partition table and master boot record (MBR) which includes the bootloader.

Figure 5-13 shows the first dialog window generated when you initiate a backup from Launch → Applications → System Tools → Administration → File Backups. This differs from the menu in JDS 2003, which simply uses Launch → Applications → System Tools → Backups.

JDS calls the first screen of the program the backup module. This module searches for files in the system and creates the backup archive. The backup module requests an archive name, type, and description.

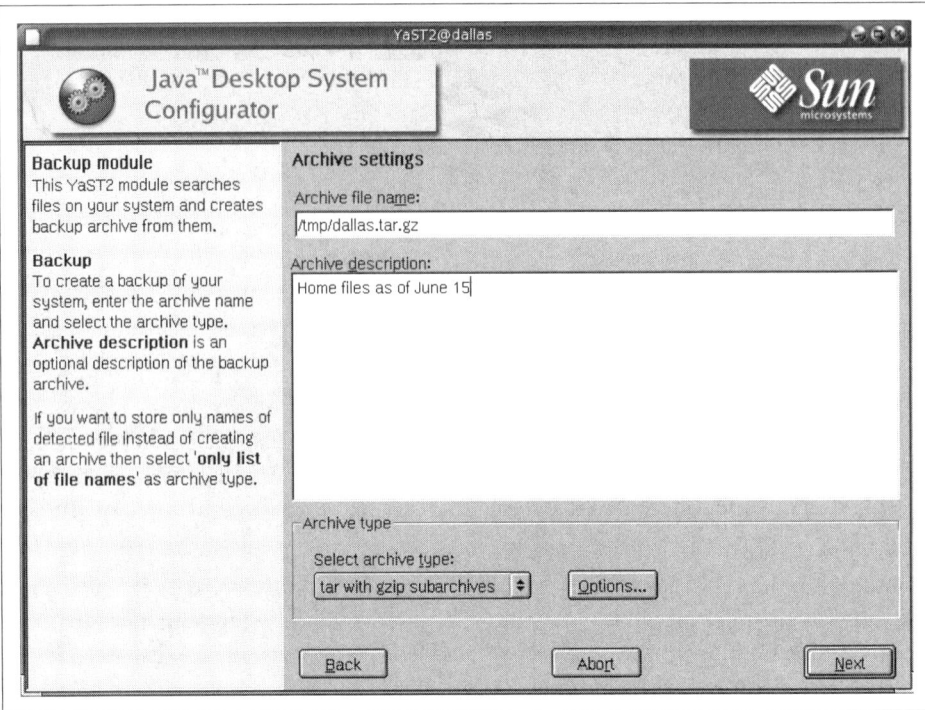

Figure 5-13. JDS file backup

In our example in Figure 5-13, we named the archive */tmp/dallas.tar.gz*. That means JDS will store the archive in the */tmp* directory and will store the archive in a compressed tar file (tar stands for tape archive, a term left over from earlier Unix times). You have an option to enter a description to help you remember what you're backing up; in this case we described the backup "Home files as of June 15."

The archive will contain files from packages that were changed since package installation or upgrade. Files that do not belong to any package can be optionally added to the archive.

If you press the Options button in Figure 5-13, Figure 5-14 appears to show the options available for storing all your data. The example shows that we chose CD-R-RW disks. The backup will create a multivolume archive to fit on the 74-minute blank disks.

The Search setting allows you to select the parts of the system you want to search and backup. Your options include:

- Search files that do not belong to any package
- Backup hard disk system areas
- Check files before creating the archive

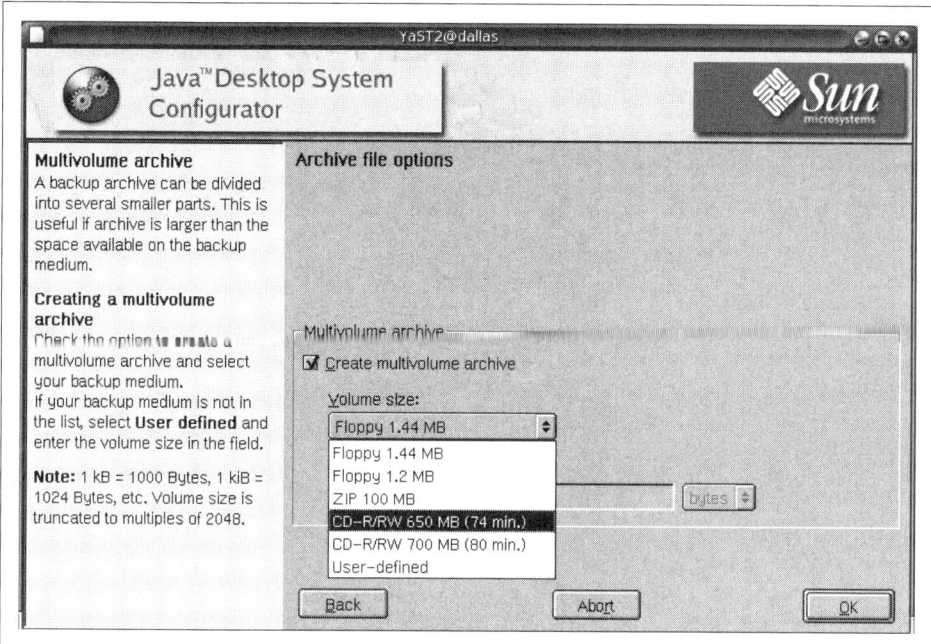

Figure 5-14. Archive Options

What Is MD5?

Professor Ronald Riverest of MIT invented the MD5 algorithm, which produces a 128-bit "fingerprint" from input. People use the MD5 algorithm for digital signature applications, where a large file must be "compressed" in a secure manner before being encrypted with a private (secret) key under a public-key cryptosystem, such as RSA. MD5 is a way to verify data integrity more reliable than other commonly used methods.

MD5 sums can be used to determine whether the file was changed. These are more reliable than checking size or modification time, but take more time.

You can also exclude areas you do not want searched, which typically include:

- */tmp*
- */var /lock*, */var/run*, */var/tmp*, and */var/cache*

You can also add directories such as */home/username/staroffice7* and */home/username/.mozilla*.

Once you choose the folders to exclude, you can send the backup module off on a search for files to include in the archive. A screen similar to Figure 5-15 will show you the progress of the search. The search takes a number of minutes and ends up by creating a list of files similar to the one seen in Figure 5-16. This is a list of files found. A check mark in the first column indicates that the file will be backed up. You can uncheck a file, and it will not be included.

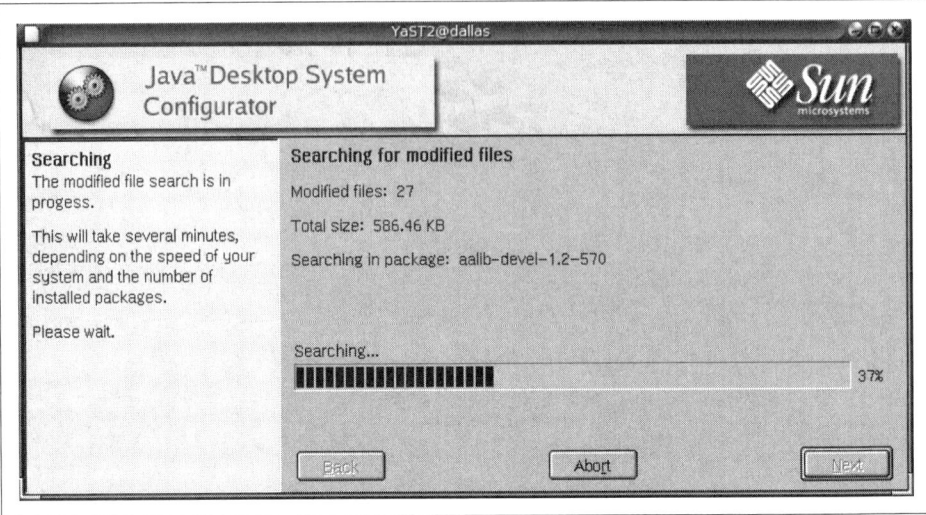

Figure 5-15. Backup search screen

Once you accept the list by pressing Next on detected file list, the backup module will begin the process of building an archive table and map. The information to restore the system exists in a file called *autoinst.xml*. The information about the files created for archives exist in the Backup summary details, as shown in Figure 5-17. You reach the backup details by clicking the details button, shown in Figure 5-18.

After the backup modules build the table and restore information, it provides you with summary information, as seen in Figure 5-18. Notice that the information in this figure provides you with the types of files archived and the location of the auto-installation profile. The screen also tells you to click Details to see more information.

The errors mentioned in Figure 5-18 were insignificant. The backup module refused to back up the unnecessary cache of Internet Explorer, installed by Codeweavers Crossover office.

In Figure 5-18, you can see the detailed summary of the backup process including the archive volumes created. They include (in this case) two files, which will fit on recorded CD-ROMs: *01_dallas.tar.gz* and *02_dallas.tar.gz*.

The next step in the process would be to create the backups on the CD-ROMs. The easiest course is to use Nautilus to create the CDs: open the desktop icon "Documents", then choose Go → CD Creator in the toolbar menu. Be sure to include *auto-inst.xml* on the disk containing *01_dallas.tar.gz*.

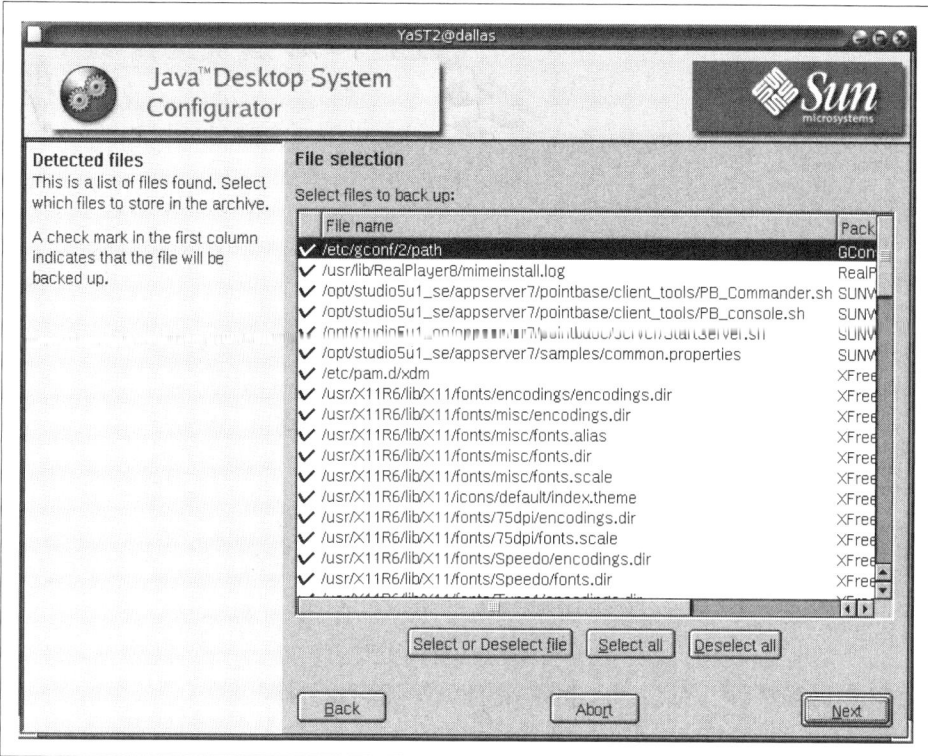

Figure 5-16. Files setected to archive

JDS Restore Module

The Restore Files program enables you to restore your system from a backup archive, such as the one we created in the previous section of this chapter. You can enable the restore module by selecting Launch → Applications → System Tools → Administration → Files Restores. This brings forth the screen in Figure 5-19.

As you can see in Figure 5-19, the instructions exist on the left sidebar. Some further explaination follows.

Restore module

    Just remember that using this is all a measure of last resort. You do not want to restore data files you may have deleted by accident from this backup archive. Use the restore function only if you have completely crashed your system and this is the only way to recover.

Archive selection

    If you use this option, specify the name of the first file you made when you backed up your system, such as *01_dallas.tar.gz*.

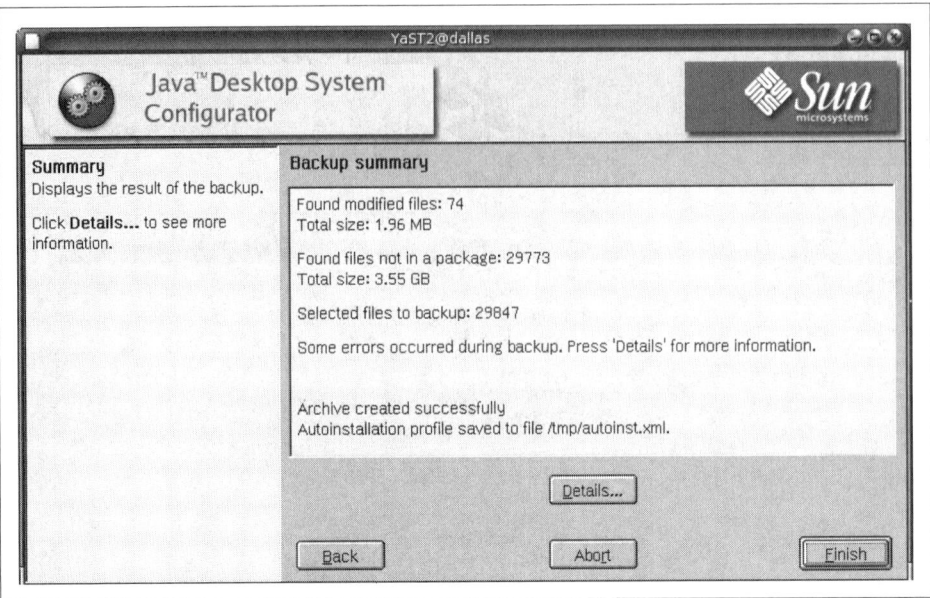

Figure 5-17. Backup summary

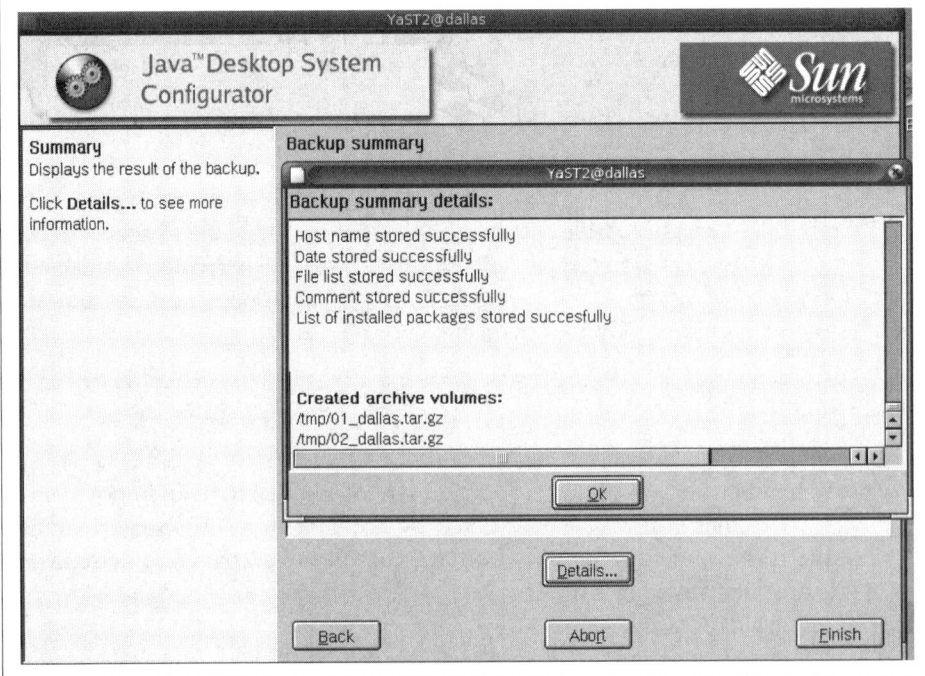

Figure 5-18. Backup summary details

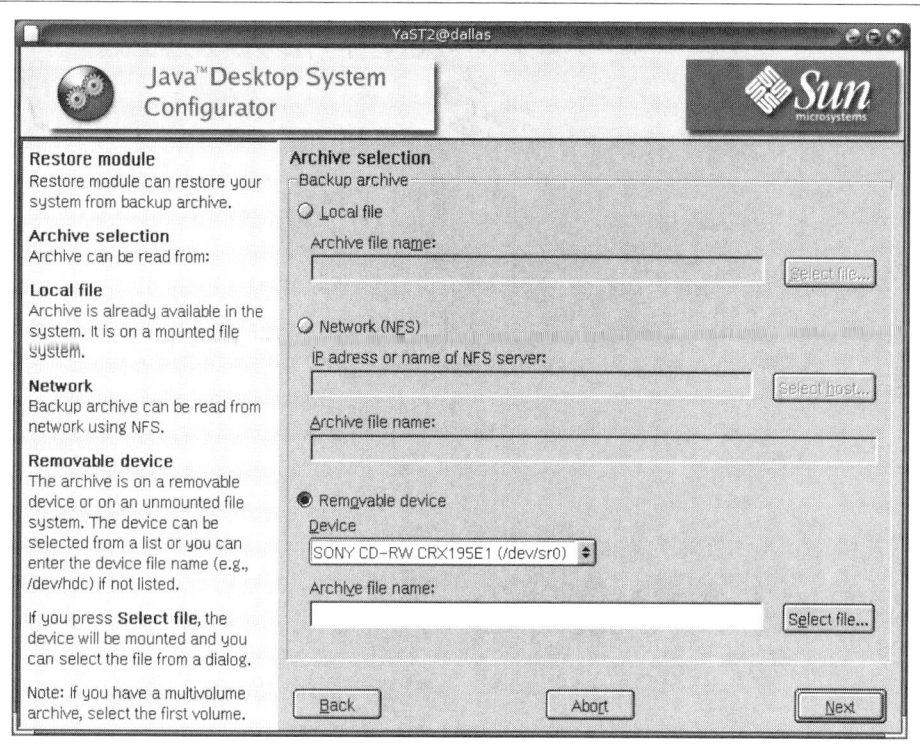

Figure 5-19. JDS restore module

Local file

> This option can be used if you copied an archive from a CD or some other off-line media to a normal disk.

Network

> Backup archive can be read from network using NFS. If your achived files exist on a server, you can mount the Network File System directory and see the file in your directory tree.

Removable device

> This is somewhat like "Local file," but mounts the disk first.

The JDS Restore Files module helps you restore your system from a backup archive. Usually, you will have reinstalled your system from the original media and then selected the restoration media. When you get the screen in Figure 5-19, you specify the location of the backup archive, such as "cdrom." In Figure 5-20, you can see the first options in the */media* directory.

Once you select the file, you will find the backup archive. For example, if you chose cdrom under files, the window would next provide a listing of the files on the CD-ROM disk. When you select the file, you will be taken back to the screen in Figure 5-19.

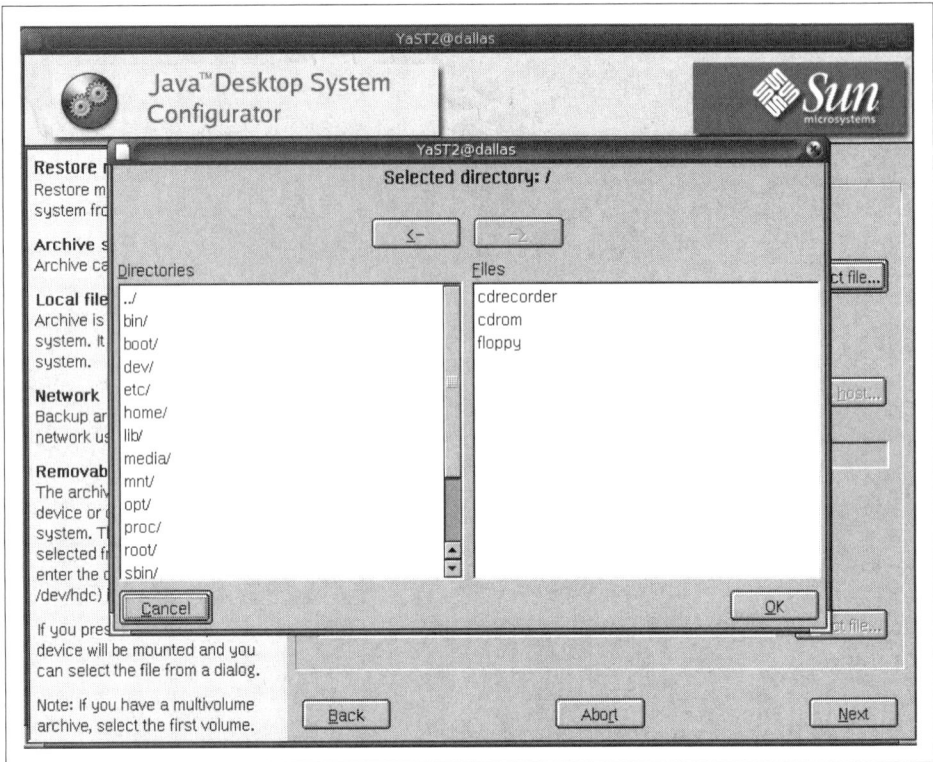

Figure 5-20. The restore module

Press Next to proceed. As you continue, a description and the contents of the individual archives displays. You can then choose what to restore from the archives.

Two options exist for:

- Uninstalling packages that may have been added since the last backup
- Renewed installation of packages that you may have deleted since the last backup

The two options allow you to restore the system state as of the last backup.

The restore module installs, replaces, or uninstalls many packages and files. Use it only if you have had a major system failure. Otherwise, to save and restore data files from your home directory, use a removable medium or store them on a server.

Maintaining and Supporting JDS

In this chapter, we addressed several issues related to keeping your system updated, installing and removing software, and protecting data. We also learned about package management. As you continue using Linux and JDS, you'll find this information

---

valuable. Your knowledge of the RPMs will have a direct bearing on how well your system performs.

Chapters 6 and 7 are where you can gain knowledge about JDS productivity applications. In these chapters, we introduce you to software you can in your everyday work life, including the web browser, email and personal information management, word processing, and instant messaging. As you progress into those chapters, you will find that the information learned in this chapter helps you understand JDS and how everything fits together architecturally.

CHAPTER 6

Using the Internet Applications

Java Desktop System bundles an excellent set of applications for managing email, contacts (address book), and calendar events, as well as web browsing and instant messaging. The most popular Internet tools, Email and Calendar, and Web Browser, are grouped together at the top of the menu that you see when you click on the Launch button, as shown in Figure 6-1. The other application covered in this chapter, Instant Messenger, is located under Launch → Applications → Internet → Instant Messenger.

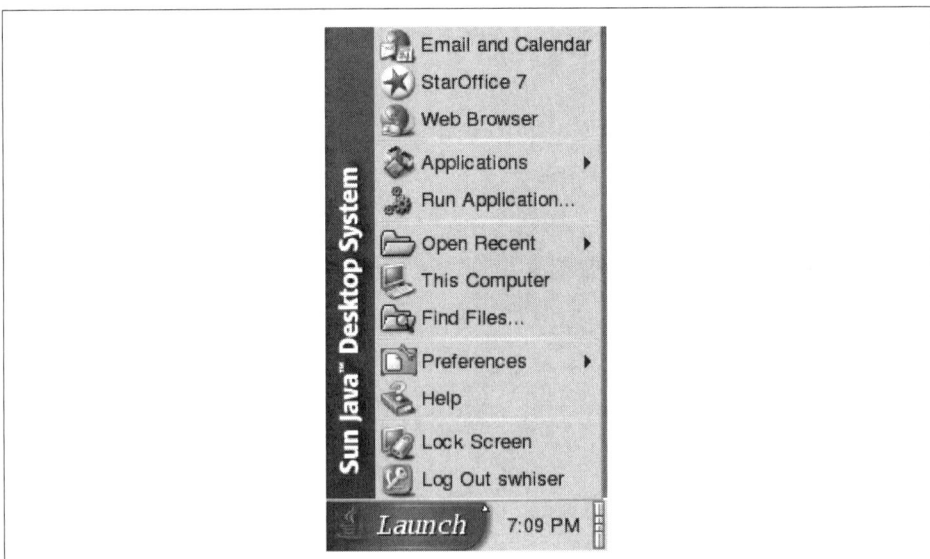

Figure 6-1. The Launch menu

Table 6-1 summarizes the functions you can perform with each application and the name of the actual program that is running.

Table 6-1. The Internet applications

JDS menu item	Program name	Function
Email and Calendar	Evolution	Email, calendar, address book, tasks, news, and weather summary links.
Instant Messenger	gaim	Chat with colleagues on the AOL Instant Messenger, ICQ, IRC, and Jabber networks.
Web Browser	Mozilla	Browse the Web, open HTML files, and manage files.

Email and Calendar

The JDS Email and Calendar program is located at the top of the Lunch menu, under Launch → Email and Calendar. (See Figure 6-2.) The program that offers all these features, called Evolution, presents five modes or dimensions of functionality, adding up to a full-fledged Personal Information Management (PIM) program:

Inbox (email)
> Compose and send email; view, reply and forward incoming email; archive important email.

Contacts (a.k.a. Address Book)
> Store names, addresses, phone numbers, and email addresses; create email Group Lists for collaborative message broadcasting.

Calendar (a.k.a. Scheduler)
> Track appointments; set alarm-bell reminders; print out weekly sheets for a do-it-yourself datebook.

Tasks
> Track ToDo items and link them with Calendar.

Summary
> One-page digest of custom-set news, weather, new email, appointments, and tasks. (See Figure 6-3.)

 Email and Calendar is very similar in layout, functionality, and use compared with popular PIMs such as MS Outlook, but excludes some of Outlook's well-known vulnerabilities.

Email and Calendar Setup

This section describes things you have to do just once to start using Email and Calendar.

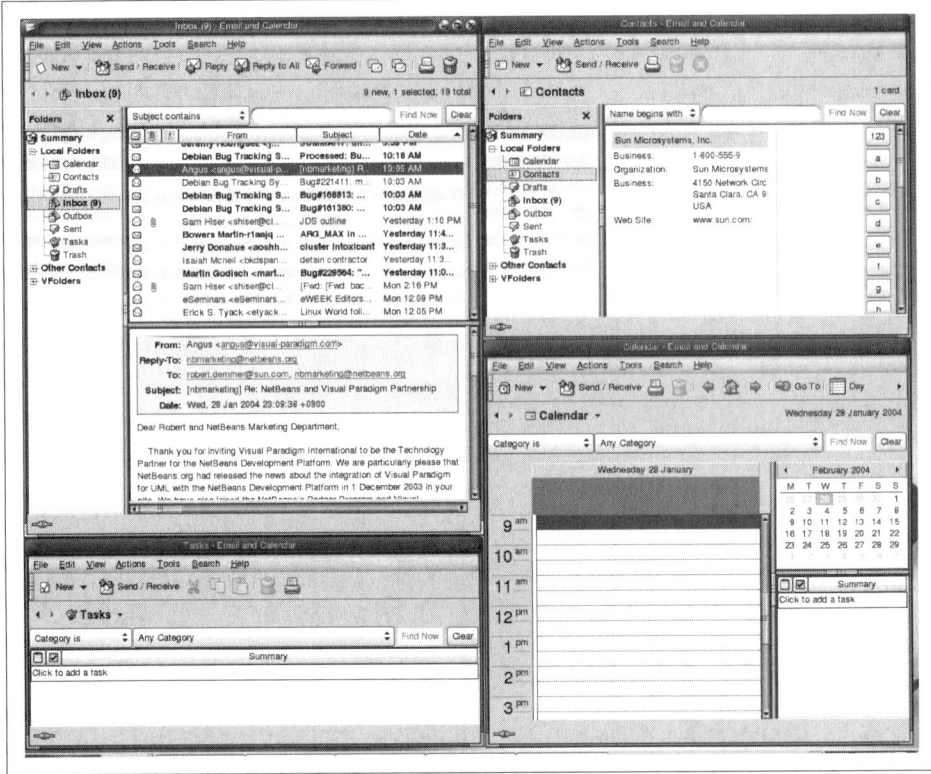

Figure 6-2. The four key dimensions of Email and Calendar

Email account setup: gathering the required information

The information you need at hand to set up an email account is not always straight-forward. Some of the data is self-evident or within ready grasp, including your email address, email USER ID, and email PASSWORD. Examples of these are shown in Table 6-2. You created these items when you opened your email account. Your Internet service provider (ISP) or Web-mail service provider can provide help if you should have any questions or difficulties with these.

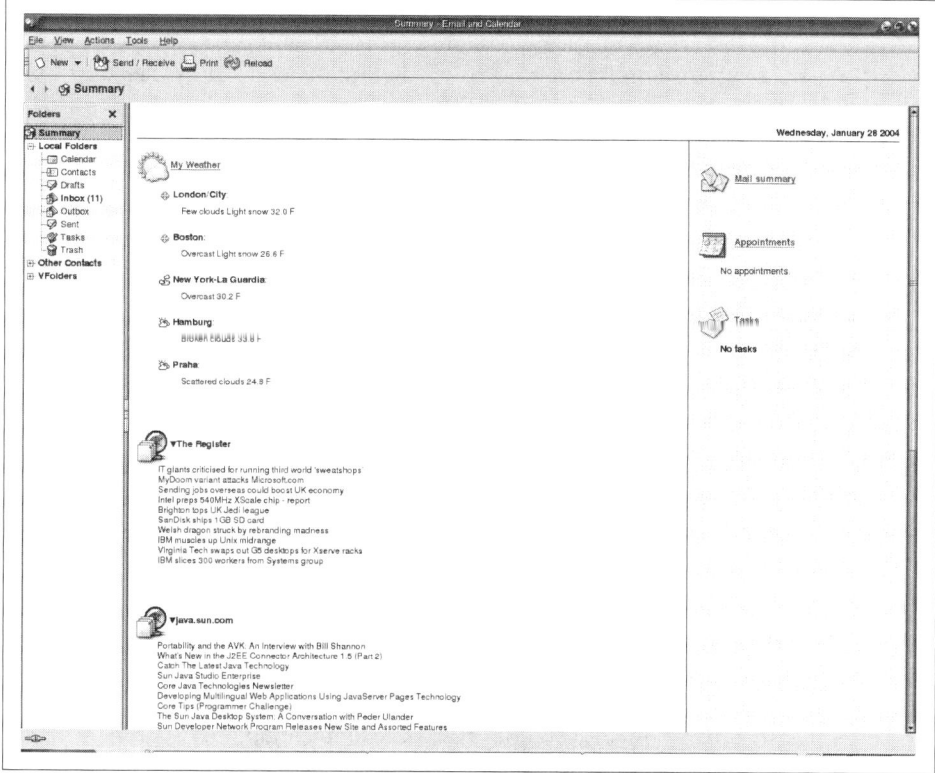

Figure 6-3. Summary is a handy view of custom links

Table 6-2. Basic information required for email setup

Email setup information	Sample input
Email address	shiser@cloud9.net
Email USER ID	shiser
Email PASSWORD	7j%8089778&L4Kd

Security note: The email password in Table 6-2 is an example of a relatively "strong" password because it is longer than eight characters and contains an apparently random mixture of alphabetical and numerical figures. An example of a "weak" password is your birthday (all numbers, four to six digits, easy to find out). Slightly less weak, but still weak, is your social security number (all numbers, nine digits, not impossible to find out). Using public information in a password courts unnecessary risk. Every user has the opportunity to trade the convenience of a short and memorable password that's weak with a more difficult, cumbersome password that's strong. A happy medium that works well in most circumstances is a memorable sequence with a fair amount of randomness. Post-It notes stuck to the frame of your monitor, showing passwords in plain view, are not recommended.

Other setup information, including the names and protocols of your incoming and outgoing email servers, may take you a bit of effort to gather by yourself. You can get them from your system administrator, ISP or Web-mail service provider. Examples are shown in Table 6-3.

Table 6-3. Required email server information

Email setup information	Sample input
Incoming (receiving) mail server type	POP
Incoming (receiving) server name	`mail.cloud9.net`
Outgoing (sending) mail server type	SMTP
Outgoing (sending) server name	`smtp-server.nyc.rr.com`

If you are a confident and self-sufficient user, gathering your email server information can be fairly easy, with some common sense and the assistance of the Web. You can look up your Incoming and Outgoing email server names by consulting the Help or Support pages of your Internet or Web-mail service provider. Alternatively, it may be even easier to go to a search engine and enter some variation of the following search strings:

- Your ISP or Web-mail service provider email servers
- Configuring your ISP or Web-mail service provider email with MS Outlook

These strings may bring up resulting links to content containing references to the mail server names of your ISP or Web-mail service provider. Double check that the search output is current, however; outdated information lasts a long time on the Web.

Generally, the following guidelines may be helpful. Your Incoming Mail Server is either a) the Incoming mail server of your ISP; or b) the Incoming mail server of your Web-mail service provider (for example, Yahoo! Mail, Gmail, or any other third-party Web-mail service that you may be using instead of your ISP). In the example setup in Figures 6-4 through 6-10, the Web-mail service provider is Cloud 9, a Web-mail service provider in the New York City region.

Your Outgoing email server is always an Outgoing email server associated with your ISP (the company providing your Internet connection). In the example setup in Table 6-4, the ISP is NYC - Roadrunner, a national Internet service provider.

Table 6-4. Sample email server names

Internet (or Web-mail) Service Provider	Incoming mail server	Outgoing mail server
AOL	`aol.enetbot.com`	`aol.enetbot.com`
Charter Communications	`pop.charter.net`	`smtp.charter.net`

Table 6-4. Sample email server names (continued)

Internet (or Web-mail) Service Provider	Incoming mail server	Outgoing mail server
Cloud9	`mail.cloud9.net`	`mail.cloud9.net`
NYC - Roadrunner	`pop-server.nyc.rr.com`	`smtp-server.nyc.rr.com`
Texas - Roadrunner	`pop-server.texas.rr.com`	`smtp-server.texas.rr.com`
Prodigy/SBC Global	`pop.sbcglobal.net`	`smtp.sbcglobal.net`
Yahoo! Mail	`pop.mail.yahoo.com`	`smtp.mail.yahoo.com`

Web-mail is an excellent idea! It allows you to read, compose, and send email from any connected computer anywhere, not just your main workstation. This can be handy for traveling or if you regularly work on different computers. Most competitive ISPs provide a Web interface for email, but dedicated Web-mail services that are *not* ISPs may provide better interfaces, features, security, and protection from viruses, spam, and in-your-face advertising.

Setting up your first email account: evolution setup assistant

Upon first booting up JDS and opening Email and Calendar (Launch->Email and Calendar), you encounter a setup wizard called Evolution Setup Assistant that leads you through a dozen screens to help you configure your first email account. Figures 6-4 through 6-10 offer an example of an email setup that works for one of the authors' configurations.

After the Welcome screen (Figure 6-4), you come to the Identity screen (Figure 6-5), where you should enter your name and email address in the appropriate fields in the Required Information section.

The information entered here (Figure 6-6) is used by Email and Calendar for header information that's displayed in the email you send.

Next, select your email server type. In Figure 6-7, POP is usually the appropriate selection. Check with your ISP, Web-mail service provider, or system administrator if you are unsure of your Server Type for receiving email. (See Figure 6-8.)

Next, enter the host name or incoming email server name in the Host field. (Some examples of common incoming [or receiving] email server names are offered in Table 6-4, in the middle column, under Incoming Mail Server.)

The wizard automatically fills in your Username, based on the front part of the email address (the part before the @ symbol) that you entered earlier (See Table 6-2). Make sure that this is the email USER ID by which your account is known to your Internet or Web-mail service provider. (See Figure 6-9.)

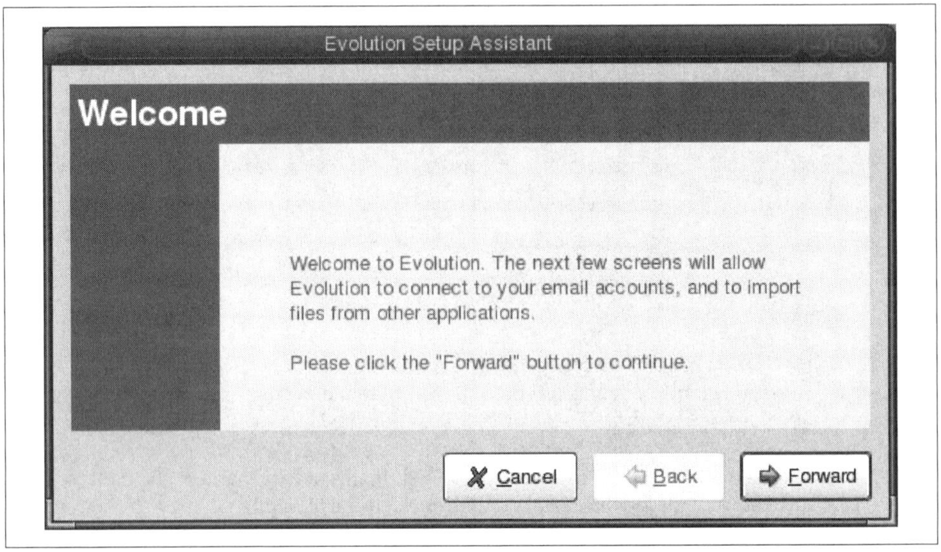

Figure 6-4. The Welcome screen

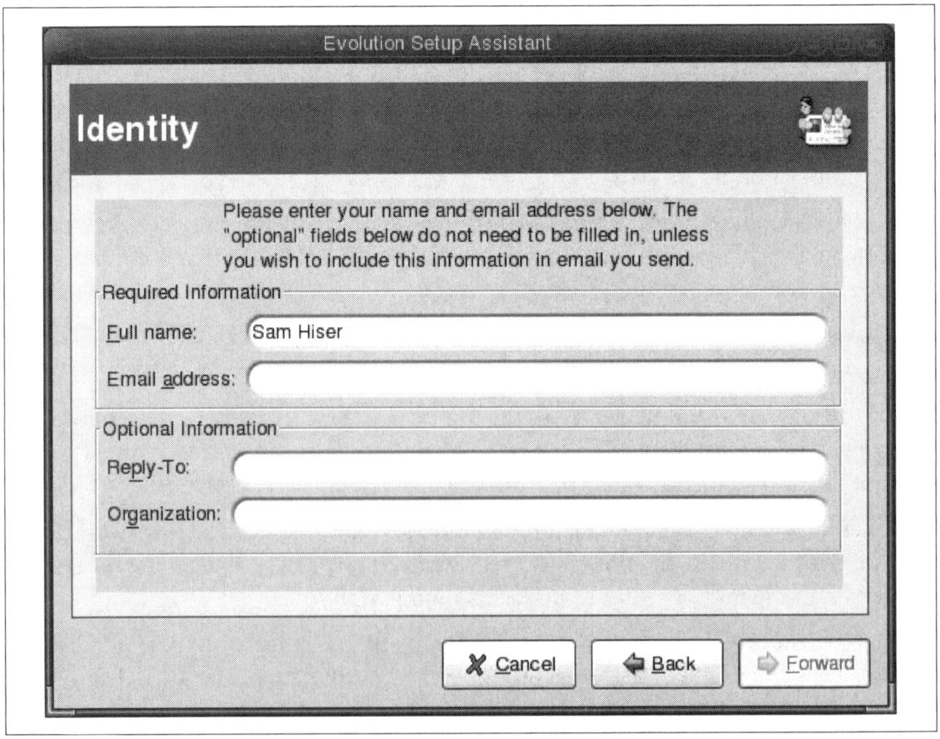

Figure 6-5. The Identity screen

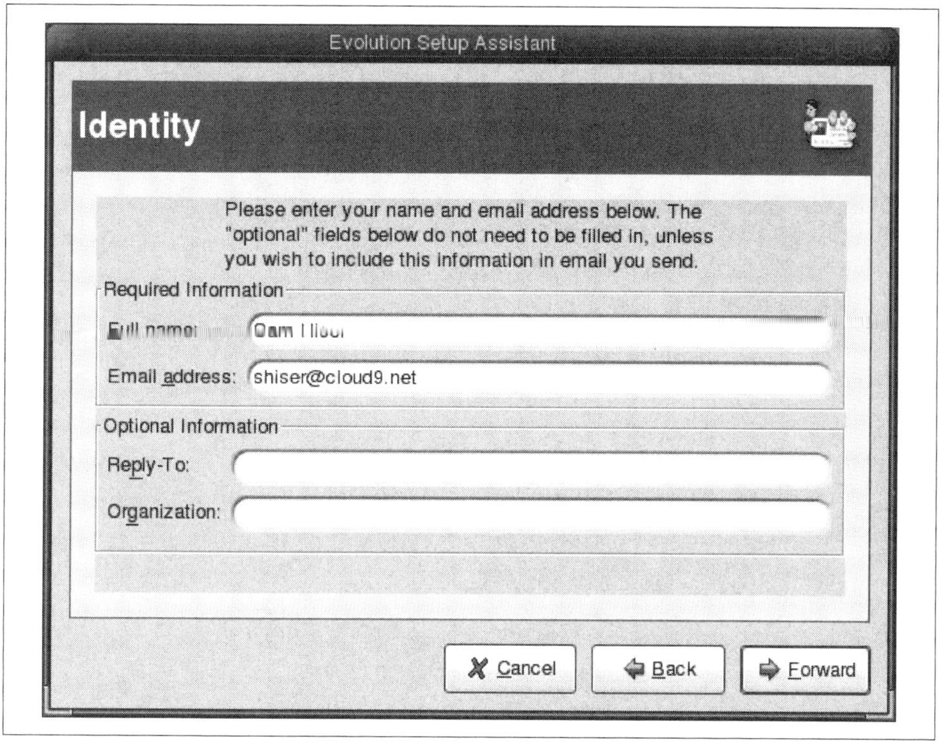

Figure 6-6. Identity screen, filled in successfully

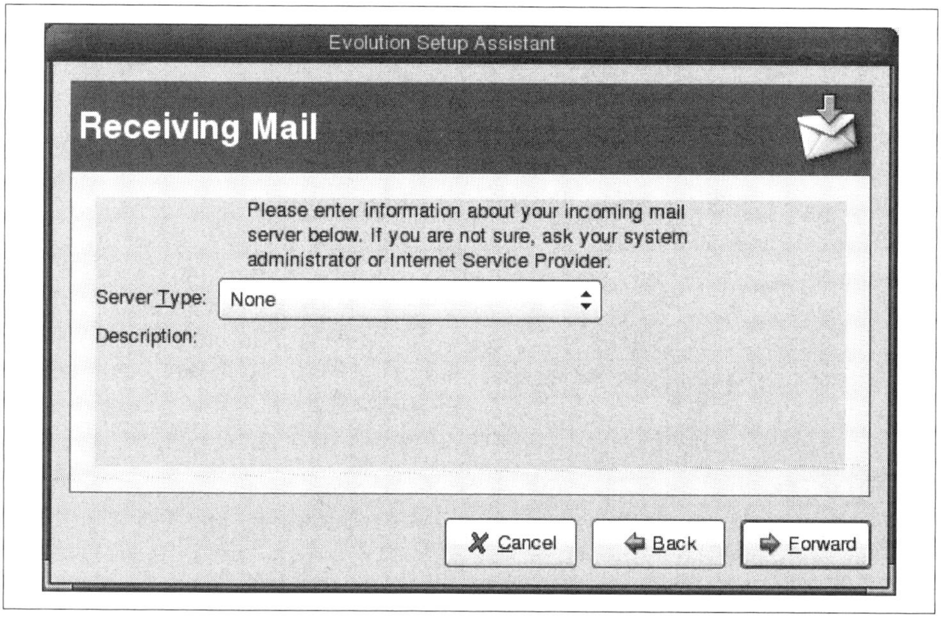

Figure 6-7. The Receiving Mail window

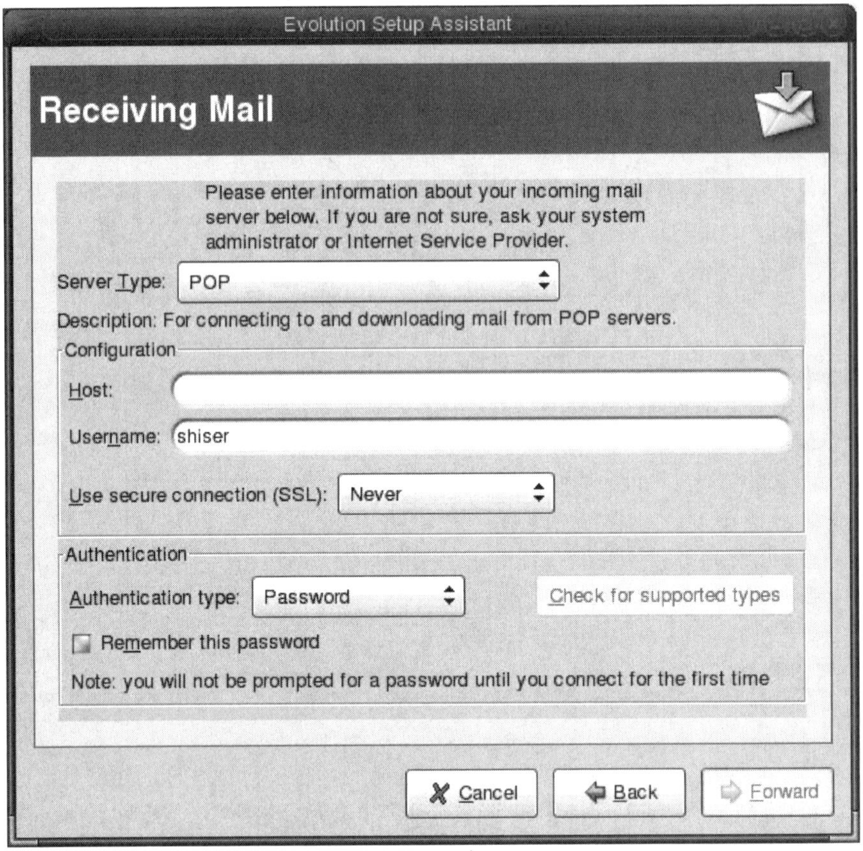

Figure 6-8. Selecting your email server

After filling in your email server information, click the Forward button and proceed to the screen for additional email options.

In Figure 6-10, you can check the box if you want to make your system automatically check your email server for new email once every 10 minutes (10 minutes is the default that's set in the spinner). You can tweak the system to check either more or less frequently than 10 minutes. Leaving it alone works fine for most users. Leaving the box unchecked altogether means that the system checks for new email only when you explicitly press the Send / Receive button, which also works fine for most users.

Message Storage option

The Message Storage option (Figure 6-10) is an important consideration if you plan to access your email from more than one computer and you are using POP mail. If this is your first email account setup on your main or primary workstation (where you plan to archive the more important pieces of email in folders), it's a good idea to

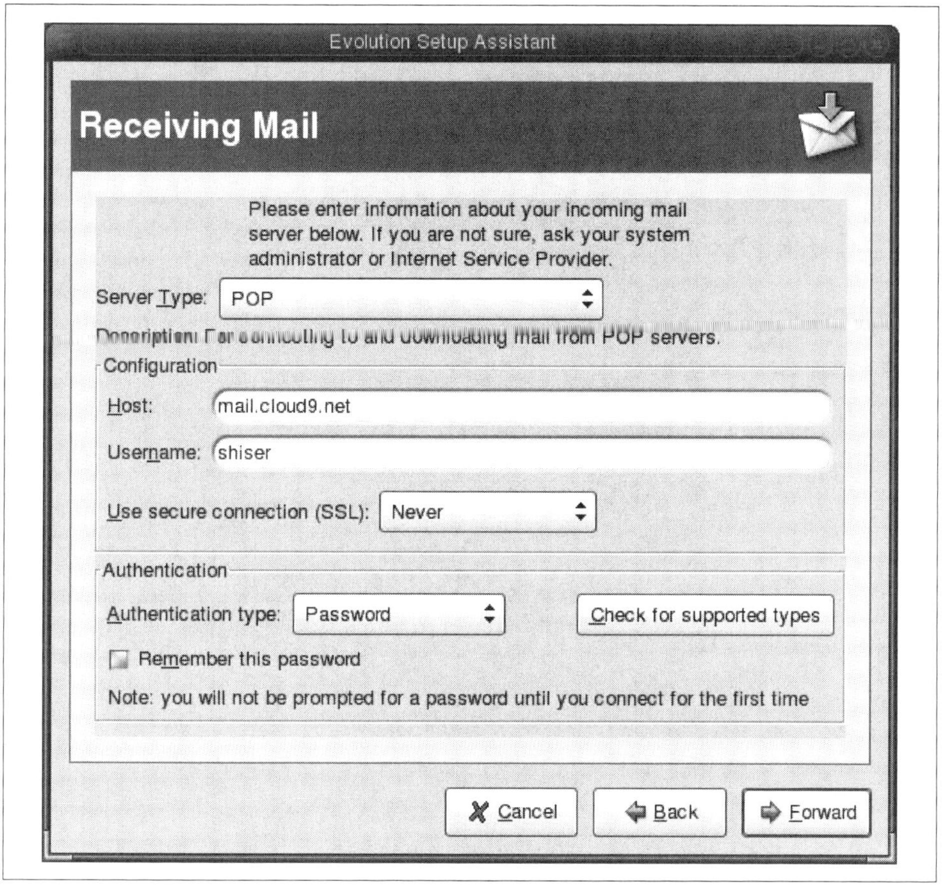

Figure 6-9. The Receiving Mail dialog, filled in successfully

leave this Message Storage option unchecked. This clears email off your ISP's or Web-mail service provider's email servers each time you access email. This is helpful because it keeps your inbox at the email server from getting full, by moving your email (when you ask to read it) to your local workstation, which has ample disk space.

Alternatively, when you are setting up a secondary workstation to access your email account (a family member's computer, for example, that you use from time to time), you may check the box "Leave messages on server" on that machine. This way, when you access email from that computer, your email stays on your ISP's or Web-mail service provider's email server until you access and download it later on from your own primary workstation. Later, you can archive your important email locally on your primary workstation, at which time it is automatically cleared out from your ISP's or Web-mail service provider's email server.

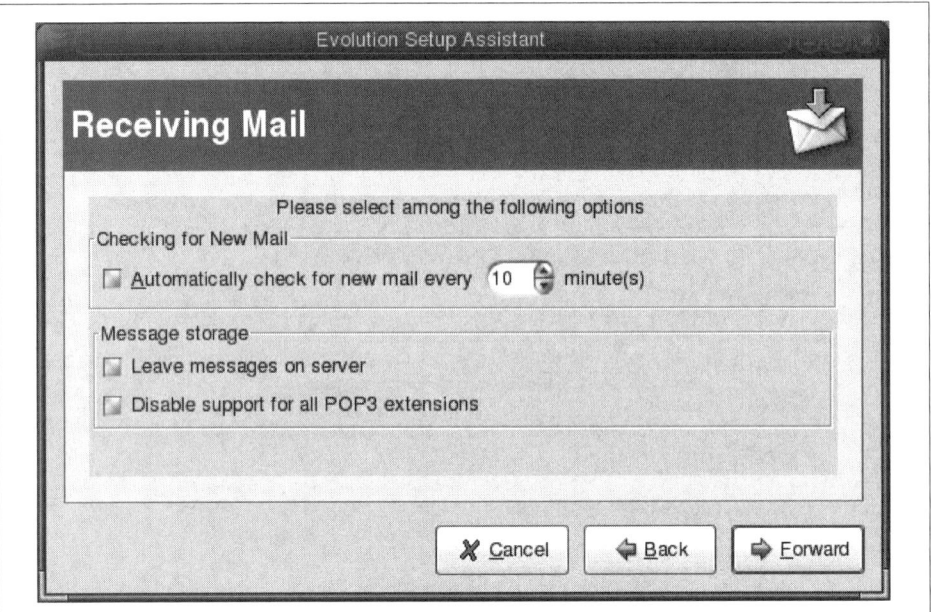

Figure 6-10. Receiving Mail

Fill in the Sending Mail screen (Figure 6-11) with the appropriate outgoing email Server Type and Host name. See Table 6-4 for examples of sending or outgoing mail server names.

In the Account Management screen (Figure 6-12), set the name for your email account as a label and set this account as the default if it's your primary or only account.

In Figure 6-12, leaving the settings as you see them is fine in most cases. The first email account you set up is always the default account. If you later set up additional email accounts, you can establish an account naming scheme that does not simply default to the email address, if doing so helps you keep track of your different accounts. You can change the default (primary) account setting here, too.

You can always go back to edit any email account settings via Tools → Settings, where you can select an account and edit its incoming and outgoing servers, and all other settings you've encountered here from Figures 6-4 through 6-12.

Next, you must choose your time zone. (See Figure 6-13.)

Finally, click the Apply button to finish the email account setup process. (See Figure 6-14.)

Download mail by clicking Send/Receive on the toolbar, near the top of the Email window. The first time you click it, you are prompted (Figure 6-15) to enter your email password. Enter it here. For convenience, you can check the box for JDS to

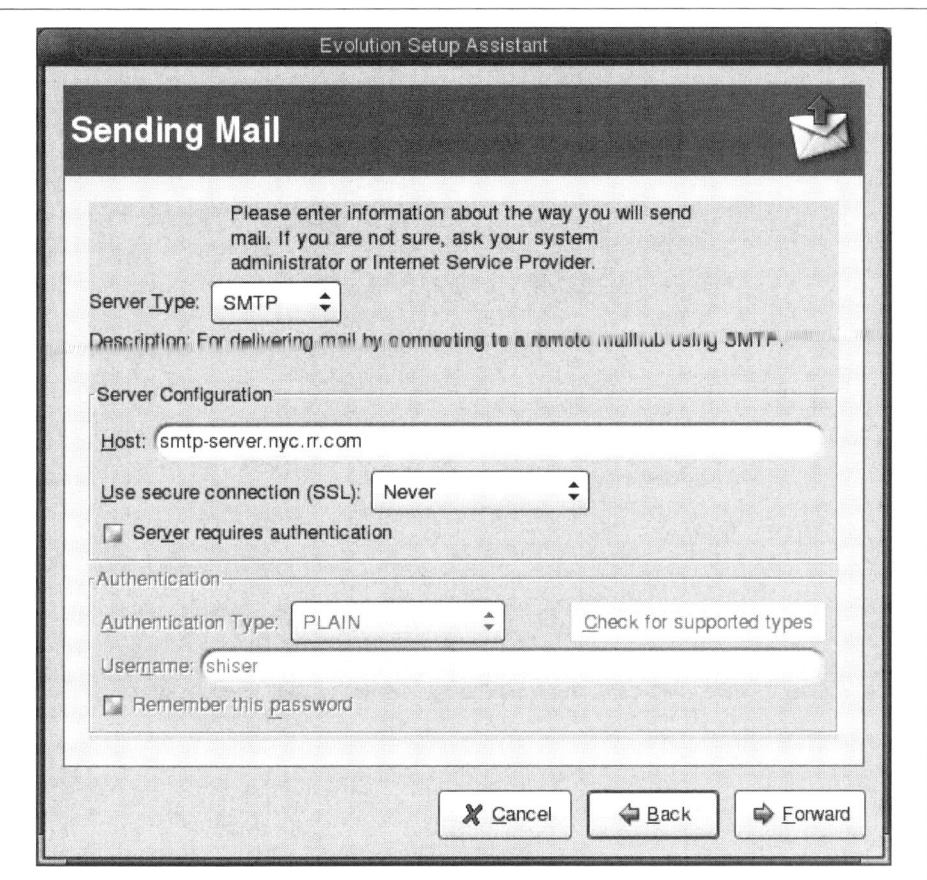

Figure 6-11. The Sending Mail screen, filled in successfully

"Remember this password," and JDS will hold your password on the system, so you don't have to reenter it each time you start up email.

If you are security-conscious, you can maintain an extra degree of password protection by leaving the Remember this password box unchecked. This requires that you enter your email password each time you click Send/Receive, or your system automatically checks the server for email. (See Figure 6-10.) For some people, the inconvenience is worth the added measure of security.

Importing Contacts (from Your Old Address Book)

If you've been using email for several years now, you very likely have a collection of friends' and colleagues' names, email addresses, phone numbers, and mailing addresses that is priceless to your daily business workflow, as well as useful for personal once-a-year occurrences like Christmas-card mailings. Anyone who has lost

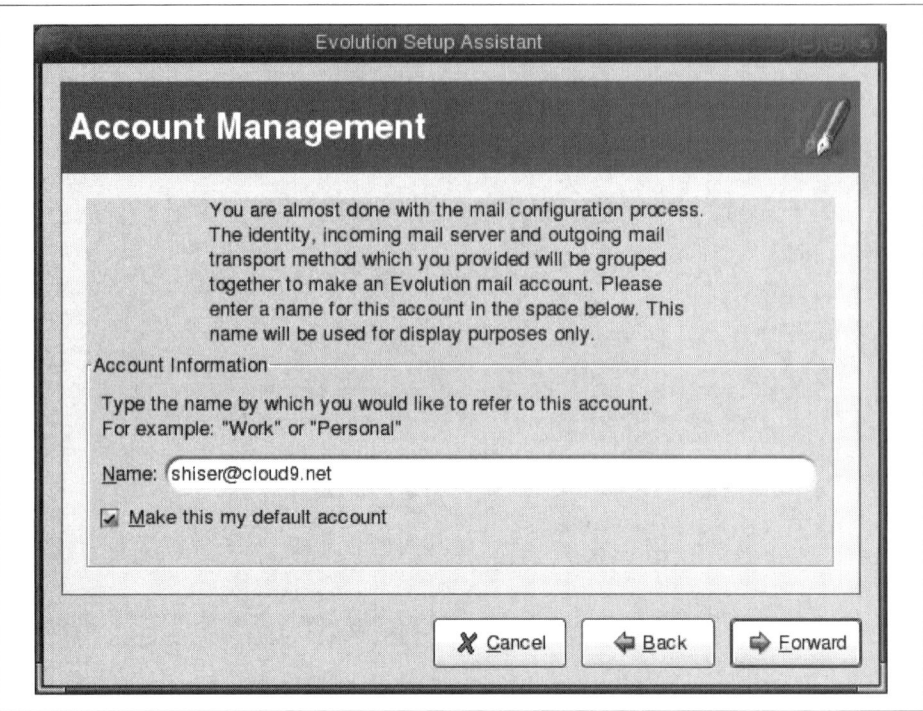

Figure 6-12. The Account Management screen

their old Filo-Fax or who has irreparably had a computer crash knows the value of the data in that address book and how long it takes to rebuild one from scratch.

Accordingly, one of the most useful procedures in JDS is to bring your personal information over from your old desktop.

Generally, importing your contacts is a three-step process:

- On your old desktop system, Save or Export your address book data as a text (*.txt*) or VCard (*.vcf*) file.
- Attach the file to an email addressed to yourself or save it on removable media (CD-R, floppy disk, or USB storage "dongle") to bring it over.
- Import the file into the Contacts folder of JDS Email and Calendar program.

Figures 6-16 through 6-23 show explicitly how to migrate Contacts information from MS Outlook (2000) on Windows XP to JDS's Email and Calendar program. If you are migrating from another platform or address book program, this series of screen shots may still be useful if you use a little imagination. Barring that, a search of the Web may yield specific documentation for "Importing Contacts to Evolution" that is applicable to your platform or situation.

Figure 6-13. The Timezone screen

In Outlook Contacts, in Figure 6-16 in select all contacts via Edit → Select All. This highlights all your contact entries.

Having selected all contacts, choose File → Save As from the Main menu.

In the Save As window (Figure 6-17), select the target folder in the Save In: drop-down at the top and enter the filename in the File Name: field. This establishes the folder or "path" and the name of the text file containing all contact data. Then, click the Save button. Note that the "Save as type:" (or file type) is automatically set appropriately to Text Only, so you don't need to change it.

Now, go to Outlook (inbox view) and click the New button at the top left. This opens an empty message window, which you should address to yourself: enter your own email address in the To: field.

Next, click the paper clip attachment icon on the toolbar to open the Insert File window. Here, you can browse or "look in" various folders to find the contacts text file

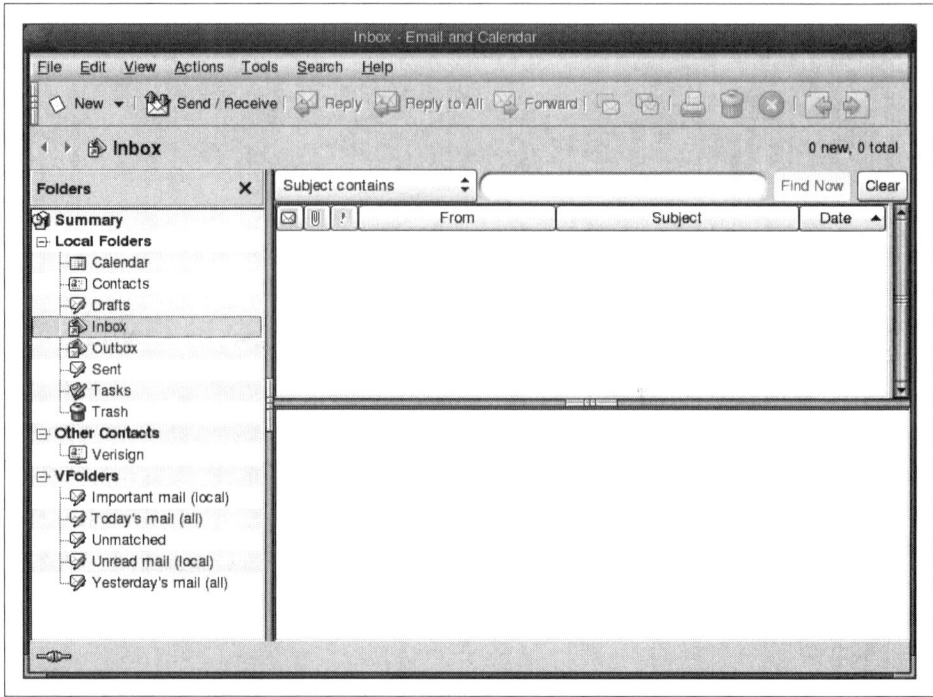

Figure 6-14. First view, once configured

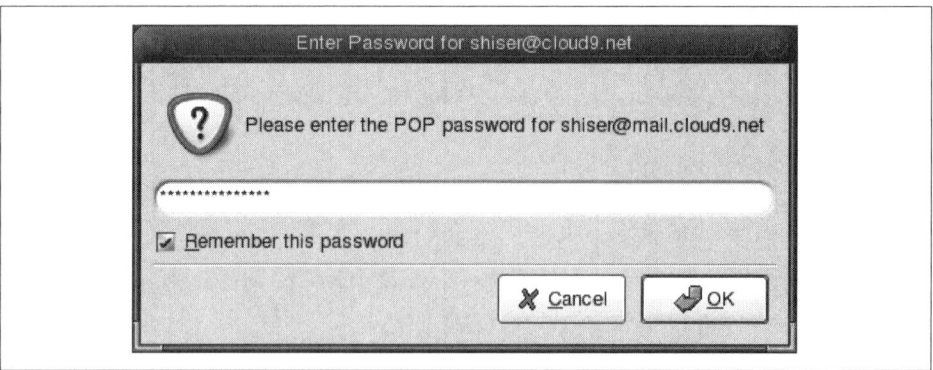

Figure 6-15. Password prompt

that you created above. (See Figure 6-17.) With a single click, highlight your contacts file and click the Insert button at the bottom right of the Insert file window. (See Figure 6-18.) This attaches the file to a message addressed to yourself. Note the attached file icon at the bottom of the open message window in Figure 6-19: it's a little notepad icon.

Next, fill in the Subject: field with something identifying this email and click Send on the toolbar.

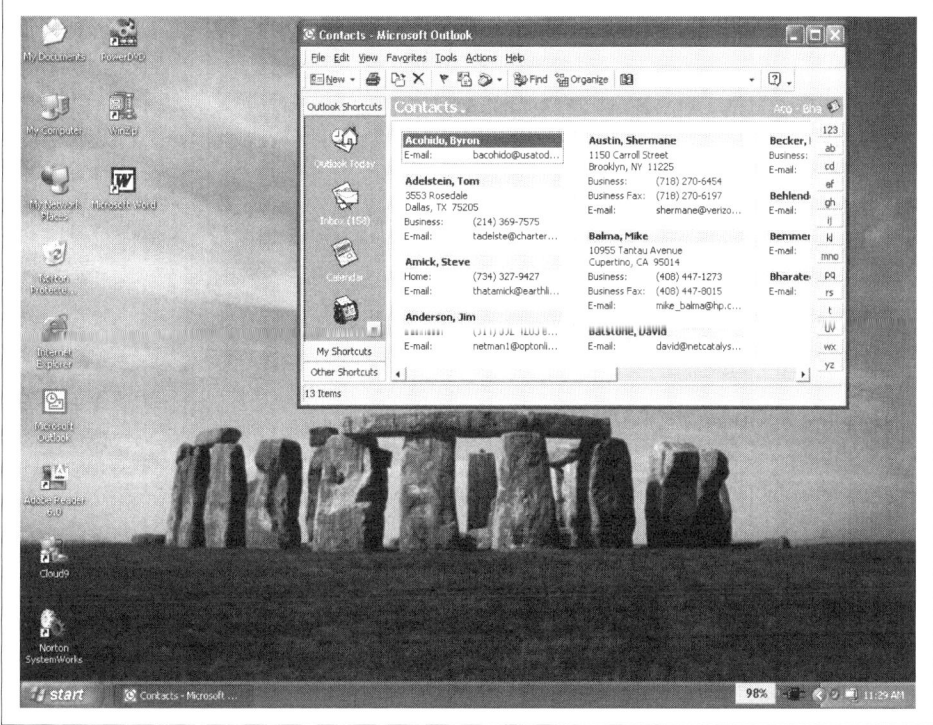

Figure 6-16. Step 1: exporting contacts from MS Outlook

Before moving on, make sure to "flush" your email outbox to ensure that your self-post has been sent. To do this, press the Send button on Outlook's toolbar.

Now that you've sent your contacts to yourself, exit Windows and go into JDS. This may require rebooting for those with a dual-boot system. For others, who are migrating to a new or different PC, it may require sliding your chair a few feet or even driving across town.

Now, in JDS, open Email and Calendar to field the email you have just sent to yourself. The attached text file icon is visible at the bottom left within the message window. Clicking on the black caret at the right side of the attachment icon opens a drop-down permitting you to choose Save Attachment.

In the Save Attachment window (Figure 6-20), select the folder (or directory) in your JDS filesystem, in which you want to save the attachment, and click OK. In the example of Figure 6-20, the folder currently selected is visible in the drop-down at the top center of the Save Attachment window, with its complete path: */home/swhiser/Documents/JDS_manual*. Use this drop-down menu or the Folders and Files panes to select your favored directory. Typically, */home/[user]/Documents* is fine for most users. Do remember where you placed the contacts file. Avoid saving to / or to */root*.

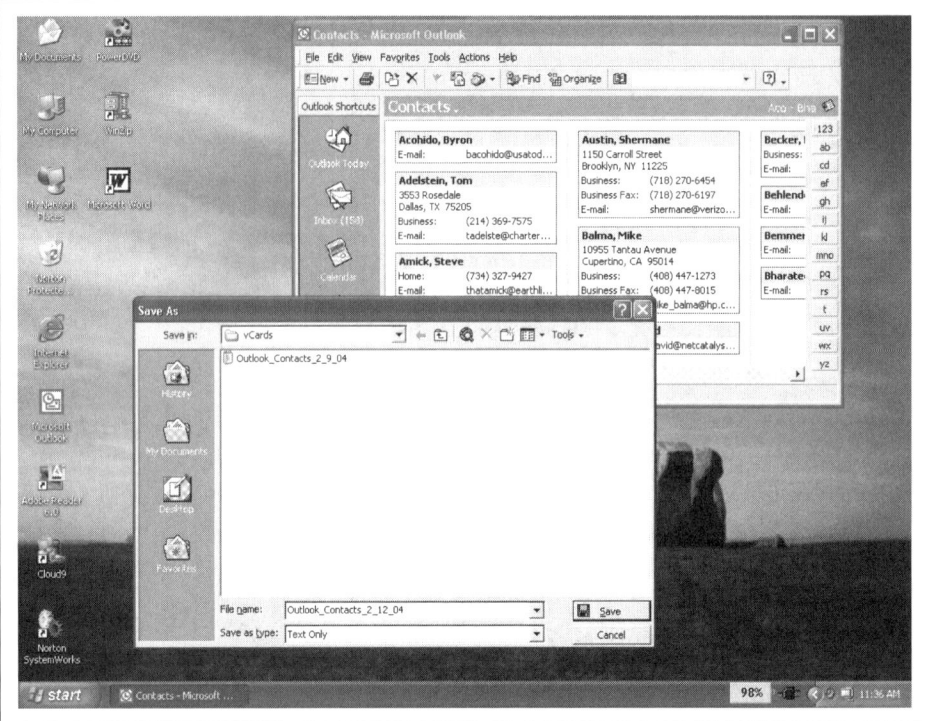

Figure 6-17. Choosing path and filename

Having collected your contacts successfully, now it's time to import the contacts data into the Email and Calendar program.

In Email and Calendar, click File → Import and follow the process through the Evolution Import Assistant.

In the Importer Type (Step 1 of 3) window, select "Import a single file" by clicking the adjacent radio button and click Forward.

Now, in the Select a File (Step 2 of 3) window, browse your JDS file system to find the name of the contacts text file you just emailed to yourself. Use the Browse button to click on the appropriate path in the drop-down menu and click on the name of the contacts text file in the location in which it had been saved earlier. Once you've found it, as pictured in Figure 6-21, click the Forward button.

Now, in the Import File window (Step 3 of 3), click the Import button.

Select the folder in which to place your contacts. Highlight the Contacts folder and click OK. This is shown in Figure 6-22.

Now in the Select importer window, choose "VCard (.vcf, .gcrd)," even if you are importing a text (.txt) file, then click OK. (See Figure 6-23.)

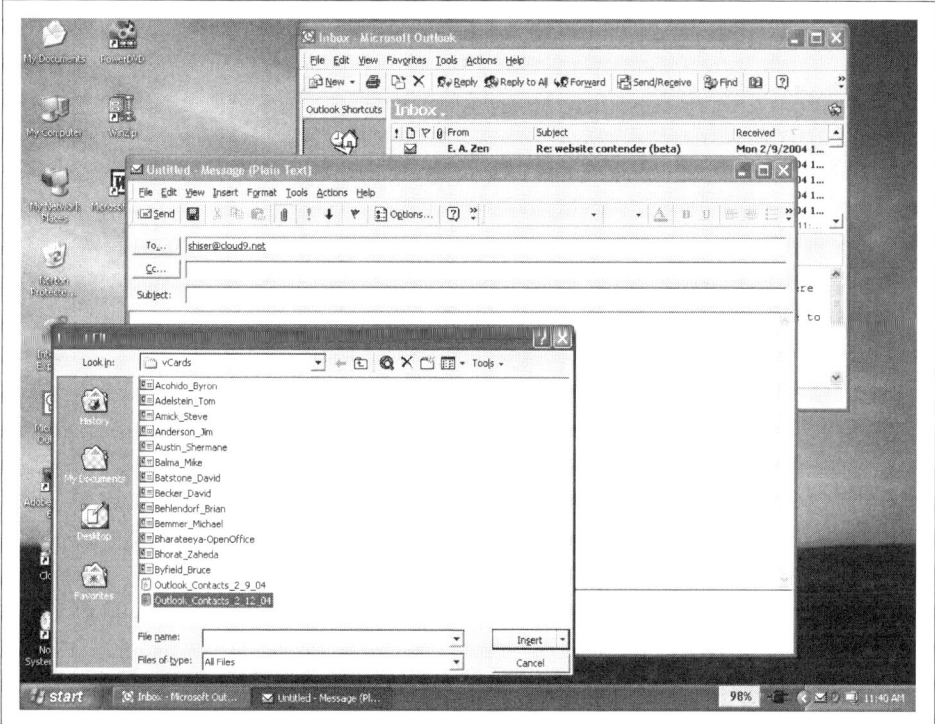

Figure 6-18. Step 2: sending contacts attached to yourself

If you have a large number of contacts—from hundreds to thousands—the importation process will take a few seconds. Patience is encouraged.

Email and Calendar Basics

If you've used a graphical email program on another computer system, the activities familiar to you there may now serve you well here. But we cover email basics here to help you warm to the new environment.

Inbox Views

On Email and Calendar's Main menu, third from left, is the View drop-down menu. Here you can customize your view of the Inbox. (The drop-down menu changes according to which dimension of Email and Calendar—Inbox, Calendar, Contacts, Tasks or Summary—is currently open.)

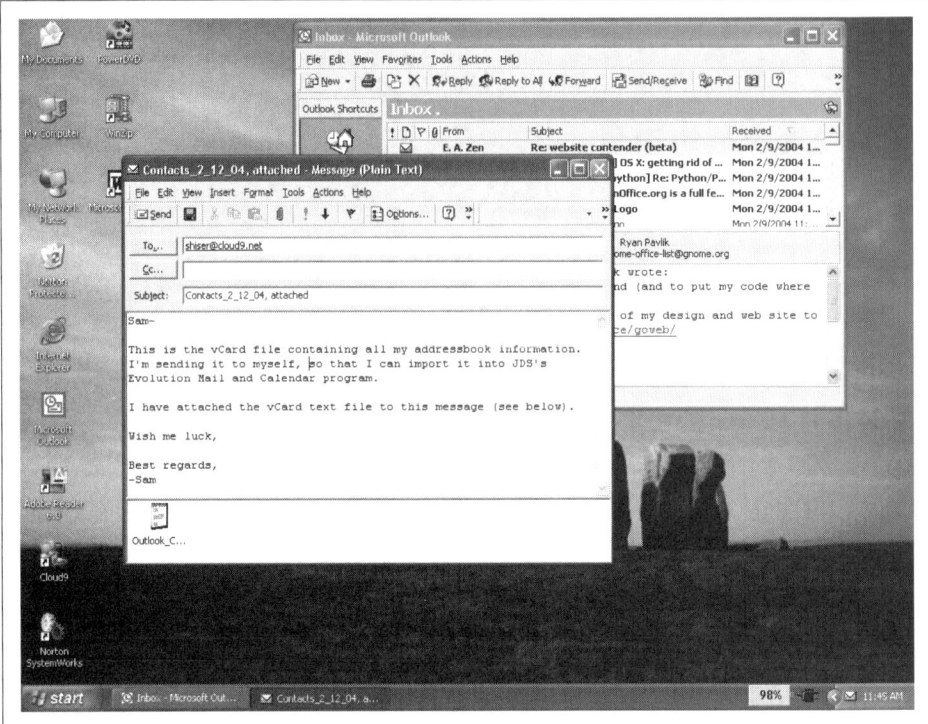

Figure 6-19. Attaching your contacts text file to yourself

The four aspects of Inbox Views for email folders are:

- Current View (of the Inbox)
- Shortcut Bar
- Folder Bar
- Preview Pane

Current View lists the mail in your Inbox, along with a Preview Pane that shows you the top few lines of a single email message. This view allows you to establish how email is sorted in your Inbox (by Subject, Sender, Status or other criteria). The Shortcut Bar and Folder Bar offer two different options for quickly navigating from Inbox to another of the dimensions: Calendar, Contacts, Tasks, or Summary.

If desired, you can uncheck all the View choices, leaving only the Inbox visible.

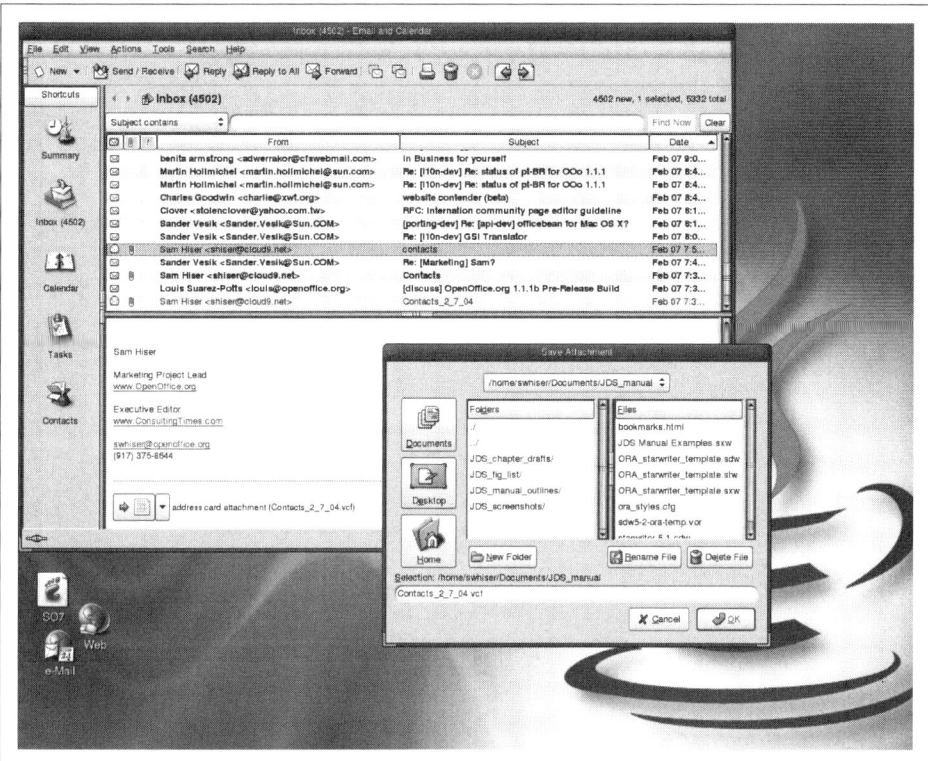

Figure 6-20. Fielding your attachment

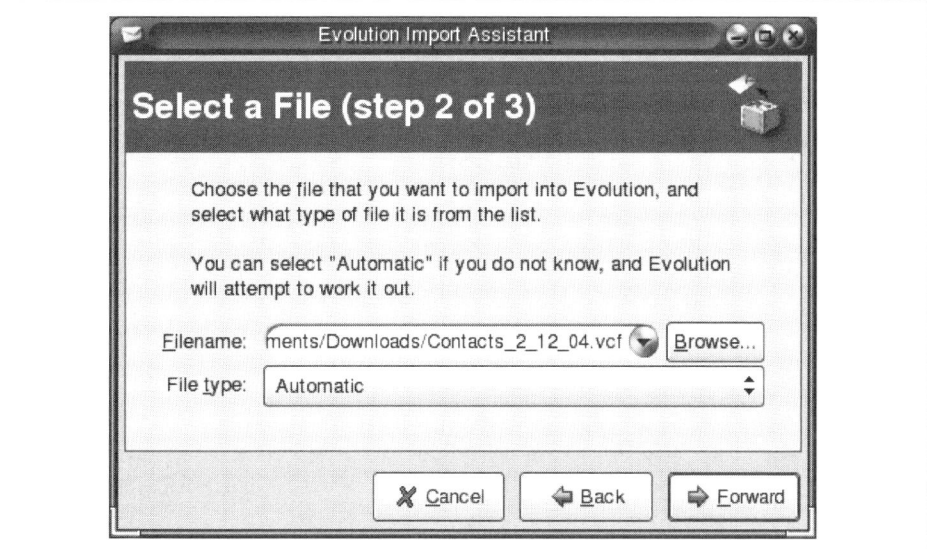

Figure 6-21. Selecting the contacts text file

Figure 6-22. Selecting the folder

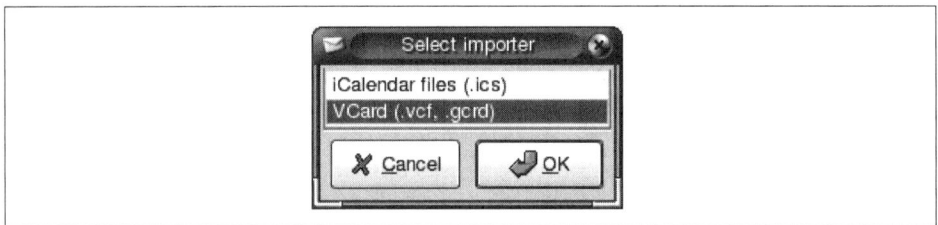

Figure 6-23. Selecting the importer

 Users report sometimes finding Preview Pane to be hidden for unknown reasons. It's likely they have inadvertently altered a setting somewhere. To restore the Preview Pane, simply go to Views on the program's Main menu and check the box in front of "Preview Pane." If the Preview Pane box is checked and you still don't see it, the divider of the Inbox and Preview Pane has been mistakenly dragged to the lower edge of the application window. Fix it by reaching down with the mouse and dragging and dropping the divider back upward to restore the Preview Pane to view.

Compose a message

At the top lefthand side of the Email and Calendar program's toolbar is the New button. Clicking it launches a fresh Compose window, shown in Figure 6-24.

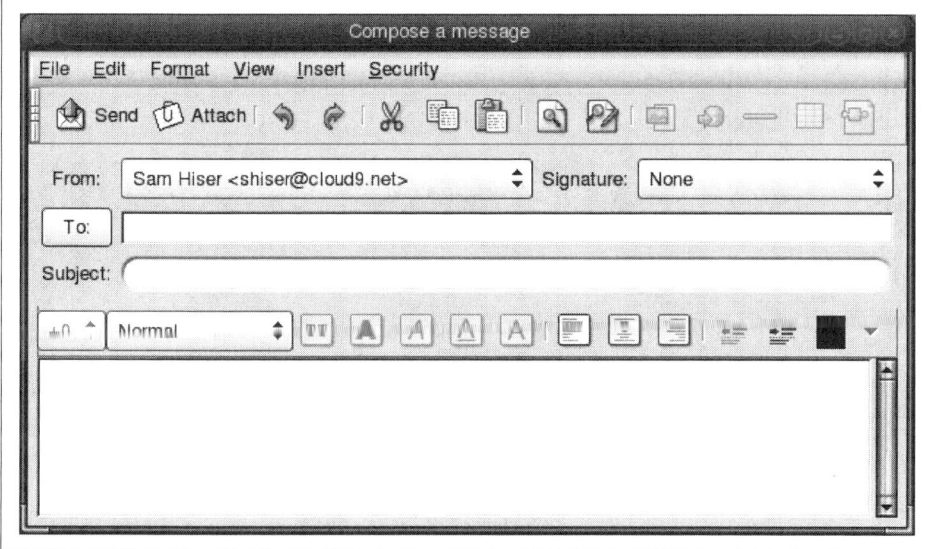

Figure 6-24. "Compose a message" window, default view

Customizing the Compose window: From, Reply-to, Cc., Bcc

If you want to include one or more colleagues on an email you are sending, invoke the "Cc Field" in the "Compose a message" window by checking the box, View → Cc Field, in the current Compose window.

Email and Calendar also provides a feature called "blind carbon copy," or Bcc field. The "To" and/or "Cc" recipients cannot see the "Bcc" person's email address in the header of the received email. To send a blind carbon copy, check the box of View → Bcc Field in the current Compose window and enter there the email address of the contact to whom you want to discretely send the email. Figure 6-25 shows a Compose window set with all email recipients visible.

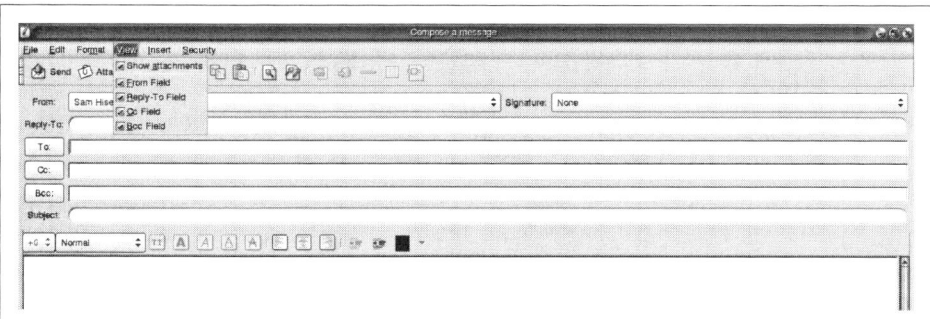

Figure 6-25. All recipients and attachments visible

Contacts: adding and deleting a record

In Contacts, click the New button at the top left of the toolbar, and a fresh blank window appears (Figure 6-26) for you to enter Name, Job Title, Organization, Email Address(es), Postal Address, Phone Numbers, and various other useful information.

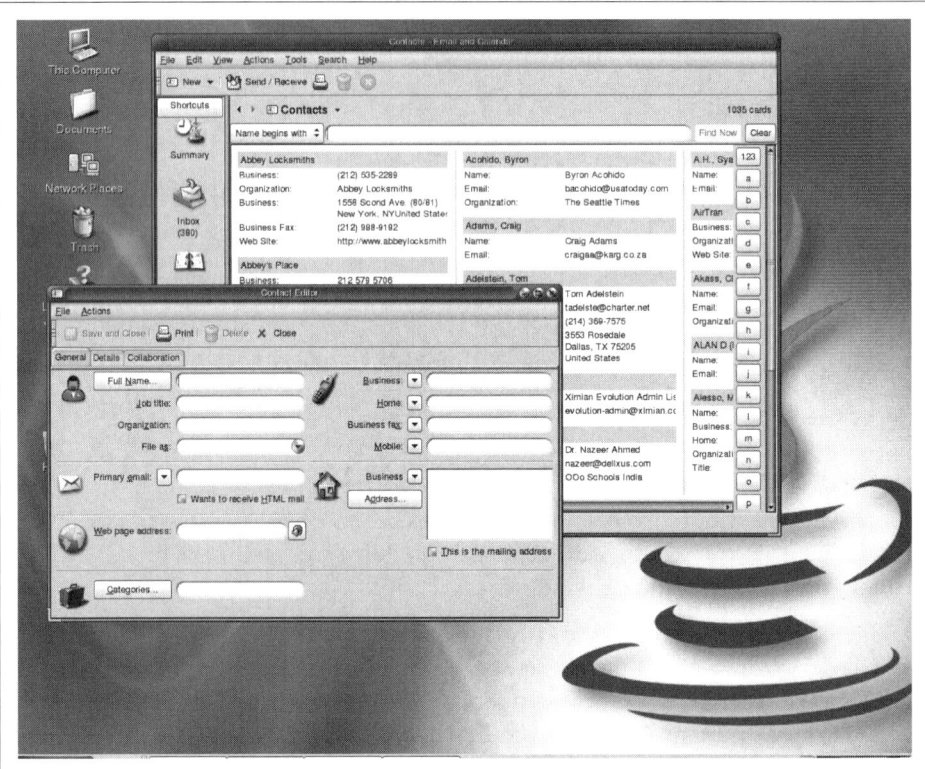

Figure 6-26. Adding a contact record

After you have finished entering the relevant information for this person or record, click the "Save and Close" button at the top left of the toolbar, and the entry is complete and saved.

There are several ways to delete an existing entry from Contacts. The quickest is to right-click on the gray name bar at the top of the record you intend to delete, then select Delete at the bottom of the menu that appears. A confirmation window next appears: press the Delete button to delete the record.

Alternatively, click on the gray name bar of the record you want to delete. It turns blue, upon the click. Then press the Delete key on your keyboard, and a confirmation window opens asking if you are sure. Proceed as above.

Calendar views

Figure 6-27 shows Calendar in "Work Week" view. You can alter the view by clicking one of the view icons on the toolbar. The four distinct views include:

Day view
> View appointments for one day in detail, at half-hour increments.

Work Week view
> View five days of the workweek—each day in a vertical column—and get a quick visual sense of your schedule. (See Figure 6-27.)

Week view
> View all seven days of a week, in grid format.

Month view
> View the whole month, in grid format.

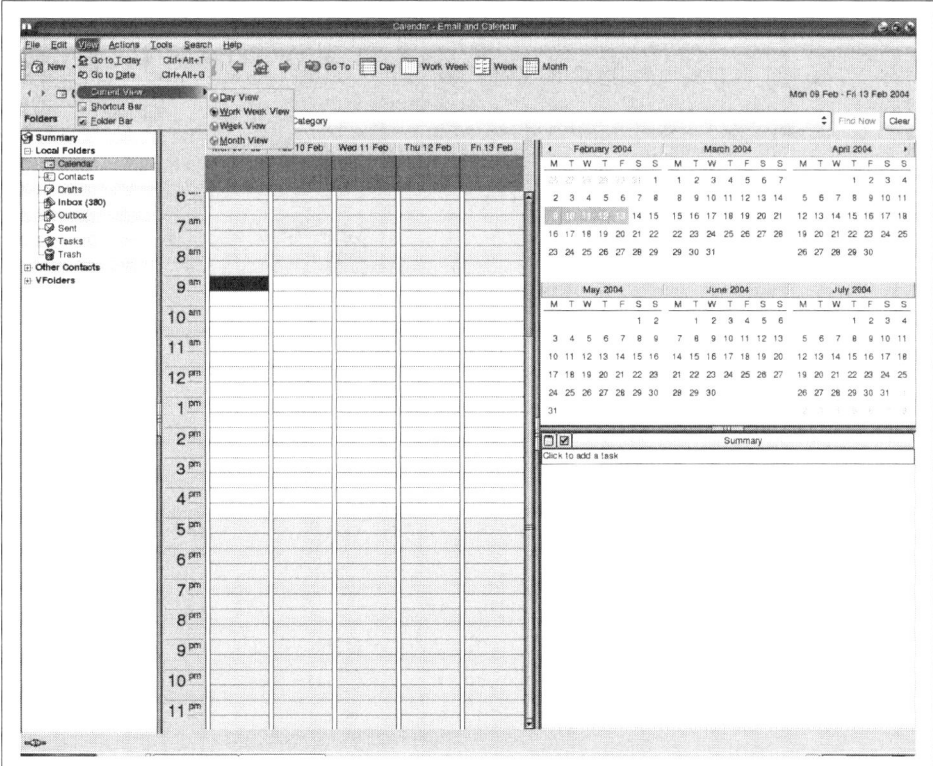

Figure 6-27. Calendar in Work Week view

An alternative way of changing view is from the Main menu: select View → Current View and choose among the four views.

Calendar: highlighting contiguous dates

Note that three views of Calendar, all except Month View, integrate a Tasks pane in the lower-right corner and a handy set of monthly calendars in the upper-right corner. There, the current date is always outlined in red.

These monthly calendars have a special feature where you can highlight any number of contiguous days, by clicking and dragging the pointer over the days, and the main calendar pane sets to those dates. Figure 6-28 illustrates an example in which the contiguous days highlighted are March 9th through March 11th.

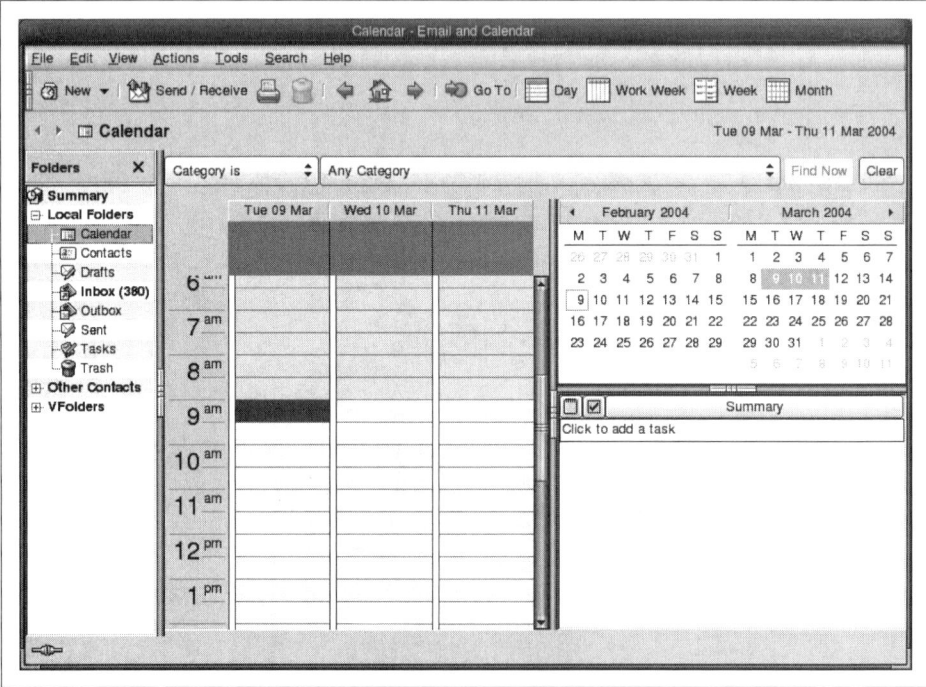

Figure 6-28. Highlighting contiguous days

In the monthly calendar at the upper right, you can move to the next or previous month by clicking the little triangle that appears at the left or at the right of the month's name. When displaying a day, you can add an event to your calendar by double-clicking on the day or a time segment within the day.

Summary: customizing News & Weather

Just like email itself, the news and weather links in the Summary dimension require an Internet connection to function.

The first time you open Email and Calendar (after the very first time you bootup JDS), the default News & Weather links visible on the Summary page may not suit your needs or taste, and they may not be relevant to your location. It is quite easy to change these links from within Email and Calendar by going into Tools → Settings and clicking on Summary Preferences in the lefthand index.

Here, click the News Feeds tab, second from left, where you see a list of available feeds in the All column at the left. The righthand column, labeled Shown, includes the News Feeds that are visible on the Summary page. You can delete feeds you don't want by highlighting the feed in the Shown column with either a right- or left-click and then by clicking the Remove button. To add a desired feed from the All column at the left, simply highlight the feed you want and click the Add button, and it will appear in the Shown column. Save your changes, as usual, by clicking the OK button when you are finished.

Email and Calendar Power Tips

JDS Email and Calendar includes some advanced features that make it a powerful and stable desktop toolset. Here, we explore a few examples that can boost your email effectiveness and overall productivity on the desktop.

Email: setting up signatures

Signatures are saved blocks of text that you can compose in advance and then set to include automatically at the bottom of email messages. Signatures can be used to simply identify you or offer a few chosen words or important hyperlinks to recipients of your email. When you enter and set Signatures, you can have them appear automatically at the bottom of every email you compose, reply to, or forward; or you can have no Signatures attach automatically, permitting you to select one manually from your list of Signatures to have more control.

To set up any number of different Signatures, run through the following steps:

1. Follow Tools → Settings and, on the left-side index, choose "Composer Preferences" about midway down.
2. Click the Signatures tab, the middle of three at the top, on the right.
3. At the right of the blank Signature(s) space, click the Add button and the "Edit signature" window pops up.
4. In the "Name:" line, enter a name that describes the Signature. (If you are going to have more than one Signature, pick a naming scheme that helps you later choose among several Signatures quickly.)
5. Now, in the larger space below, enter the Signature itself.

   A standard personal Signature is your Name, followed by your Email Address. Signatures used in connection with work often have Name, Title, Company, and Email Address.

 If you go to the trouble of deploying a marketing, aesthetic, or humor-
ous message in a Signature, please make it unique, poignant, clever,
funny, or acerbic. Boring Signatures are no less sinful than spam! (See
Figure 6-29.)

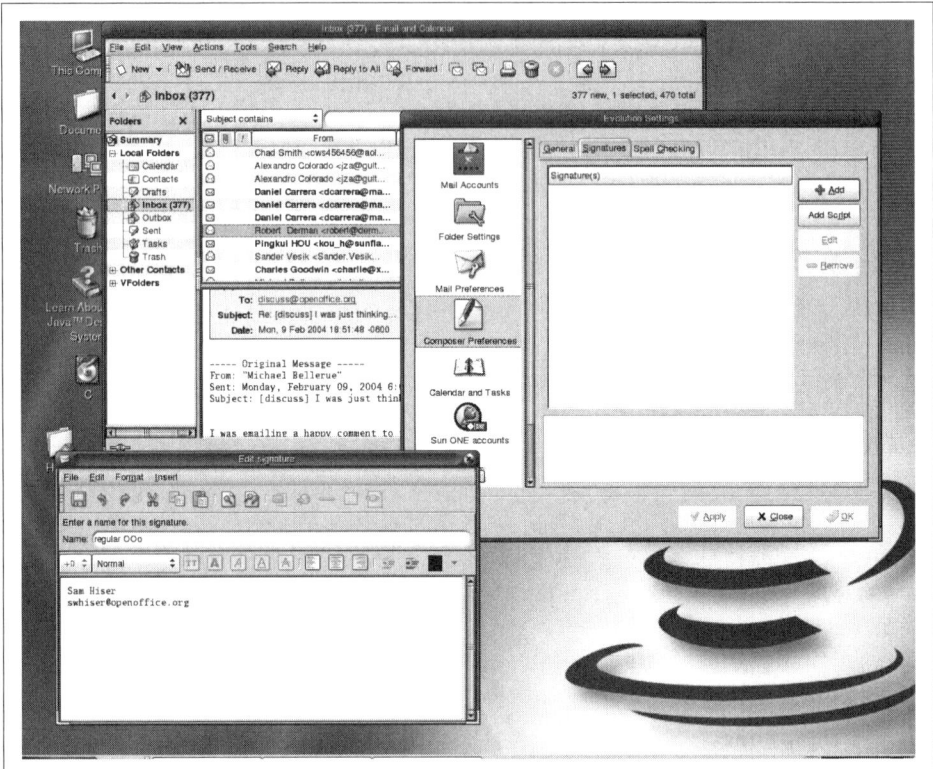

Figure 6-29. Creating a Signature

After entering the Signature text in the "Edit signature" window, select File → Save
and Close, or click the Save icon at the top left of the toolbar. Repeat the procedure
to add additional Signatures, if desired. You may later edit existing Signatures via
this method, too.

An alternative method for adding Signatures is through the Evolution Email Account
Editor via Tools → Settings at the Mail Accounts dialog. Here, highlight any email
account and click the Edit button on the right side of the dialog box. This opens the
Evolution Account Editor, where, at the bottom right, you find an Add Signatures
button. Clicking Add Signatures opens up the Edit signatures box, where you can
repeat the Signature creation process described above.

Email using security and encryption

JDS Email and Calendar includes features for integrating email with the robust Public-Key Infrastructure (PKI) encryption software that runs on JDS. With encryption integration, security-conscious users benefit from being able to key-sign or authenticate their outgoing email—that is, to verify that the email truly comes from them and has not been altered by a third party. They can also send encrypted email to others as well as de-crypt email that arrives in encrypted form from other parties.

To use these security features, JDS users need a public and private key-set and need to be able to set up either PGP (Perfectly Good Privacy, *www.pgp.org*) or GPG (GNU Privacy Guard, *www.gnupg.org*) on their system. The operation of the PGP or GPG encryption software products that implement secure email are beyond the scope of this book.

The JDS email security features are enabled in Tools → Settings under Mail Accounts. Click an account in the list to highlight it and then choose Edit. The tab that appears on the far right, labeled Security, is where you enter your PGP or GPG Key ID and establish other desired settings for email authentication and encryption services.

Contacts: creating Contact Lists (or Groups)

Active email users may find Contact Lists indispensable. These let you create lists of multiple names for sending a single email message to many people simultaneously and for making sure that no relevant person is forgotten each time you have information to convey to the group. This can be considered a low-grade form of spam, so Contact Lists should be used carefully, with forethought. However, when used judiciously, Contact Lists can save a great deal of repetitive effort.

To create a new Contact List, go to your Contacts and right-click the gray name bar of any existing Contact entry. A drop-down list appears with "New Contact List…" second from the top. (See Figure 6-30.) Click on "New Contact List…" and up pops the "Contact List Editor" window.

To create a new Contact List, proceed to type in a Name for the new list. Then you can either manually enter email addresses, clicking the Add button each time, or drag and drop existing email contacts into the list window. When you finish building the new contacts list, click the Save and Close button at the top lefthand side of the toolbar. (See Figure 6-31.)

JDS Instant Messenger (IM)

Instant messaging, sometimes called chat, has moved from primarily a teenager's social medium to an important communication tool for professionals. It complements email and traditional tools such as the telephone, in many collaborative settings. One key

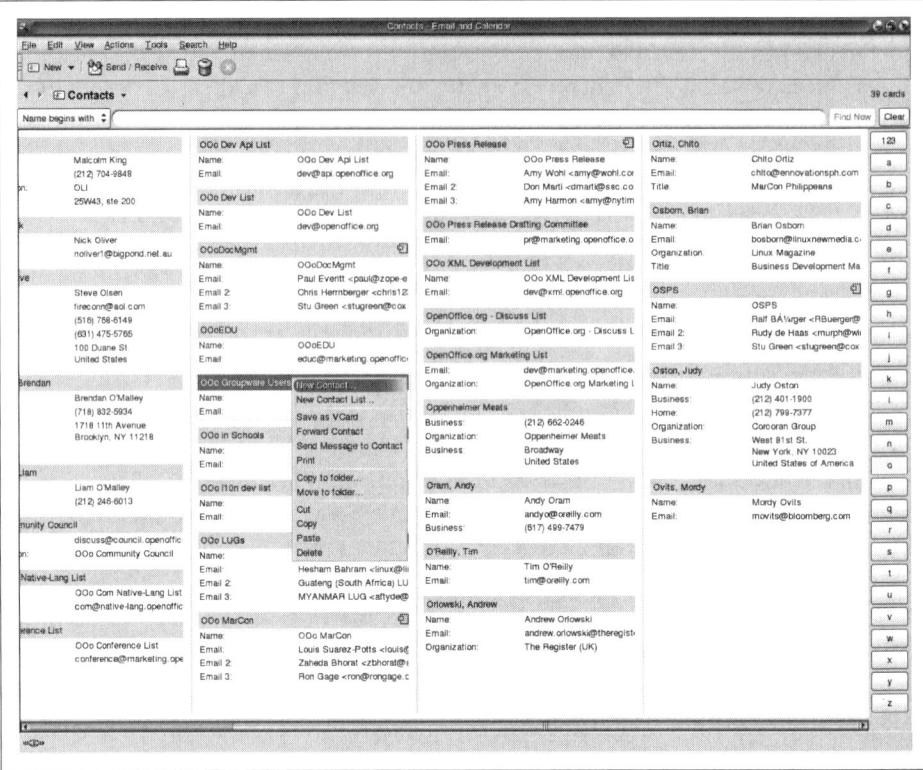

Figure 6-30. Creating an email Group

benefit of instant messaging in a business context is the speed and immediacy it offers for making contact and exchanging information through the desktop, at no cost.

Many different forms of instant messaging are offered by large Internet providers and other services. Luckily, the instant messaging tool in JDS supports many of them. JDS's Instant Messenger is based on *gaim*, a multiprotocol Internet chat client. Instant Messenger is located in JDS under Launch → Applications → Internet → Instant Messenger.

Through JDS's Instant Messenger, you can chat with members of any of the following instant messaging and chat networks:

- AOL Instant Messenger ("AIM")
- ICQ
- IRC
- Jabber

Figure 6-31. Contact List Editor awaiting input

Chat services or protocols not supported by JDS include:

- MSN
- Yahoo!
- Zephyr

Previously, software limited instant messaging participants to communicate only with members of their own network, where they shared the same communication protocol. For example, only a short time ago, AIM members could chat only with other AIM members but not Jabber members. Now programs such as JDS's Instant Messenger are solving the fragmentation of the instant messaging networks.

With Instant Messenger, you can maintain accounts with multiple instant messaging networks and change instant messaging services as you chat with different buddies, or even run chat sessions from different networks simultaneously. It's still impossible, however, to hold a single multi-person chat session with people across different chat networks because the instant messaging services still use different protocols.

If you absolutely must chat with members of certain chat networks that are unsupported by JDS's Instant Messenger, you may be able to solve the problem by downloading additional software. JBuddy Messenger is another multi-protocol chat client that works with several IM networks, not covered by JDS's Instant Messenger, including AIM, ICQ, JBuddy, Lotus Sametime, MSN, and Yahoo!.

Help for downloading and installing JBuddy Messenger is available online at Sun's JDS Support Forum, *http://supportforum.sun.com/sjds/*. JBuddy Messenger software is located at *http://www.zionsoftware.com*.

IM Setup

Here we cover the procedures necessary to set up your Instant Messenger account.

Sign up a new account, get a screen name

To use Instant Messenger, first you need to have a Screen Name or sign up to create a new account and Screen Name with one of the above-mentioned instant messaging networks. Table 6-5 tells you where to go to set up your account and Screen Name among the various networks. Take your pick.

Table 6-5. Set up a new account

Chat network	Sign up for a screen name
AOL Instant Messenger (AIM)	http://my.screenname.aol.com/
ICQ	http://web.icq.com/register
Jabber	http://www.jabber.org/user/userguide/#register
Netscape/AIM	If you already have an @netscape.net email address, your existing Netscape email USER ID and PASSWORD functions as your IM Screen Name and Password.

Technically oriented users may enjoy reading up on the different instant messaging protocols available, since the services and functionality that each one offers varies. Each of the web sites for the instant messaging services provides useful information on its respective network, protocol, and features. There is also a useful (although incomplete) survey of the different instant messaging and chat protocols on the gaim software developers' web site, *http://gaim.sourceforge.net/protocol.php*.

Go to the Screen Name registration page of your chosen chat network and follow the procedure there for establishing a Screen Name and Password. Typically, you are asked to provide an email address and possibly additional information such as your birth date.

Once you have established your Screen Name, you can set up your account in Instant Messenger and begin chatting.

Account setup

To set up your first chat account, open the JDS Instant Messenger program via Launch → Applications → Internet → Instant Messenger. The Login window appears. Enter your Screen Name and Password in the respective fields. (See Figure 6-32.)

Figure 6-32. Awaiting screen name and password input

In the Screen Name field, the phrase "<New User>" indicates that you have no Instant Messenger accounts set up yet. Highlight the phrase and press the Delete key or just type your Screen Name over it while it's highlighted. Then press the Tab key, enter your Password, and click the "Sign on" button. This immediately opens the Buddy List window on your desktop, and you are ready to chat. This also establishes your default Instant Messenger account, which the program remembers the next time you open the program. (See Figure 6-33.)

 Users sometimes have difficulty logging in if they do not adhere to the upper- or lowercase pattern originally established in their Screen Name or Password. Your chosen chat network determines whether your Screen Names and Passwords are case-sensitive.

You can see the first (default) IM account information in Figure 6-34, which you automatically entered when you first performed account setup.

You may have additional different instant messenger accounts and Screen Names by which others know you on a different chat network. To add one or more of such accounts to your JDS Instant Messenger program, go to the open Buddy List window (this window is always open and on your desktop when you start Instant Messenger) and select Tools → Accounts, which opens the Accounts window. Here you can add additional IM accounts, as necessary.

Figure 6-33. Entering Screen Name and Password

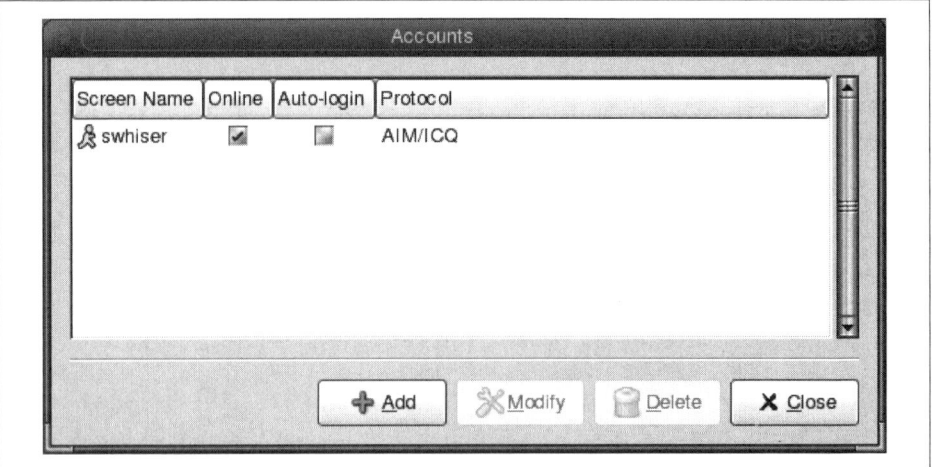

Figure 6-34. Instant messaging account information

IM Basics

Here we cover the basic tools for using JDS's Instant Messenger.

Sign on

Once your Screen Name and Password are entered into the Login window correctly, click the "Sign on" button. Your Buddy List appears on your desktop, and you are logged into Instant Messenger.

 If you are on a network behind a firewall, such as a company's local area network, it may be difficult for you to sign on to Instant Messenger. In such circumstances, consult your system administrator, who may be able to configure a proxy.

Note that upon each subsequent occasion when you open Instant Messenger, your default Screen Name and Password is entered and all you need to do is click "Sign on." Even this step can be bypassed, as we see in the next section.

When you first open the program and see Buddy List, the main window is blank. The Buddy List, shown in Figure 6-35, already contains one Group called "OSSI & OGIP." Later, we discuss how to manage Buddies and Groups.

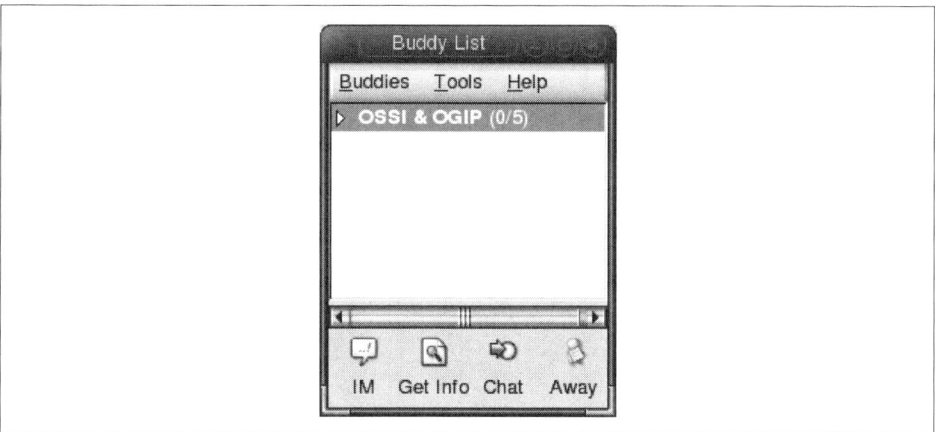

Figure 6-35. Buddy List

Auto-login

You can save a keystroke by setting up Auto-login, if you want Instant Messenger to automatically log you in when you first open it.

In Buddy List, go to Tools → Accounts to open the Accounts window. There, the Auto-login column is second from the right. You can check the box of the account or accounts for which you want to establish auto-login.

Auto-login saves a few extra mouse-clicks at the start of each IM session and is especially useful if you have a single, default, IM account that you use all the time; it's also useful to signal to your Buddies that you're available for "IM-ing."

Keep in mind that auto-login has its drawbacks. Logging into your IM account always signals to other "IM-ers"—those who have your Screen Name entered into their Buddy Lists—that you are at your workstation and available to chat. In many cases, such as when you are very busy, you may not want to signal to others that you are available, since an instant message from them might be distracting. At times like this, you may want to open your Instant Messenger program to see who among your Buddies is online, but you would like to stay "offline" to them. In this case, auto-login would add mouse-clicks to your workflow. So, your "Auto-login" settings are worth some consideration and should optimally be based on what you prefer to do *most* of the time.

Begin to chat

If you know someone's Screen Name on the instant messaging service that you signed up with, you can begin chatting immediately. (It's probably more efficient to add them into your Buddy List immediately, especially if you will be chatting with them in future. See the section "Adding buddies.")

At the bottom of the open Buddy List window on your desktop, click the IM button on the extreme left. The New Message window opens (Figure 6-36) and prompts you for a Screen Name. Enter the other party's Screen Name and click OK.

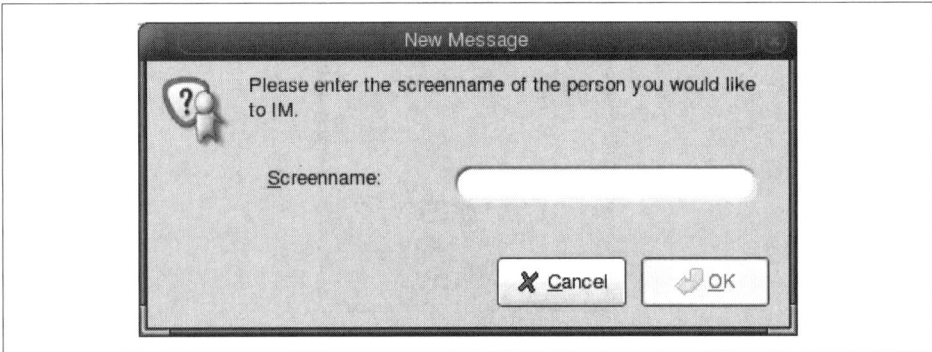

Figure 6-36. The New Message window

This opens a Conversation window, shown in Figure 6-37, and you're ready to begin an instant messaging session.

See in Figure 6-37 how the window is labeled *gpbazzini*. That is the Screen Name of the person with whom you are about to chat. Note also the tab at the upper left of the upper panel, which is also labeled with the other chat party's Screen Name. When you are holding multiple chat sessions at the same time, the tabs come in handy, allowing you to move easily among the different conversations. (Opening a single chat session with multiple parties is a different capability (discussed later in the section, "Multiparty chat.")

Type text into the bottom window (where the cursor sits when the window first opens) and press Enter. Each time you press the Enter key, the latest message you typed is transmitted to the IM session partner's Conversation window, assuming she is logged on to the instant messenger service on her workstation. Her replies will come right back in sequence into your Conversation window.

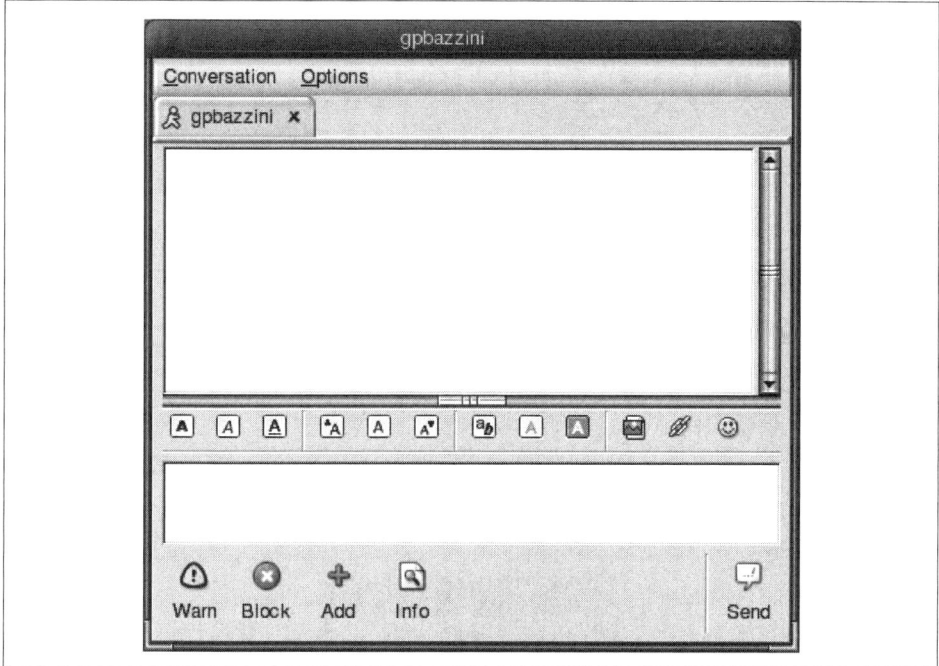

Figure 6-37. The Conversation window

The Buddy List

In the context of instant messaging, a "buddy" is someone with whom you regularly want to chat. A buddy could be a spouse at their workplace, a sibling, a best friend, an acquaintance, or a work colleague. Often one's Buddy List includes many, if not all, of those kinds of people. Later, we'll show how to organize buddies into groups.

The Buddy List is critical to productive chat. Without it, you would need to remember all friends' or colleagues' Screen Names, which would add many unnecessary key-strokes and likely make you quickly lose interest in IM.

The Buddy List is also the departure point for making most adjustments to your account, preference, and privacy settings in your JDS Instant Messenger program.

Adding buddies

To add a Buddy, go to your Buddy List window (Figure 6-35) and select Buddies → Add a Buddy. This opens the Add Buddy window (Figure 6-38), where you can enter the Screen Name and Alias of your Buddy.

The Alias is your label for that Buddy as it is later listed visibly in your Buddy List. For example, in Figure 6-39, the alias Tom represents Tom Adelstein, the coauthor of this book, whose Screen Name is not as easy for Sam to mentally associate with him. The longer your Buddy List, the more important it is to create easy Aliases.

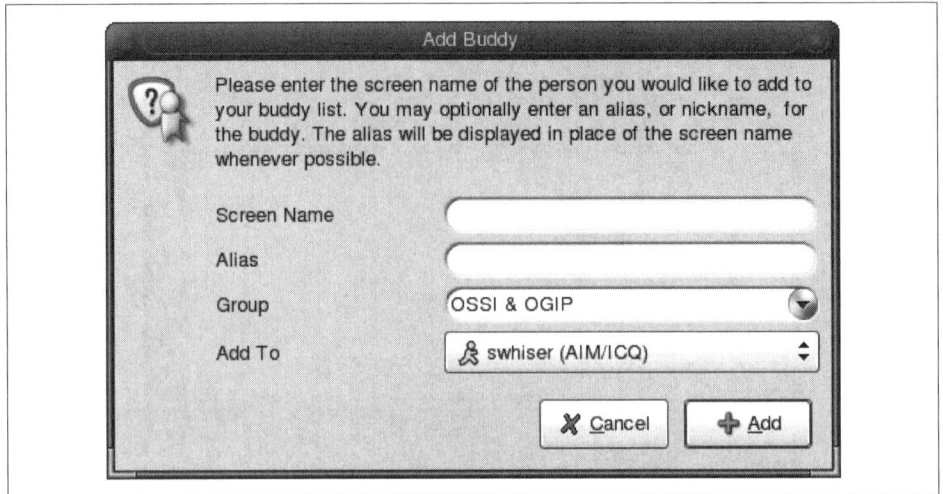

Figure 6-38. The Add Buddy window

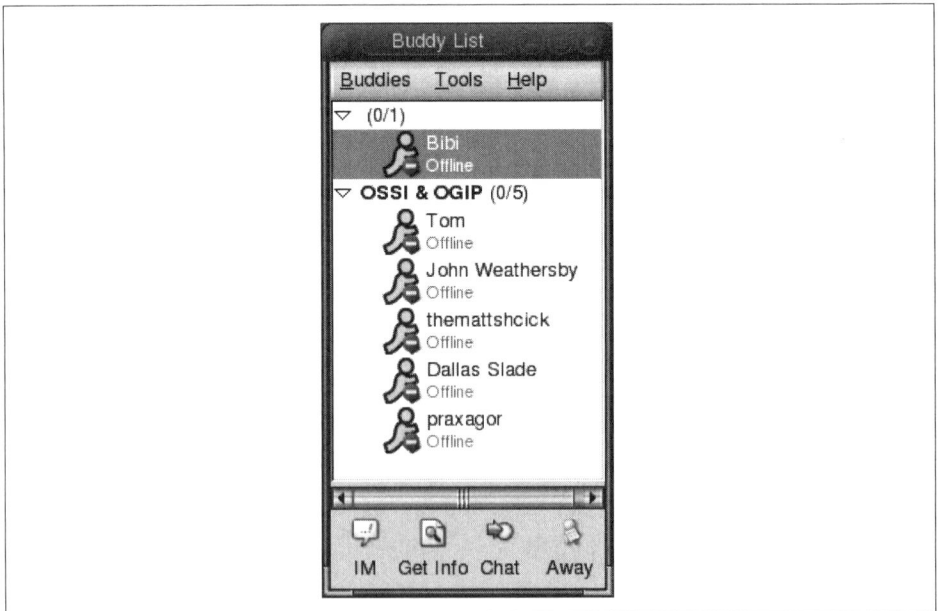

Figure 6-39. The Buddy List with Groups displayed

 The Alias feature is useful because it is often not easy to recognize someone by his or her Screen Name. For example, with the hypothetical Screen Name Moochy007, it is easy to forget the real person behind it. On the other hand, some people are impossible to forget.

Begin to chat with buddies

To start a chat session with someone in your Buddy List, go to the Buddy List and double-click the Alias of the Buddy with whom you'd like to chat. This action calls up a Conversation window, ready for your input. Type in your message, then press Enter, to transmit. Away you go.

Add a group

As said earlier, you can find your buddies more easily if you organize them into groups. To add a new group to your Buddy List, go to your Buddy List and select Buddies → Add a Group. This opens the Add Group window into which you can enter the name you make up, then press the Add button. Use a naming scheme that helps you quickly identify the different Groups that you establish over time in your Buddy List. Figure 6-39 shows a Group called "OSSI & OGIP."

The Conversation window

When you or one of your correspondents starts an instant messaging session, as we have shown, a Conversation window is active. Your keyboard entries appear in the lower window as you type. When you press Enter after typing, your input is sent to your partner. It also appears in your upper window after a parenthetical time-stamp, followed by your Screen Name, both of these in a color that distinguishes your own contributions to the conversation from your partner's.

The Conversation window also offers tabs representing the different chat conversations that are open simultaneously. Each tab is labeled with the other party's Screen Name. You can maintain multiple chat sessions with different people, while using the tabs to navigate from one to another. The people on the respective other ends do not know you are chatting with others.

If you have multiple instant messaging accounts and are logged on to more than one at once, the Conversation window menu offers a useful Send As feature, which permits you to change the account that you send a message from. You could change Screen Names in mid-chat, but this may only achieve confusion. It is more likely you will start multiple sessions using different services.

Conversation Text Customization

The Conversation window lets you change the size and the color of your message text, as well as providing the usual bold and italic forms. Font customization features are accessed among the buttons that are between the upper and lower panes within the Conversation window.

Conversation inserts

The Conversation window offers buttons permitting you to insert image files and hyperlinks to web content you want to refer to in a message. There is also a button to insert a variety of smiley faces to liven up your IM communications. The insert buttons are located between the upper and lower panes, at the right.

What's that little keyboard icon in the top right?

This mysterious icon, which comes and goes, is one of the most interesting and useful design features of Instant Messenger.

The little keyboard icon is like a busy signal. When it appears, it signals that the person with whom you are chatting is typing on his keyboard.

In a conversation, it is often polite to wait until the other party is finished talking before one speaks; otherwise you interrupt, which may be considered rude. So too in instant messaging and chat: if you see the other party is typing, you may do well to wait until they have sent their message to respond.

Multiparty chat

Instant Messenger permits chat with many participants at the same time. A host, the person who first creates a multi-party chat session, invites other individuals to join it. The host must first go to her Buddy List and select Buddies → Join a Chat. This opens the Join Chat window where the host:

- Selects which of her accounts to join
- Enters a name for the multi-party chat session
- Sets the Exchange number (4 is the default)

IM Power Tips

Instant Messenger offers numerous features and configuration preferences. In this section, we highlight just a few interesting ones. As always, you can gain a lot by spending a few minutes exploring the application's settings, buttons, and menu items to learn about features that may enhance your own ways of working and playing.

Chat between IM and cell phone

Instant Messenger allows you to send text messages to SMS-enabled cellular phones. Moreover, the recipient's text message replies appear on your desktop, like a standard instant messaging session.

At your Buddy List, click the IM button, at the bottom left of the window, to open the New Message window. (See Figure 6-36.) In the Screen name line, enter +1, followed by the cell phone number to which you intend to send the text message, and click OK. (See Figure 6-40.)

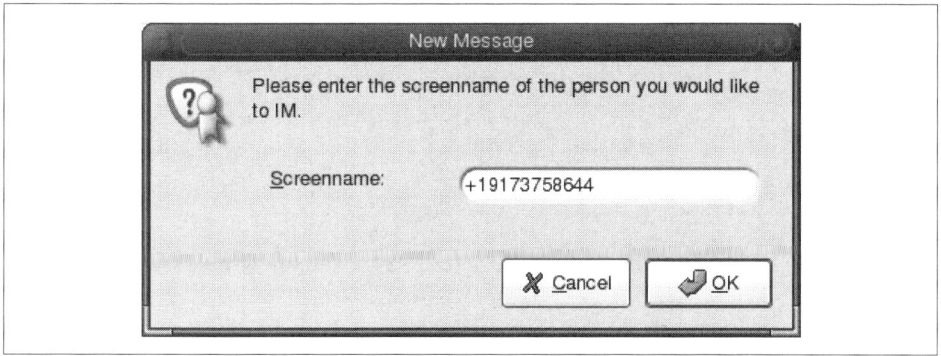

Figure 6-40. Sending a text message to a cell phone

This opens a new Conversation window, where you can chat with the holder of the cellular telephone. They can reply as they would in a conventional text conversation.

For this feature to work, it is necessary that the cell phones with which you want to communicate have SMS text-messaging features that are accessible and enabled by their cell phone service provider. Check with your telecoms provider to confirm the service. Additionally, messaging services are not uniformly established yet and certain countries may not accommodate IM-to-cell connections for various reasons.

If you are able to connect, though, this is an exciting feature.

Disable (or enable) sounds

If you have been using instant messaging, you know that there are sounds associated with a message received and with other messaging events.

There are occasions—such as when you are using IM as a back-channel on a multi-member conference call—when you should disable sounds on your desktop, so everyone on the call is spared hearing the Message Received beeps going off in the background. If everyone kept sounds enabled, imagine the flurry of beeps that would be audible on the call, when the opposing party, in a heavy negotiation, finally announces the details of something important, like *pricing*.

To disable sounds when receiving a message, go from your Buddy List to Tools → Preferences → Sounds → Sound Events and uncheck the box next to Message Received. This stops your machine from beeping upon each incoming instant message.

Other sound events you can control from this window include:

- Buddy logs in
- Buddy logs out

- Message received
- Message received begins conversation
- Message sent
- Person enters chat
- Person leaves chat
- You talk in chat
- Others talk in chat
- Someone says your name in chat

Here, you can make permanent changes or restore the default settings.

Managing "Away Messages"

You can send an Away Message if you leave your desk for a few minutes. This is a polite way to tell your Buddies that you are not available, especially if you leave during a chat session.

The system defaults to automatically sending an Away Message if you do not touch the keyboard for one minute. The system's default Away Message reads, "Slightly less boring default." You can change this default message and adjust the time period to your preference via Buddy List; go to Tools → Preferences and click on Away/Idle. This window also lets you deactivate the Auto-away feature, so it stops sending Away Messages automatically. If you do that, the only way to send an Away Message is manually via Tools → Away, where you can choose an appropriate message (or the default) from the drop-down box.

To edit, to add new, or to erase unwanted Away Messages, go from your Buddy List via Tools → Preferences to Away Messages, where the tasks are self-explanatory. You can also add or remove Away Messages more directly from Buddy List via Tools → Away → New Away Message or Tools → Away → Remove Away Message, where the actions should also be intuitive.

Privacy Control

Instant Messenger offers fine-grained control over whom you permit to contact you. This is a very important feature, because instant messaging can seriously disrupt your attention on the desktop. Without Privacy Control, instant messaging is useful only in personal or social contexts and can scarcely be used in business settings. It also allows users to maintain large Buddy Lists, while permitting only a few chosen individuals to make incoming contact.

To control privacy, go from your Buddy List to Tools → Privacy, where the window offers a variety of choices via a drop-down list. (Figure 6-41.) Among Privacy settings, the following choices are available:

- Allow all users to contact me
- Allow only the users on my buddy list
- Allow only the users below
- Block all users
- Block the users below

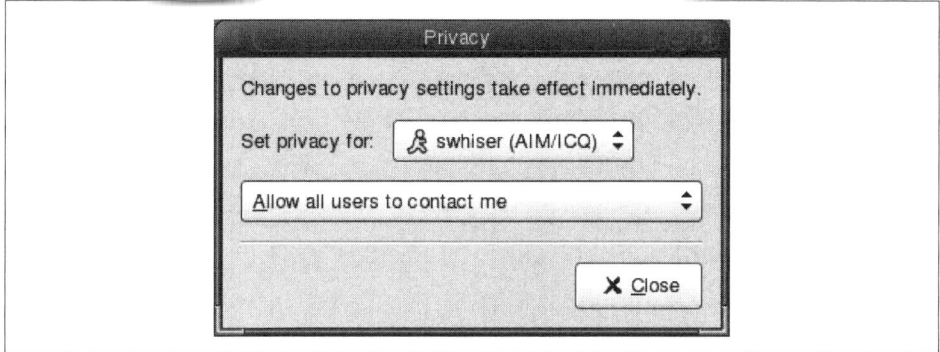

Figure 6-41. Privacy window, in default mode

In the Privacy window, you can establish different privacy settings for each of your different instant messaging accounts, using the "Set privacy for" drop-down in the Privacy window. Figure 6-42 illustrates a restrictive privacy policy setting, in which the user has permitted instant messaging access to only two colleagues.

Transferring files

JDS Instant Messenger is in the beginning stages of offering the ability to transfer files over an instant messaging session. File transfer is supported to varying degrees by the different instant messaging services and protocols.

Generally, you can send and receive files that are less than 1 MB in size; however, protocol support must exist at both ends of a file transfer for success. Trial-and-error is a good way to see whether file transfer works for you with certain colleagues. Support may sometimes be present but undocumented.

Figure 6-42. Adjusting privacy settings

Web Browser

The JDS Web Browser, shown in Figure 6-43, is located on the main Launch menu. It is a popular and well-established program called Mozilla, containing five desktop tools:

- Navigator (web browser)
- Mail & Newsgroups (email client)
- Composer (HTML editor)
- Address Book (address book)
- IRC Chat (IRC chat client)

In this chapter, we cover only the web browser functions. We don't discuss Mail & Newsgroups or Address Book in this book because we already cover JDS's Email & Calendar program for email and contacts. For information on Composer, interested users are encouraged to consult the Mozilla documentation (or documentation on the StarOffice or OpenOffice.org HTML editor module, too). IRC Chat is also covered by the Mozilla documentation.

Web Browser Setup

In this section, we cover basic customization of your web browser. This is particularly useful if you have been computing for a while in another environment and need to bring over your important legacy information tools such as bookmarks.

Figure 6-43. The Web Browser, as-is, out of the box

Resetting your Home Page

The default setting for the Home Page on your JDS Web Browser is *http://www.sun.com*. If you want to set a different Home Page, select Edit → Preferences → Navigator, where, in the middle section labeled Home Page, you can enter a new URL on the Location line.

The example in Figure 6-44 illustrates resetting the Home Page to Google. Now, each time you launch web browser, Google is the first screen that opens up. (See Figure 6-45.) Google is an excellent first screen for many people, because when they launch a new browser, finding information is often the first thing to do. Other frequent choices people make for their first screen include their Web-mail service, such as Yahoo! Mail, their personal Web-log (blog), or their company extranet.

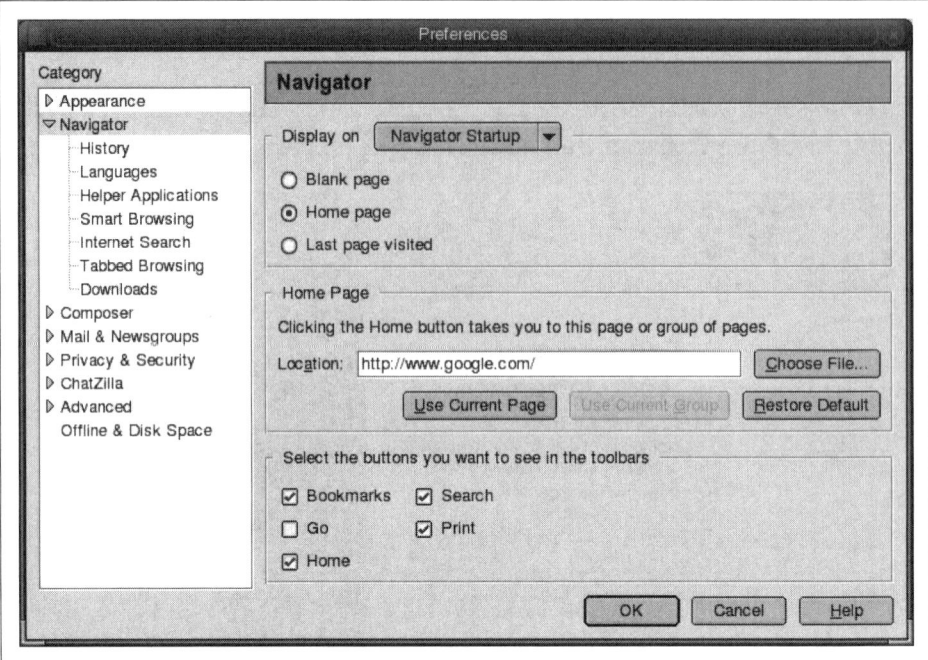

Figure 6-44. Resetting the Home Page

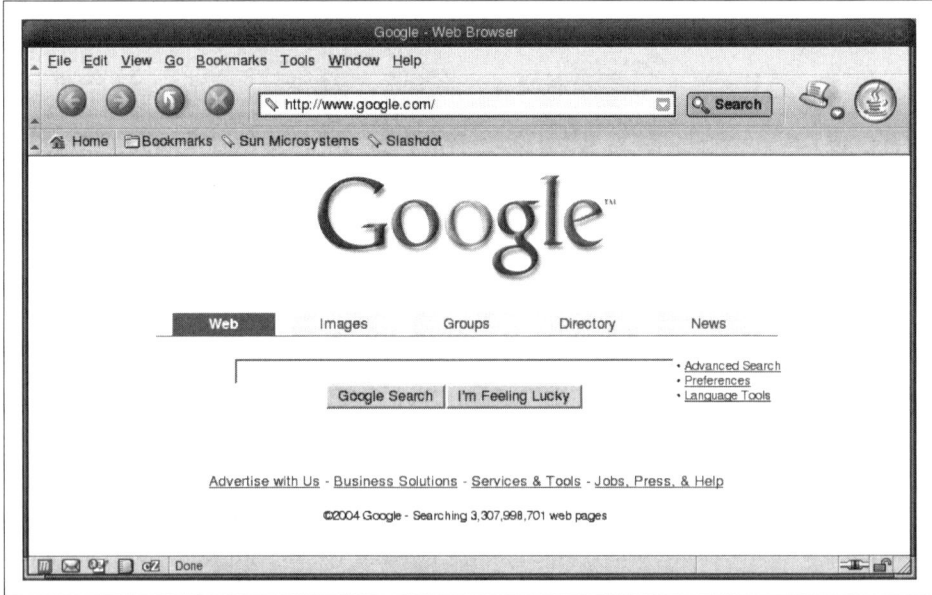

Figure 6-45. The new Home Page

Launch shortcuts

Since the web browser gets heavy usage on most people's desktops, it helps to place a Launcher icon on the desktop or on the Taskbar panel for one-click access to open the web browser.

Adding Launcher Icons

Maximize your speed in opening applications by adding Launder icons to the Taskbar panel, the desktop surface, or both. Clicking once on an icon is generally easier than three clicks through a series of menus.

You can easily add a Launcher icon by dragging and dropping the existing icon from the Launch menu. (Using this method, the original icon does not disappear from the Launch menu.) Simply select Launch → Web Browser, for example, and click and hold the mouse button, while dragging the icon to your preferred destination, then release the mouse button.

This is a tricky procedure for first-time users (especially in landing on the Taskbar panel), so a little mouse dexterity is required. You can quickly undo any mistakes with a right-click on a poorly placed icon: select Remove From Panel (when the icon is on the Taskbar panel) or Move to Trash (when the icon is on the desktop).

When you are already in your web browser, a convenient way to launch another instance of the browser is with the keyboard shortcut, Ctrl-N. (This keyboard shortcut works in most applications, launching a new instance of the currently live application window.)

Importing Favorites or Bookmarks (from your old desktop environment)

If you have built up a large collection of Favorites (also known as Bookmarks) in your previous desktop browser, or even a small but high-quality set, you may be more productive on your new JDS system if you can import them at the first opportunity.

The environment depicted in Figures 6-46 through 6-48 is Windows XP with MS Outlook (2000) and Internet Explorer.

Importing Favorites (Bookmarks) varies, depending on the environment from which you are moving, but generally involves the following steps:

1. Save or Export Favorites (Bookmarks) to a file.
2. Email the Favorites (Bookmarks) file to yourself.
3. Import the Favorites (Bookmarks) file into your JDS Web Browser.

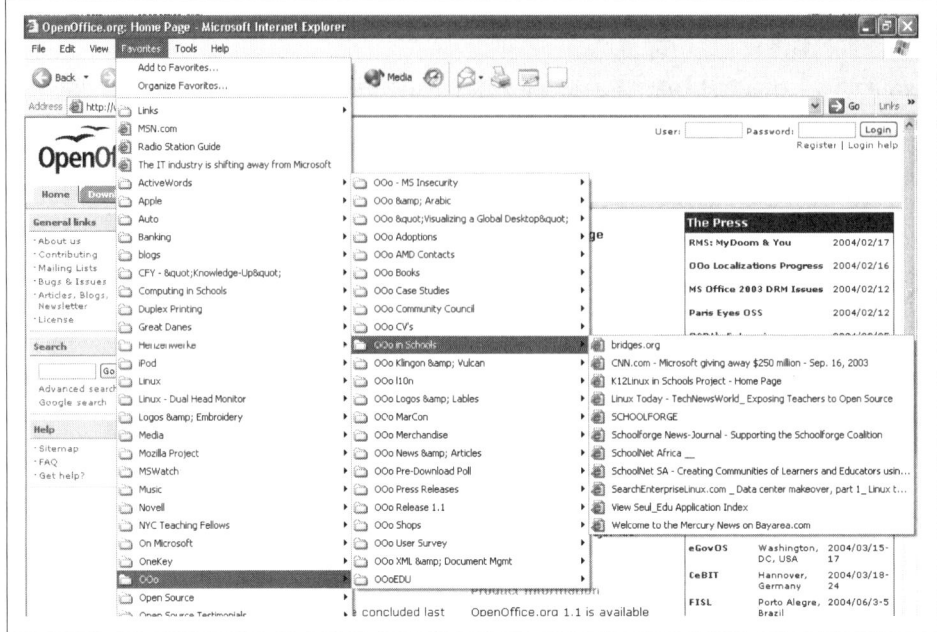

Figure 6-46. A plethora of Favorites

Note on terminology: If you are confused, you have a right to be. "Favorites" in the Windows environment is called "Bookmarks" in JDS. However, recall that, even in Windows, the default filename—when you export and save your Favorites—is *bookmark.htm*. It's a mad, mad, mad world.

Step 1: exporting Favorites from Windows XP. First, open Internet Explorer and select File → Import and Export… to open the Welcome screen of the Import/Export Wizard, shown in Figure 6-47.

Click the Next button, which takes you to the next screen. Then select Export Favorites in the "Choose an action to perform" pane. Click the Next button, which opens a window called Export Favorites Source Folder, shown in Figure 6-48.

Designate from which folder you want to export Favorites. It's the "Favorites" folder at the top of the tree, as seen in Figure 6-48. Highlight the Favorites folder with a single click, and then click the Next button.

Here, as illustrated in Figure 6-49, tell the wizard the path and filename of the file you want to create to hold your exported Favorites data. Figure 6-49 uses the default path *C:\Documents and Settings\User\My Documents* and the default filename *bookmark.htm*. These should work fine for most users, but you can also designate your own path or a different filename. In either case, you need to remember the

---

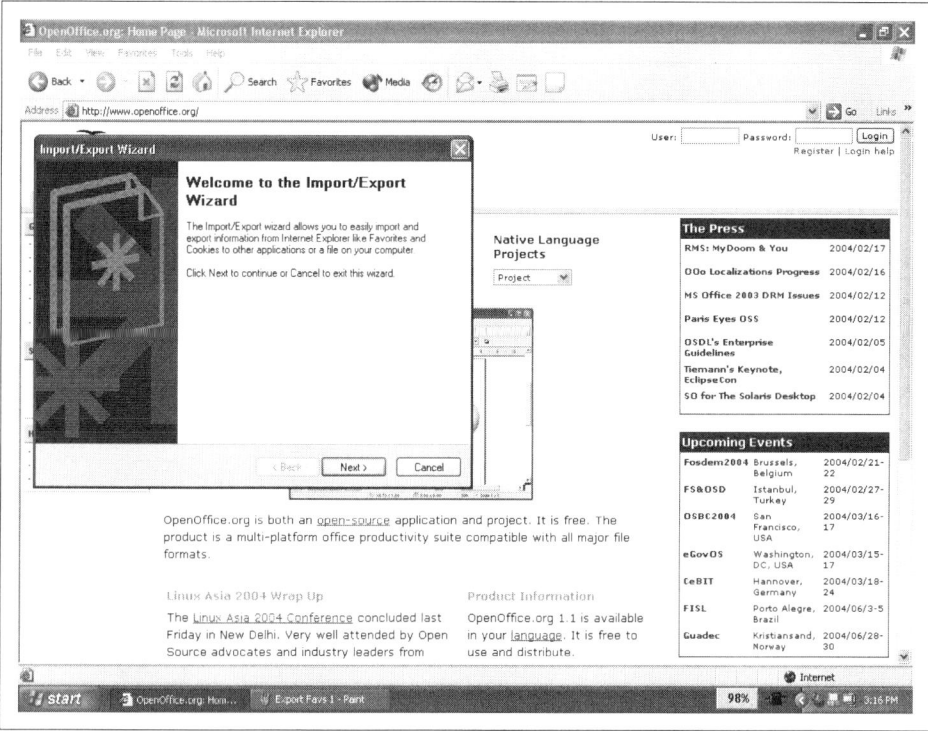

Figure 6-47. The Import/Export Wizard

filename and its path (i.e., where it's located in your filesystem) to complete importing Favorites to JDS. Watch out if you already have a file named *bookmarks.htm* at this location: it will be overwritten.

Click Next, then the Finish button.

If you used the default filename and path and all goes well, your favorites will have been successfully exported to a file named *bookmark.htm*, located in the *C:\Documents* and *Settings\User\My Documents* directory. Keep this in mind for Step 2.

Now you'll get a small window saying that you "Successfully exported favorites."

Step 2: email your Favorites to yourself.   Next, send the Favorites file you just created over to your JDS desktop. (This assumes that JDS is already configured to receive email.) Do this by attaching the *bookmark.htm* file to an email message, sending it to yourself, and fielding it on the other (JDS) system.

This procedure is similar to the one described earlier in this chapter for emailing your address book contacts data to yourself. Refer to the section called, "Importing Contacts (from your old desktop environment)," in the Email and Calendar section of this chapter.

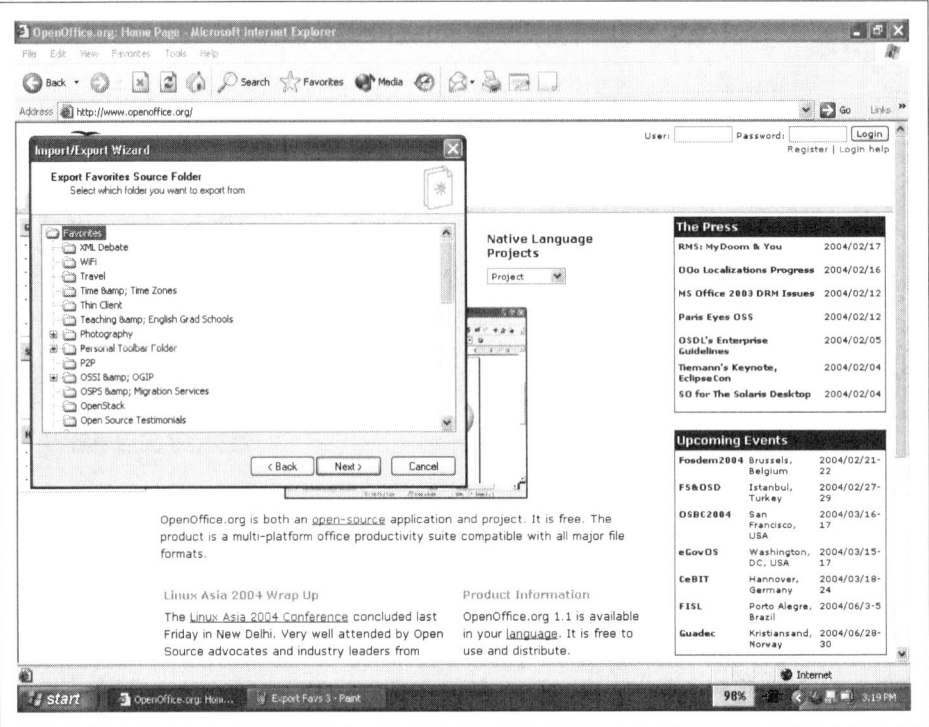

Figure 6-48. Picking the source folder

Step 3: import your Favorites into the JDS Web Browser. Leave your Windows XP environment and move over to JDS.

Open JDS Email and Calendar and click the Send/Receive button on the toolbar to receive your email. Reasonably soon, you can find your Favorites file attached to an email in your Inbox.

Open the email by double-clicking on it in your Inbox. Figure 6-50 shows an open email message. Then scroll down to the bottom of the email, where you'll find the attachment, and click on the caret. On the drop-down menu, click Save Attachment, and the Save Attachment window pops up. Here, as shown in Figure 6-51, you can choose the target directory where you want to place the file, by browsing through the Folders pane. You can also change the filename in this window if you want, or create a new folder with the eponymous button.

Now, to import your Favorites into your web browser, open your JDS Web Browser and click Ctrl-B. Alternatively, click on Bookmarks in the browser's Main menu. This produces a drop-down list where you should click "Manage Bookmarks..." Either the keyboard shortcut or the menu option opens the Bookmark Manager window.

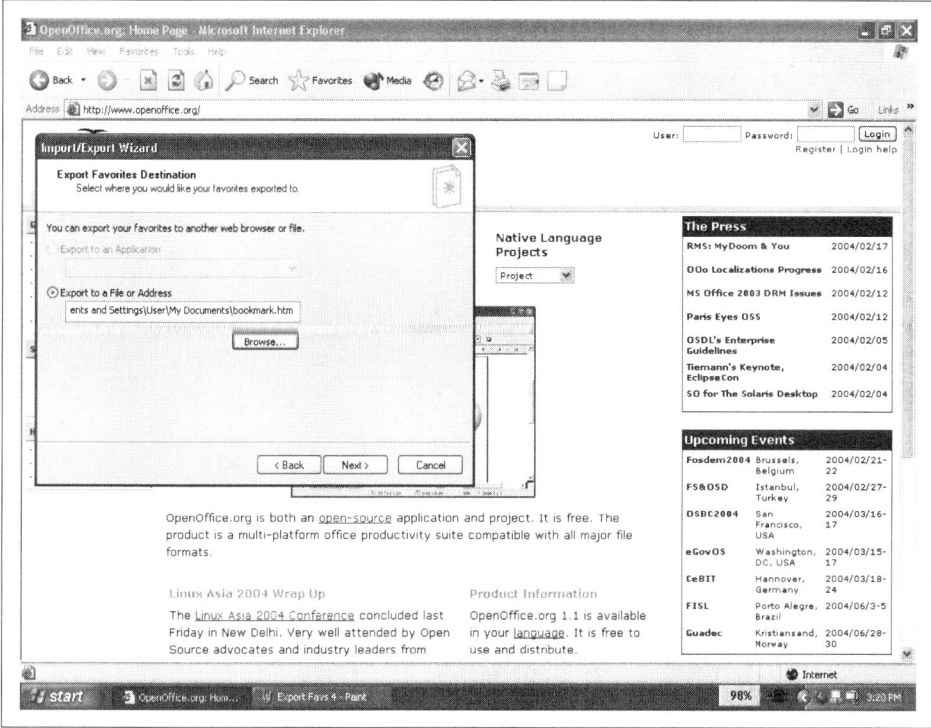

Figure 6-49. Export to a file

Here, in the Bookmark Manager window, selecting Tools → Import opens the "Import bookmark file" window. Here, you can search for and select the file you just emailed to yourself. (Figure 6-52.) The Bookmark Manager window is covered more extensively below in the "Web Browser Power Tips" section.

In this example, we saved the *bookmark.htm* file from our email to the path */home/swhiser/Documents/JDS_manual*, where it sits unperturbed. Click on folders until the correct path appears in the "Look in:" drop-down menu, at the top. When you are in the correct folder, the file you are looking for should be visible in the main pane, as shown in Figure 6-52. Click once on the filename; it becomes highlighted and appears in the "File name:" field. Finally, click the Open button to import your bookmark folders and bookmarks.

If you already had a number of bookmarks and folders set up in your JDS Web Browser, they should still be there. But you may need to do some pruning, rearranging, or refiling in the list. Each additional import you perform appends the contents of a bookmarks or Favorites file to the end of the existing bookmarks list in your web browser.

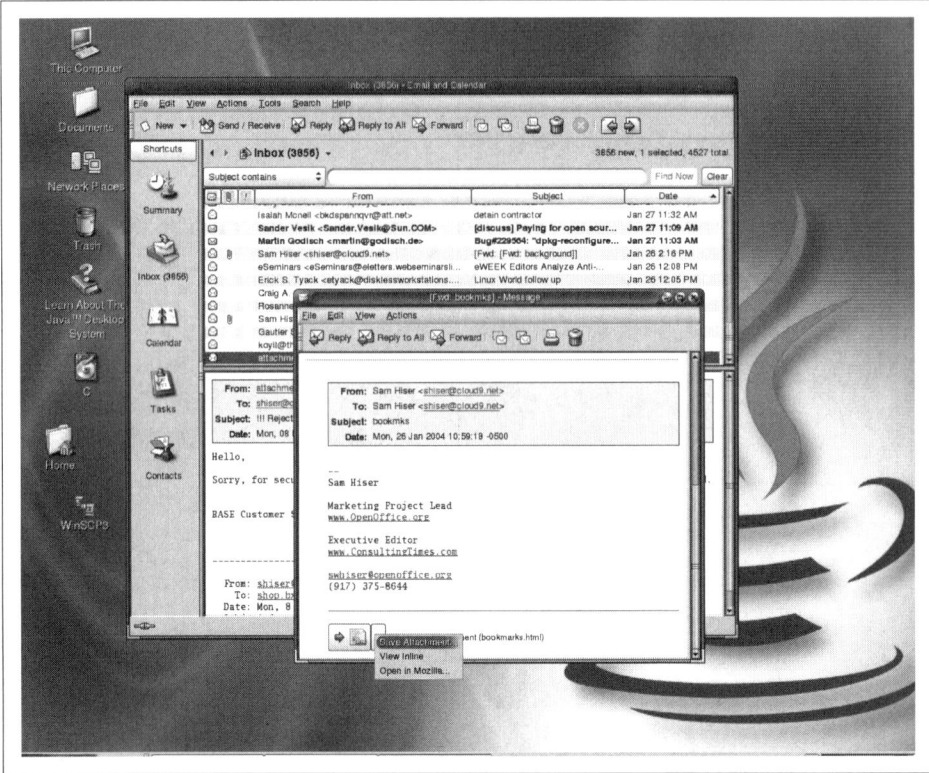

Figure 6-50. Saving an attachment

Web Browser Basics

As a desktop tool, the web browser is among the simplest and most intuitive programs. Enter a web address and away you go. But since the web browser is so important in the repertoire of desktop tools, and since people use their browser a lot, it really pays off when users take some time to learn a few extra features and tricks.

The JDS Web Browser is based on Mozilla. There are quite a few nice features in this program that can enhance your ability to find and store information quickly for current and future reference.

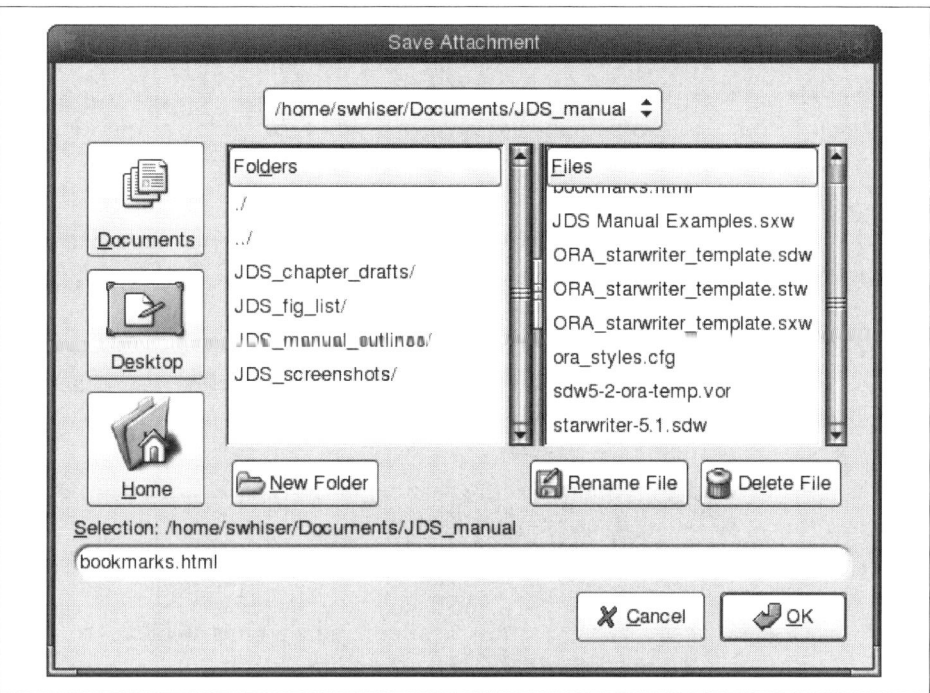

Figure 6-51. The Save Attachment window

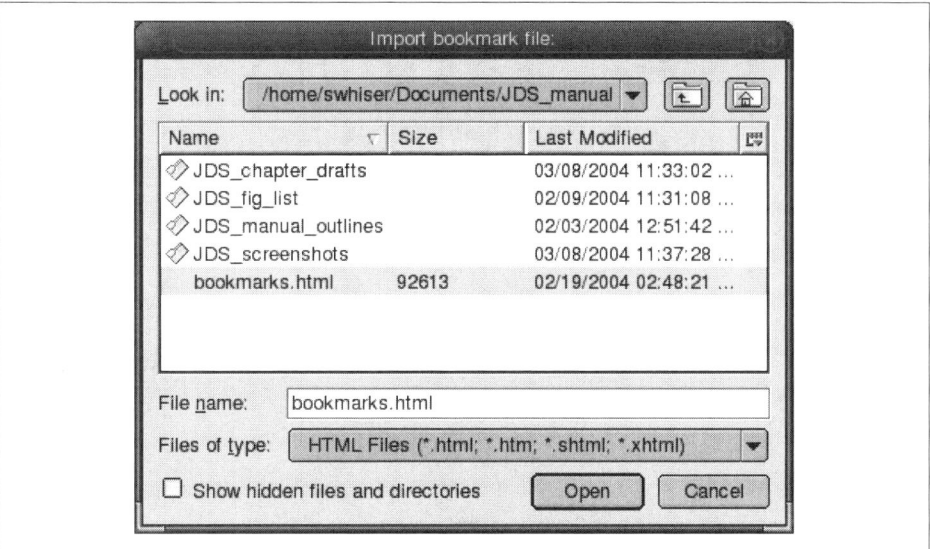

Figure 6-52. The Import bookmark file: window

Elements of the web browser

The web browser has a full toolset for surfing and searching the Web. The basic tool elements are located in familiar places and provide functionality that users from other popular desktop environments make no effort to pick up quickly. (See Figure 6-53.)

Main Menu

The top-most menu of the browser. It contains eight elements, similar to many other desktop application interfaces: File, Edit, View, Go, Bookmarks, Tools, Windows, and Help.

Location Bar

The white bar at the center of the browser's toolbar, just below the Main menu. The place in which to type a URL when surfing the Web.

Search Button

Just to the right of Location bar, the Search button can be set to your favorite search site, for one-click searching.

Personal Toolbar

Just below the Location bar and Search button, this bar can be set to contain your favorite frequent web links or folders containing groups of links.

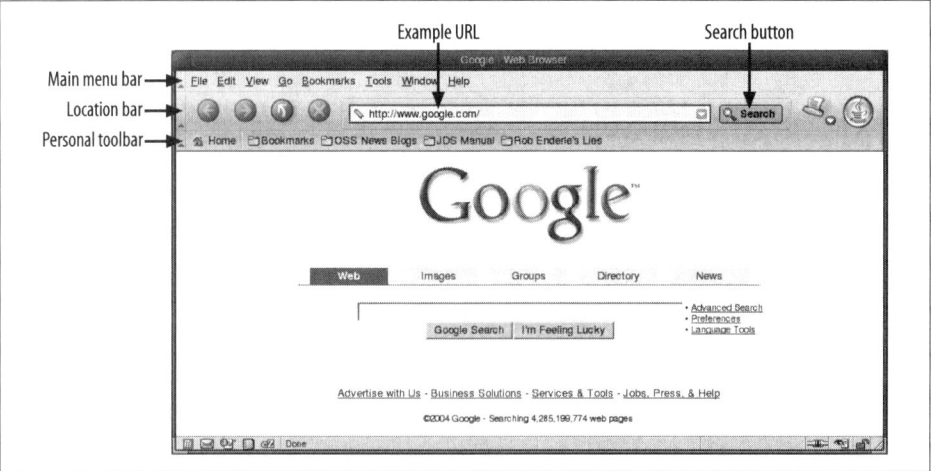

Figure 6-53. Basic elements of JDS web browser

Entering a URL directly

One prominent basic feature of the web browser is the Location bar, the white field that sits prominently at the center of the browser's Navigation toolbar, just below the Menu bar, at the top. You can enter a URL there by manually typing in the name of the web site you wish to visit. Often, you can just type the core name or keyword of the company or site. For example, you can get to Apple Computer's web site by fully typing **http://www.apple.com**. But for a popular site like this one, try just typing **apple**; the browser's native intelligence, in combination with the Google search engine, should find the right site. (See Figure 6-54.)

Figure 6-54. Entering the URL at the Location bar

Be aware that sometimes *www* does not belong in certain URL sequences. Always check the precise punctuation of a URL and make sure that uppercase and lowercase appear as they are supposed to, because some URLs require exact input.

Clicking hyperlinks

Hyperlinks are the elements of text within a web page on which you can click to go elsewhere; they are usually highlighted in blue and underlined. (Figure 6-55.) If they are objects or graphics in a web page, they are often not highlighted, but you can still click on them. In either case, when they are clicked, they take you to another web page. Hyperlinks are also commonly referred to as "links."

Adding a Bookmark

If you want to return later to this web site in Figure 6-55, the best way to store its URL in your web browser is by using the handy Bookmarks feature. Press Ctrl-D or click Bookmarks on the browser's Main menu and select Bookmark This Page from the top of the drop-down list. This automatically places the URL of the current web page at the very bottom of your Bookmarks List.

See the sections, "Managing Bookmarks" and "Filing Bookmarks," for more advanced ways of using Bookmarks.

Web Browser Power Tips

We've chosen the power tips in this section because they are easy to learn. But they could significantly increase your productivity as well as your enjoyment of the browser.

Figure 6-55. Hyperlinks in an exemplary Home Page

Quick entry for URLs

If there is a keyboard shortcut to win the Academy Award of Desktop Keyboard Shortcuts, it is web browser's Ctrl-L. In the JDS Web Browser, this places the cursor in the browser's Location bar. When there is a URL already in the Location bar—which is most of the time—this shortcut also highlights the whole URL, so you can immediately type in a new keyword or the URL of the web page you wish to visit, and the previous URL is automatically replaced.

Managing Bookmarks

Advanced users come to rely heavily upon a large list of Bookmarks, just as many rely upon an extensive and well-ordered file cabinet in a business or home office. The larger the Bookmark list, the more helpful is an intelligent filing scheme that simplifies and speeds a search for that all-important web site or article.

We've already shown how to import your Bookmarks from your old desktop environment in the section, "Importing Favorites or Bookmarks" (from your old desktop environment); here we go deeper into the ways you can manage Bookmarks.

The Bookmark Manager window is where you can create and organize Bookmark folders and create a sort of filing cabinet for all the web information that's important to you.

To open the Bookmark Manager window, illustrated in Figures 6-56 and 6-57, select Bookmarks → Manage Bookmarks… from your browser's Main menu.

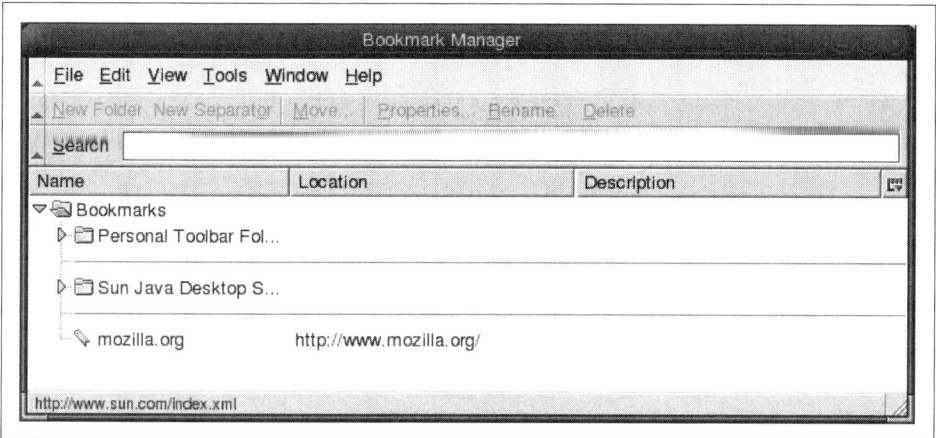

Figure 6-56. Bookmark Manager window, out of the box

Creating Bookmark folders

Just like folders on your desktop, folders within your Bookmarks can be organized into a convenient tree structure. This is increasingly useful as the number of Bookmarks builds up.

To create a new Bookmark folder, select the Bookmarks drop-down off the Main menu and click on "Manage Bookmarks..." that calls up the Bookmark Manager window. (See Figures 6-56 and 6-57.) First, highlight, with a single mouse click, the folder immediately below where you want the new folder to be placed. Then, click the New Folder button, located at the far left on the Bookmark Manager toolbar. This action brings up a window called Properties for "New Folder," where you can enter the name and a description of the new folder. Finish by clicking the OK button.

Filing Bookmarks

Filing a Bookmark is one step more sophisticated than just adding a Bookmark (See the section, "Adding a Bookmark."). It's what you do when you have already added Bookmark Folders to establish a filing system for your Bookmarks.

To File a Bookmark, simply select the Bookmarks drop-down from the browser's Main menu and click on "File Bookmark…" that calls up the File Bookmark window, where you can highlight a specific destination folder, with a single mouse click, and then press the OK button. Note how, in Figure 6-58, when the File Bookmark

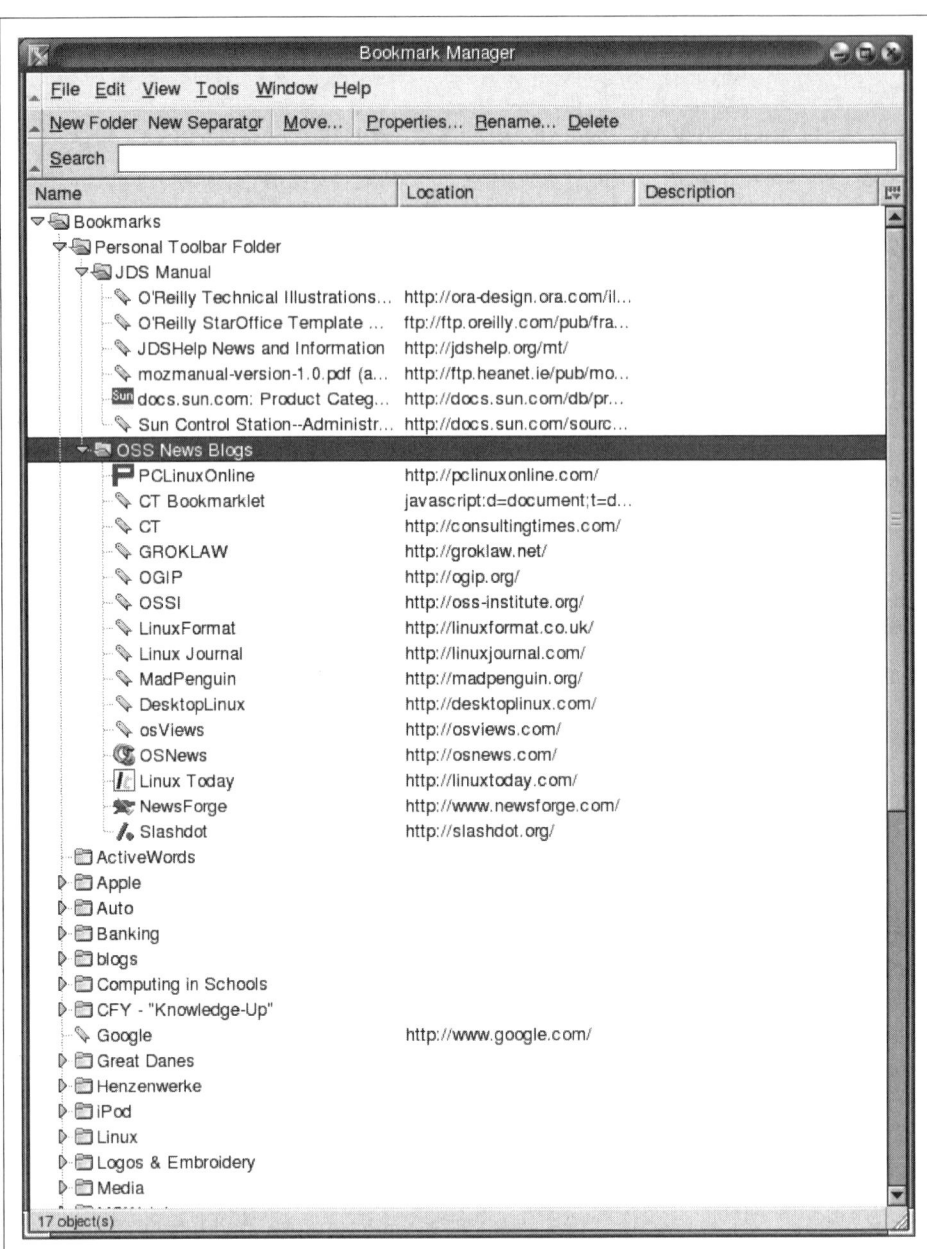

Figure 6-57. Bookmark Manager, after a few years of use

window appears, the name and URL of the current web page are automatically
entered in the Name and Location fields.

Figure 6-58. Filing a Bookmark

In the File Bookmark window, you can also alter the name of the web site (as it appears in your Bookmarks list) and enter a Custom Keyword that permits faster access to the web page that you are filing. (This is a terrific feature, covered in more detail in Custom Keywords.)

Personal Toolbar

The JDS Web Browser's Personal Toolbar is located just below the Location bar. (See Figure 6-53.) Out of the box, the Personal toolbar has only a Home icon, a Bookmarks icon (which works identically to pulling down the Bookmarks drop-down from the Main menu), and a Sun Microsystems folder icon. But you can add more folders and individual web site links to this toolbar to make your web browser really sing in *your* key. (See Figure 6-59.) The example in Figure 6-54 shows the folders we have added already to our Personal Toolbar, "JDS Manual" and "OSS News Blogs." We have taken away the Sun Microsystems folder icon.

To add the current web site to the Personal Toolbar, select Bookmarks → File Bookmarks… on the browser's Main menu (just as in the section, "Filing Bookmarks"). Having called up the File Bookmark window, now click once on the Personal

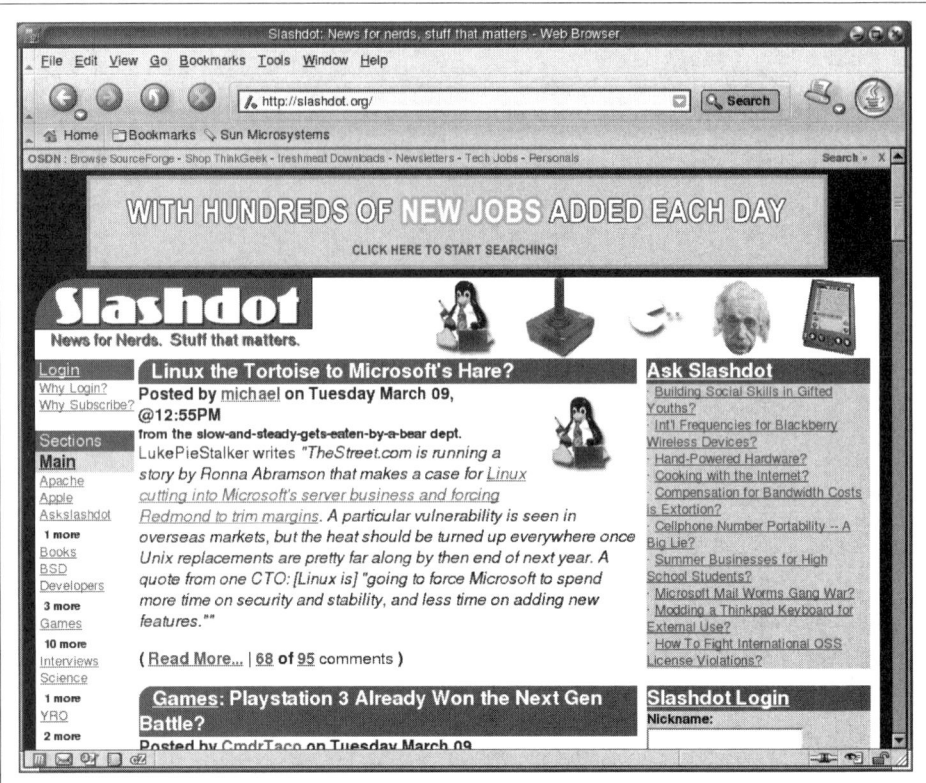

Figure 6-59. Among our most frequented web sites . . .

Toolbar Folder in the Destination: pane. (See Figure 6-60.) This highlights the Personal Toolbar Folder, and now you can press the OK button.

In Figure 6-60, notice that while the web site name and location were automatically entered in their respective fields, we took pains to give our new Personal Toolbar item a keyword. (See Figure 6-61.) See the section, "Custom keywords," for additional information about assigning keywords to your Bookmark entries.

In addition to adding a single link or web site to the Personal Toolbar, you can add an entire folder that works as a drop-down menu full of bookmarks. This allows you to pack more links into the limited real estate up there on the Personal Toolbar.

Adding a folder to the Personal Toolbar is just as easy as adding a link. In the web browser, select Bookmarks → File Bookmarks... from the Main menu. In the File Bookmarks window, highlight the Bookmarks Folder with a single click, then click the New Folder button at the bottom right of the File Bookmarks window. This opens a Properties for "New Folder" window. Next, simply type the name of your new folder into the "Name:" field (the description is optional) and click the OK button.

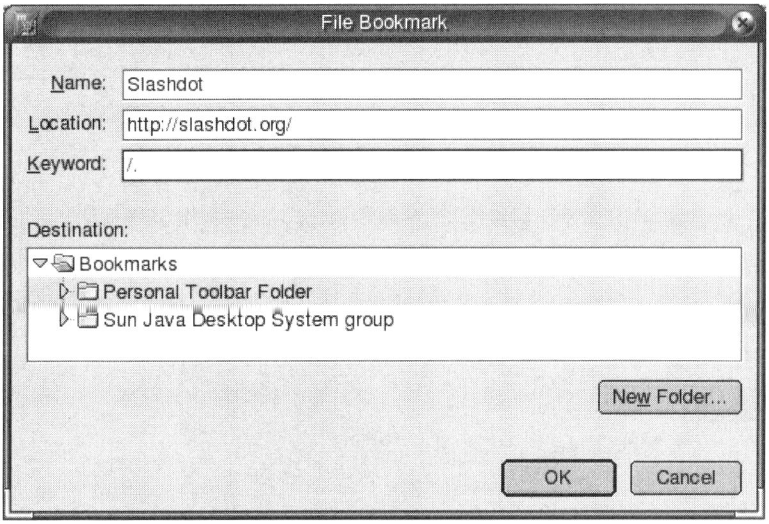

Figure 6-60. Filing a link in the Personal Toolbar Folder

Figure 6-61. Slashdot is filed in the Personal Toolbar Folder

Using File Bookmark window is the fastest way to add a new folder to the Personal Toolbar. But you can also add or otherwise manage Bookmark links and folders by calling up the Bookmark Manager window via Bookmarks → Manage Bookmarks… of the Main menu.

As an example of where alternative methods are available to achieve the same result, Figure 6-62 illustrates using Bookmark Manager to drag and drop a newly created folder to its rightful place in the Personal Toolbar. It's typical: there is usually more than one way to "skin the cat" on the desktop.

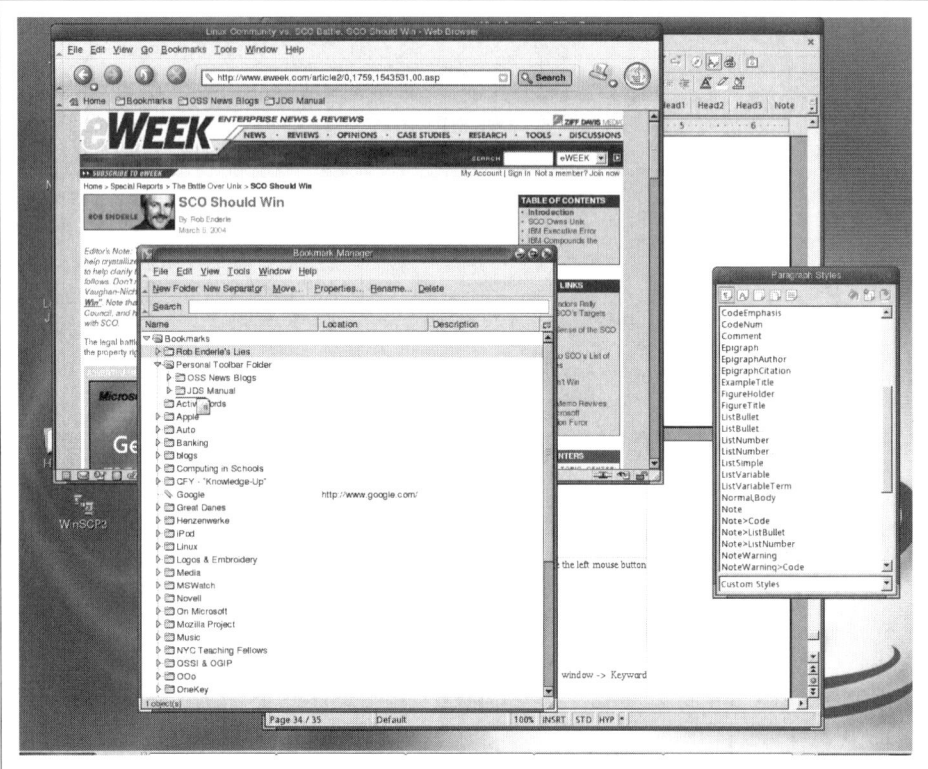

Figure 6-62. Dropping a new folder into place

Custom keywords

This is a superb feature. The JDS Web Browser permits you to set your own keywords to rapidly launch important or favorite web pages. In the earlier example, Figure 6-60, we set up a quick two-keystroke keyword for the Slashdot Home Page. You can create custom keywords for any web page you wish. Once you make using custom keywords a habit, your web browsing will positively smoke!

You can set a custom keyword when you file a Bookmark. Call up the File Book-mark window by selecting the Bookmarks drop-down on the browser's Main menu and by clicking "File Bookmark…". In the File Bookmark window, you'll see the highlighted web page's name and location. Now enter a keyword in the Keyword field and click OK.

 The keyword we chose that's reflected in Figure 6-60 is "/," which is deliberately short and fast to type because the two keys are adjacent on the (standard U.S. English) keyboard. This keyword is also easy to remember. It's a good idea to plan your keyword assignments to be short and easy to remember, unless you are not lazy. Guess what web site our other favorite Keyword, "goo," stands for?

Alternatively, you can set custom keywords for web pages that are already filed in your Bookmarks list by going into Bookmark Manager, where you can highlight a particular Bookmarked web page and click on the Properties button. This action calls up the Properties for "[Name of web page]" window, where you can type in the new keyword in the Keyword field and click OK.

Search

There are four ways to enjoin a search with the web browser:

- Enter a term in the Location bar and double-click the Search button.
- Highlight a term in a web page and choose Web search for "[term]" in the right-click menu.
- Go to your favorite search site and do a regular search there.
- Enter a term in the Sidebar Search field and click the Sidebar Search button.

The most attractive benefit of the highlight and right-click method (the second on the list) is that the action is quick and calls up another instance of the web browser. This allows you to pursue the search in a different browser instance, without losing your place at the original page.

One quick way to go to Google is to simply click the Search button on the Location bar. This takes you to the Google Home Page, where you can enter a search in the main search field there. (See Figure 6-53.) The Search button is set by default to call up Google, but you can set the button to call up one of eight different search sites by selecting Edit → Preferences → Navigator → Internet Search. There, in the Default Search Engine section, you can select a different search engine.

Sidebar

The Sidebar (Figure 6-63) also offers similar search capabilities.

Figure 6-63. Searching for "Godot" from the Sidebar

 If you can't find your Sidebar, it's hidden by default. To reveal it, simply click F9 or go to the browser's Main menu and select View → Show/Hide, where you should click on Sidebar. An unhidden Sidebar tucks away nicely against the left edge of the browser, just like a sock drawer.

Tabbed browsing

Tabbed browsing enables you to open numerous web pages within a single instance of Web Browser, where you can move to a page by clicking its tab. (Figure 6-64.)

To open a new tab in Web Browser, press Ctrl-T. You can also open a web page link in a new tab by right-clicking on the link and then clicking "Open Link in New Tab" in the menu that appears.

In Figure 6-64, you can see some of our favorite open source news blogs across the Tab Bar. At the far left of the Tab Bar is a button that allows you to open a new tab, and at the far right is a button for closing the current tab.

Combining Tabbed Browsing with Search and active use of the Sidebar offers a powerful toolkit of facilities for your web research repertoire.

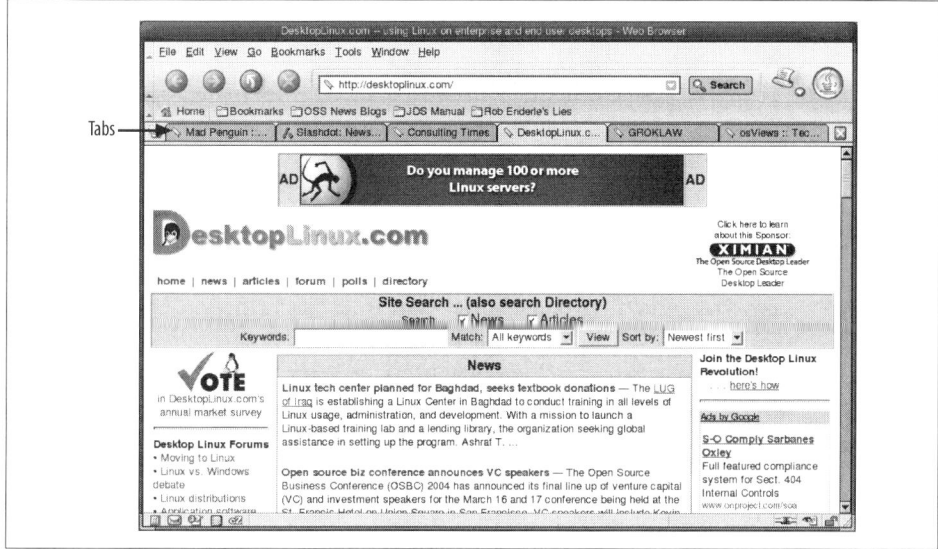

Tabs

Figure 6-64. Tabbed browsing

Pop-up blocking

JDS's Web Browser has a setting to prevent unwanted pop ups (and "pop unders," too) from disturbing your pristine work flow. Pop ups are among the most annoying web developments to pop up in recent years, so it's great to have control of these exploitative, attention-grabbing techniques.

To turn blocking on, go to Edit → Preferences → Privacy & Security → Popup Windows. There you can check the box "Block unrequested pop-up windows." You can also elect to play a sound when a pop-up window is blocked or to display an icon in the Navigator status bar.

Allowing certain pop ups

Note that some pop ups are desirable. Pop-up blocking can prevent some important features at certain web sites from working, such as login windows for banks and online shopping sites.

You can add exceptions to pop-up blocking, through the Popup Manager window. To call up Popup Manager, go from the web browser's Main Menu to Tools → Popup Manager → Manage Popups. This opens the Allowed Web Sites window. Here, you can add specific web sites to a list of pop-up-blocking exceptions. You can remove sites from this list, too.

To set a new pop-up exception, as you come across a site you want to deal with, select Tools → Popup Manager → Allow Popups From This Site. This is a different route that opens the same Allowed Web Sites window but has the current web page's information already entered in the Add field. Just click OK to add the site to the pop-up-blocking exceptions list.

Cookies

JDS's Web Browser offers extensive cookie management features through the Cookie Manager. We cover the basics of blocking, unblocking, and editing cookies here.

Cookies are small pieces of information that certain web sites store on your computer's hard drive when you visit that web site. Cookies contain information about you or your computer, allowing the serving web site to identify you in certain ways when you return to that site. For example, some web sites require sign-on or even password access; it is the cookie information stored in your browser that permits you to avoid reentering this data each time you return to that web site. So cookies provide a measure of convenience to users that can also be commercially beneficial to owners of web sites.

Users and observers have different opinions about whether or how cookies may invade personal privacy. The choice to block cookies is up to the individual user: how much convenience are you are willing to trade away for possibly better privacy?

If you want to avoid receiving a cookie from a specific web site, go to the Home Page of that site and select Tools → Cookie Manager → Block Cookies from this Site. This calls up a window with the message, "Cookies from this site will always be rejected." Press OK.

If you have blocked cookies from a web site and wish to unblock them, select Tools → Cookie Manager → Unblock Cookies from this Site. This likewise calls a window with the message, "Cookies from this site will not be blocked." Press OK.

You can also open Cookie Manager (Figure 6-65) to view and remove all cookies that already may be stored in your computer. From the browser's Main menu, select Tools → Cookie Manager → Manage Stored Cookies. In Cookie Manager, you can scroll through all the cookies on your computer. The left column, Site, is the one you want to check, because it identifies the web site from which the cookies came. The second column, Cookie Name, is usually indecipherable, but you can ignore it.

Remove cookies individually using the Remove Cookie button, at the bottom of the window, or wipe them all out together using the Remove All Cookies button. You can also highlight a contiguous group of cookies for removal—for example, a number of cookies that all come from the same site—by highlighting one cookie, holding down the Shift key, and pressing the up or down arrow key to highlight the cookies you'd like to remove. Then press the Remove Cookie button.

Managing history

Web Browser keeps track of the most recent web sites you've visited in two places: the Location bar (where you enter URLs) and in a History window. By default, all the

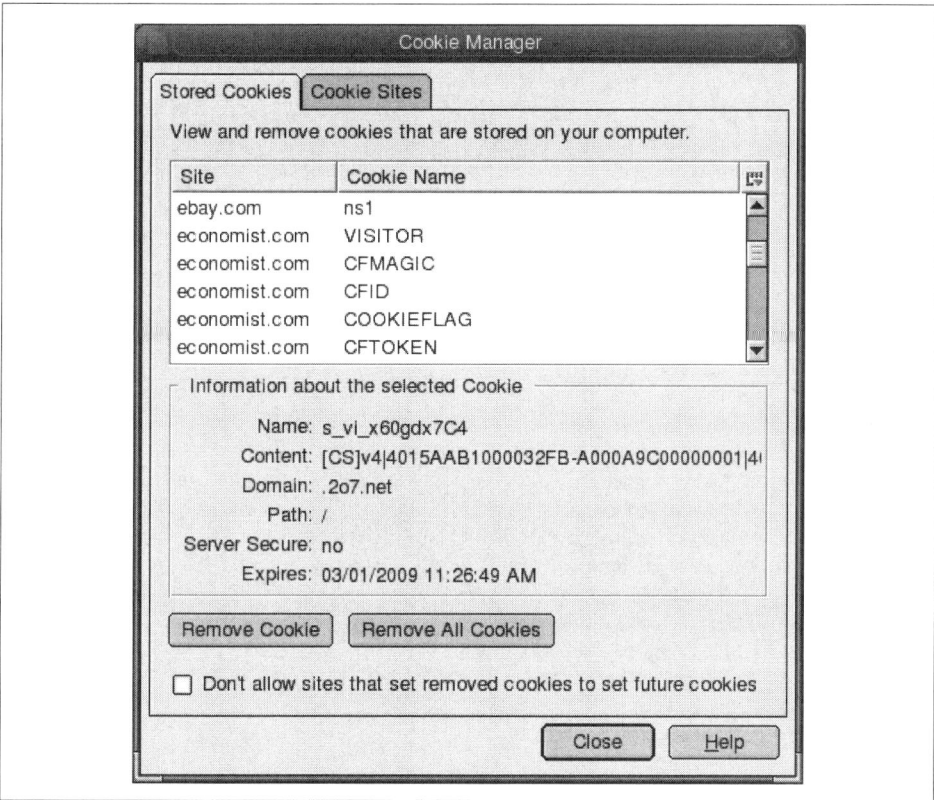

Figure 6-65. The Cookie Manager

sites you've visited for the past nine days are stored in your history. A much shorter list is in the Location bar.

To see the sites you've recently visited in the Location bar, click on the downward-pointing caret, at the right end, inside the Location bar. That produces a drop-down list of recently visited web sites. Scroll down the list and click on any URL to quickly return to that site.

A more comprehensive list of past URLs appears in the History window. (Figure 6-66.) Call up this window by pressing Ctrl-H or selecting Go → History from the browser's Main menu.

Clearing history

To clear your browsing histories, go to the browser's Main menu and select Edit → Preferences... → Navigator → History. There, you can independently clear the history in the Location bar and the contents of the History window. You can also increase or decrease the number of days of history stored by Web Browser.

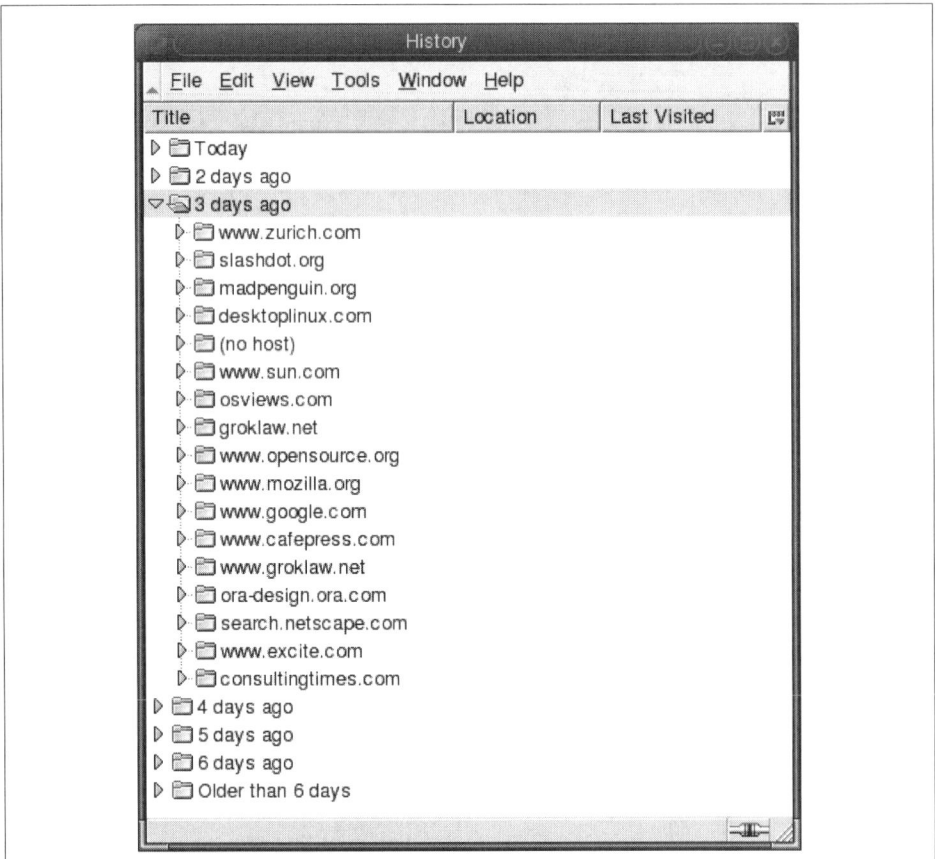

Figure 6-66. The History window

You can also delete individual web sites within your History window, without clearing all of them. Open the History window (Ctrl-H), right-click on the URL you want to remove, and select Delete.

Turning off the history function

You can't turn off the Location bar's history collection function; you can only clear it manually. However, you can turn off history collection in the History window. At the browser's Main menu, select Edit → Preferences... → Navigator → History. In the Browsing History section, set the "Remember visited pages for the last ___ days" field to 0.

Master password security

JDS's Web Browser also offers a master password that protects sensitive information stored by the browser such as web site passwords and digital certificates. You were

---

prompted to enter a master password when you (or your system administrator) first set up the system.

You can manage your master password from the Preferences window. Select Edit → Preferences... → Privacy & Security → Master Passwords, where you can change, reset or establish how often the system asks you to confirm your master password. (See Figure 6-67.)

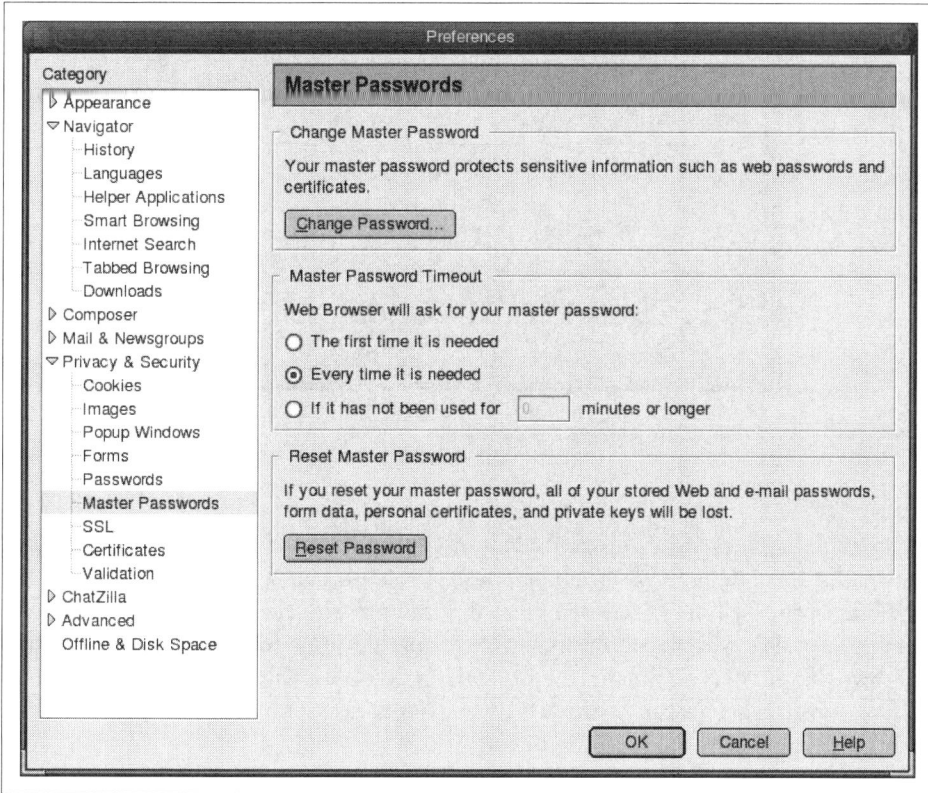

Figure 6-67. Manage your master password

Manage passwords

Security-conscious users can also manage web site passwords by deleting them or by blocking them from being saved from certain important web sites. This adds a beneficial layer of security for protecting access to personal financial information or sensitive personal data, such as credit card information or order history.

To manage your web passwords, go to the browser's Main menu and select Tools → Password Manager → Manage Stored Passwords. This opens the Password Manager window (Figure 6-68), where you can remove sensitive web sites' passwords individually or all together. You can also create a list of web sites for which the browser never saves the password. To create or manage the list of web sites for which you wish to block password storage, click over to the Passwords Never Saved tab (shown in the background of Figure 6-68).

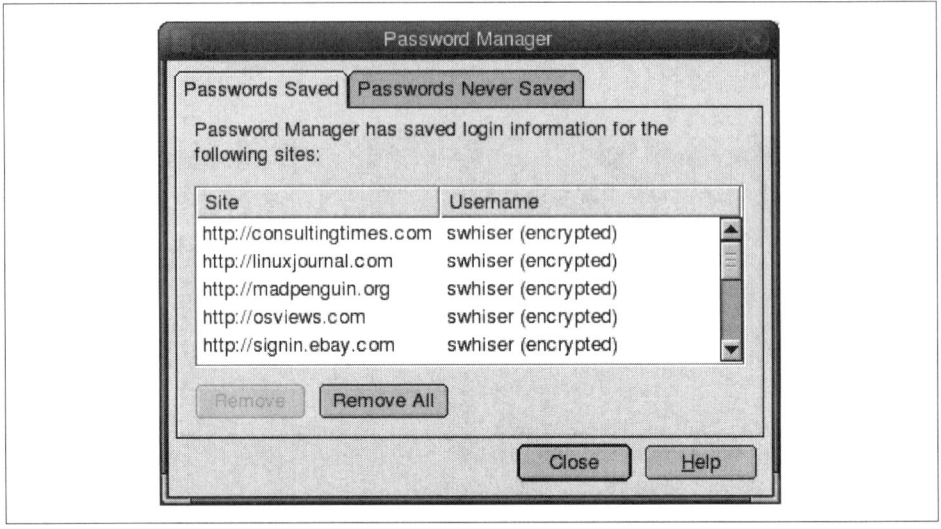

Figure 6-68. View of the "Passwords Saved" tab

Macromedia Flash

Many animations on the Web, and a growing number of forms and other advanced web features, are done in Macromedia Flash. JDS automatically supports Flash in the web browser so that JDS users can view and interact with these pages. The explosive growth of Flash's features and popularity makes this an important component of the JDS browser. Flash is an illustration of how Sun has been willing to incorporate commercial, proprietary features into JDS to provide users with what they need, on top of an essentially open source software base.

In addition to supporting Flash transparently in the web browser, JDS also permits you to export Impress presentations in the Flash format for distribution or display on the Web. See Chapter 8 for details.

CHAPTER 7

Word Processing with StarWriter

StarOffice Writer (also known as "StarWriter") is the word processor module included as one of six key components of StarOffice. StarWriter is a state-of-the-art software application, designed in look, feel, and function to be familiar to users of Microsoft Word. Yet StarWriter offers surprising new stability and flexibility. It allows you to create or import and edit text documents and publish them to a number of widely accepted file formats, including open standard XML and some new formats for small handheld devices.

Like JDS itself, StarOffice is distinguished by its stability on the system. Its other hallmark is the tight integration of its word processor, spreadsheet, and all other modules, which leads to a strong consistency in features, menu placement, and ease of use. The StarOffice modules are listed in Table 7-1. Covering modules in separate chapters (as we do for simplicity) risks giving the impression that they feel or behave like separate applications. In fact, the opposite is true: the modules work smoothly and consistently together as a holistic set of desktop tools.

Table 7-1. The modules of StarOffice

StarOffice module	Function
StarWriter	Word processor
StarCalc	Spreadsheet
StarImpress	Presentation
StarDraw	Graphics editor
StarHTML	Web (HTML) editor
StarMath	Math formulas editor

We cover StarWriter exclusively in this chapter, and StarCalc and StarImpress together in Chapter 8. We omit the remaining modules because they are less frequently used, and their features and functions are well supported in the leading reference texts and online documentation.

StarWriter Basics

This section focuses on the most commonly used features and may be sufficient for most users to get their work done on StarWriter. But you are also encouraged to read the section "StarWriter Power Tips" to increase your repertoire of features for creating and handling more complex and larger documents.

Launching StarWriter

Start StarWriter from the Launch menu by clicking on the StarOffice 7 button, second from the top. This brings up the "Templates and Documents - New Document" window, where you can select the New Document icon in the left-side index, then Text Document from the list in the central pane. (See Figure 7-1.)

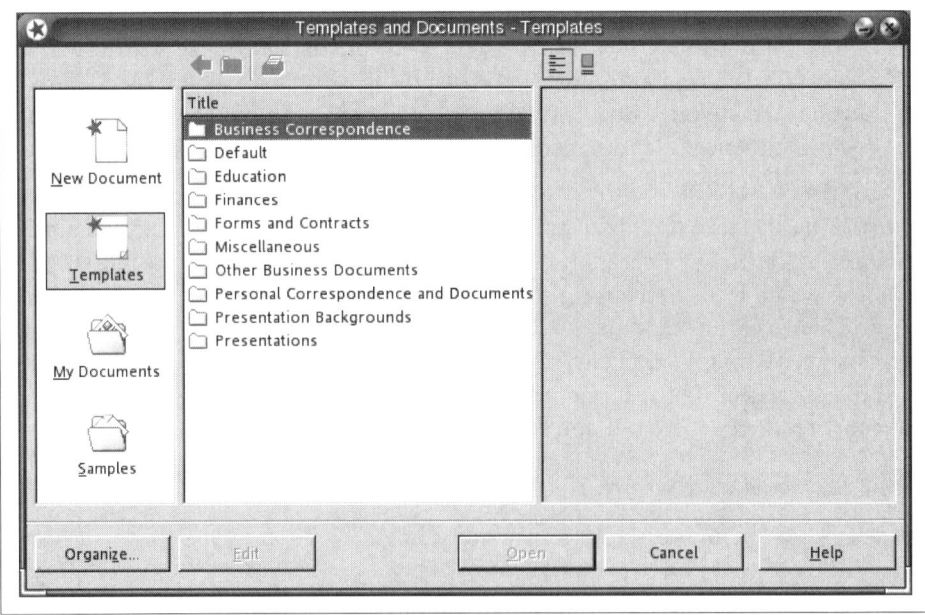

Figure 7-1. Start with a blank or choose a template

 You can also launch StarWriter directly if you have created a dedicated launcher icon on the desktop, task bar or both. See "Adding a Home Directory to Your Desktop" in Chapter 3, where the process for adding a launcher icon is demonstrated. It's possible to create a dedicated launcher icon for each module of StarOffice (StarWriter, StarCalc, etc.), which is especially useful to do for the modules you use often.

Initial Setup

The first time you launch StarOffice, the application runs a setup wizard to take you through a few steps for initial setup and configuration. Because this is a one-time procedure, we placed the initial setup instructions toward the end of this chapter in the section "StarOffice Initial Setup."

Opening Files

There are two ways to open a file:

- From the desktop or from within a folder, click on an icon that represents a StarOffice or MS office file. This will open StarOffice and display the file for editing.
- In StarOffice, select File → Open. In the Open window, browse through the file-system and select the desired folder and filename, then click the Open button.

 MS Office files—i.e., those in the *.doc* format—open in StarOffice in the same way a native StarOffice document opens. You can edit the MS Office document and save it either in its own format or in StarOffice's native format.

Saving Files

After editing a document, select File → Save. A new file is saved to the user's */home/[user]/Documents* directory by default. You can also save a file to its current or the default directory with one click of the Save Document icon on the Function bar.

If you need to select a different target directory or change the filename or file type, select File → Save As. The Save As window, shown in Figure 7-2, appears. Here you can make the appropriate selections and click the Save button. This window is explored further in the following section.

Saving as different file types

If you open an existing document, it is saved by default in its original format. Thus, if you receive an MS Office file from a colleague and edit it, you get an MS Office file in return. That's usually what you want, so you can exchange documents with everyone and not force your word processing choice on them (as new versions of MS Office itself are wont to do as a form of planned obsolescence).

Sometimes, however, you need to save a document in a different format; we describe some of those situations in the section "Saving or Exporting to Common File Formats." The most common reason to change the file type is when you create a new StarWriter document and want to save it in MS Word format. By default, new documents are saved in StarWriter's native format (although that default is easy to

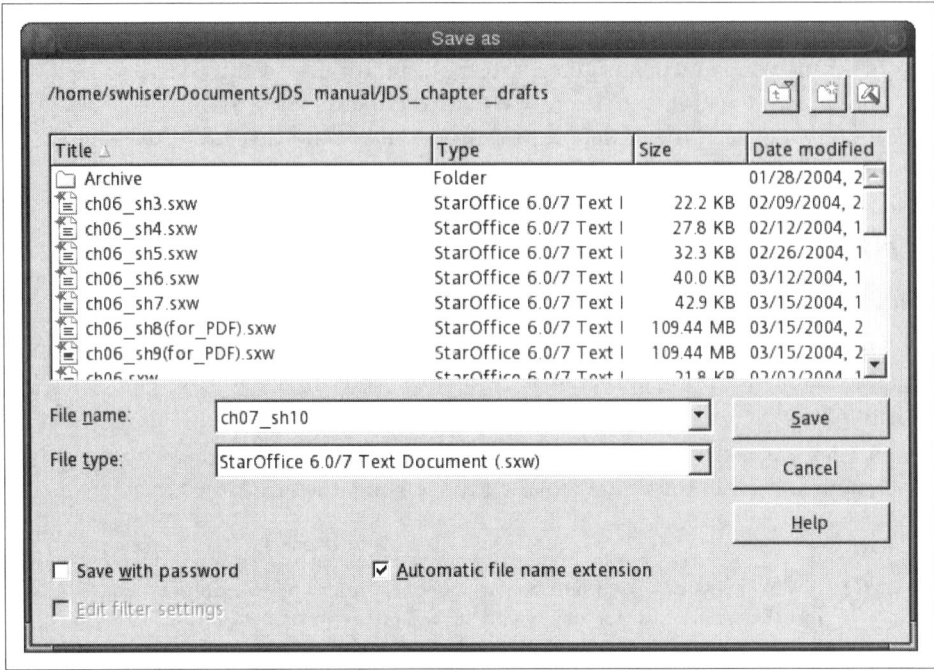

Figure 7-2. The Save As window

change; we show you how later). The formats supported by StarWriter are listed in Table 7-2. To choose a new file type, select File → Save As to open the Save As window. Here, you can make the appropriate selections and click the Save button.

Table 7-2. Save files in many formats or file types

File format	File extension (suffix)
StarOffice 6.0/7 Text Document *	.sxw
StarOffice 6.0/7 Text Document Template	.stw
MS Word 97/2000/XP	.doc
MS Word 95	.doc
MS Word 6.0	.doc
Adobe PDF	.pdf
Rich Text Format	.rtf
StarWriter 5.0	.sdw
StarWriter 5.0 Template	.vor
StarWriter 4.0	.sdw
StarWriter 4.0 Template	.vor
StarWriter 3.0	.sdw
StarWriter 3.0 Template	.vor

Table 7-2. Save files in many formats or file types (continued)

File format	File extension (suffix)
Text	*.txt*
Text Encoded	*.txt*
HTML Document (StarOffice Writer)	*.html;.htm*
AportisDoc (Palm)	*.pdb*
DocBook (simplified)	*.xml*
Pocket Word	*.psw*

Note that most of the file types in Table 7-2 are available as a save option in the Save As window. (See Figure 7-2.)

Benefits of a Good Standard Format

StarWriter's so-called native default file format is OASIS XML, based upon the OpenOffice.org/StarOffice implementation of the World Wide Web Consortium's specification for XML (eXtensible Markup Language).

Translation: "It's a good thing. StarWriter's file format is open, it's standard, and it's not controlled by a single entity."

StarOffice and OpenOffice.org users are helping us have a more compatible world by supporting open file format standards.

The Save Progress Indicator

When saving a document, you may notice that StarWriter displays a progress bar at the very bottom edge of the program window to indicate where in the save process you may be. The progress bar comes and goes very quickly when saving small documents, so its principal benefit comes with large documents that take more than a few seconds to save. The indicator is reassuring when StarWriter becomes inactive while performing a long document save.

Feature Comparisons

One of the most common complaints lodged by new users—or by people trying to delay a forced migration to a new office suite—is, "It doesn't have [my favorite] feature. It's missing the one thing I need to get my work done!"

The truth is that StarWriter has most of the features offered by MS Word—plus a few significant ones Word lacks and that make StarWriter more suitable for large and multichapter documents. It's just that the corresponding features may be located in a different place or labeled under a different name in StarOffice.

Table 7-3 can help you acclimate to the new terminology and layout of StarWriter.

Table 7-3. Features in MS Word 2000 and StarOffice 7

Feature name	MS Office2000	StarOffice 7
AutoCorrect	Tools → Autocorrect	Tools → AutoCorrect/AutoFormat
AutoNumbering	Format → Bullets and Numbering	Format → Numbering/Bullets...
Compare Documents	Tools → Track Changes → Compare Documents	Edit → Compare Document...
Envelope	Tools → Envelopes and Labels	Insert → Envelope...
Go To	Edit → Go To	Edit → Navigator
Header and Footer	View → Header and Footer	Insert → Header, chk 'default' Insert → Footer, chk 'default'
Insert Clip Art	Insert → Pictures → Clip Art	Tools → Gallery
Labels (create)	Tool → Envelopes and Labels	File → New → Labels
Master Document	View → Outline	File → New → Master Document File → Send → Create Master Document
Mail Merge	Tools → Mail Merge	Tools → Mail Merge View → Data Sources
Page Numbers	Insert → Page Numbers	Insert → Fields → Page Number
Record Macro	Tools → Macros → Record New Macro	Tools → Macros → Record Macro
Styles	Format → Styles	Format → Styles → Catalog Format → Styles → Load Format → Stylist
Table (insert)	Table → Insert → Table	Format → Autoformat... Insert → Table
Track Changes	Tools → Track Changes	Edit → Changes → chk 'Record,' chk 'Show'
Word Count	Tools → Word Count	File → Properties → Statistics

Names of the Toolbars

The important toolbars of StarWriter—to which we refer often—are the Main menu, the Function bar, the Object bar, and the Main Toolbar. (See Figure 7-3):

Main Menu
> Contains File, Edit, View, Insert, Format, Tools, Window, and Help; this is where you go with the mouse to execute most commands in StarWriter. You can view the menus, also, by using the Alt key, along with the first letter of the menu name (Alt-F for the File menu, for instance). The function-key (F-key) alternatives to many common commands are listed in Table 7-6.

Function Bar
> Contains the Open a Recent Document drop-down menu, Open New Document, Open File, Save, Document, Edit File, Export to PDF, Print File and other icons that are handy for one-click execution of the most common functions.

Object Bar

Contains the Document Styles drop-down menu, Fonts & Font Size drop-down menus, Bold, Italics, Underlines, indents, bullets & numbering, and character coloring, all available with a few clicks.

Main Toolbar

Contains Insert Table, Insert Fields, Insert Objects, Spellcheck, Data Sources, and other tools. This toolbar lies along the left edge of StarWriter.

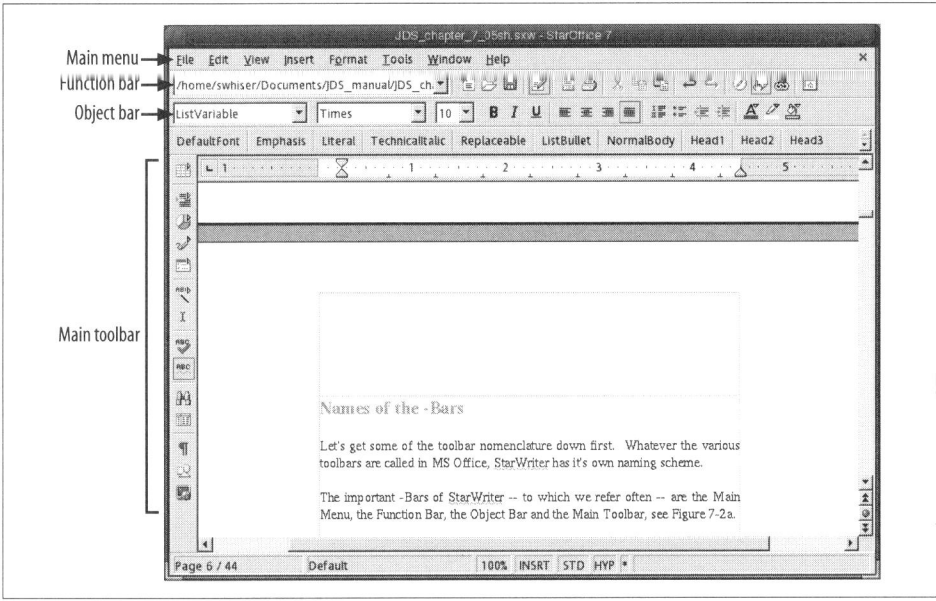

Figure 7-3. The toolbars of StarWriter

These are merely the default toolbars that are visible out-of-the-box. Others can be invoked by customizing the toolbars. See the section just below. The additional toolbars available include:

- Table Object Bar
- Numbering Object Bar
- Frame Object Bar
- Draw Object Bar
- Control Bar
- Text Object Bar/Graphics
- Bezier Object Bar
- Graphics Object Bar
- Objects

- Text Object Bar/Web
- Frame Object Bar/Web
- Graphics Object Bar/Web
- Object/Web
- User-defined no.1

Customizing the Toolbars

You can hide any of the toolbars (except Main menu) by unchecking their names in the top half of the context menu that opens when you right-click in the empty space within any of the toolbars. (See Figure 7-4.)

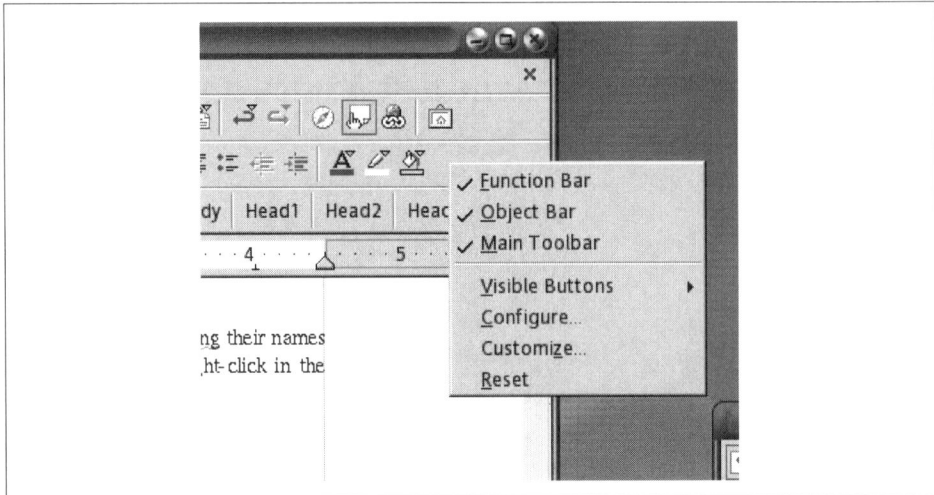

Figure 7-4. The context menu for configuring toolbars

You can further rearrange elements and redesign toolbars to your personal preference by choosing any of the other four choices in the bottom half of the contextual menu:

Visible buttons
> Check off or uncheck (to hide) which buttons/icons appear on that Bar

Configure…
> Customize and allocate which toolbars are available

Customize…
> Calls the Customize Toolbars dialog, offering a grand array of buttons to add to any toolbar in the list

Reset
> Restore the default configuration for all toolbars

Changes made using these commands apply to the specific toolbar on which you right-clicked to call the context menu.

 If you pause to study the StarWriter toolbar names, you'll be glad you did. Quiz on Monday!

Basic Formatting

This section covers basic formatting techniques for short and simple documents. The later "Power Formatting" section covers formatting techniques generally employed for larger, more complex documents.

One-click character formatting

When most word processor users think of document formatting options or styles, they think of bold, italic, underlining, fonts, font sizes, indentations, and other visible effects on text. If you're experienced with word processing, you know to look on the Object bar for the basic character formatting buttons, and you know these buttons can help you execute quick formatting changes in one click.

Figure 7-5 illustrates the available buttons for creating direct effects, which include such fancy changes as coloring text and creating bulleted or numbered lists. In addition to font-change Object bar buttons such as B, I, and U, you can use familiar keystroke combinations (Ctrl-B, Ctrl-I, and Ctrl-U) after selecting text that you wish to change.

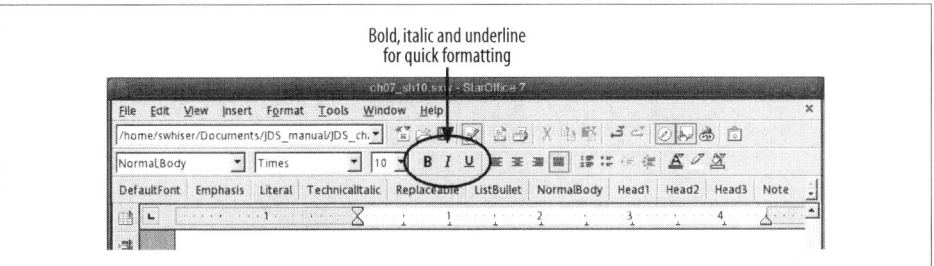

Figure 7-5. The formatting buttons on the Object Bar

When you apply manual formatting changes, whether from the Object bar buttons or the Format drop-down menu (Figure 7-6), StarWriter changes the format of the whole word when the cursor is simply located somewhere within the word at the time you invoke the change. There's no need to highlight the whole word. This saves extraneous mouse maneuvers or keystrokes. Direct changes can be made one at a time to sequences of characters or to whole paragraphs.

Character formatting

The Object bar shown in Figure 7-5 contains the most often used operations for altering text. If you have more unusual needs, such as applying a different font, highlight the character or characters you want to change using the mouse or arrow keys, and then select Format → Character... from the main menu at the top of the window. This reveals the Character window shown in Figure 7-7.

Paragraph formatting

You can indent, align, set borders, and generally manipulate paragraph formats via Format → Paragraph... on the Main Menu, shown in Figure 7-6. The Paragraph window is shown in Figure 7-8. If you use the mouse or arrow keys to highlight multiple paragraphs first, changes are applied to all selected paragraphs. If you don't highlight anything, paragraph changes affect the paragraph in which the cursor is currently placed.

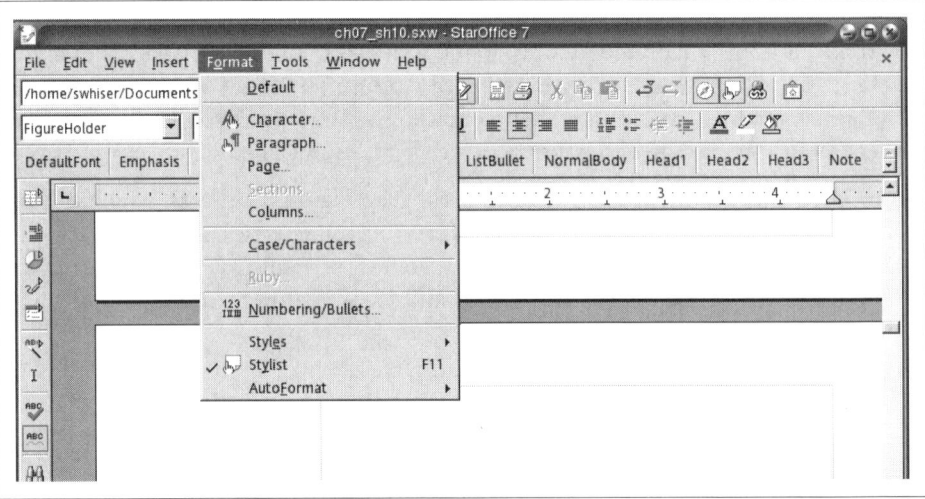

Figure 7-6. The Format drop-down on the Main menu

Unlike characters and paragraphs, invoking page format control through Format → Page... (Figure 7-9) lands you in the realm of general Styles, which we cover later. To create a page format or style that you can reuse repeatedly, see "Adding new styles (or creating styles)."

Inserting headers and footers

Headers and footers are the textual (or other) content that you want to repeat at either the top (header) or bottom (footer) of every page of a document or section. Before you fill in any information, headers and footers appear as empty banners or frames at the top and bottom (respectively) of each page.

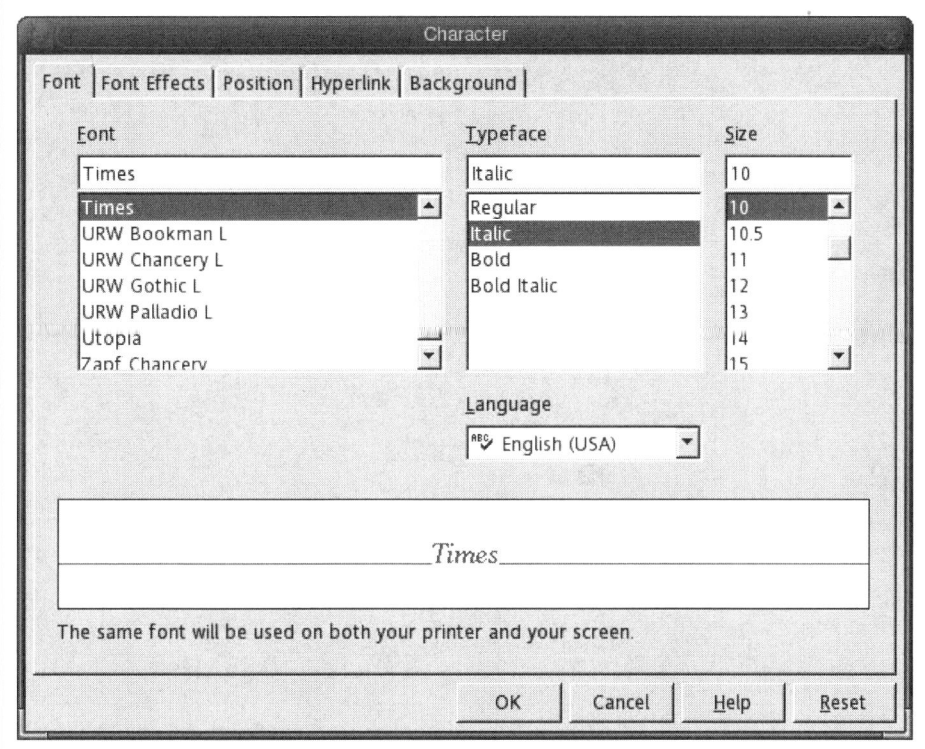

Figure 7-7. The Character window

To insert a header, go to the Main menu, select Insert → Header and check Default in the drop-down menu. This opens a header frame into the current document where you can type or enter the appropriate content that appears at the top of every page of the document.

Inserting a footer is the same as inserting a header, but select Insert → Footers and check Default.

To change headers or footers in the middle of a document, see the section "Changing headers or footers in mid-document."

Page numbering

Most documents show page numbers in a header or footer. To generate automatic page numbers, insert a header or footer (depending on where you intend the page number to go, at either the top or bottom of each page) and place the cursor inside the live header or footer frame by clicking once there. Then go to the Main menu and select Insert → Fields. This invokes a drop-down menu with the following choices:

- Date
- Time

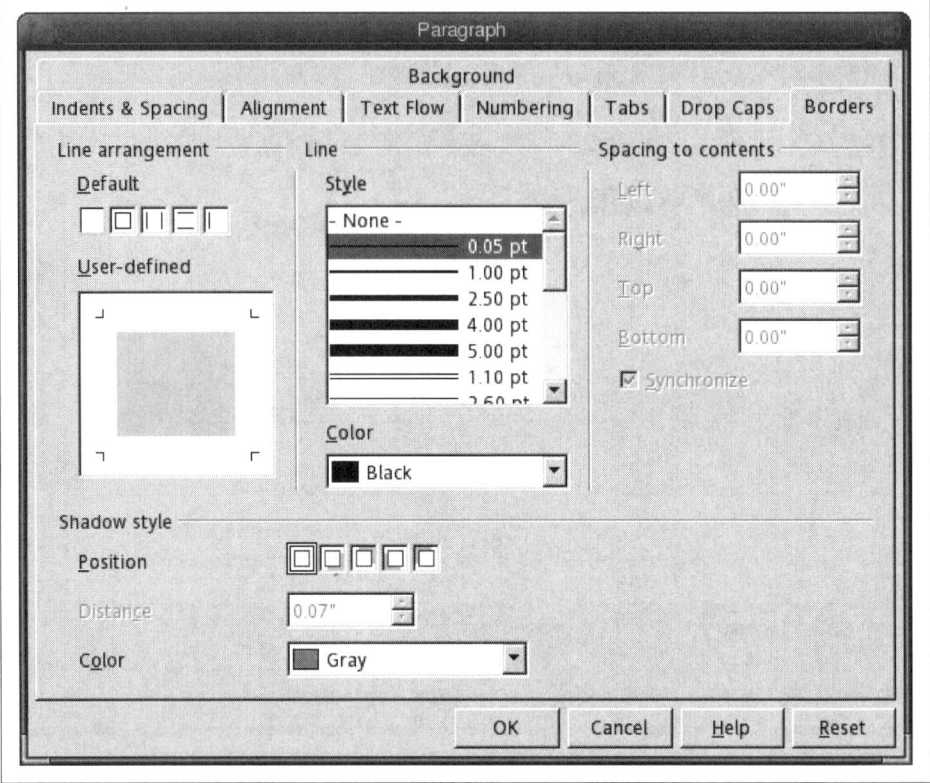

Figure 7-8. Paragraph window

- Page Number
- Page Count
- Subject
- Title
- Author
- Other

Selecting the Page Number choice inserts the page number automatically at the location of the cursor. (See Figure 7-10.)

Sometimes it's appropriate to create page numbering in a header or footer that states the page number as well as the total number of pages in the document. Such a format would read "Page 16 of 96," for example. In this case, place the cursor in the target location in the header or footer and type **Page** followed by a space, insert Page Number as shown above, type **of** followed by a space, and insert Page Count from the same drop-down menu.

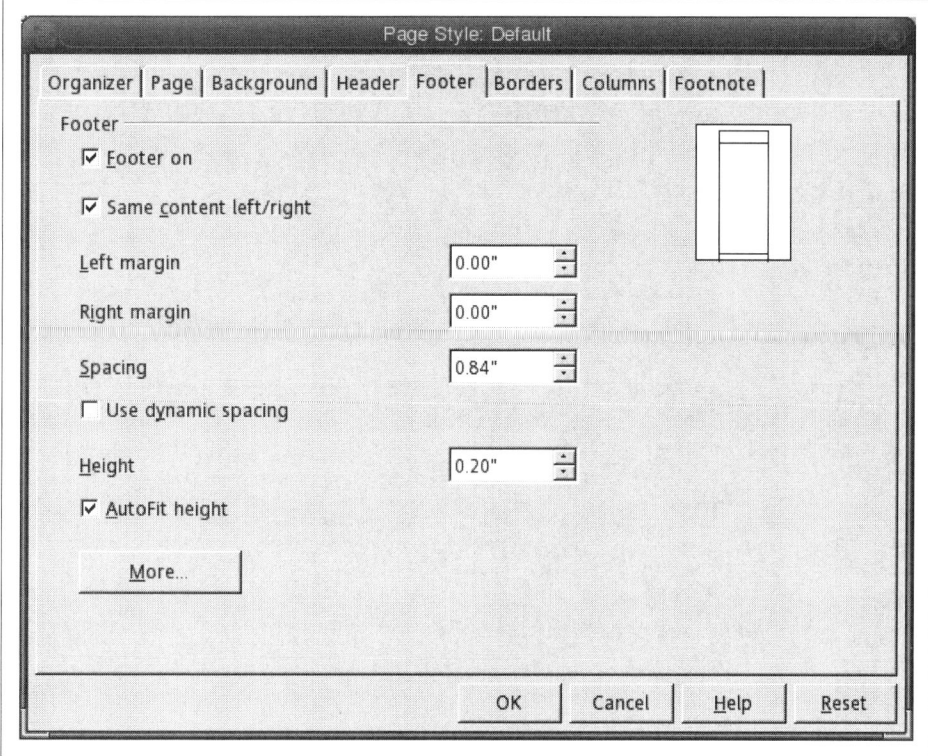

Figure 7-9. Page window

To change or restart page numbering at a certain point in a document, see the section "Changing page styles in mid-document."

Inserting the filename

Sometimes it's useful to have a document's filename, or even the whole path with slashes, entered into a header or footer. This helps identify—especially in the document's printed form—the location of the digital source of the document for subsequent retrieval.

To insert a filename, first insert a footer as described earlier.

Then press Ctrl-F2. Alternatively, place the cursor in the footer, select Insert → Fields, and choose Other in the drop-down menu. This invokes the Fields window.

Next, in the Document tab, in the Type column, click on File name. This will invoke the Format column on the right side of the Fields window.

Finally, click on Path/File name (or any desirable variation offered) and click the Insert button at the bottom of the Fields window.

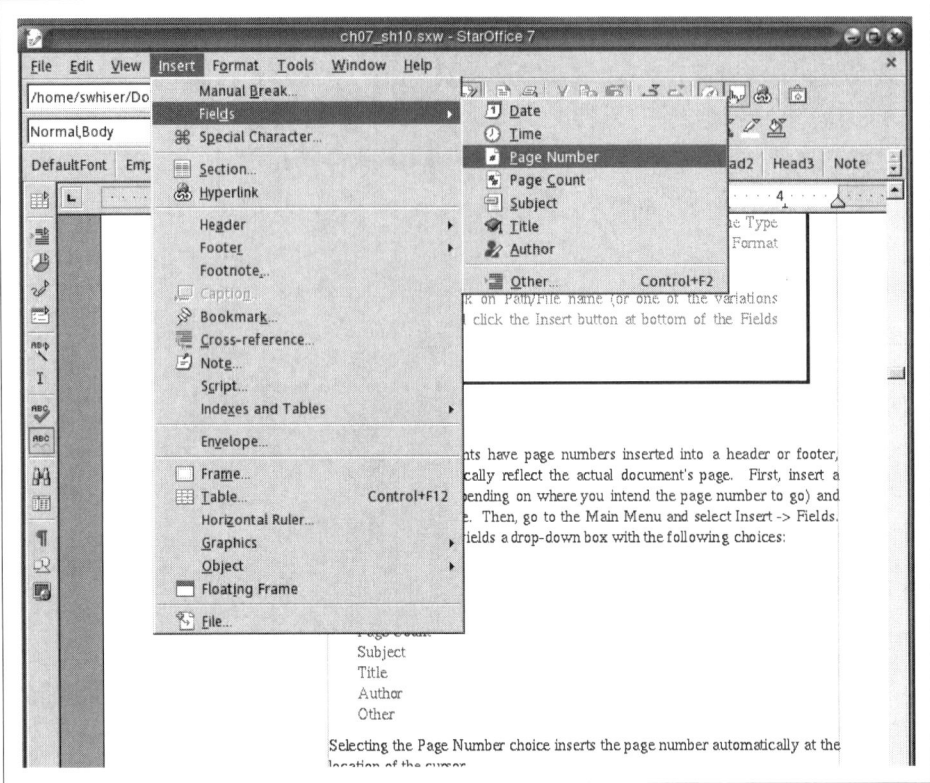

Figure 7-10. Inserting page numbers

Introducing Templates and Styles

Templates and Styles are the advanced document formatting tool sets of StarWriter. While we cover their use below in the "StarWriter PowerTips" section, it may be helpful to prepare you here with an overview of what they can do.

Introducing Templates

A template is a preformatted file or document that is used as the basis for creating other similarly formatted documents. Using a template saves the effort of formatting documents the same way over and over again. What we call "Templates" in context of StarWriter is the whole tool set for storing and managing templates, as well as creating new documents from template files.

 A StarWriter template file is distinguished by its suffix or file extension, *.stw*, while StarWriter text document has the *.sxw* extension.

Template files are linked to the documents that are created with them. It may help to imagine the template file, or the source file, as the "parent" and the derived document as the "child." Parent-to-child linkage is one of the principal benefits of using Templates. What's powerful is when you have a large number of "child" documents in your Documents folder, for example, you have the ability to update the formatting of all those files in one stroke by altering the formatting of the "parent" template file.

We cover the Templates tool-set in the section "Templates."

Introducing Styles

Styles refers to the strong formatting features of StarWriter that permit you to maintain a growing catalogue of stock and custom compound formats for characters, paragraphs, and pages that you can use over and over across all your documents. Like Templates, Styles brings power to your desktop repertoire by helping you eliminate repetitive tasks.

 The Styles tool set is accessed when you open the Stylist palette simply by pressing the F11 function key or via Format → Stylist from the Main menu. Try opening the Stylist just to see what's there. It generally takes a lot of use to become familiar with Styles, so don't be put off by the complexity at first.

In one example, a style applied throughout a document—a certain type of heading for instance—can be altered in one stroke when you modify that particular style in your Styles Catalog. The modification to the style will ripple through your document, saving the repetitive tagging of possibly many instances of that heading. Such features are most useful with large and heavily formatted documents such as chapter works, technical documentation, research reports, and white papers.

We cover Styles in the section "Styles."

Basic Printing

You can print the current document in one stroke by simply clicking the printer icon on the Function bar. (See Figure 7-11.)

Alternatively, you can gain additional control of printing via the Print window. Select File → Print from the Main menu, or simply press Ctrl-P. Here, you can choose a non-default printer (if one is set up), a limited page range, or a different number of copies for the current print job. You can also elect to print to a file. (See Figure 7-12.)

Instructions on setting up your printer(s) in JDS are located in Chapter 3.

When to Avoid Using Templates and Styles

Templates and Styles, together, form StarWriter's rich feature set for eliminating repetitive formatting tasks. Their power, however, is matched by their complexity: they take substantial effort to master. Some suggest they are not widely useful for this reason; but the power and discretion, as always, is in the hands of the circumspect user.

You can be successful working with documents while avoiding Templates and Styles for quite a while. This can work well, for example, with one-of-a-kind documents that you can afford to create from scratch and format manually from the Function bar or via Format on the Main menu. Likewise, many users have a do-it-yourself approach to templates involving manual renumbering of the filename of the evolving drafts of a document, or using plain old letters or forms stored in one's folders to quickly create a similar new document. If you are comfortable in such desktop habits, they're hard to criticize.

As soon as groups of your documents become repetitious or share similar formatting characteristics (at the page-, the paragraph-, or the character-level) and as your documents grow in length, using Templates and Styles begins to make more sense. Every user is equipped to judge for himself the appropriate time to dive into the more advanced features in the StarWriter tool set. We cover Templates and Styles in some depth in the "StarWriter Power Tips" section.

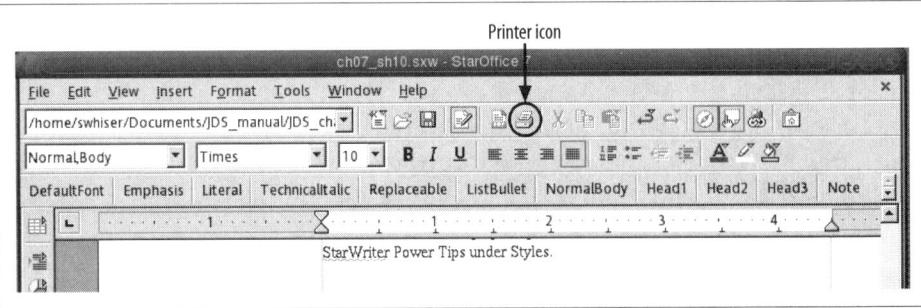

Figure 7-11. The Printer icon on the Function Bar

StarWriter Power Tips

With its many file format output options and its use of open XML formats, StarWriter encroaches upon the territory of professional-grade desktop publishing software. Well, it should. StarWriter offers features, tools, and capabilities that surprise users of consumer-grade word processors. This section assembles tips on formatting

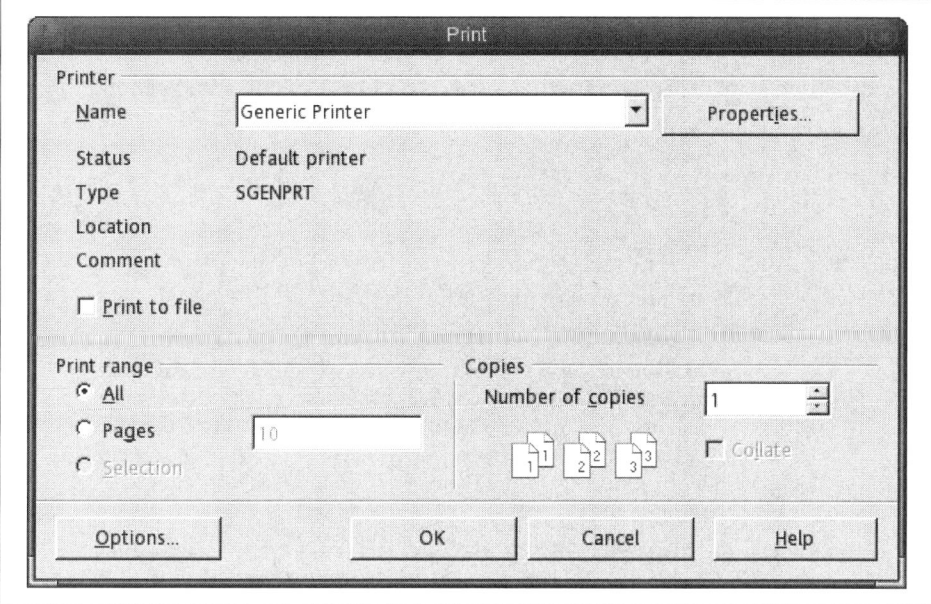

Figure 7-12. The Print window

techniques that apply to large, complex documents that demand careful planning and efficient formatting control. Such documents might include:

- Manuscripts divided into chapters
- White papers
- Technical documentation
- Newsletters

Keep in mind that any features or techniques covered in this section may still be useful, too, in any of your small document production.

Saving or Exporting to Common File Formats

StarOffice facilitates saving files in several different file types, including some very useful document standards such as PDF. By choosing the format in which you save a document, you can ensure your work is viewable and editable in different software environments: Windows, Mac, Solaris, and others.

Saving in the MS Word file formats

Chose File → Save As… from the Main menu. In the Save As window, open the File Type drop-down menu and select the desired MS Office file format version; choices include:

- Microsoft Word 97/2000/XP (*.doc*)
- Microsoft Word 95 (*.doc*)
- Microsoft Word 6.0 (*.doc*)

See Figure 7-2 for details of the Save As window.

If you are asked to share a document with an MS Word user, ask precisely which version of MS Office your collaborating partners are using or are likely to use. This is necessary because the later MS Office file formats are not compatible with earlier versions of their file format. For example, users of Word 6.0 cannot read or edit files produced in the later Word 2000 file format.

You can solve such file format incompatibilities by persuading your office colleagues and supply chain partners to convert to the open XML file format used in StarOffice and OpenOffice.org. Before they get around to that, the PDF format offers a fair chance at guaranteeing readable (though not editable) documents.

Export as Adobe PDF

In your current document, click the small, red Export to PDF icon on the Menu, and the Export window opens with File Type preselected to Adobe PDF. Notice in Figure 7-13 that the Export window is similar to the Save As window.

Enter the file name, choose a folder in which to save the new PDF file, and press the Save button.

You can achieve the same result by selecting File → Export as PDF and filling out the Export window as instructed above.

Sending a document as an email file attachment

StarWriter offers a host of facilities for exporting or sending the current document to others through one or two mouse clicks. To send the current document as an attachment to an email, select File → Send → Document as Email… and this calls up the JDS Email and Calendar program, along with a new Compose window with the current StarWriter document already attached. (See Figure 7-14.) Fill in the address and subject lines, perhaps add a few words in the message window, and press the Send button.

This feature sends the file attached automatically in the native or default StarOffice open XML (*.sxw*) file format.

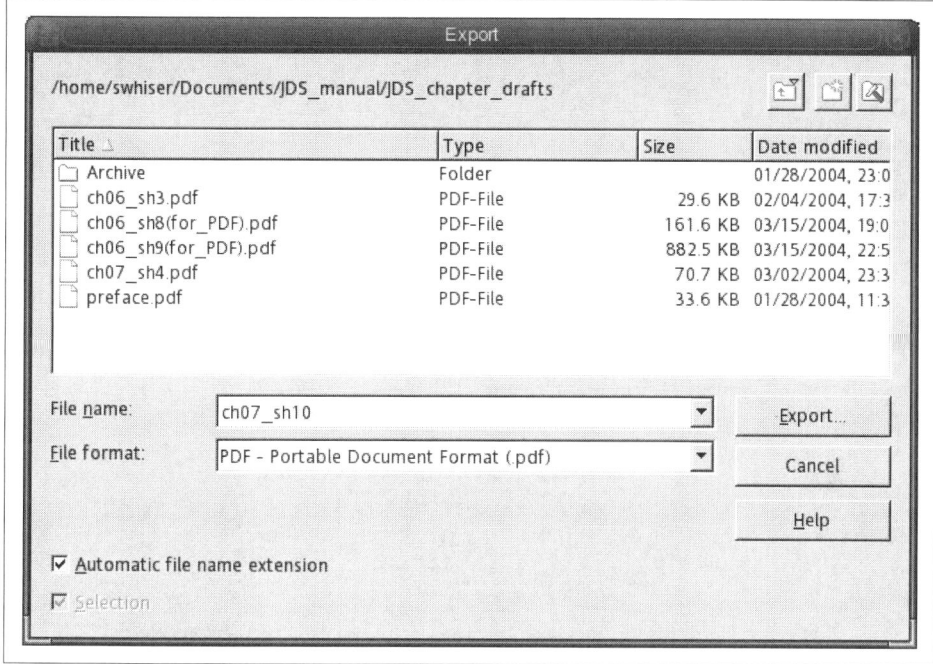

Figure 7-13. The Export window

Sending a document as a PDF attachment to an email

To send the current document as an Adobe PDF attachment to an e-mail, select File → Send → Document as PDF Attachment... The PDF Options window appears and lets you select a page range or the whole document, and the amount of file compression. The default compression setting, Print optimized, is fine for most purposes.

You can achieve a similar result in more steps by exporting a file to PDF into a folder and then manually attaching the PDF to an email message. For the inconvenience of a couple added steps, you get a copy of the distributed PDF file saved in your filesystem, which may be useful later.

Power Formatting

For small and one-time documents, the tools we've shown you so far in this chapter can make you very productive. But if you're concerned about maintaining a consistent format across many documents, and producing large documents with multiple chapters, you should move on to the power features in this section.

Frames

A frame is a rectangular window you can insert into a document. It is much like a picture frame and is useful for holding formatted text, graphics, titles, sidebars, and

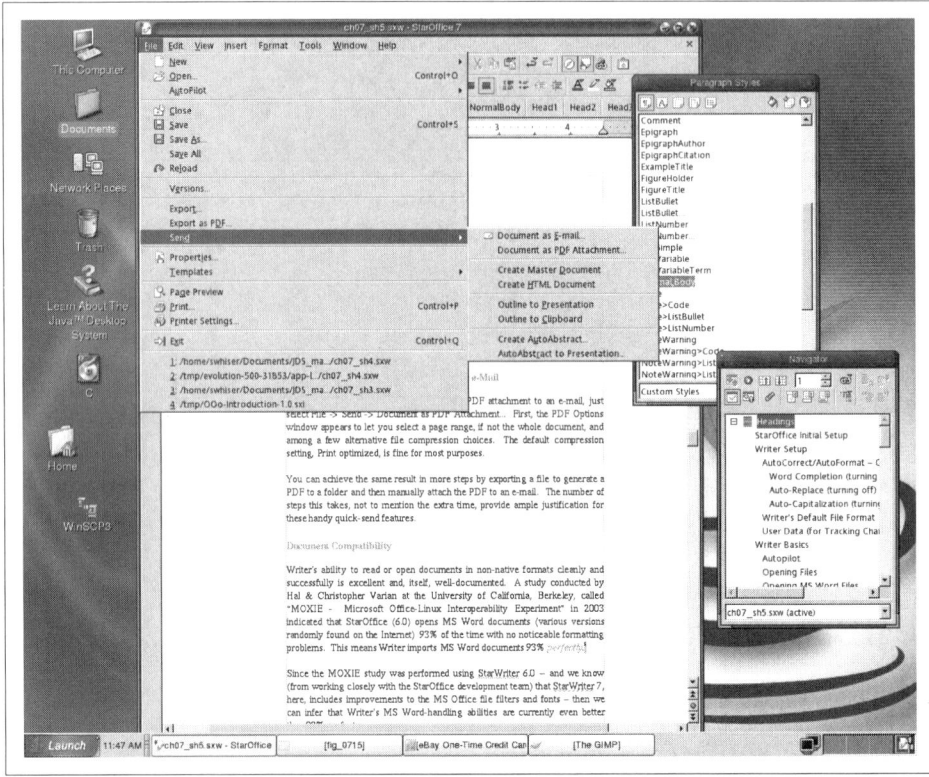

Figure 7-14. Sending a document as email

other content that you want to set apart from the main text in your document. You can even put frames within frames.

To insert a frame into your document, place the cursor in the target location and select Insert → Frame from the Main menu. This opens the Frame dialog, where you can establish the dimensions, location, and other characteristics of the frame, as shown in Figure 7-15.

The Frame dialog gives you options for selecting the characteristics and features for your frames: size, anchor point, position, background color, word-wrap characteristics, links, and text flow, among other things.

Linking text frames

Linking frames together permits text to flow automatically through several designated frames that have been placed into a document. For example, in a newsletter or article, you might wish to highlight a specific passage with a larger and more visible font to give the skimming reader a quick sense of the subject, to lure them into reading the whole thing. However, with limited space you may not be able to fit the whole highlighted passage into a single frame. In such a case, simply insert three

PDF: A Format for All

In a world of mixed computer systems, Adobe PDF is one of the most universally accepted file formats. It has other virtues, too:

File size

> PDF files, depending on the type of content, can be smaller than the StarOffice- or MS Office-original files from which they were generated, making them preferable to other file types when they are sent as an email attachment or downloaded from the Web.

Readability

> PDF is suitable for the most professional print jobs. It renders fonts and graphics within documents attractively and sometimes better than the originating application.

Portability

> PDF can be read on every modern computer system. Most users on any major operating system platform already have Adobe Acrobat Reader installed, allowing them to view most PDF files painlessly. Do keep in mind that StarOffice-generated PDF files must be viewed in Adobe Acrobat 5.0 or later.

Security

> PDF is a comparatively secure format because files can't be edited as they can in a StarWriter or Word document. With a fixed format such as PDF, your work is less subject to unpredictable alterations by others.

In summary, Adobe PDF is an efficient and readable format. Send your work as a PDF file whenever a read-only format is appropriate and sufficient.

---

frames and set them to link together so that the text you enter can flow automatically through the frames.

In the Frame dialog Options tab, shown in Figure 7-16, you have the opportunity to set the frame linkages by entering the names of the previous frame or next frame using the drop-down lists where all existing frame names are visible. Once the frames are inserted and linked, you can paste in the desired text and format it for best effect.

If you view the Navigator (by pressing function key F5 or selecting Edit → Navigator), you can see a list of all the frames in your document. This permits you to jump through your document to specific frames quickly. See the section "Navigator" for further information on navigating frames.

Borders

Formatting a paragraph with borders can be an effective way to structure information in a document. The bordered paragraph styles you create can be named, stored, and reused again and again.

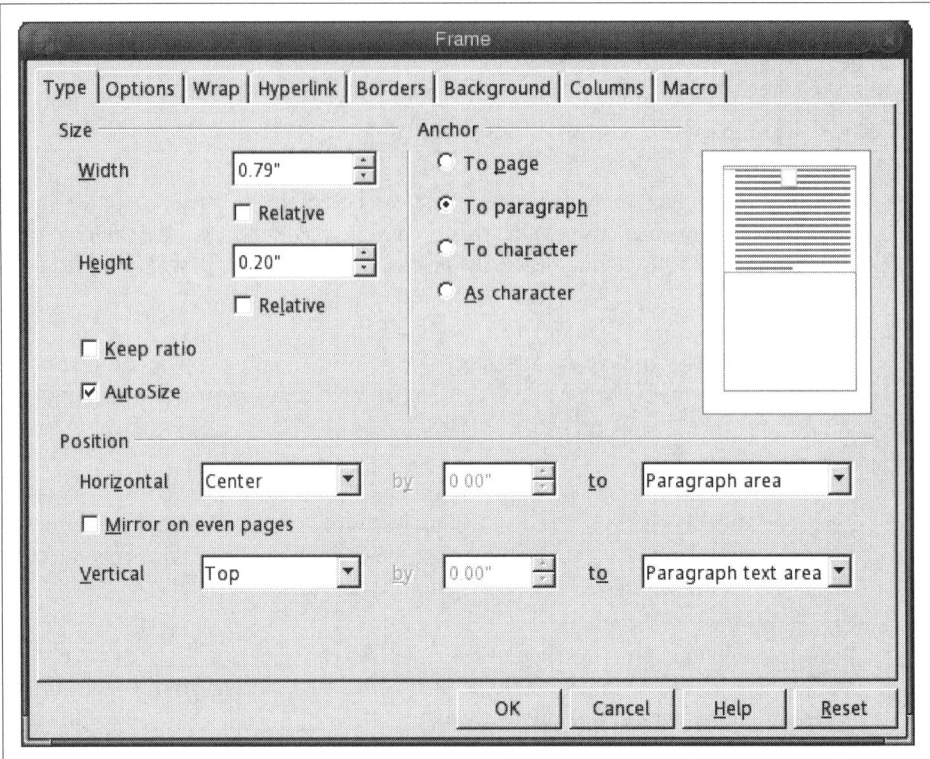

Figure 7-15. The Frame window

To design a bordered block of text or paragraph for one-time use, select Format →
Paragraph → Borders tab (Figure 7-17) from the Main menu.

Here, you can design the outlines, background colors or shading, drop shadow,
spacing, and other features of your bordered paragraph.

To design a style for a bordered paragraph that you can reuse many times, use Styles.
Press Ctrl+F11 to invoke the Styles Catalog and create a new paragraph Style using
the Borders tab. Styles are explained in the section "Adding new styles (or creating
styles)."

Sections

Sections are named areas in a document or blocks of text, graphics, or objects that
you can use to prevent text from being edited, to show or hide text, and to repurpose
text and graphics from other StarOffice documents. You can also use sections to
employ a different column layout from the one prescribed by the current page style.

To insert a section into the current document, select the text or area you wish to be
contained in the section and select Insert → Section from the Main menu. Figure 7-18

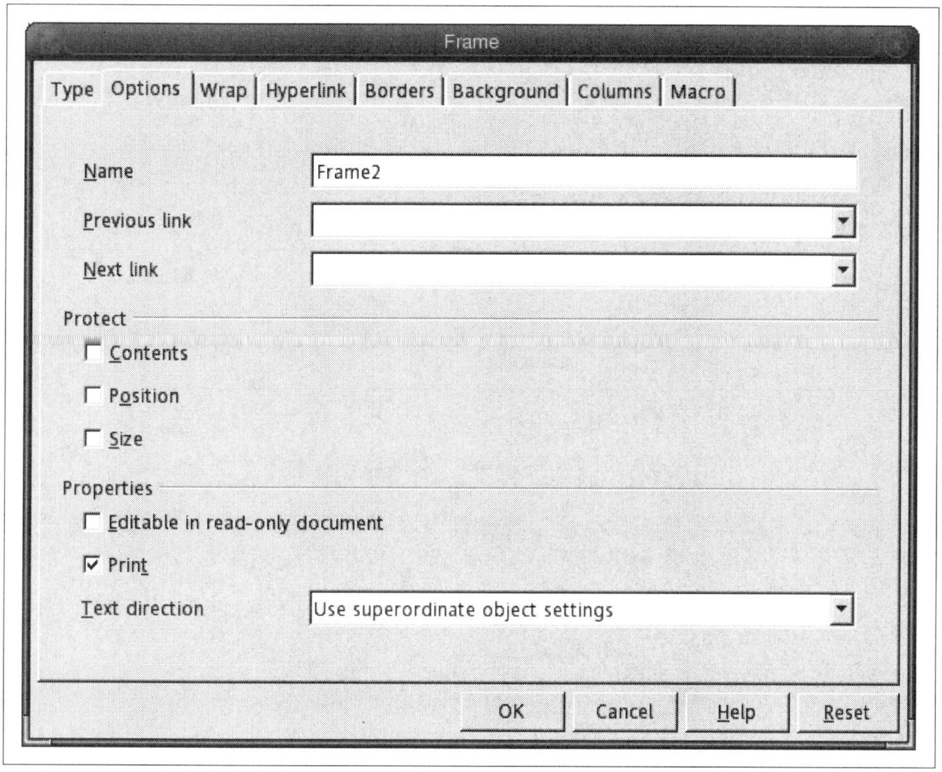

Figure 7-16. Linking text frames

illustrates the facilities available in the Insert Section dialog, that permit you to link, write-protect, hide, or format the section and its contents.

A section contains at least one paragraph. When you select text and create a section, a paragraph break is automatically inserted at the end of the text.

You can insert portions from a text document, or an entire text document, as a section into another text document. You can also insert portions from a text document as links in another text document, or even in the same document. (See Figure 7-18.)

An inserted section is defined, like a header or footer in a StarWriter document, by fine gray lines, so it's clear where the section begins and ends. To enter a new paragraph either just before or just after a section, click once, either before or after the section boundary, and press Alt+Enter.

Generating a Table of Contents

For longer written work that is structured with chapters or headings, it is convenient to exploit StarWriter's ability to autogenerate a Table of Contents. This feature is often used because manually generating tables and indexes is extremely time-consuming and repetitive—especially for larger documents.

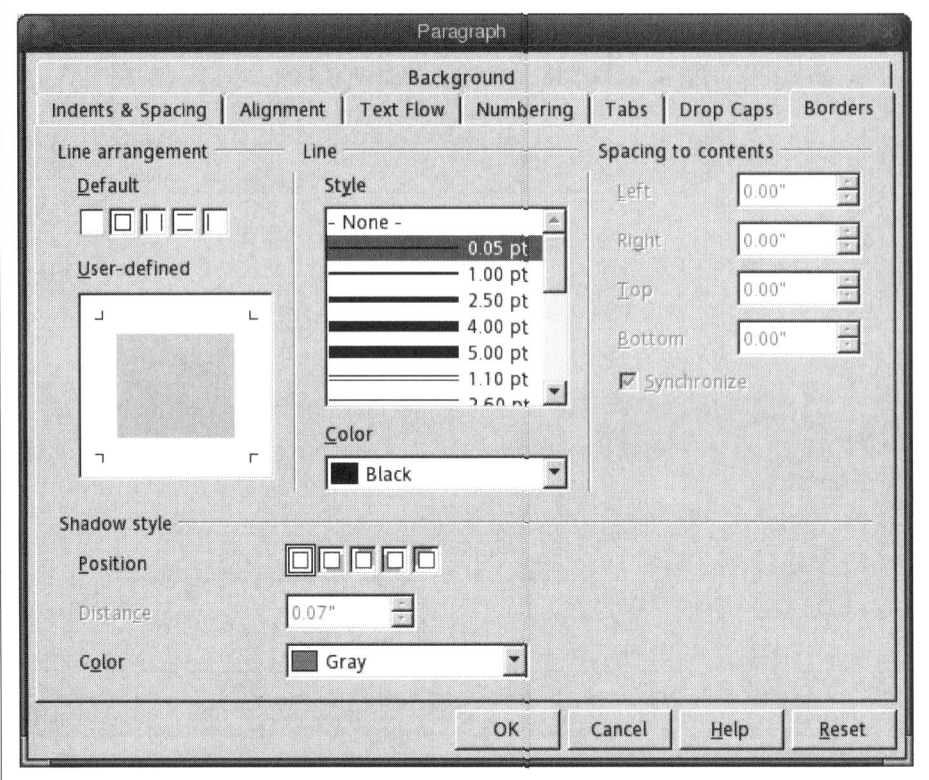

Figure 7-17. The Paragraph window, Borders tab

To generate a table of contents that picks up the headings you've inserted into your document, choose Insert → Indexes and Tables and then, from the drop-down menu, Indexes and Tables.... once again. You can then insert a generic table of contents simply by pressing the OK button of the Insert Index/Tables window, as shown in Figure 7-19.

You can generate a number of different kinds of indexes and tables, including:

- Table of Contents
- Alphabetical index
- Illustration index
- Index of tables
- User-defined
- Table of objects
- Bibliography

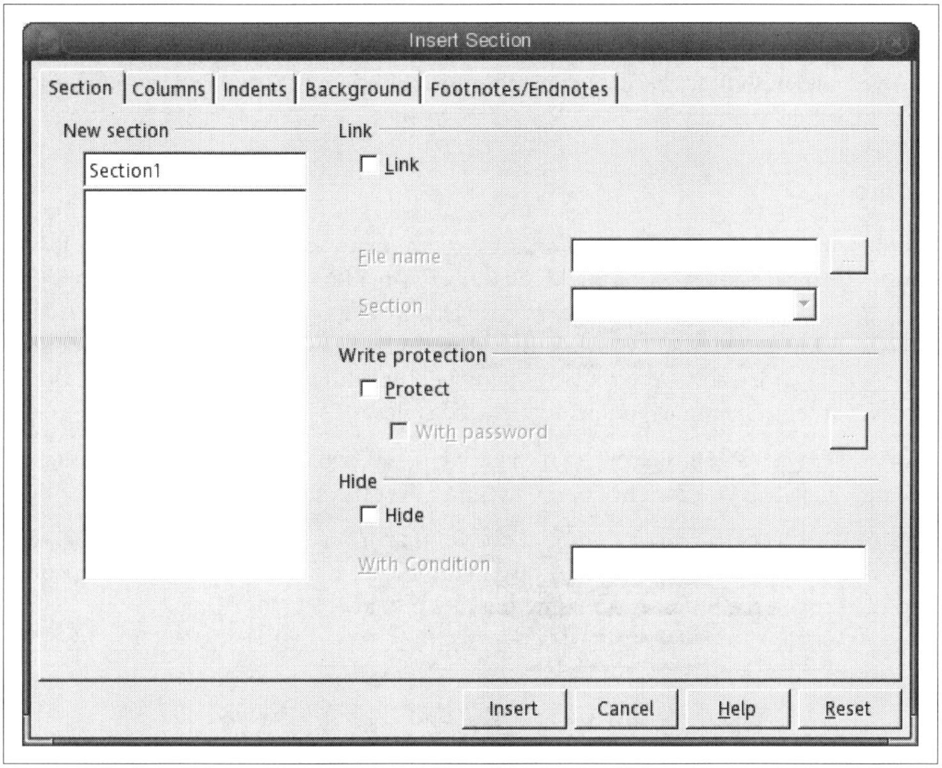

Figure 7-18. The Insert Section window

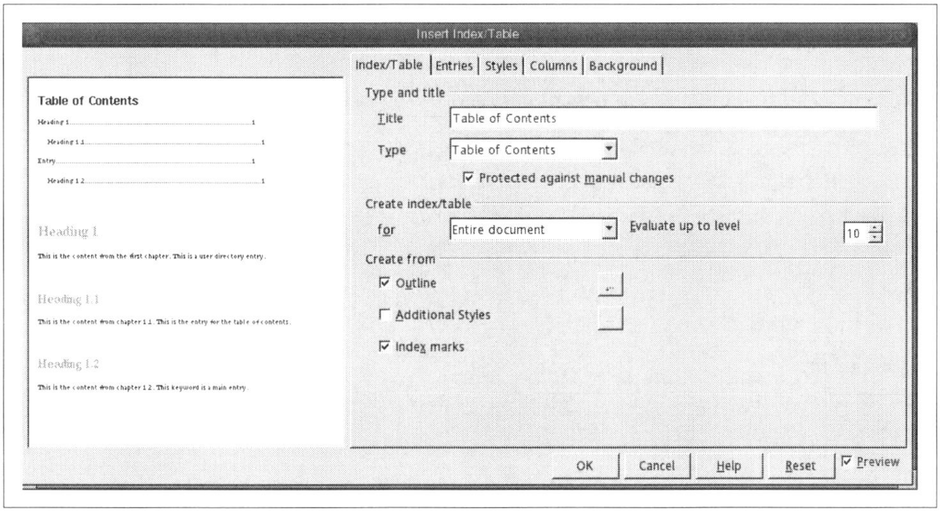

Figure 7-19. The Insert Index/Table window

From the Insert Index/Table dialog, you can designate the type of index or table, its layout, and other characteristics. You can design the number of heading levels involved and reformat the index or table to make it more legible, distinctive, and effective.

Styles

Styles is one of the most powerful and important features of word processing. If you find yourself formatting a particular character, word, paragraph, page, or other element of your document the same way, over and over, you should consider saving yourself a lot of time (and preventing errors) by using an existing style or defining your own new one. If you work with many people and want them all to make documents that look the same, you definitely need styles.

Put another way: any formatting you can apply to text can be turned almost as quickly into a style, which you can then apply over and over through a couple of clicks.

Figure 7-20 shows the button on the Function bar (third from the right, highlighted) with which you can quickly open the Stylist to begin manipulating Styles. You could also easily open the Stylist by pressing the function key, F11.

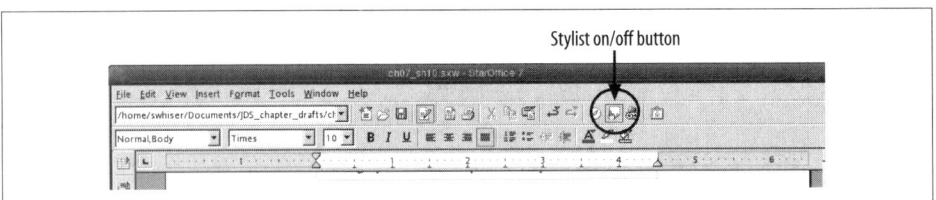

Figure 7-20. The Stylist on/off button

Once open, the Stylist lets you toggle among the five different style types or style categories:

Paragraph Styles
> Set formatting for a whole paragraph, note, sidebar, list, frame, table, or other collection of set-off text

Character Styles
> Format a word, single character, or selection of characters

Frame Styles
> Set formatting for frames that might include such content as text, a bulleted text or list, graphics, charts, or other frames

Page Styles
> Apply an entire set of Styles to a whole page; this is the tool to apply to chapters and title pages

Numbering Styles
> Select from a variety of numbering formats for numbered lists

---

To switch from one style category to another, simply click the corresponding icon at the top left of the Stylist's toolbar.

The Stylist

The interface to StarWriter's Styles is a floating palette called the Stylist. It is invoked by pressing the function key, F11, or the Stylist On/Off button on the Function bar. The Stylist On/Off button looks like a page with a tiny hand on the lower-left corner. The default state of Stylist is to open in Paragraph Styles with the Automatic mode, as shown in Figure 7-21.

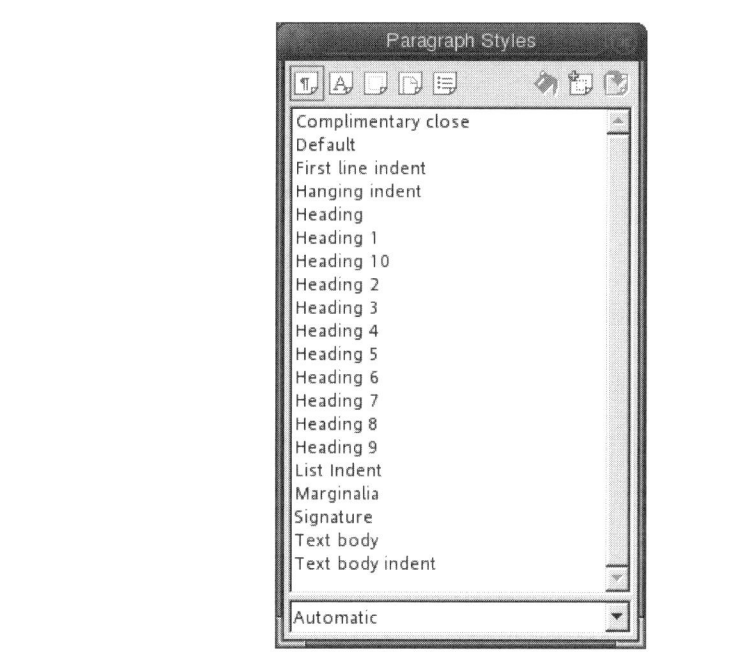

Figure 7-21. The Stylist opens to Paragraph Styles

Clicking through the icons on the Stylist's toolbar, you begin to get a feel for the different styles that come with StarWriter out of the box.

First example: applying a character style

One of the simplest things to do with the Stylist is to apply one of its default character styles. Click on the Character Styles icon (second from left, showing an A) at the top of the Stylist. This reveals all the default character styles available (the window is in "All" mode by default).

To apply a bold style, for example, highlight the bold character style (at the top of the list by default) with a single click and then click once on the paint can icon, third from the right at the top of the Stylist. (See Figure 7-22.)

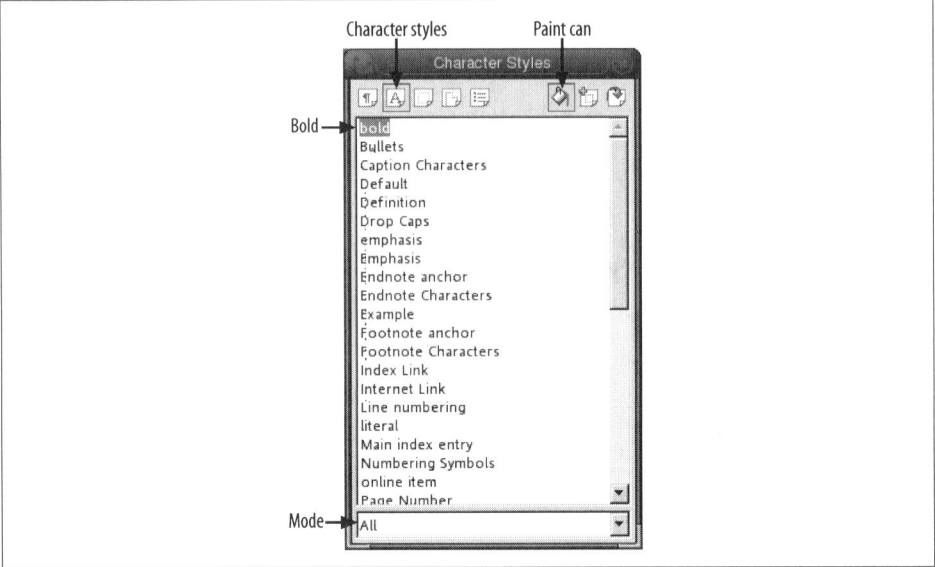

Figure 7-22. The Stylist, ready to paint bold

When you invoke the paint can, your cursor turns into a little paint can tool that makes it easy to apply your chosen style with precision. Click on a word you wish to embolden, or draw the paint can cursor across some text. The paint can now give you a Midas touch, which makes bold everything on which you click. You can turn off the style by pressing F11, clicking on the X icon at the top right of the Stylist box, or choosing a different style.

Stylist view modes

There are too many styles to show conveniently at one time in the Stylist window, so there's a way to view different subsets of all available styles.

The Stylist View Mode drop-down menu is at the bottom of the Stylist. Each mode shows a particular subset of styles you may be interested in at a particular moment. For instance, the view mode can limit you to seeing styles related to lists, or related to formatting a page for HTML (a web page). There is also a view mode, Custom Styles, to show styles that you or your colleagues have added to the document. If you decide you do want to see all styles available for your document, select All Styles in the menu.

What makes Styles View Modes even more complicated is that the different view modes vary according to the current style type in which you're sitting. The Stylist

View Modes available vary by context, according to which type of style you are in (whether Paragraph, Character, Frame, Page or Numbering Style). (See Table 7-4.)

Table 7-4. Stylist view modes

Paragraph	Character	Frame	Page	Numbering
Hierarchical	Hierarchical	Hierarchical	Hierarchical	Hierarchical
All	All	All	All	All
Applied	Applied	Applied	Applied	Applied
Custom	Custom	Custom	Custom	Custom
Automatic	n.a.	n.a.	n.a.	n.a.
Text	n.a.	n.a.	n.a.	n.a.
Chapter	n.a.	n.a.	n.a.	n.a.
List	n.a.	n.a.	n.a.	n.a.
Index	n.a.	n.a.	n.a.	n.a.
Special	n.a.	n.a.	n.a.	n.a.
HTML	n.a.	n.a.	n.a.	n.a.
Conditional	n.a.	n.a.	n.a.	n.a.

Modifying styles

We've already shown you how to change a particular paragraph or set of characters. You can make similar changes to styles. For instance, if you want list items indented differently from the default indentation used in a list style, you can edit the list style and make it indent each list the way you want. When you modify a style, it immediately takes effect on all existing items in the document, as well as items you create afterward. In this section, we'll show you how to modify a style; a later section shows you how to create an entirely new style so you can do things the inventors of StarWriter didn't anticipate.

> Quick-flowing styles modification is one of the key productivity benefits for using Styles versus manual or direct formatting. It permits efficient formatting of large documents for work that is likely to be used by many different people or reformatted repeatedly for different purposes.

To modify a style, press Ctrl-F11 to bring up the Style Catalog. The resulting window is shown in Figure 7-23. You can also invoke the Style Catalog from the Main menu by selecting Format → Styles → Catalog....

The Style Catalog displays different styles, depending on the style set at the cursor's current location. This can be very convenient; if you want to modify a certain style throughout an entire document, just place the cursor on one example of that style and proceed to modify it.

Figure 7-23. The Style Catalog

With the Style Catalog open, highlight the style you wish to alter and click the Modify button at the right of the Style Catalog window. This opens the Style Settings window for the style highlighted in Figure 7-23 called "Normal, Body." The Style Settings window is shown in Figure 7-24: here you can change any characteristic that is available for modification. The characteristics you can adjust include:

- Name
- Text flow
- Linkages
- Font
- Size
- Indent
- Alignment
- Spacing
- Tabs
- Capitalization
- Background color
- Borders

An alternative way to modify a style is to right-click on the style in the Stylist and choose among the choices New, Modify or Delete. When you click Modify, the Style Settings window opens and you can make the desired changes.

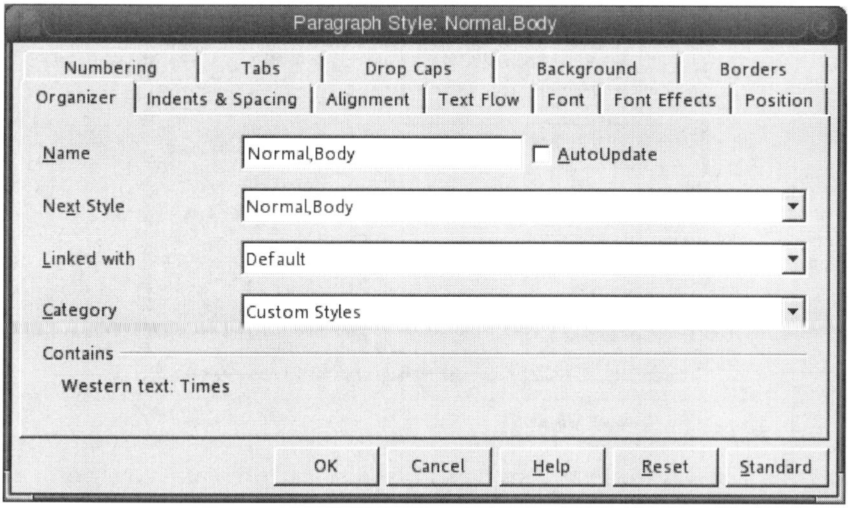

Figure 7-24. The Style Settings window

Updating styles

Short of creating a whole new style from scratch, you can quickly change an existing Style by applying the format of a selected character, paragraph, or page.

To update a particular style, press the function key, F11, to open the Stylist. Next, click the icon of the style type you want to update: Paragraph, Character, or Page. Then, click once in the document in the place where you want to copy/update the style from. For example, you may be "borrowing" paragraph formatting that you had previously applied manually. Next, in the Stylist click on the style name you wish to update. Then, finally, click the Update Style icon at the far right of the Stylist toolbar.

Adding new styles (or creating styles)

Although StarWriter comes with many predefined Styles, specialized documents sometimes have elements that don't fit into one of the predefined styles. StarWriter makes it easy to create new Styles, too.

To add a new style to the Stylist, first open the Stylist by pressing F11. Next, pick a style type and highlight an existing style in Stylist that's similar to the new one you wish to create (if such a style exists). Right-click that style and select New…. This opens the Style Settings window shown in Figure 7-24. Here you can set all the characteristics you want for the new style, including its category.

There are two alternative ways to add a new style. One is by clicking the New Style from the Selection button, which is the second button from the right, at the top of the Stylist. This opens the Create Style window, where you can choose a new style from the given list and enter a name for the new style, as shown in Figure 7-25.

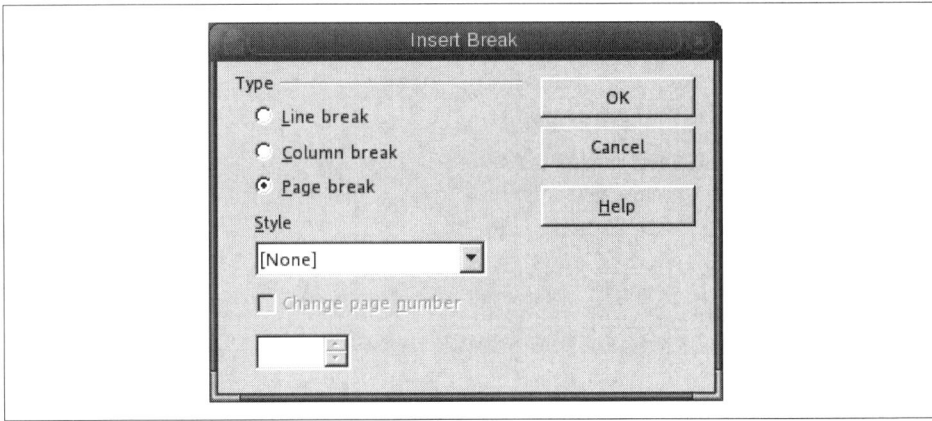

Figure 7-25. The Create Style window.

Perhaps the best way to create a style that doesn't closely resemble any existing style is to press Ctrl-F11 to open the Style Catalog. Then click the New… button on the right side. This opens the Style Settings window where you can make all the desired selections to create your new style.

Changing page styles in mid-document

Some documents contain multiple page formats for such things as title, chapter, end-note, and footnote. To change the page style midway through a document, start by inserting a manual page break where you need to make the change. Place the cursor just after the last character on the page before the change and select Insert → Manual Break… from the Main menu. This opens the Insert Break window, shown in Figure 7-26, where Page Break is the default type of break. Before pressing OK to insert the manual page break, select the page style you want to follow the break. You may need to create a new page style to accommodate the new formatting.

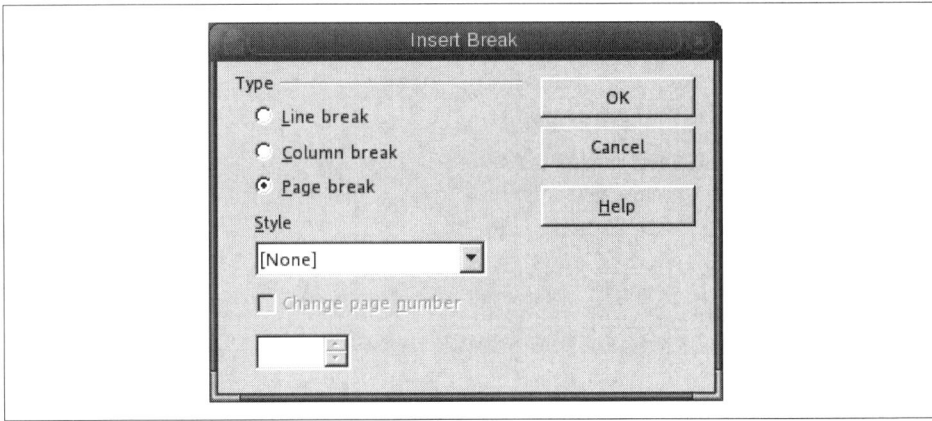

Figure 7-26. The Insert Break window

Changing headers or footers in mid-document

If you need to have the headers or footers change somewhere within your document, insert a manual page break and deploy a different page style with different header or footer content or formatting. Keep in mind that you may need to create a new page style to accommodate the different headers or footers. See "Adding new styles (or creating styles)" for information on deploying a different page style.

Changing page numbers in mid-document

This feature is useful in making transitions between different sections of a document, such as from the front matter (where pages are often numbered with lower-case italic Roman numerals) to the beginning of the text (where numbering may start over again from 1.

Follow the guidelines given in the section "Changing headers or footers in mid-document." The window that asks you to confirm that you want to insert a manual page break includes a check box labeled "Change page number"; if you check this box, a page number appears in the small box beneath. You can type in a new number or press the arrow buttons to increase or decrease the number. See Figure 7-26, where the spinner is located below the Style drop-down menu.

Mirrored (odd and even) page formats

Mirrored page formatting is also known as right- and left-page formatting, or odd- and even-page formatting. It is used for two-sided printing in printed books such as this one, or other bound documents. The mirrored page format is also useful for any long document that will be printed on a two-sided or duplex printer. To print in duplex mode, see the section, "Advanced Printing," later in this chapter.

This formatting technique employs different Page Styles that alternate on the left and right page so that page numbers are located at the outer edge of the pages. Often, other information such as chapter and book title are also moved from one side of the header or footer to the other, to achieve a mirrored effect.

Creating a work in the mirrored page format requires adding two new Custom Styles, described in "Adding new styles (or creating styles)." We'll repeat the directions here, customizing them for mirrored pages.

1. Call up the Style Catalog by pressing Ctrl-F11. Set the style type drop-down menu at the top to Page Styles and the mode drop-down menu at the bottom to Custom Style, as shown in Figure 7-27.

2. Click the New… button in the window at the right. This calls up the Page Style settings window, shown in Figure 7-28, where you should enter a name for the new style, such as "Mirrored Left Page."

3. Click over to the Page tab. In the Layout settings section under Page layout, select Mirrored. Over at the left, set Margins, Inner to about two inches. (See Figure 7-29.)

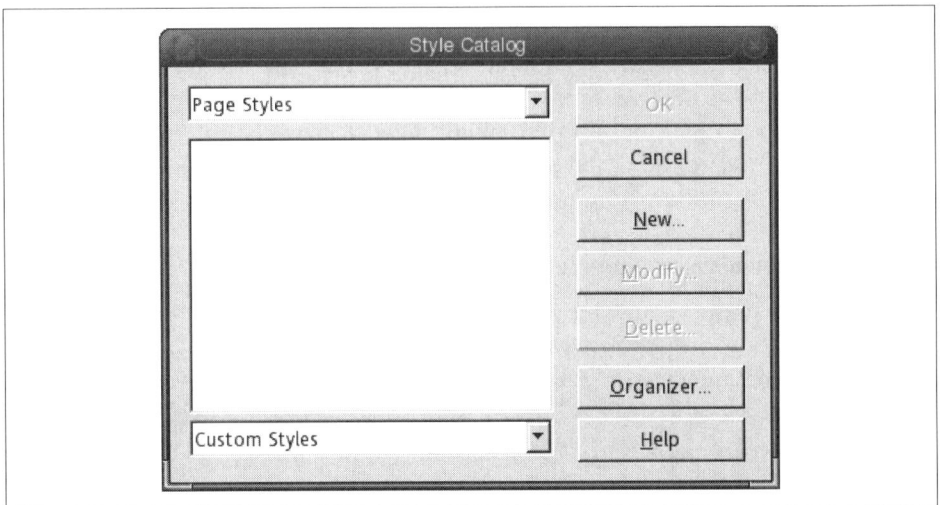

Figure 7-27. Style Catalog: adding a new page style

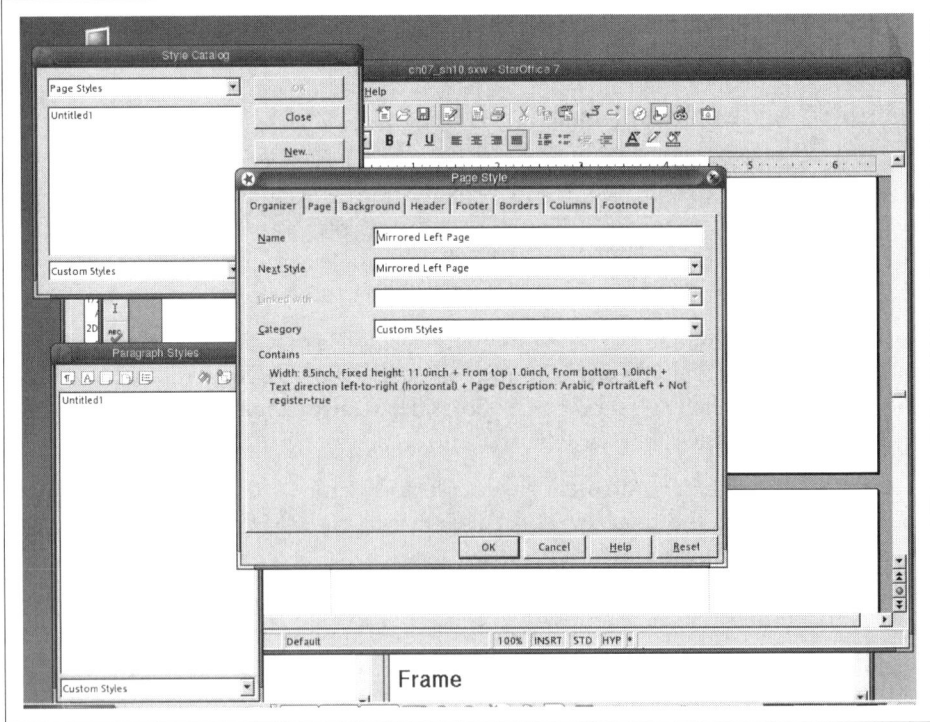

Figure 7-28. The Page Style settings window

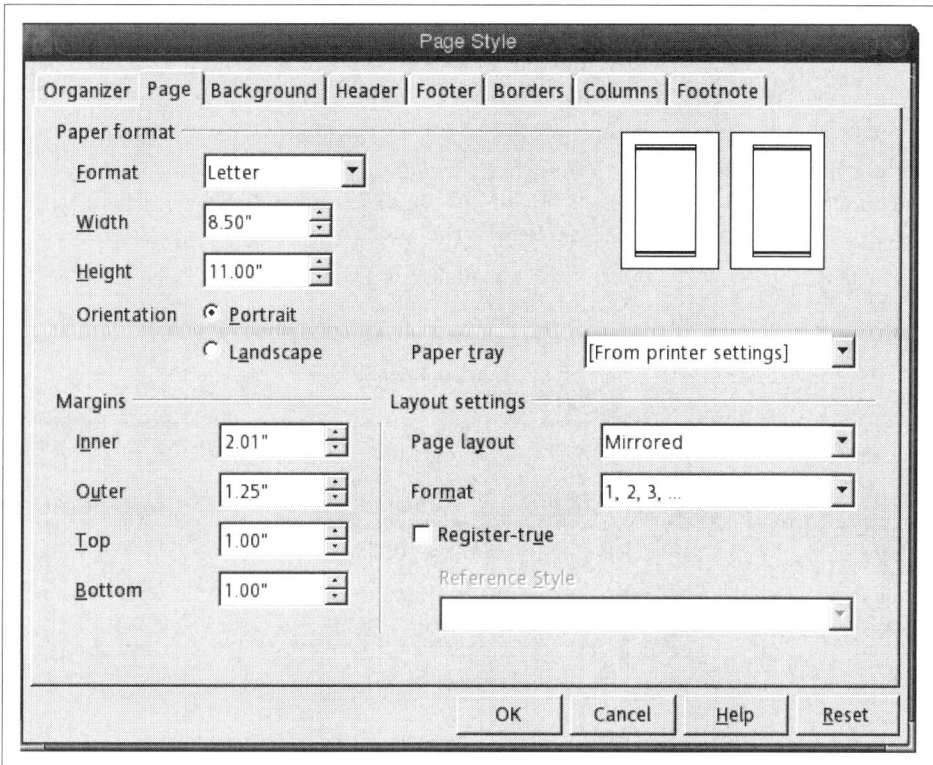

Figure 7-29. The Page Style, Page tab

4. Click over to the Header tab and check the box to turn on headers. Uncheck the box labeled "Same content left/right."

5. Click over to the Footer tab and check the box to turn on footers. Uncheck the box labeled "Same content left/right." Click OK to close the Page Style settings window.

6. Repeat the procedures just described to create a new style called "Mirrored Right Page."

Having established these two new styles, go back to the Style Catalog and modify both styles to ensure that the Next Style box in each one is set to the other. For example, in the custom style called "Mirrored Right Page," the Next Style drop-down menu should read, "Mirrored Left Page"; and in the custom style called "Mirrored Left Page," the Next Style drop-down menu should read, "Mirrored Right Page." See Figure 7-30, which shows sample Style settings for the Mirrored Right Page style.

Duplex Printing Makes Sense

Duplex page formatting is used in documents to exploit printers that support duplex (two-sided) printing. This saves paper!

Duplex printing is a good habit, especially for school administrators to encourage in their teachers and students. Such eco-friendly and cost-efficient behavior goes a long way and will migrate into the workplace as the students grow up.

You can print in duplex mode manually, incurring some headaches, or do it with an extra printer attachment called an automatic duplexer.

While you may demur at the up-front cost of a duplexer, the paper-savings justify the habit over the long life of a workgroup-quality laser printer.

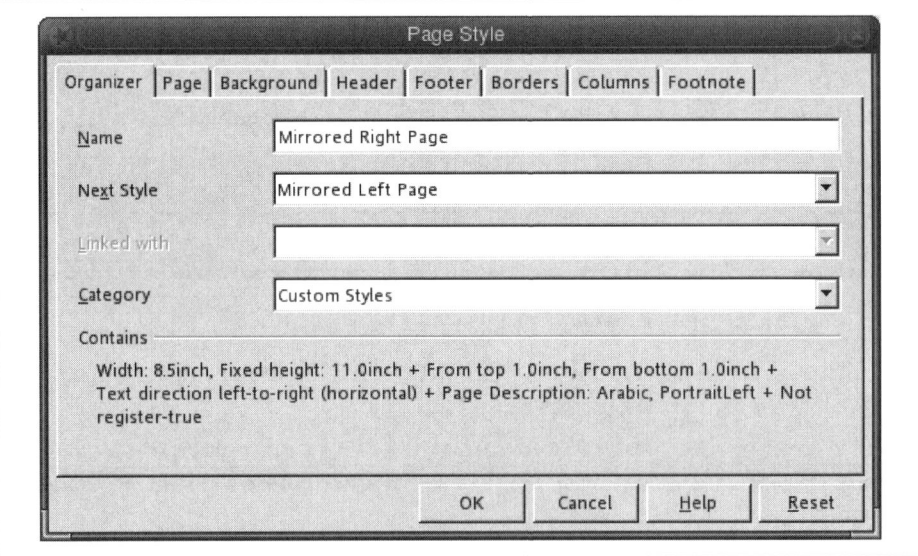

Figure 7-30. Designating the Next Style

Load (transfer) styles

You can transfer styles into the current document from another document or template by selecting Format → Styles → Load…. from the Main menu. This calls up the Load Styles window, shown in Figure 7-31. Here you can specify a file containing the styles you want, and load any or all of these styles by checking the desired boxes along the bottom of the window.

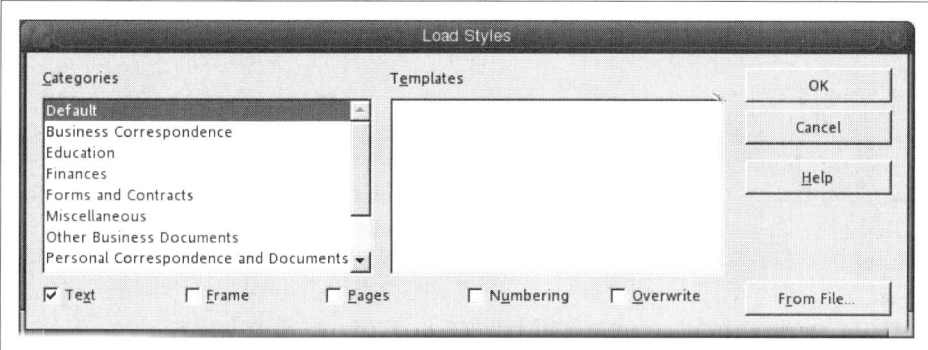

Figure 7-31. The Load Styles window

Templates

A variety of stock templates and a facility for creating, editing, importing, and managing templates are included with StarWriter. You can access templates by clicking StarOffice 7 on the Launch menu to open the Templates and Documents window. Then highlight the Templates icon on the left-side index, as shown in Figure 7-32.

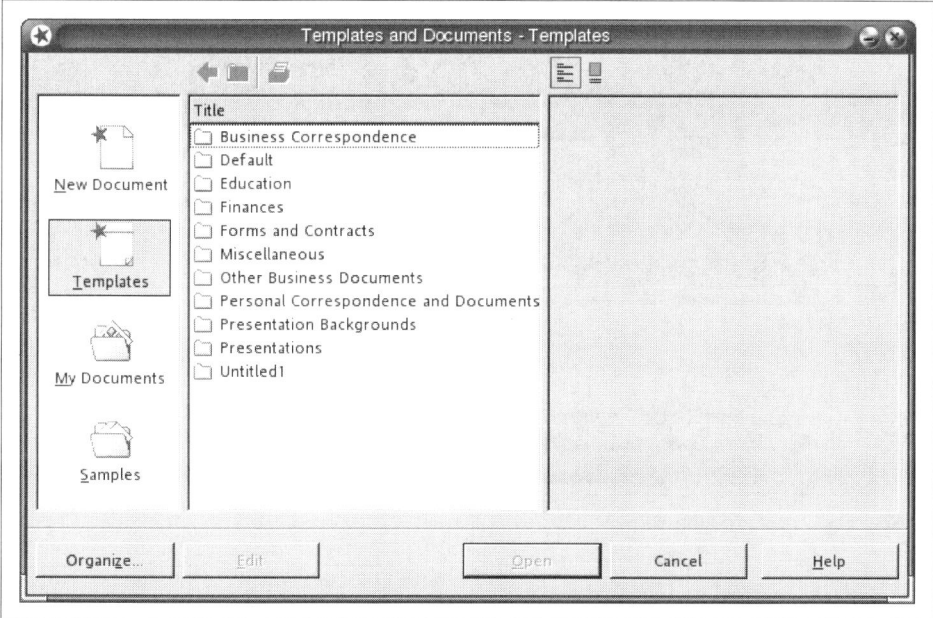

Figure 7-32. Templates and Documents - Templates window

Here, you can open one of the various stock templates and work away: edit and save it just as you would a normal document. Documents created this way, however, are linked to the template file from which they were derived. See "Template linkages" for further details.

Saving your own document as a template

Any of the documents you've created in your file system can perform as a template. Quite often users repurpose old files such as office memoranda, fax cover sheets, or business letters, and use them to create new documents by simply replacing a few key words. This practice is fine and works well for many people; however, users could be more productive if they took full advantage of StarWriter's template management facilities and particularly its linkage abilities further below.

Creating a new template

To create a new template, open a new text document (or use an existing document from your file store) and make the necessary formatting adjustments that you'd like to have in your template. Now, select File → Templates → Save... from the Main menu. This calls up the Templates window, shown in Figure 7-33, which permits you to name the new template and select a template folder or Category in which to store it. You can create any number of your own personal templates and store them this way.

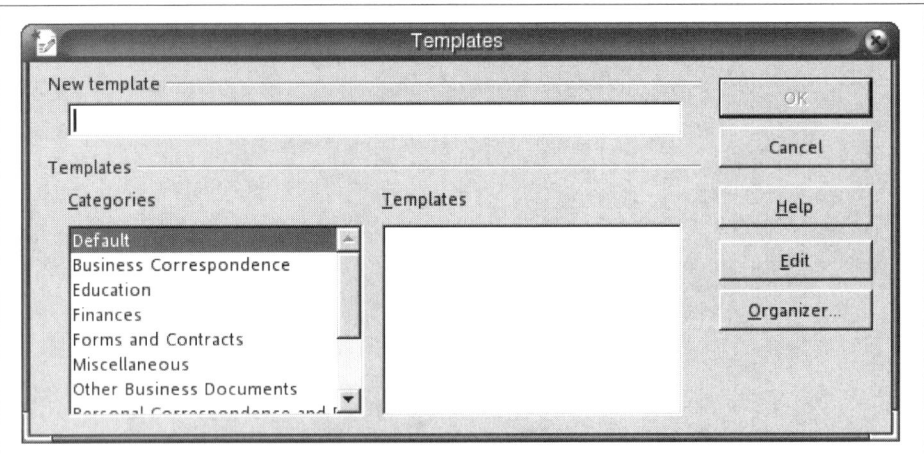

Figure 7-33. The Templates window

Files saved as templates this way automatically have the *.stw* file extension appended.

Editing templates

You can edit or generally treat a template file just like any other; however, we recommend editing a template with special care, since it can be easy to open a template file and then save it by mistake as a normal StarWriter *.sxw* file—which would interfere with the templates linkages and storage location.

One direct way to edit a template is to select Launch → StarOffice 7 from the Launch menu. This opens up the Templates and Documents window directly in the Default folder. Click around the Templates folders to find the template you want to edit. Click once to highlight it. This lights up the Edit button at the bottom of the window, second from the left. Clicking the Edit button opens your template, ready for edits. When you save via this route, the proper directory path and file format appear automatically in the Save dialog, so there's less opportunity to mishandle your template inadvertently.

Managing templates

You can also save any of your own documents as a template or, later, move them into one of the Templates folders/categories using the Template Manager. Access the Template Manager from the Main menu by selecting File → Templates → Organize…. (See Figure 7-34.)

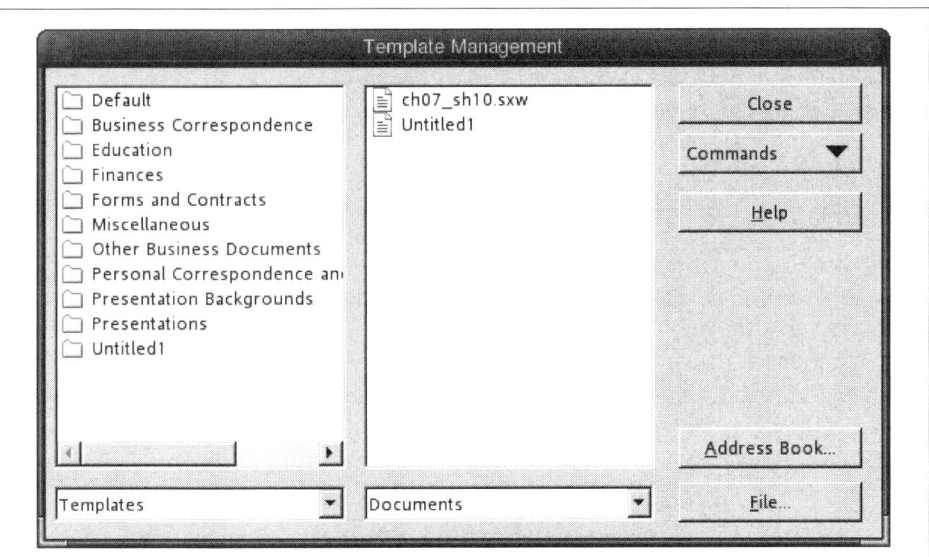

Figure 7-34. The Template Management window

You can browse documents in the righthand pane of the Template Manager and drop them into folders in the templates pane on the left.

Template Manager also offers facilities for importing, updating, and adjusting printer settings associated with templates.

Importing Templates

The template files you encounter in the Template Management window's Default folder are actually stored in */home/swhiser/staroffice7/user/template* directory on the system. The templates you encounter in all the other Template Management folders are actually stored in the */home/swhiser/staroffice7/share/template/english* directory. (This allows individual users in a multi-user installation of StarOffice to change their own default master templates without affecting the same change for all other users on the network.)

To import template files from MS Word or from any trusted outside sources (including useful ones you find on the Web), you could manually copy the templates into the respective directories above, and they will show up in the folders you expect in the Template Management window. Templates copied in this way are also available when you use the AutoPilot to create documents from templates.

You could also use the Import Templates feature in the Templates Management window to get external templates into the correct place and into the proper file format (*.stw*). This ensures that templates and the files derived from them maintain their linkages (see "Template linkages").

Additionally, a third way to import a template would be to select File → Save As, choose "StarOffice 6.0/7 Text Document Template (.stw)" as the File Type, and set the path to the appropriate one of the two directories, mentioned above.

Template linkages

Template files are linked to documents derived from those templates. When you have a large number of documents in your file system that were created from a certain template (call them "subdocuments"), you can update the formatting of all subdocuments in one stroke by altering the Styles or general formatting of the source template file. Then, each time you open one of the subdocuments, you are prompted to accept or reject the formatting alterations that were made to the source template, as illustrated in Figure 7-35.

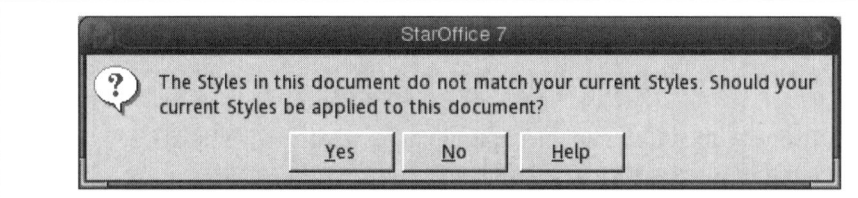

Figure 7-35. Okay the format changes to a subdocument

Linkage is broken, however, if you later save the source template file via File → Save As or via the Save icon on the Object bar; so you should always save a template file via File → Templates → Save… if you want it to remain linked to its subdocuments or to keep using it as a template.

Change the default template for all new text documents

As mentioned earlier, the standard blank document that opens up when you select File → New → Text Document from the Main menu is based on a default template file that is saved in the Templates and Documents - New Document window. (See Figure 7-36.)

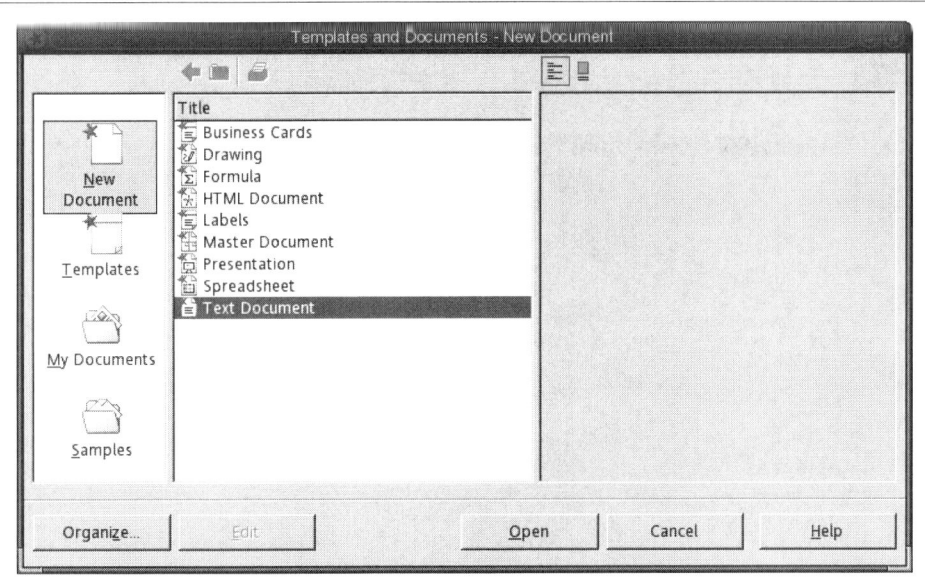

Figure 7-36. Templates and Documents - New Document window

To change the default template for all new text documents, first create a new template with the desired formatting (and add custom styles, if desired), as described earlier in "Creating a New Template." Save it by selecting File → Templates → Save… (Figure 7-33), enter the filename (let's call it *newdefault*), and click once on Default in the Categories pane at the left to save it in that folder.

Then, go into the Template Management window by selecting File → Templates → Organize… and double click in the left pane to open up the Default folder, where you find your new template file, *newdefault*. Click once upon it to highlight *newdefault* and click on the Command button at the far right to view the drop-down choices. Select Set As Default Template at the bottom of the list.

To restore the original Text Document default template, simply click the Command button once again and select Reset Default Template → Text Document.

Autopilot: quick document creation

Autopilot is like Templates on steroids. It offers a way of creating customized documents that are much like templates, but it is a wizard that takes you through a few steps to customize the new document rapidly before launching it. Autopilot is, therefore, a useful tool for first-time users who wish to get up and running in StarWriter quickly.

Access Autopilot via File → Autopilot, where you see a drop-down list, as shown in Figure 7-37.

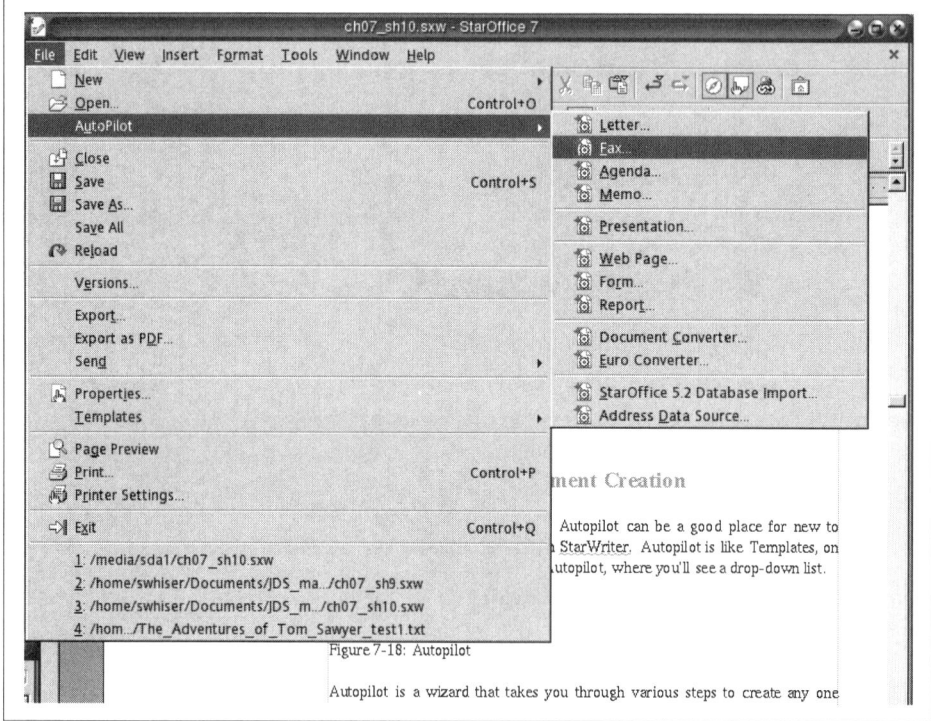

Figure 7-37. The Autopilot

Autopilot is a wizard that takes you through various steps to create an individual document from a generous list of different document types:

- Letter
- Fax
- Agenda
- Memo
- Presentation
- Web Page

- Form
- Report

The resulting documents may not come out perfectly suited to your taste, but they are a good way to get up and running in document creation quickly. (See Figure 7-38.)

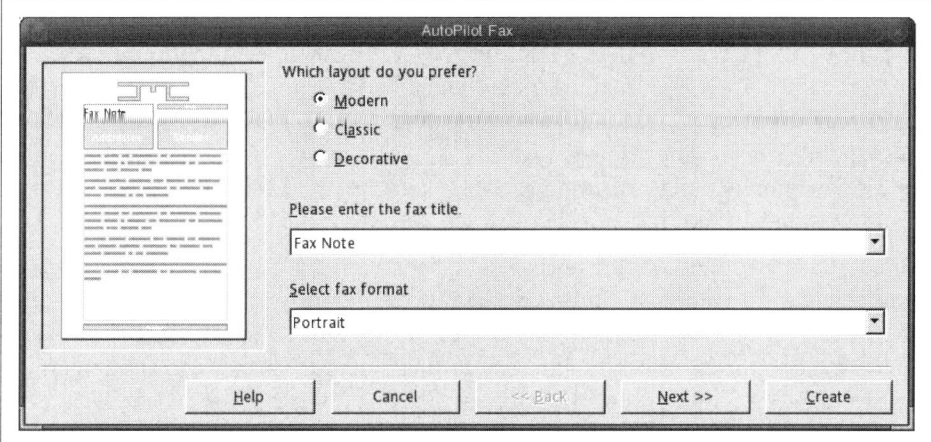

Figure 7-38. Creating a fax document with Autopilot

Autopilot also contains several different utilities for converting documents and currency figures within documents, as well as importing old StarOffice (5.2) database files and address book contact information.

Master Documents

A master document is helpful for creating large chapter works. It is a lightweight and small document, similar to a stand-alone table of contents. Rather than containing the text of a complete work, a master document contains merely links to the separate chapter files where the text actually resides. This makes editing and generally moving around and manipulating a master document a quick and snappy experience because the system never maintains a whole, large bulk of (mostly unused) data in computer memory.

There are two different ways to create a master document. One way is to create all the subdocuments first, create the master document, and then link the subdocuments to it. The trick to this method is to use the *same template* when you create all the subdocuments. The alternative way is to generate a master document and subdocuments from an existing document.

 Using subdocuments with different templates or styles will result in a mess!

To use the first method, create your subdocuments as usual from a uniform template. Then create the master by selecting File → New → Master Document. This opens a new master document template, as well as the Navigator, which pops open onto the desktop. You will notice that the master document's toolbar is a little different from usual. To hook up your first subdocument, go to the Navigator and select Insert → File (the Insert button is fourth from left on the Navigator's toolbar). This calls up the Insert window, which allows you to browse your filesystem for the appropriate subdocument. Click once on the chosen file, then click Insert. Repeat the process for each additional subdocument you want to add to the master.

To use the second method, make sure your document has a Heading 1 paragraph to mark where each chapter should start; the process described here breaks up the document at these Heading 1 paragraphs and turns them into separate chapters in separate files. Go to the document you intend to break up into master and subdocuments and select File → Send → Master Document. This opens a window called "Name and Path of Master Document," where you should enter the name and choose the folder to hold your new master document and the subdocuments that will be generated.

In the example shown in Figure 7-39, Mark Twain's *The Adventures of Tom Sawyer* (a free eText downloaded off the Internet and formatted) has been exported to create a master document and many subchapter files. You can see in the Navigator, at the left, that each subchapter appears as a separate file. The name of the new master document was named by the user (*TS1_MD.sxg*) and can be seen at the top center of the StarWriter window above the Main menu. And all the subdocuments are accordingly named *TS1_MD1.sxw* through *TS1_MD28.sxw*.

 Beware that complex formatting in the original document may be lost in the resulting master and subdocuments. The tools described in this section are best applied to documents with simple, consistent formatting.

Collaboration with Documents

When several people create and edit a document together, by passing the draft around, it becomes useful to turn on changes tracking. This allows each person's changes and deletions to appear in a different color, while the document circulates for drafting.

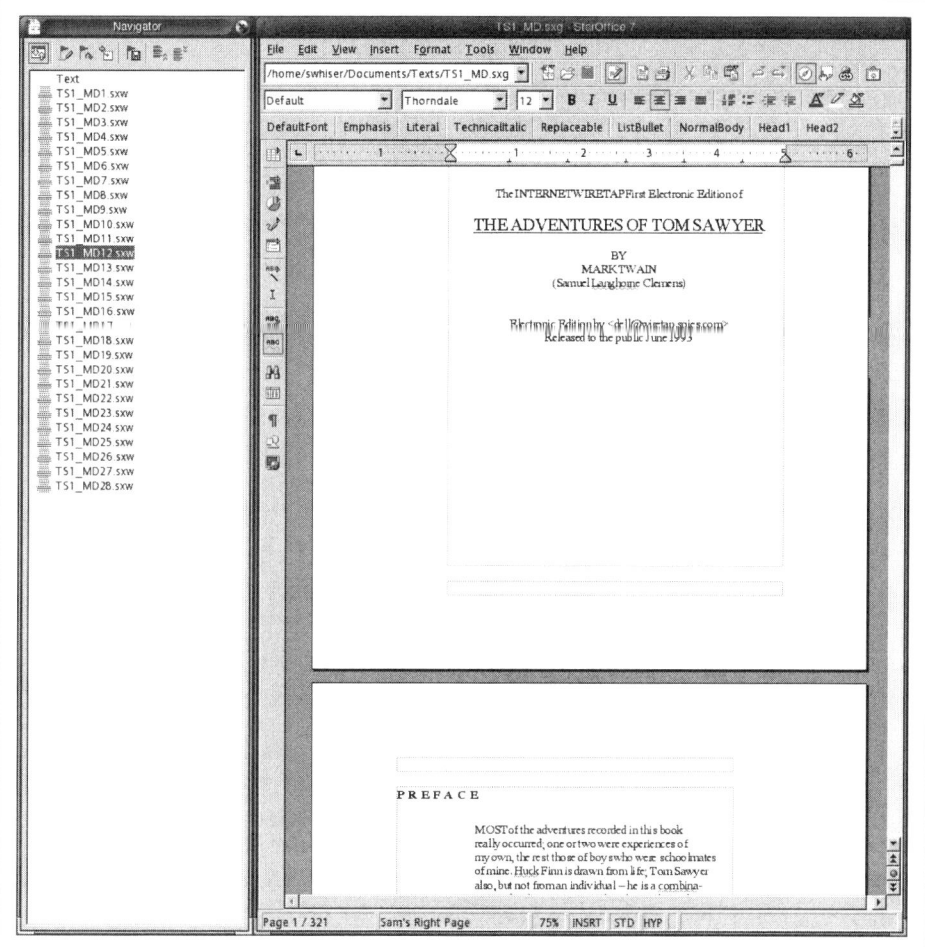

Figure 7-39. "Tom Sawyer": master document with subchapters.

Changes Tracking

To turn on Changes Tracking, select Edit → Changes from the Main menu and single-click both Record and Show. Once turned on, these settings "travel" with the document when it is saved, and stays on until someone unchecks them and saves the document again.

Advancing Collaboration

Changes tracking (a.k.a. "red-lining") is a useful wordprocessing feature, but it does not solve collaboration problems as robustly as software designed to support multiple, simultaneous edits. Systems that permit stronger forms of collaboration include the Wiki (a system for letting people update web pages simultaneously), version control systems (which keep track of all changes over the life of documents, and allow multiple versions to exist simultaneously), and whiteboards or similar multiuser systems.

By contrast, projects that depend on changes tracking in wordprocessors require a leader who assigns the document to different people in order, and some form of numbering in the title of a document (*sales_report_kate_01*, *sales_report_joe_02*, and so on). To see how you can benefit from using a form of version control provided by Star-Writer, see the section "Version control."

Comparing documents

To compare two different documents, open the first document and select Edit → Compare Document.... This opens the Insert dialog, where you can select or type in the name of the second document. Click the Insert button at the bottom right of the window. The insert procedure merges the two documents and shows the results, using the changes tracking feature, as if you had started with the second document and edited it to create the first. Typical results are shown in Figure 7-40.

Version control

StarWriter's version control features allow you to keep track of numerous versions of a document from within a single file. This both saves disk storage space and provides ready and quick access to older versions of a document. Thus, if you make edits that you later regret, you can back them out. If somebody asks when a change was made, you can review earlier versions of the document.

Version control is accessed via the Main menu under File → Versions.... This launches the versions window. See Figure 7-41.

To save a new version of a document in which you're working, choose File → Versions... from the Main menu and click the Save New Version button at the top left in the versions window. The Insert Version Comment window (Figure 7-42) pops up, permitting you to enter a few phrases to remind yourself and your collaborators later what changes you made and why. Documenting what you've done here lets you also distinguish versions later, without having to open each one.

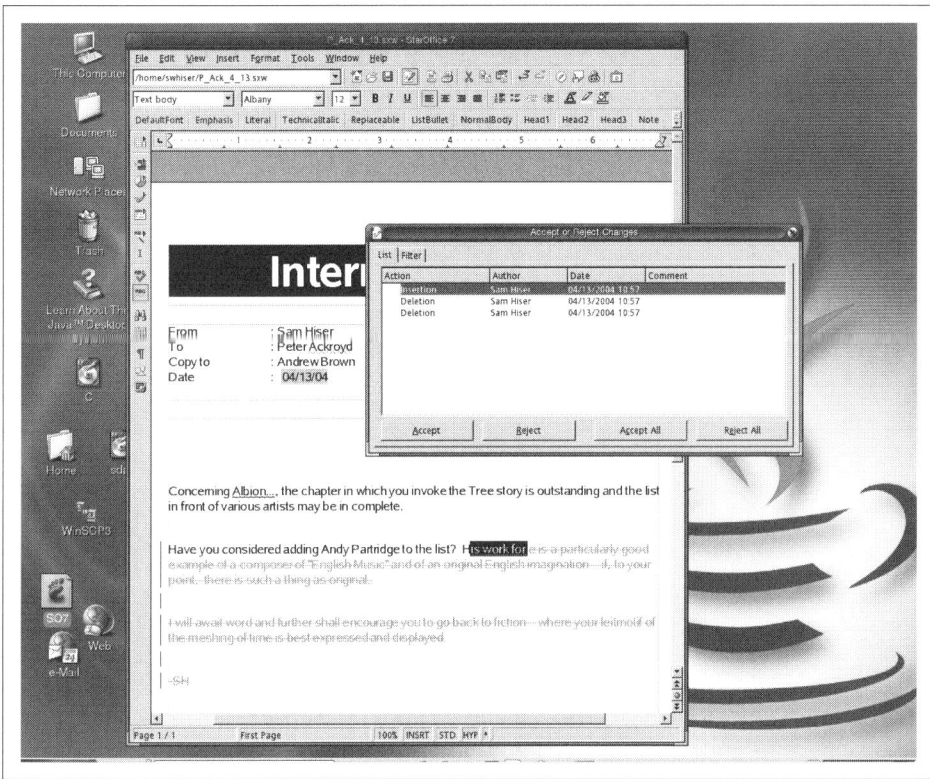

Figure 7-40. Differences display as red-lined content

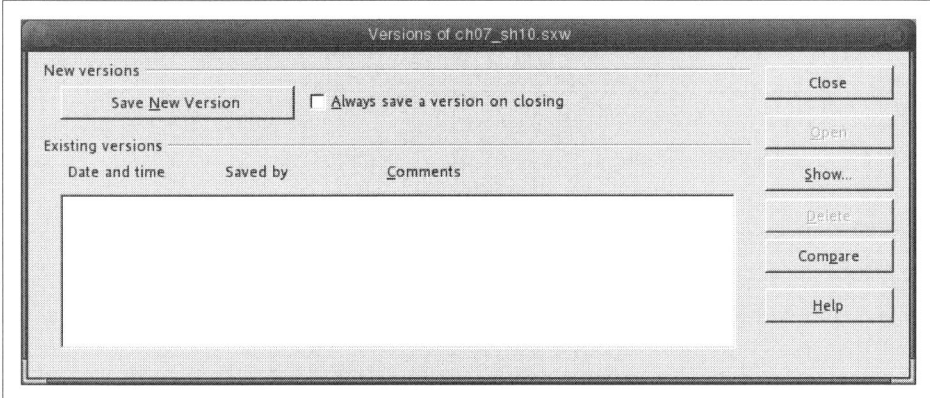

Figure 7-41. The Versions window

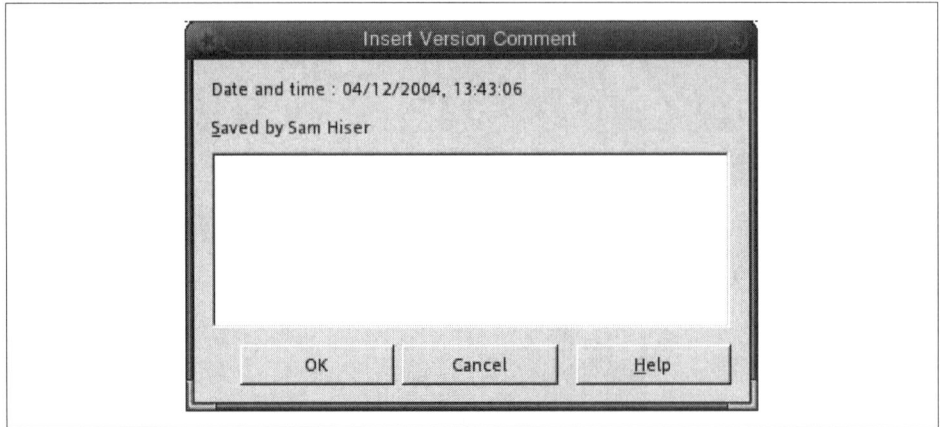

Figure 7-42. The Insert Version Comment window

 If you use File → Save As... to save a version in which you are work-ing, none of the version information is preserved; you have instead cre-ated a spanking new document. You could, of course, start again with this new document as a base, and use version control once again for future changes.

To open a specific version of a document listed in the versions window, choose File → Versions…, highlight the desired version, and click the Open button. This opens the respective version of the document as a *read-only* file. You can, if you wish, save this version as a separate document, with no reference to other versions, past or future, by using the File → Save As… menu option.

To track and show changes from one version to another, click the Compare button in the versions window. This highlights all version differences (just as when using the Edit → Compare Document feature) in a document and gives you the chance to accept and reject each change.

Navigator

The Navigator is a floating panel, like the Stylist, that adds horse-power to your movements within a document. The Navigator is turned on or invoked by clicking the Navigator button on the Main menu, just to the left of the Stylist button, or by pressing the function key F5.

Figure 7-43 shows the Navigator with the major categories, Headings, Tables, and Text frame collapsed. If you click on the plus sign in front of any of those categories, such as Headings, all headings within your current document are revealed, like in Figure 7-44.

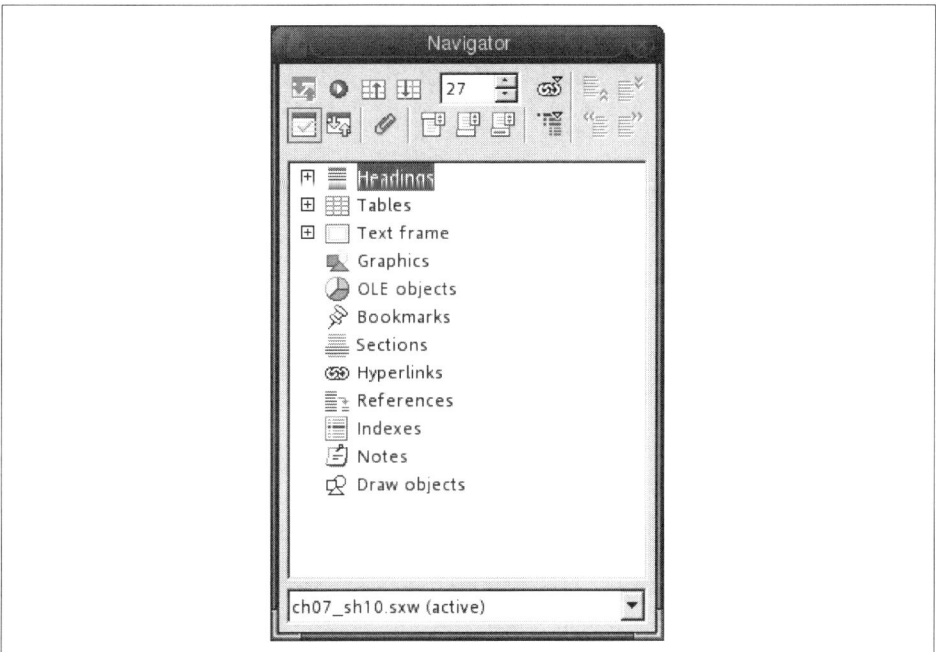

Figure 7-43. The Navigator, collapsed view

In addition to Headings, Tables, and Text Frames, Navigator displays and a variety of different object types in its panel, allowing you to move quickly among sections and types of elements in a document.

Keyboard Shortcuts

Table 7-5 lists the most common keyboard shortcuts that users find valuable for speeding up document composition. The shortcuts are faster than using mouse and drop-down menus because the keystrokes allow you to keep both hands on the keyboard. Some people in danger of developing Repetitive Stress Syndrome through excessive use of the mouse can find these shortcuts of particular value.

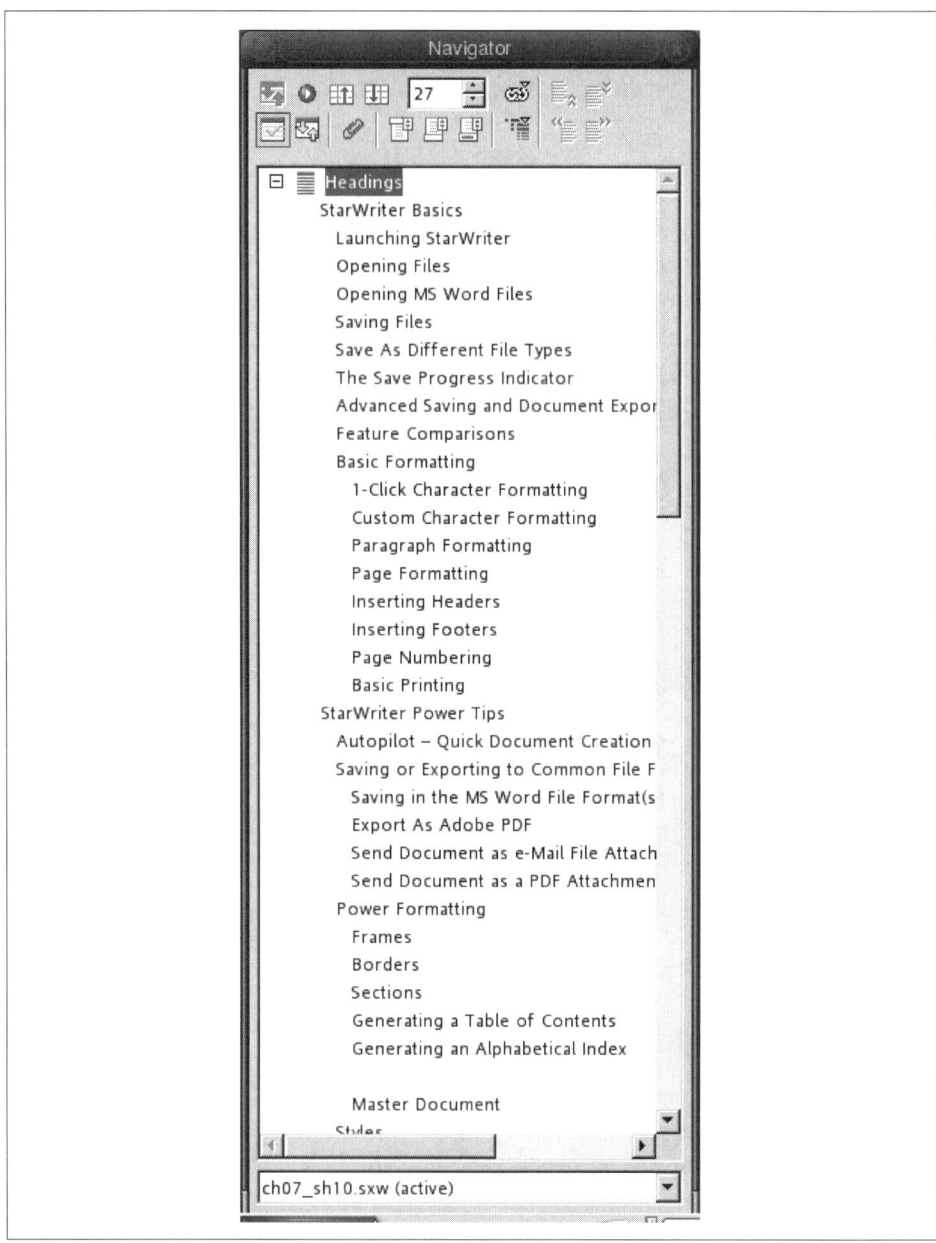

Figure 7-44. The Navigator with Headings exploded

Table 7-5. Common keystrokes to avoid the mouse

Function	Keystrokes
Copy text	Ctrl-C
Cut text	Ctrl-X
Paste text	Ctrl-V
Bold text	Ctrl-B
Italic text	Ctrl-I
Underline text	Ctrl-U

Function key defaults

Table 7-6 is a chart that may be useful to users who take full advantage of the function keys in MS Office and need to reacclimate to the slightly different default function key mappings in StarOffice.

Table 7-6. Function key defaults by comparison

Key	MS Word2000	StarOffice 7
F1	Help	Help
F2	Move text or graphics	Formula bar
F3	Insert Autotext	Run AutoText entry
F4	Repeat last action	Data Sources
F5	Choose Go To command	Navigator Pane on/off
F6	Go To next pane of frame	Toggle to next Toolbar or Pane
F7	Choose the Spelling command	Spellcheck
F8	Extend a selection	Extended selection on
F9	Update selected fields	Update fields
F10	Activate the Menu Bar	To Menu Bar
F11	Go To next field	Stylist Pane on/off
F12	Choose Save As command	Numbering on/off

Custom keyboard mappings

The function key mappings reflected in Table 7-5 are merely default settings. Users and system administrators are free to change them to reflect their personal or organizational taste or habit by selecting Tools → Configure... → Keyboard. (See Figure 7-45.) Adjustments to the function key defaults can be helpful in the desktop migration process.

There are well more than 12 functions that can be mapped to the 12 F-keys. To Microsoft's credit—or reflecting their well-documented obsession with features—

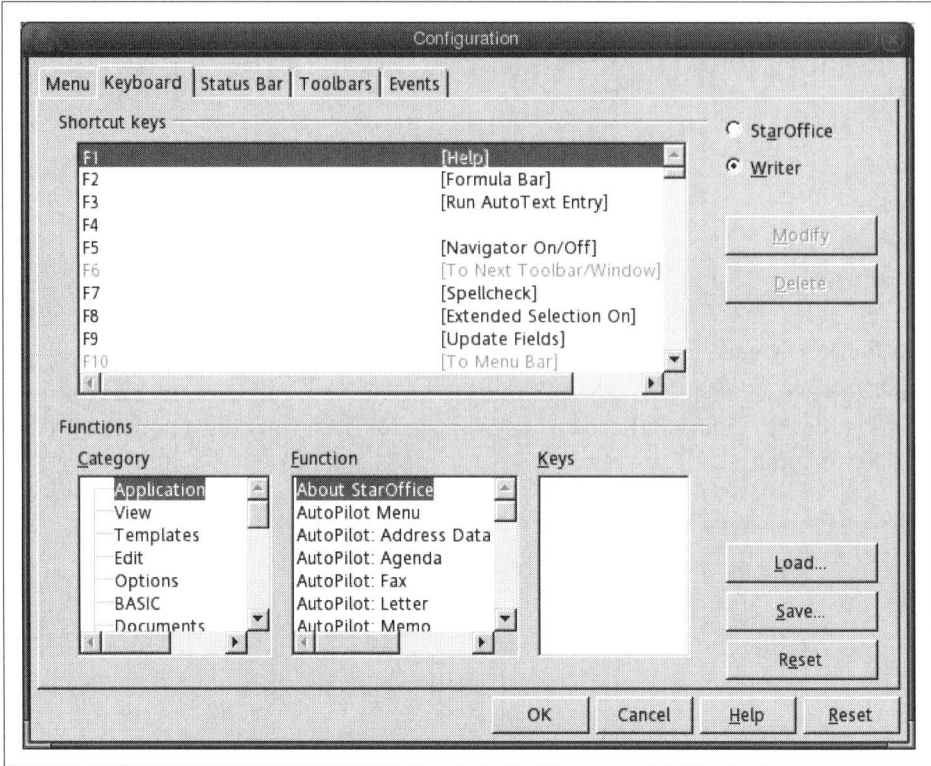

Figure 7-45. Configuration window, Keyboard tab

MS Office 2000, as one example, provides a total of seven different modes for its function key associations. Their modes include:

- F[1–12]
- Shift + F[1–12]
- Ctrl + F[1–12]
- Ctrl + Shift + F[1–12]
- Ctrl + Alt + F[1–12]
- Alt + F[1–12]
- Alt + Shift + F[1–12]

StarOffice offers four modes—F[1–12], SHIFT + F[1–12], Ctrl + F[1–12], and SHIFT + Ctrl + F[1–12]—which is still overkill for most users, and yet leaves many openings for custom keyboard mappings that can aid speed and productivity.

To alter your default keyboard mappings, select Tools → Configure… and click on the Keyboard tab in the Configuration dialog. (See Figure 7-45.) Here, in the Short-cut keys pane, select the function key whose mapping you want to change. Next, select a Category and Function from those respective panes in the lower half of the Configuration dialog and click the Modify button. This effectively remaps the function performed by the function key you selected. Repeat the procedure for as many function keys, as desired.

In the upper-right corner of the Configuration dialog, note the two radio buttons, one for StarOffice and the other for StarWriter. The latter one is selected by default. If you want to alter keyboard mappings for all modules of StarOffice and not just for StarWriter, click once on the StarOffice radio button and follow the procedure above.

Searching Documents: Find & Replace

To find and replace characters in a document, press Ctrl+F to open the Find & Replace dialog. Alternatively, you can access the dialog from the Main menu by selecting Edit → Find & Replace…. (See Figure 7-46.)

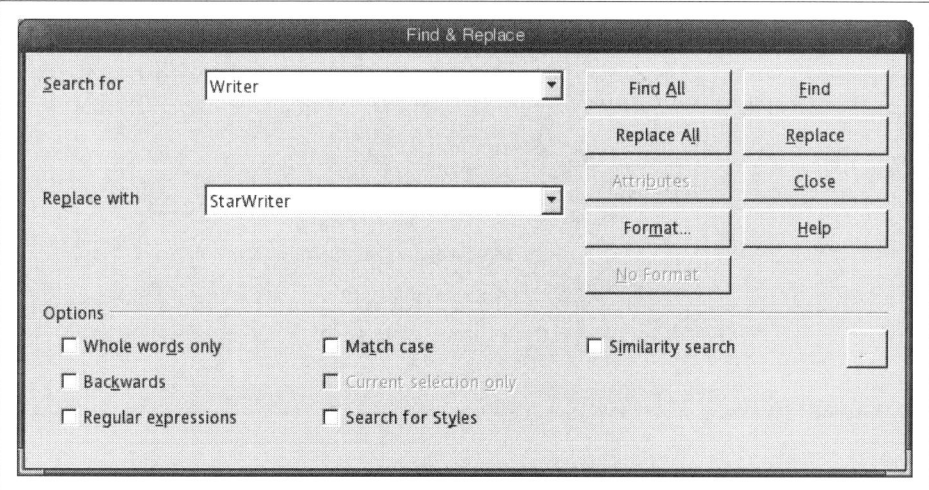

Figure 7-46. The Find & Replace window

Enter the term you're searching for in the "Search for" field (top left). If you want to change it, enter the term you'd like to replace it with in the "Replace with" field. Proceed by pressing the Find button at the top right of the window, and the search locates the term you're searching for in the nearest location in the document, after the placement of the cursor.

Continue by pressing the Replace button, wherever appropriate. If you come to a term that you don't want to replace, just press the Find button again to advance to the next example of the search term.

It may be a good idea to place the cursor at the beginning of the document before commencing Find & Replace. You can also go from the current point to the end of the document and let the search process start over from the beginning of the document when you are prompted to do so.

Insert Hyperlinks

Inserting hyperlinks—references to URLs on the Web—into documents has become essential. To insert a link, choose Insert → Hyperlink from the Main menu. This invokes the Hyperlink window, where you can enter the name of the link (complete with http://) in the Target field and the text for the link in the document in the Text field, second from the bottom of the window. Other options are also offered, as shown in Figure 7-47.

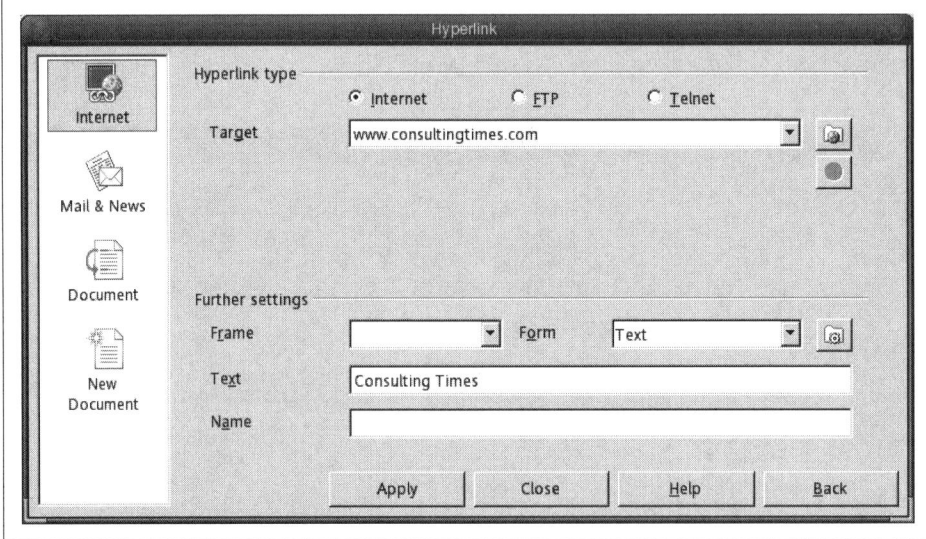

Figure 7-47. Inserting a hyperlink

Click the Apply button at the left of the series of buttons across the bottom of the window, and your text will appear highlighted and clickable in your document. Test the link to see that it was spelled, punctuated, and typed correctly. If it is correct, clicking on the link in your document wakes up your browser with the target web page in it, and produce a little surge of joy in your heart.

Naming your hyperlinks is a good idea because that enables you to move quickly among them with the Navigator, where the link names are listed in outline form and clickable. (See the Hyperlinks item in Figure 7-43 for details.) To enter a name in the Hyperlink window, type a short, but descriptive, sequence in the Name field at bottom of the dialog before you click the Apply button.

Word Count

Journalists, authors, and editors depend on this feature for their daily bread, so they can be forgiven for their oft-reported anxiety at missing word count. In fact, word count is present in StarOffice and OpenOffice.org but in a mysterious location. The feature is located in MS Word under Tools → Word Count, but in StarWriter it must be sought under File → Properties → Statistics. (See the Feature Comparison chart, Table 7-3.)

Password-Protecting Documents

You can secure StarWriter documents from unwanted access by saving files with password protection turned on. When saving with File → Save As, simply check the "Save with password" box and enter and confirm your password when you are prompted to do so during the save. (See Figure 7-48.)

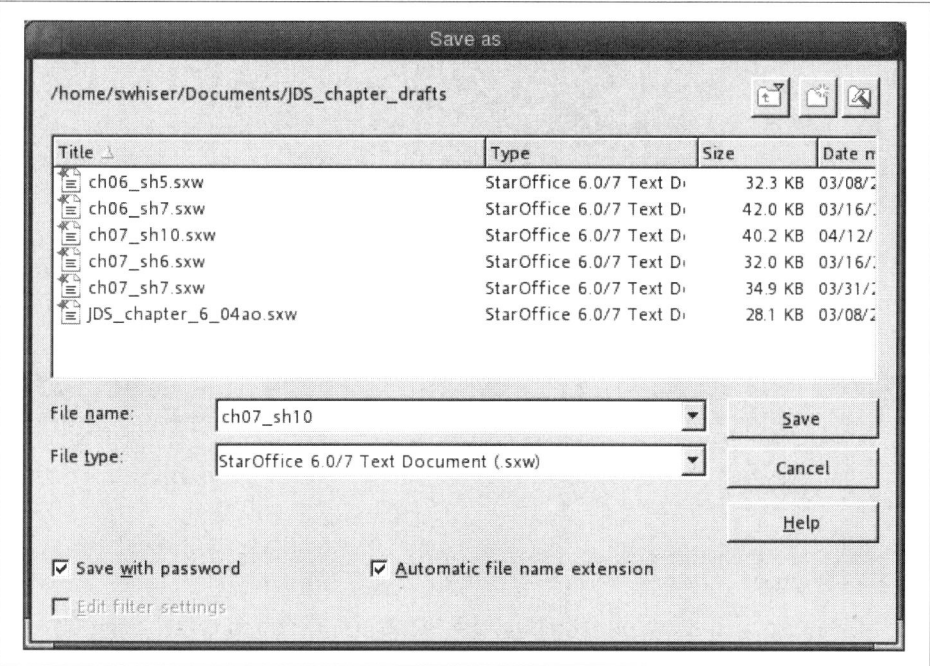

Figure 7-48. Password-protecting a whole document

To turn off whole document password protection at any time, simply choose File → Save As, uncheck the "Save with password" box, and complete the save.

StarWriter offers a variety of ways to protect your documents against alterations to Revision Markings, Sections, Frames, Graphics, Objects, Indexes, and Tables. Consult the system Help under "passwords: protecting content."

StarOffice Initial Setup

The first time you run StarOffice in JDS, you are prompted by the installation wizard to establish a few important settings used by the program. Rather than an installation, this is more like the final stages of user setup and should only take you a few minutes.

Launch StarOffice by selecting Launch → StarOffice 7 and the StarOffice Installation wizard begins. (See Figure 7-49.)

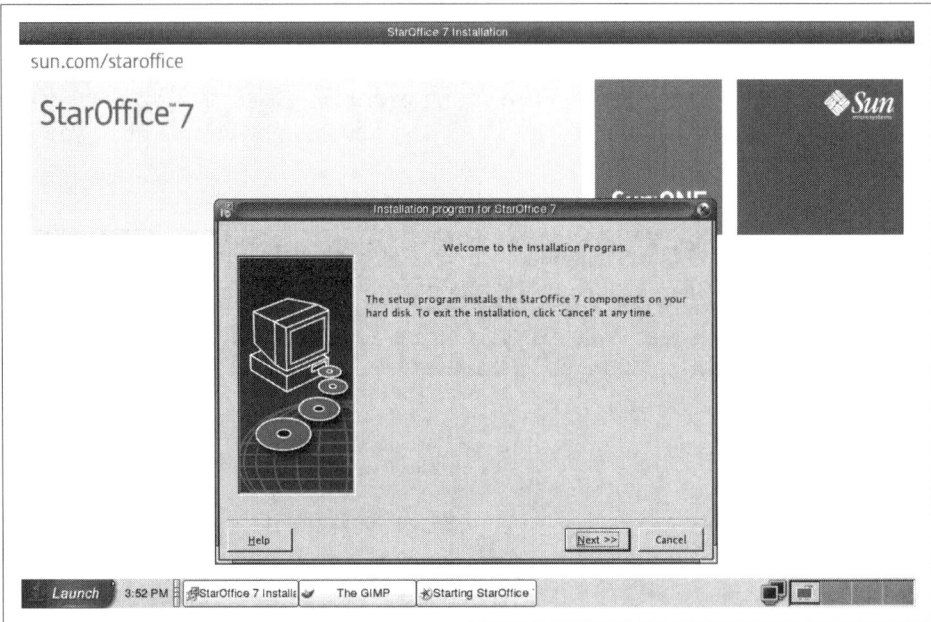

Figure 7-49. The Installation wizard begins

Click the Next button to show Figure 7-50.

"English US" is selected by default. Just click Next, unless you need to choose another language. This takes you to Figure 7-51.

This screen is much like a user-oriented README file. The screen has useful tips on a few items about migration, program features, and where to get further up-to-date information on StarOffice. Use the scrollbar at the right to skim through it. Click Next to advance. (See Figure 7-52.)

Read the terms of the license agreement, then scroll down all the way to the bottom of the license text, check the box labeled, "I accept the terms of the Agreement," and click Next.

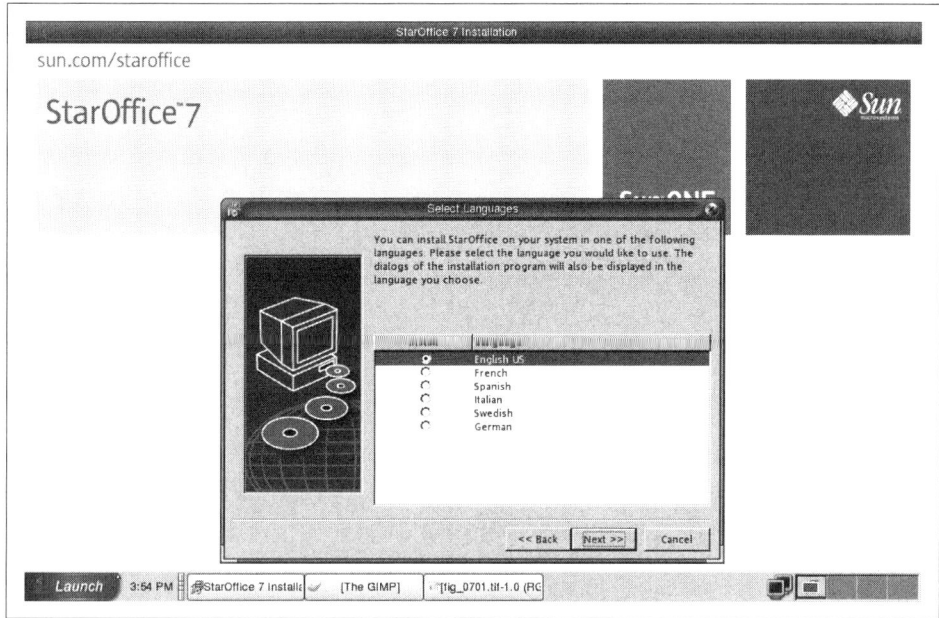

Figure 7-50. Select your language

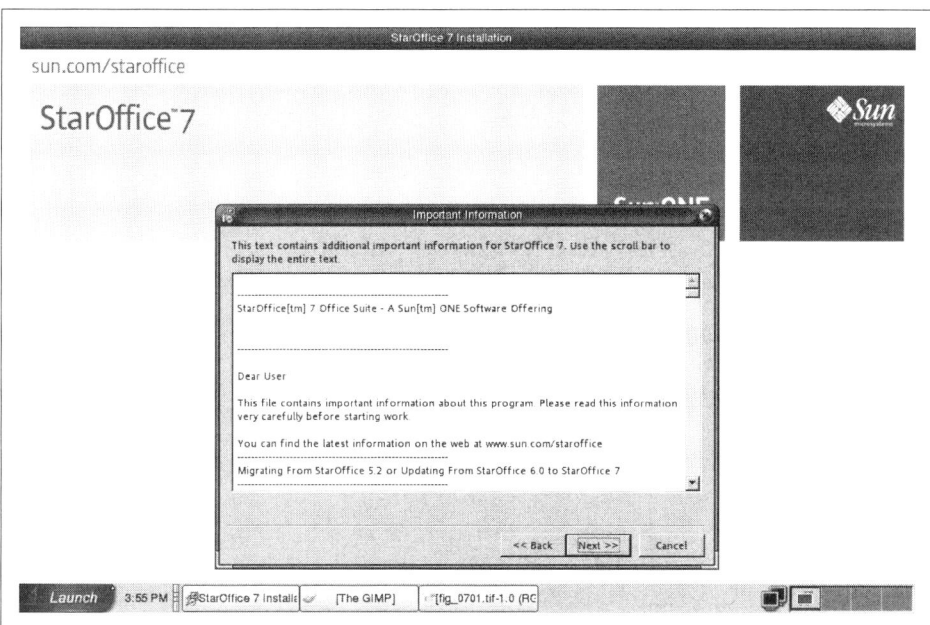

Figure 7-51. Important information

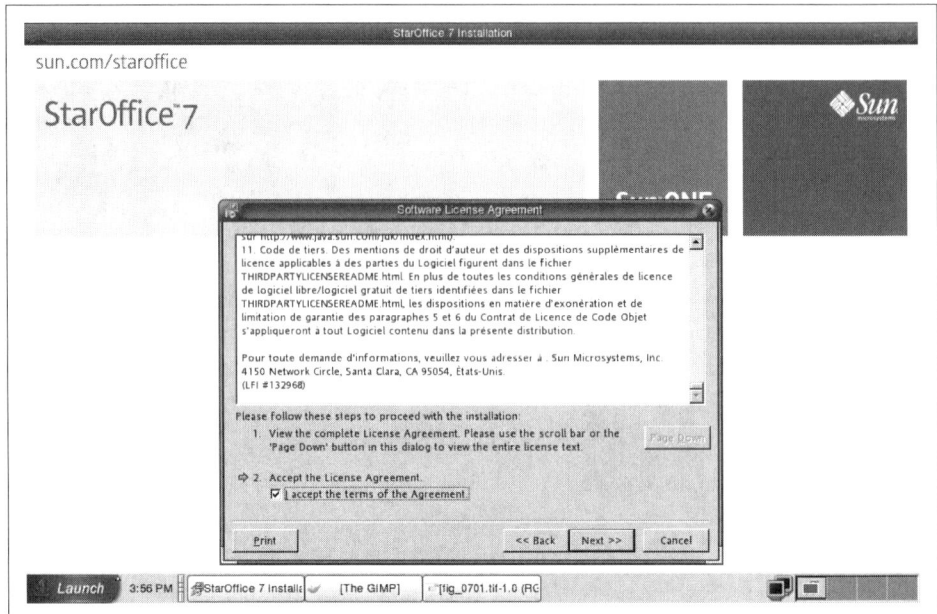

Figure 7-52. The StarOffice Software License Agreement

If you disagree with the terms of the licensing agreement, and you do not check the "I accept" box, you will not be able to complete the setup procedure. At this point, each time you launch StarOffice you will run through the setup wizard until you check the "I accept" box to complete the setup procedure.

Figure 7-53 shows the User Data form.

Enter your personal information in the form. Some people habitually skip over user data entry, leaving the fields blank on this screen. Before you do that, please note that the program uses some of this data from this form to perform certain functions.

StarOffice uses the First Name/Last Name/Initials fields, for example, in the changes tracking feature discussed earlier in this chapter. If you leave your user data blank here, your changes to a collaborative document will appear in the same color as the edits done by the most recent person to make changes. Enter your name here if you want changes tracking to give your edits a different color from those done by other editors of the same document.

In the next screen, Figure 7-54 the default "Workstation Installation" setting is appropriate for most users. (That's because StarOffice was already installed "locally" within the JDS environment when you completed the JDS installation.) Leave the setting where it is, at "Workstation Installation," and click Next for Figure 7-55.

You are strongly recommended to stick with the suggested default directory, */home/ [user]/staroffice7*. Click Next to show Figure 7-56.

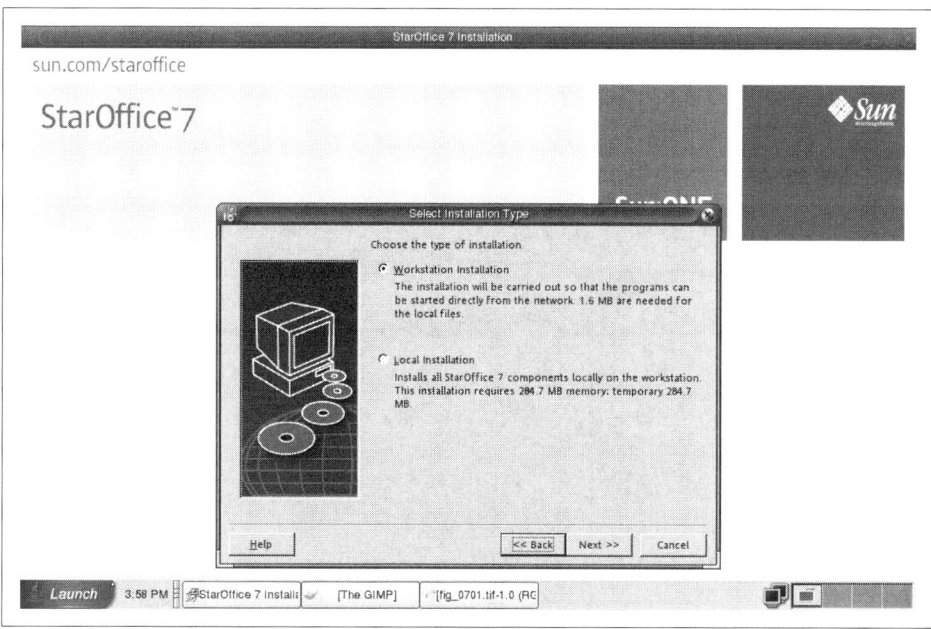

Figure 7-53. Enter User Data

Figure 7-54. Installation type

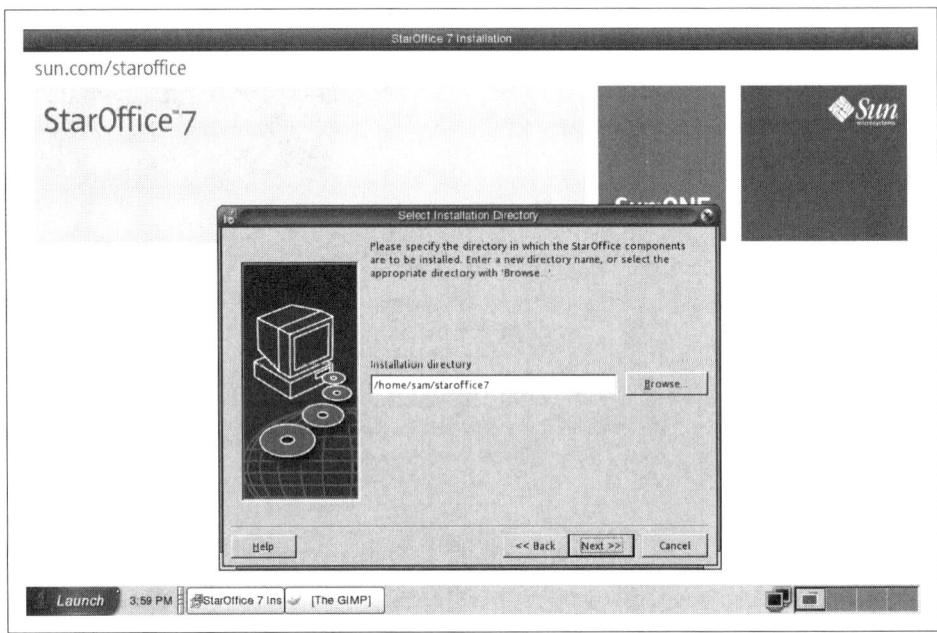

Figure 7-55. Installation directory

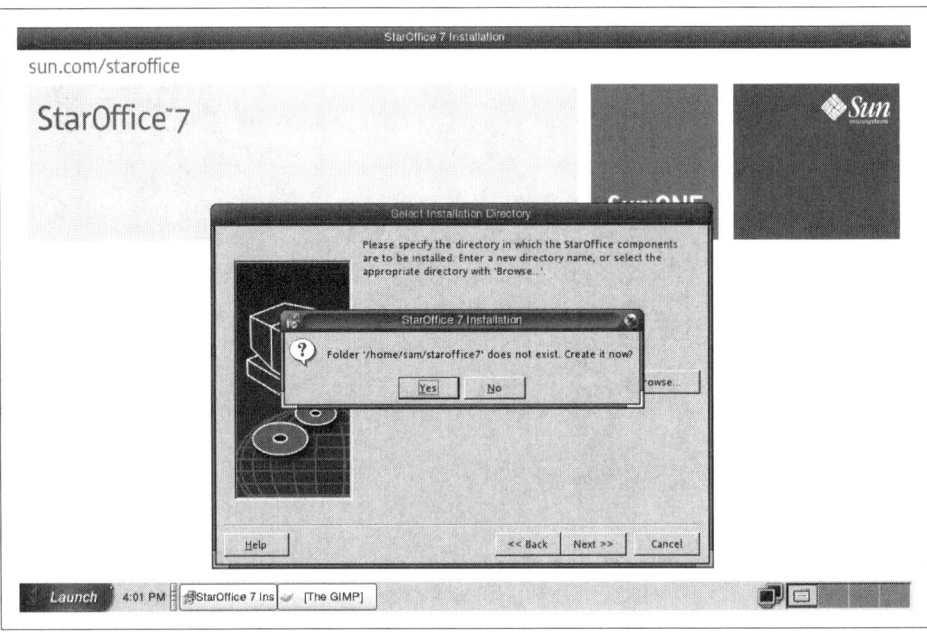

Figure 7-56. Create the directory

Click Yes to create the suggested installation directory and show Figure 7-57.

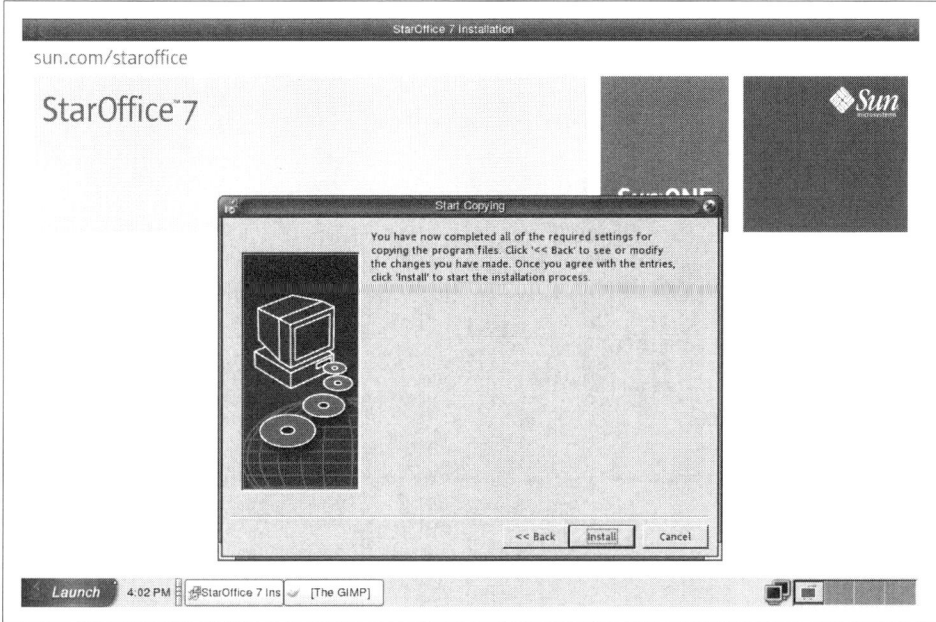

Figure 7-57. The Start Copying screen

Click Next to start the installation process, which ends by showing Figure 7-58.

Click Complete to finish the installation.

StarWriter Customizations

In an accident of convenience and relevance, we have already covered Customizing the Toolbars and Custom Keyboard Mappings.

In this section, we touch upon further ways you can customize StarWriter's settings and behavior to adapt it to the way you prefer to work. We show how to configure Launcher icons to make it faster to open the program. A substantial number of people report their displeasure at a few of the default settings, so we show you how to change certain unpopular defaults here, too.

StarOffice offers a daunting number of ways to customize settings. Many of these adjustments are simply uninteresting to most users, so we do not address them in this book. A quick browse of the five tabs under StarWriter's Tools → Configure… (Menu, Keyboard, Status bar, Toolbars, Events) would offer a good sense of the scope of StarWriter's customization possibilities for the advanced user or system administrator.

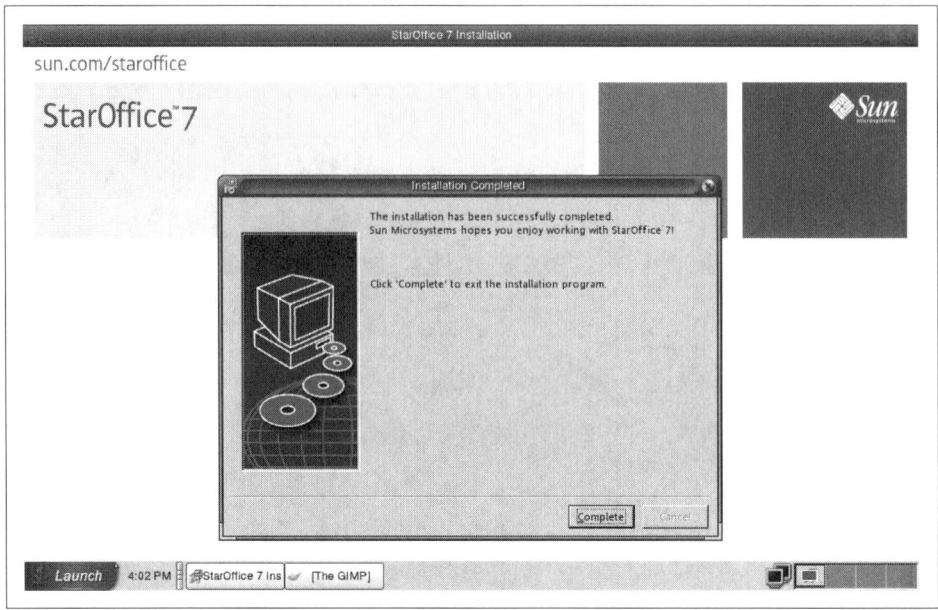

Figure 7-58. Installation completed

Add an Icon on the Desktop or Panel

Instead of bringing up StarWriter's Template window via Launch → StarWriter 7, some users may prefer to open StarOffice to a new document more directly. To save a few extra mouse clicks to gain speed, you can add a Launcher with a StarWriter icon to either the desktop or the Main Panel, or to both.

You can add separate Launchers to open each of the StarOffice modules directly. Here's the easiest way to set up a Launcher specifically for StarWriter on both your desktop workspace or the edge panel across the bottom of your desktop.

Right-click on an open space on the edge panel and select Add to Panel → Launcher from menu → Office → StarOffice 7 Text Document. This will place a StarWriter icon onto that location on your edge panel on which you may click to quickly launch a StarWriter blank document.

To add the same Launcher icon to the desktop space, simply drag and drop the Star-Writer icon you've just created on your edge panel onto your desktop workspace. This places a duplicate Launcher icon on the desktop, if that location is useful to you.

You can remove the edge panel icon by right-clicking it and selecting Remove From Panel on the context menu that pops up. To remove the desktop icon, right-click upon it and select Move to Trash in the context menu.

You can use Launchers some of the time and Templates and Documents when appropriate or necessary. Typical of the desktop, there is usually more than one way to accomplish the same task.

Adjusting Unpopular Default Settings

StarOffice is set by default to automatically complete words, replace certain characters, and capitalize initial letters in a new sentence. If you feel auto-correction to be intrusive while you are typing, the auto-correct settings are easy to adjust to be less intrusive or to turn off completely.

Word Completion (turning off)

StarWriter's Word Completion feature comes turned on by default. Some users find it distracting or annoying to have the word processor program appending the ends of words before they finish typing them. Others are content to ignore the completion action and leave the default alone.

If you like StarWriter to complete your words, simply press the Enter key when its recommendations are felicitous; otherwise press the space bar to reject the program's offering.

To turn Word Completion off, select Tools → AutoCorrect/AutoFormat → Word Completion and uncheck the box before the phrase "Enable word completion" near the top of the window. Then click the OK button. (See Figure 7-59.)

Auto-Replace (turning off)

If you find Auto-Replace to be invasive—such as when you attempt to type "(c)" and it keeps replacing your keystrokes with the copyright symbol, ©—you have two options: turn off Auto-Replace altogether (Figure 7-60), or edit the replacement list. (See Figure 7-61.)

Editing the replacement list is straightforward. Select Tools → AutoCorrect/AutoFormat and go to the Replace tab. (See Figure 7-61.) There, highlight the offending element and either press the Delete key or enter a different target result in the "With:" field.

To turn off the Auto-Replace function, select Tools → AutoCorrect/AutoFormat and click on the Options tab. The top-most option is "Use replacement table" with two checkboxes in front. By unchecking both boxes in the [M] and the [T] columns, you can turn off the specific substitutions listed in the replacement table. (See Figure 7-61.) You can turn off all the other specific automatic replacement actions, too, by unchecking the respective boxes under [M] or [T] as you go down this list in the Options tab. (See Figure 7-60.)

Note in the Tools → AutoCorrect/AutoFormat window that the left-most Replace tab, Figure 7-61, contains the list of default replacements. This list is based on the

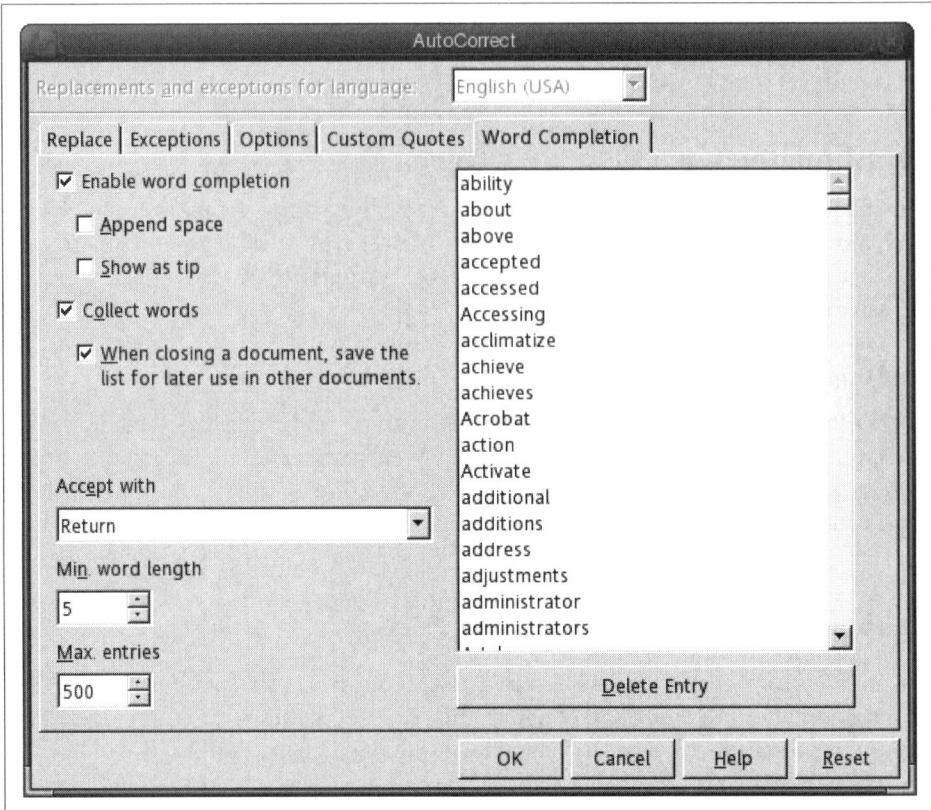

Figure 7-59. Turning off Word Completion

StarOffice developers' extensive knowledge of common keystroke errors and frequently-used symbols (such as the copyright symbol). Leaving Auto-Replace turned on can aid your compositional productivity, especially if you customize the replacement list to make your own most frequent word, character, or symbol replacements.

Auto-Capitalization (turning off or making exceptions)

StarWriter is set to automatically capitalize the next character you type after a period. It also decapitalizes a second uppercase character typed in a sequence. This is beneficial most of the time when we fail to strike the Shift key, which is surprisingly often; however, when we type abbreviations or when we type acronyms that demand two initial capitals, these AutoCorrect actions are unwanted.

If the Auto-Capitalization feature offends your sensibilities or disturbs your workflow, you can turn it off by selecting Tools → AutoCorrect/AutoFormat and clicking on the Options tab. (See Figure 7-60.) Uncheck the two boxes under the [M] and [T] columns in front of the second option, "Correct Two Initial Capitals," and the third option, "Capitalize the first letter of every sentence."

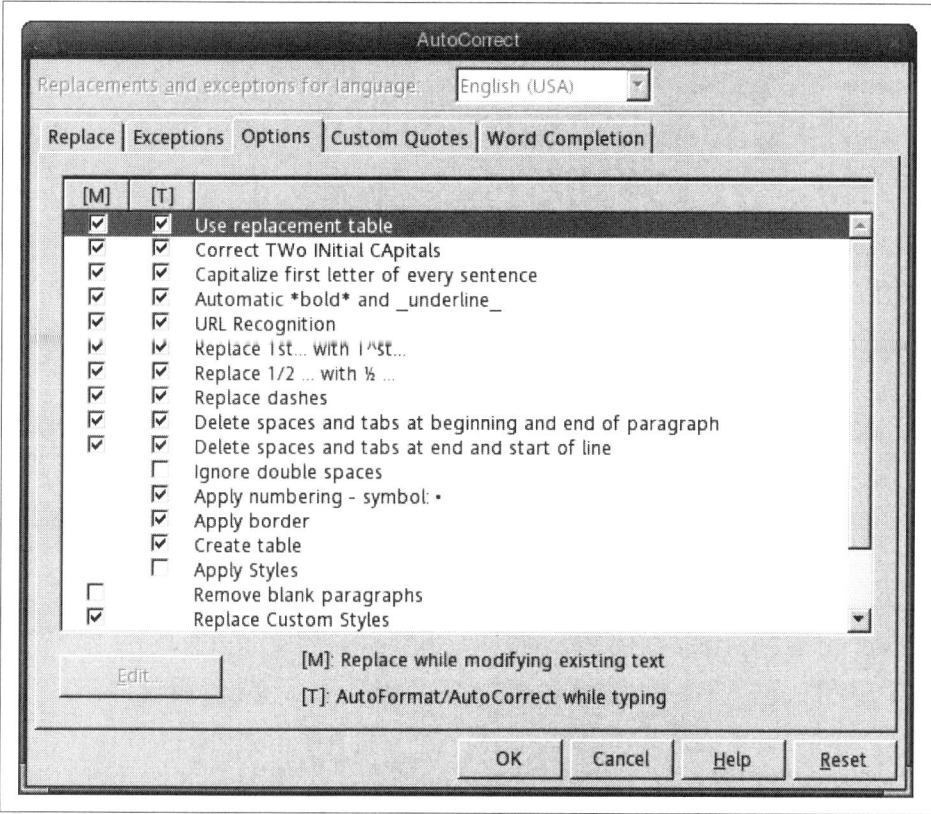

Figure 7-60. Turning off Auto-Replace

Auto-Capitalization can be very helpful when you integrate it into your typing repertoire. Consider keeping the feature turned on, while tweaking its exceptions to make the Auto-Capitalization work for you instead of against you. You can adjust Auto-Capitalization exceptions by selecting Tools → AutoCorrect/AutoFormat and proceeding to the Exceptions tab. (See Figure 7-62.)

Here, at the Exceptions tab, you can add abbreviations you repeatedly use to the "Abbreviations (no subsequent capitals)" list in the upper window. These entries permit Auto-Capitalization to automatically capitalize the first letter of a new sentence, while it will not make such an invasive adjustment after any of the abbreviations listed.

Also at the Exceptions tab, you can add to the list of words or acronyms that demand two initial capitals. The default entries already there provide a source of examples. (See Figure 7-62.)

For example, members of the software development communities often abbreviate OpenOffice.org as "OOo" and StarOffice as "SO," deploying many variations of

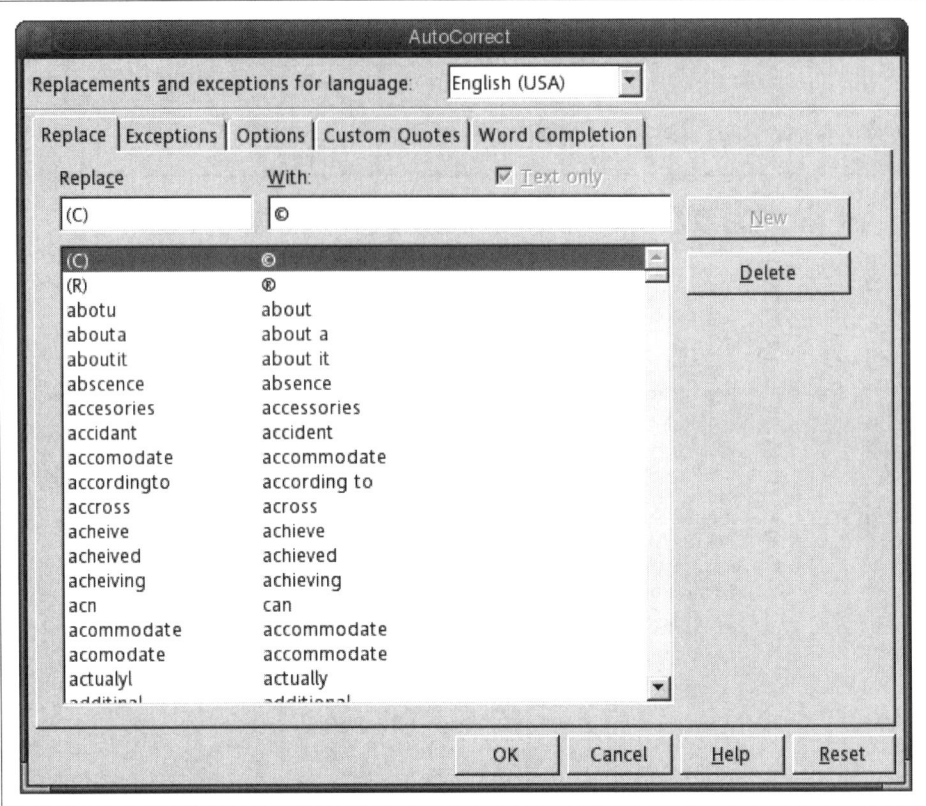

Figure 7-61. The default replacement list

these acronyms. One of the first things members need to do after installing a fresh version of either of these programs is to reset their Auto-Capitalization Exceptions to speed their work. The details within Figure 7-63 show the variations of the "OOo" and "SO" abbreviations that have been added to the Exceptions tab.

User Data (for Tracking Changes)

When you (or your system administrator) initially set up StarOffice in JDS, you were asked to enter your name and some additional information into the setup wizard. StarOffice uses the name you entered for the Changes Tracking feature.

Double check that your name is registered in the User Data section, just like in Figure 7-63. If you or your system administrator skipped entering your name in the User Data section, the changes tracking feature does not differentiate your edits or additions from those of your collaborating colleague. If you don't plan on using changes tracking, this is not be a problem for you.

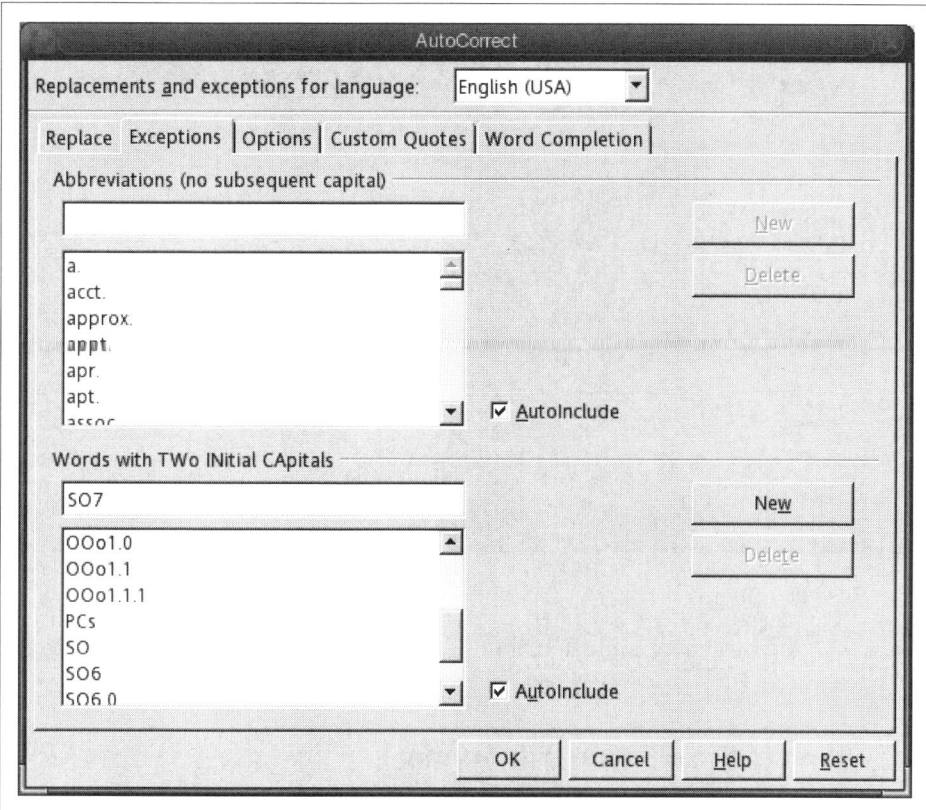

Figure 7-62. Tweaking Auto-Capitalization

If you want your information entered, go to Tools → Options → OpenOffice.org → User Data and make sure at least your name appears.

When you turn on Changes Tracking via Edit → Changes, check Record, and check Show, the changes you make show up in one color (initially red). When you save the document with changes, others, with whom you collaborate, can open the document and see your changes in red. New changes they make now show in a different color: blue. Additional collaborator's edits or additions each get different colors (red, blue, magenta, green, etc.).

StarWriter's File Format

StarOffice comes set to save your files in the native StarOffice/OpenOffice.org format, which is the open XML file format called OASIS XML, by default. If you are in a Microsoft environment or collaborate with users of MS Office—and who therefore use the MS *.doc* file format—you may feel it appropriate to save all your StarOffice-created documents in the MS *.doc* format. To avoid extra key strokes each time you

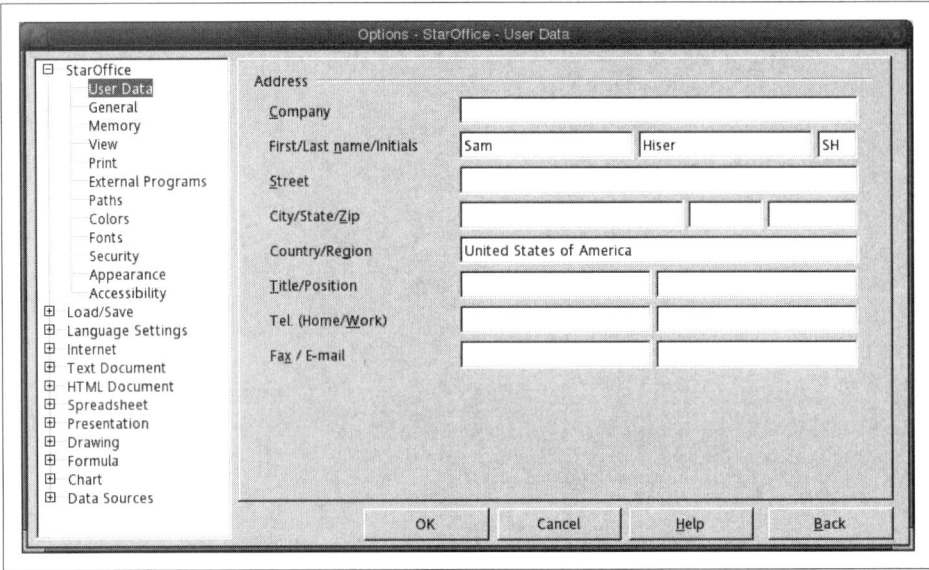

Figure 7-63. Entering user data

save a file, or reduce user confusion about the appropriate file format to save to, you can change StarOffice's default file format to MS *.doc* format.

Defaulting to the MS Word File Format

To set StarWriter to automatically save files in the MS Word *.doc* file format select Tools → Options, then choose Load/Save in the left index of the Options dialog. In the index under Load/Save, click on General. This opens the Options-Load/Save-General dialog. Here, in the "Standard file format" section, your "Document type" drop-down is already set on "Text document." Leave that as is. In the "Always save as" drop-down at right, change the selection to one of the three available MS Word versions:

- Microsoft Word 6.0
- Microsoft Word 95
- Microsoft Word 97/2000/XP

and click the OK button. Use your best discretion when choosing which version. The Microsoft Word 97/2000/XP has the most users at large; however, if your environment or people with whom you correspond most use one of the earlier versions (6.0 or 95), then that reality would inform your choice.

Document Compatibility

StarWriter has evolved an excellent ability to read or open documents in non-native formats. In 2003, a study conducted by Hal & Christopher Varian at the University of California, Berkeley, called "MOXIE - Microsoft Office-Linux Interoperability Experiment" indicated that StarOffice (6.0) opens MS Word documents (various versions randomly found on the Internet) 93 percent of the time, with no noticeable formatting problems. This means StarWriter imports MS Word documents 93 percent *perfectly*.[*] StarWriter 7, included with the JDS system you are running, does even better.

In fact, because MS Word users face incompatibilities trying to share files amongst themselves across the different versions of Word, StarOffice is more compatible with MS Office files than MS Office itself! This is because StarOffice opens all MS Office versions automatically. For example, users of (the older) MS Word 6.0 cannot open or read files in the native MS Word2000 file format. Users of the newer program are forced to "save backward" if they want their work to be accessed.

[*] *http://www.acmqueue.com/modules.php?name=Content&pa=showpage&pid=55.*

Troubleshooting Incompatibilities

You will encounter file incompatibilities sooner or later as you open or save documents in MS Office formats using StarOffice. Typical problems include some of the formatting or fonts appearing out of alignment, usually in headers or footers. Complex elements such as tables, frames, and graphical objects can sometimes appear in undesirable places or get "totally munged." These, like all incompatibilities, are frustrating, but they are not likely to represent the end of the world—or even the end of your career. That's because you know how to handle them, psychologically, as well as practically. Here are a few suggestions for what to do.

- Breathe deeply three times.

- Evaluate how much time it takes you to tweak the new document back into proper shape (a few minutes is appropriate for a simple or short document).

- If the problems are extensive (or it's a large or complex document), ask your correspondent to go back to the original document and *save it as a web page in HTML* (in Word2000, this can be done by choosing File → Save as Web Page…) and then try opening that document in StarOffice. If that's successful, you can convert the document to many different possible formats, including the MS Office *.doc* format again.

- If an MS Word document imports but comes in only partially out of kilter, consider rebuilding the document in StarWriter one paragraph, frame, table, or object at a time, using cut & paste into StarOffice. The time spent cursing your luck and pounding the table in frustration is typically equal to the five or six minutes it takes to rebuild modest-sized documents.

- If a read-only format is acceptable, ask your correspondent to go back and *export the original document to Adobe PDF*, in which format the work is almost guaranteed to be readable on any other system.

- Keep a licensed version of MS Word (2000 or higher is recommended) installed on your JDS box or nearby. See Chapter 9, where we discuss Crossover Office, its installation, and its value to productivity.

- If you are a system administrator or manager considering a switch to JDS and StarOffice in your organization, take some time to evaluate your legacy files. If you do that, file incompatibilities should not often come as a surprise. The ones that are the most frustrating and most common arise during the normal flow of business, often when users share documents while collaborating across the different systems in their extra-company supply-chain or across different system environments from school to home. You can probably discover these through testing in advance. Such document incompatibilities are manageable with sufficient thought and experience.

- Document incompatibilities tend to be minimal once an organization or household has completely standardized on a single file format and desktop environment, or has established ways of functioning effectively in the world of heterogeneous systems. Compatibility will improve in the future as open standard formats and system components gain wider adoption. If you are reading this book, then you are participating in this important trend to open standards.

CHAPTER 8

Spreadsheets and Presentations Using StarOffice

We cover the StarCalc and StarImpress modules of StarOffice together in this chapter because they are, on aggregate, less frequently used than the word processor. For economy's sake, we offer no "Power Tips" section here as we did in Chapter 7 for StarWriter. Nevertheless, our coverage of basic spreadsheet and presentation methods is designed to stimulate you to further independent exploration of the menus and features that should advance your desktop skills to the next level.

In particular, StarCalc offers advanced users powerful macro-programming and management facilities (via OpenBasic) and powerful database interactivity through the Data Sources features. While these tools are beyond the scope of this work, we encourage users to seek further documentation.

StarCalc

StarOffice Calc (also known as "StarCalc") is the spreadsheet program included in the StarOffice office suite. Users familiar with recent versions of Microsoft Excel will feel at home in StarCalc. In basic features and functions, StarCalc is comparable to Excel.

In this section, StarCalc Basics, we cover basic functionality with an added focus on some unique features presented by StarCalc. We also point out a few of the spreadsheet module's shortcomings.

StarCalc Basics

While StarCalc offers about 90 percent compatibility with MS Excel's functionality and file format, you are likely at some point to have trouble locating a familiar old command or discover a problem importing an MS Excel file.

Advanced spreadsheet users in particular are hampered by StarCalc's inability to run MS Office-originated Visual Basic macros. (There are work-arounds that we'll discuss at the end of the chapter.) More than the other modules of StarOffice, StarCalc calls for adjustments from MS Office users.

Opening Files

Select File → Open from the Main menu, choose the desired file in the dialog window, and click the Open button.

Alternatively, you can open this dialog window more quickly from the keyboard by pressing Ctrl+O.

The third way to open a spreadsheet file—either a StarCalc file or a Microsoft Excel file—is simply to click on the file icon. StarCalc launches with the file open and is ready to go.

 The spreadsheet, illustrated in Figure 8-26, is an Excel file, as denoted by the *.xls* suffix in the filename at the top center of its workspace frame. This large file (or "Workbook," as it is called in StarCalc) has 17 sheets and opens cleanly every time in StarCalc, with no errors. Although it is a large workbook with many calculations—fitting for a 10-year financial statement projection—it has simple formulas and labels that give no trouble to StarCalc's file importation facilities. Spreadsheets, originating from other applications, are generally proven to import more cleanly than text or presentation document-types because their contents tend to be simpler and more uniform.

Saving Files

To save the current file to its current folder location, simply select File → Save from the Main menu.

Alternatively, from the keyboard, simply press Ctrl+S.

If you need to select a new folder into which to save the file (such as when saving a new file for the first time), select File → Save As... from the Main menu. Choose the folder location and the filename in the dialog and press the Save button. (See Figure 8-1.)

Exporting a File as PDF

To export the current spreadsheet into the Printable Document Format (PDF), select File → Export as PDF... from the Main menu. Optionally, select the target destination folder in the Export dialog, enter or change the filename if you choose, and press the Export button.

Alternatively, you can export directly as PDF, using the dedicated Export to PDF icon on the toolbar. Clicking the icon opens the same Export dialog as the procedure just described.

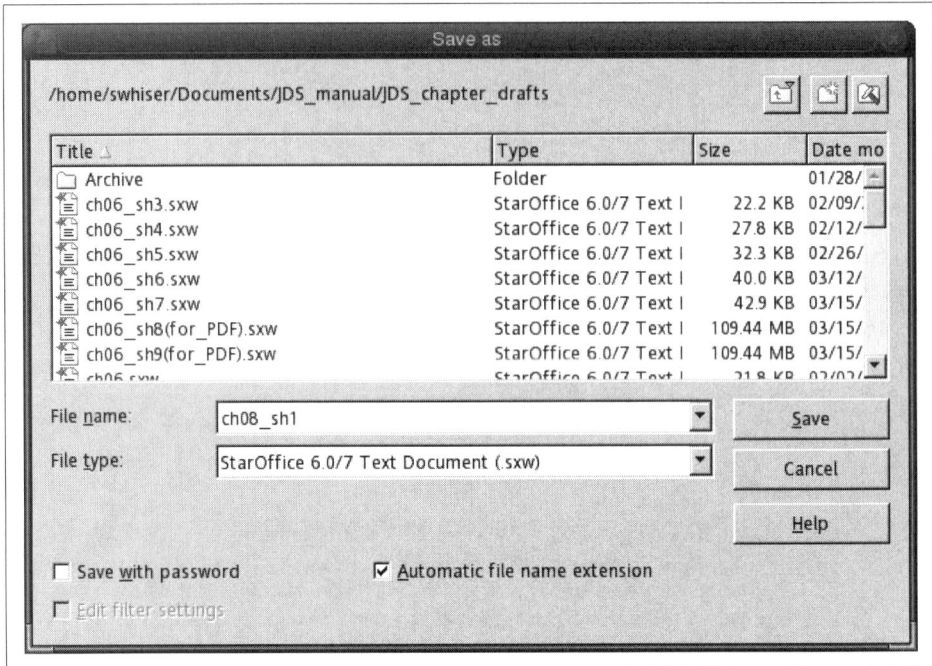

Figure 8-1. The Save As dialog

This procedure generates a PDF file from the current document and stores it in the designated file on your filesystem. This document is viewable with the PDF Document Viewer on your system (Adobe Acrobat Reader 5.0 for Linux) and by any other user with Adobe Acrobat Reader 5.0 and above.

Sending Files as Email Attachments

StarCalc offers convenient ways to send spreadsheets attached to an email message.

Send as PDF

To send the current file attached to an email message as a PDF file, select File → Send → Document as PDF Attachment... from the Main menu. This opens the PDF Options window (Figure 8-2), where you can select a page range and compression amount, or leave the options alone and just press the Export button. This action calls up the Email and Calendar program and simultaneously opens a new message window with the current spreadsheet file attached. Enter an address, subject, and body and send it as you would a typical email message.

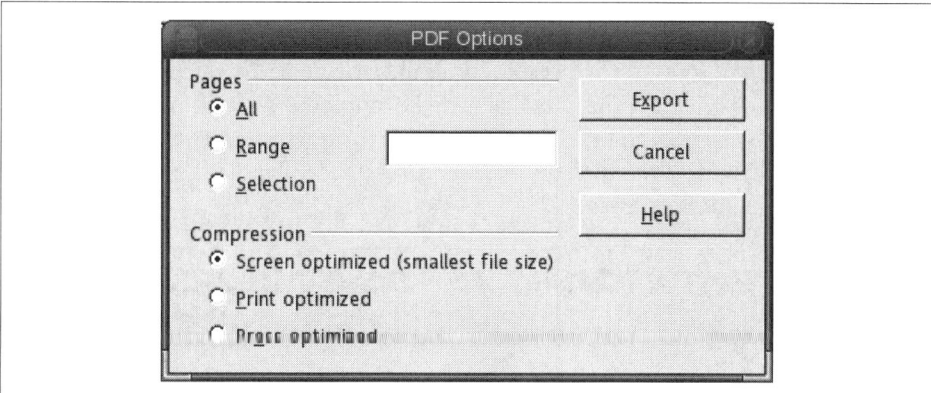

Figure 8-2. The PDF Options window

Send as StarCalc file

To send the current spreadsheet in its native StarCalc file format (with the file extension *.sxc*), simply select File → Send → Document as Email from the Main menu. This calls up your Email and Calendar program and simultaneously opens a new message window with the current spreadsheet attached in its native file format. Fill out the message as you normally would and press the Send button.

Entering Numbers

Entering numbers into a cell is straightforward. Simply place the cursor in the target cell, type the desired number, and press the Enter key.

Note that numbers appear flush-right in a cell by default.

Entering Labels (Text)

To enter a label in a cell—that is, a word rather than a number—place the cursor in the target cell, begin the character sequence with a ' (single quote) character, finish typing the rest of the characters, and press the Enter key.

For example, the column heading "Sales" would be entered as **'Sales**, followed by the Enter key.

Labels appear flush-left in a cell by default.

Autofill

This feature is designed to speed up common repetitive tasks. Autofill permits you, in one stroke, to fill in either a column or row of numbers that automatically increase by one. This is often useful when first creating a new table or spreadsheet. In the case of labels, Autofill simply repeats the label across the cell range you specify.

For instance, after entering the year 2004 (as a number and not as a label) in cell B-3, simply highlight the cell by clicking it once. At this point, you will see a small black square at the bottom-right corner of the cell. Grab the square with a left mouse click and, with the left mouse button pressed, drag the square across the cells you want to fill with numbers. Release the mouse, and the numbers will fill in consecutively. Figure 8-3 shows the result of this autofill procedure, in which the default action is to automatically increase the numbers by one in sequence. The result is similar when autofilling a column of numbers.

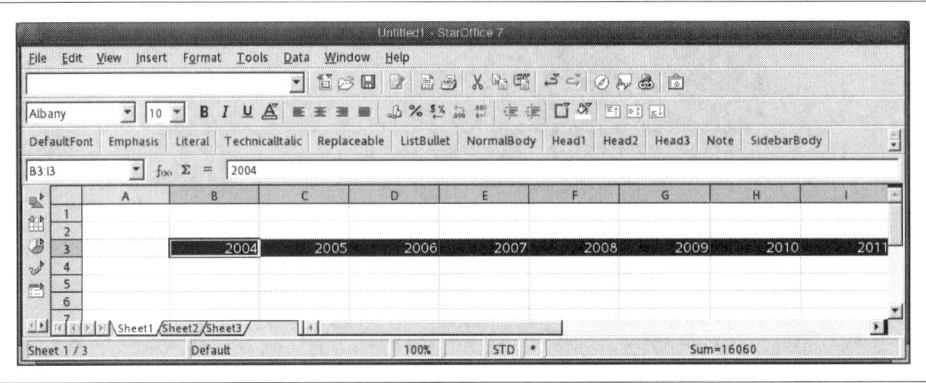

Figure 8-3. Autofill saves time-consuming repetition

Entering Simple Formulas

Formulas begin with an equal sign (=). To calculate the result of 1+1, for example, type **=1 + 1** and press Enter.

To calculate a result based on other cells, type **=** in the cell where you want the result to appear, then click on the first cell in the formula. This highlights the cell in a red outline. Type an operator such as **+** and click on the second cell. This highlights that cell in a red outline. You can keep entering as many operators, followed by cells or other values, as needed. Finally, press Enter and the result appears in the target cell.

Using the example in Figure 8-4, with the cursor in cell B9, type **=**. Next, click on cell B5, and type **-**. Next, click on cell B7 and press the Enter key. The result appears in cell B9.

Note that the Formula Field in the above figure contains the formula we just described, **=B5-B7**. The alternative way of creating the same formula is to simply type it directly into the Formula Field. First, click once on cell B9. Then click once on the empty Formula bar and type **=B5-B7**. Press the Enter key. The result is the same.

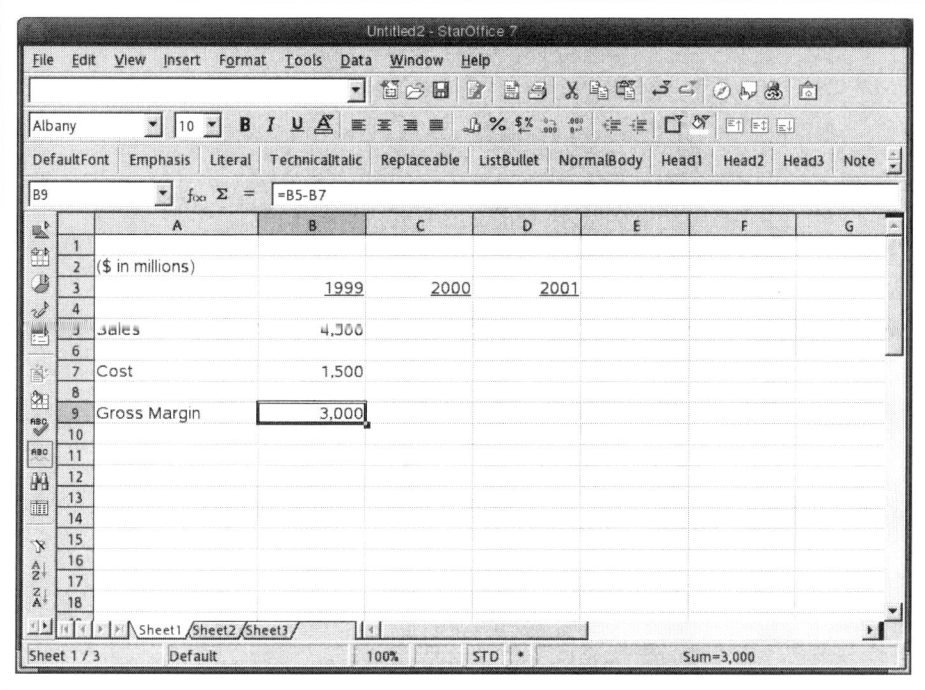

Figure 8-4. Formulas begin with the equal sign

Summing a Column of Numbers

To quickly sum an existing column of numbers, highlight the target result cell with a single click. Then, click the Sigma icon on the Formula bar. This automatically highlights in blue the most likely nearby column of numbers to be summed. (See Figure 8-5.)

If the highlighted group is appropriate, press the Enter key and the result appears in the target cell. (See Figure 8-6.) If you find you have not chosen the set of cells you wanted, you can grab the small blue square at the bottom right of the highlighted column and adjust the grouping to the precise numbers you want to sum. Then press the Enter key.

Moving Cell Contents

It's easier to move a range of cells in StarCalc than it is to move a single cell entry. This task is the one that gives the most people trouble when they are adjusting to the new environment of StarCalc, but it is quite simple once you've done it once or twice.

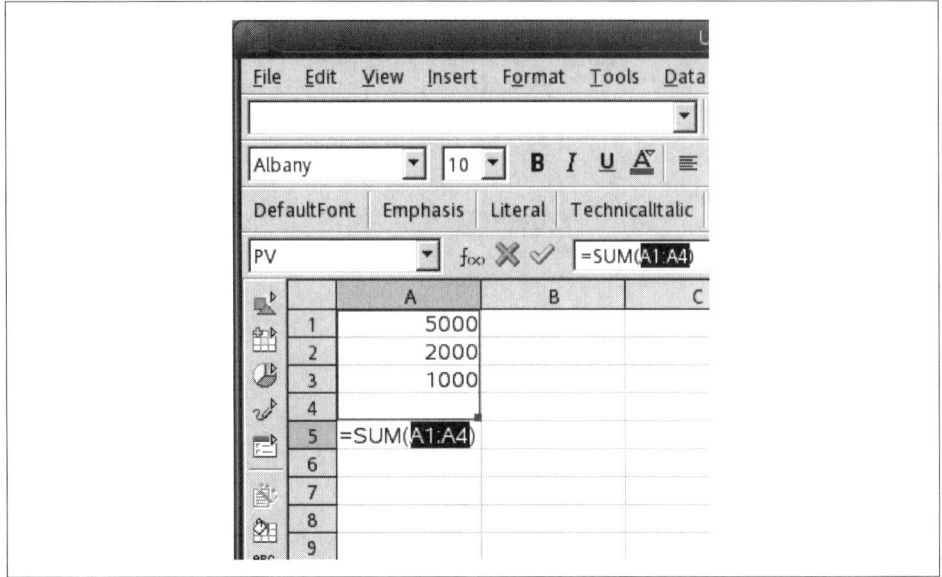

Figure 8-5. Clicking upon the Sigma icon

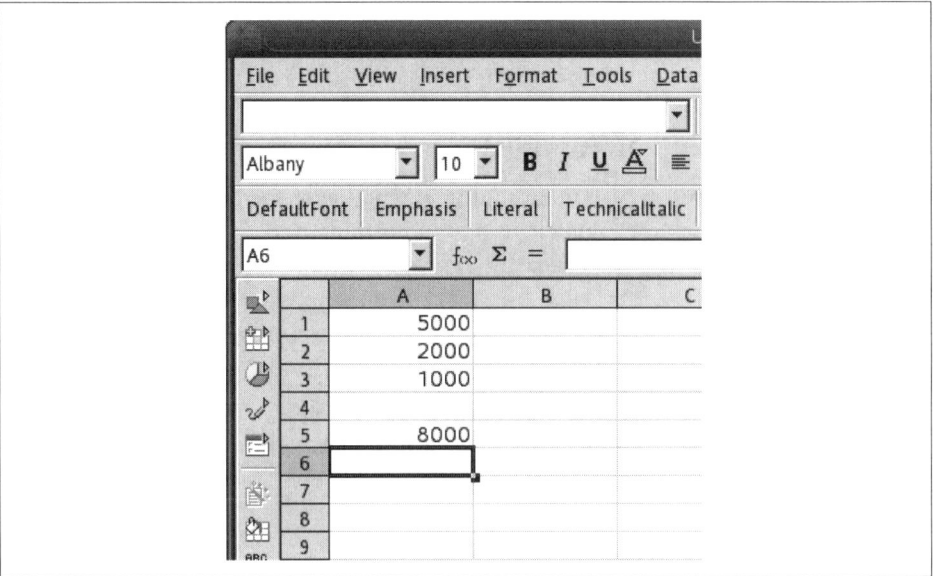

Figure 8-6. The Sigma is for summing

To move a range of cells, simply highlight the range by left-clicking in one cell at an extreme corner of the range, and, while holding the left mouse key down, drag the mouse pointer across the rest of the cells in the range. When the whole range is blackened, release the left mouse key. Go back with the mouse pointer and make a single mouse click anywhere in the blackened range to grab the range and move it to its new location. Drop the range of cells in its new location by simply releasing the left mouse button.

Moving a single cell entry requires the same procedure, but highlighting a single cell usually proves troublesome for new users. That's because the highlight motion with the left mouse button requires the user to left-click on the cell, move the mouse pointer outside the cell and back, release the mouse button, and then go back to grab and move the highlighted cell.

 MS Office offers a single motion to move a single cell, while StarCalc requires a double motion involving first a highlight then a move. Initially, the StarCalc process is annoying because it's more complicated, but in the end, it's effective and not that difficult. Still, this feature difference gets many complaints and is likely to change in future versions of StarOffice.

Adjusting Widths and Heights

To change the width of a column, bring the mouse pointer up into the grid's column headings, labeled A, B, C, etc. Note how the mouse pointer changes to a double horizontal arrow when it rolls over any column divider.

While the arrow is visible, simply move it to the right or left to increase or decrease the width of the column immediately to the left of the divider.

To put a column back to its default width, right-click on the column heading to call up the Column Width dialog. Check the empty box labeled "Default value" and press the OK button. The column now snaps back to its default width (0.89 inches).

To adjust the height of a row, apply the procedure shown earlier for adjusting column width, but with the mouse cursor on the tops or bottoms of a row heading, at the left edge of the page.

To restore a row's default height, apply the procedure shown earlier for restoring the default column width, but at the left edge of the page on the desired row heading.

Merging Cells

To merge multiple cells together, first highlight the group of cells you want to merge, then select Format → Merge Cells → Define from the Main menu. This creates one cell that contains the contents of the cells in the range you highlighted. StarCalc's recognition of data can be quite sophisticated. For instance, if one column contains Jun and another contains 3, the date 06/03, followed by the current year, appears in the merged cell.

Basic Formatting

Most spreadsheet users find that a few cell-formatting commands carry them through most of their work.

The Object Bar

The quickest way to format numbers and labels in the cells of a spreadsheet is to use the formatting buttons across the Object bar, shown in Figure 8-7. Most office tool users are familiar with the Bold, Italic, and Underline buttons, as well as the justification and simple number formatting buttons.

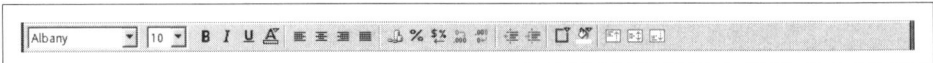

Figure 8-7. The Object bar

If the formatting choices offered by the Object Bar prove too limiting, apply more customized formats through the Format → Cells... path off the Main menu. This displays the Format Cells dialog box, with a bewildering range of formatting options, just a few of which are discussed in the following sections.

Underlining a cell

To underline an entire cell or range of cells, the Borders palette is the best tool. Highlight the range you wish to underline, then click on the Borders icon on the formatting toolbar to open the Borders palette, and click on the underline button in the palette, as illustrated in Figure 8-8.

Note in Figure 8-8 how the activated underline icon is highlighted on the Object bar and has a dark outline around it (the outline is blue on your screen). This visual cue is used consistently across the Object bar to indicate that formatting features are active wherever the cursor presently rests.

Underlining a cell label

Underlining a cell label is different from using Borders to underline the entire cell. To underline a cell label, highlight the label you want to underline and click the underline icon on the formatting toolbar (just as with typical word processors). (See Figure 8-9.)

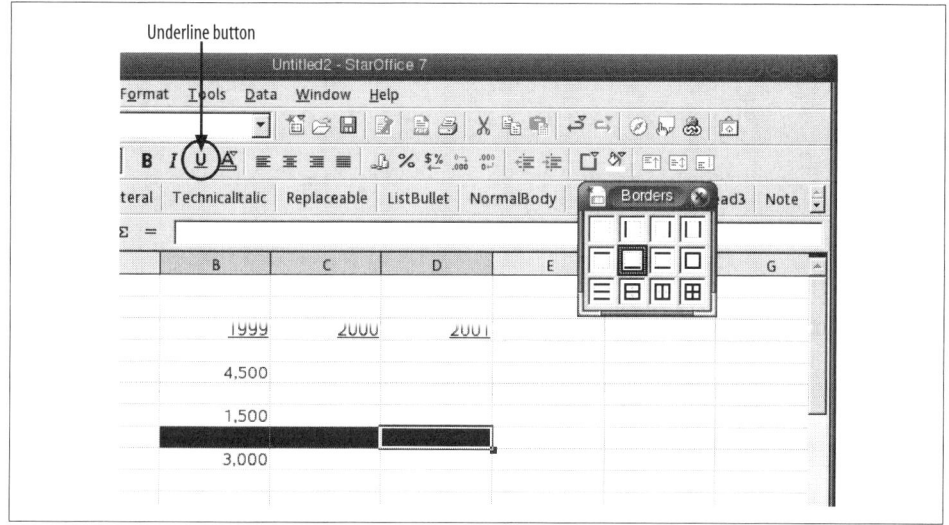

Figure 8-8. Borders palette is the tool for underlining cells

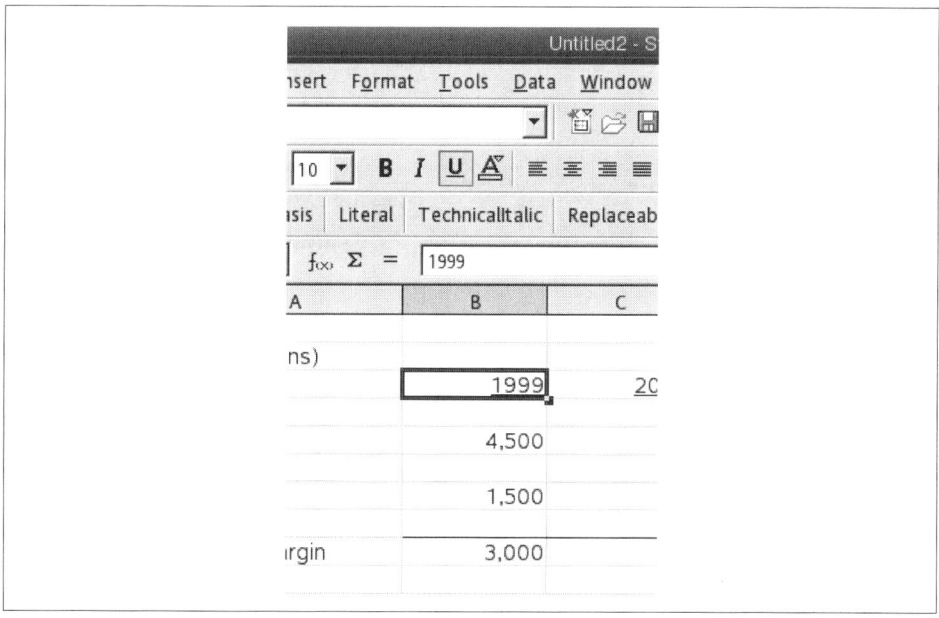

Figure 8-9. Underlining a label

Cell background color

Perhaps you'd like to dress up a simple table of numbers or make the bottom line you're trying to emphasize stand out by giving the cell backgrounds a little color. This is easily done by invoking the Format Cells dialog. First, highlight the range of cells you'd like to color. From the Main menu select Format → Cells… and click the

Background tab, shown in Figure 8-10. Choose a color on the color palette with a single click and click the OK button.

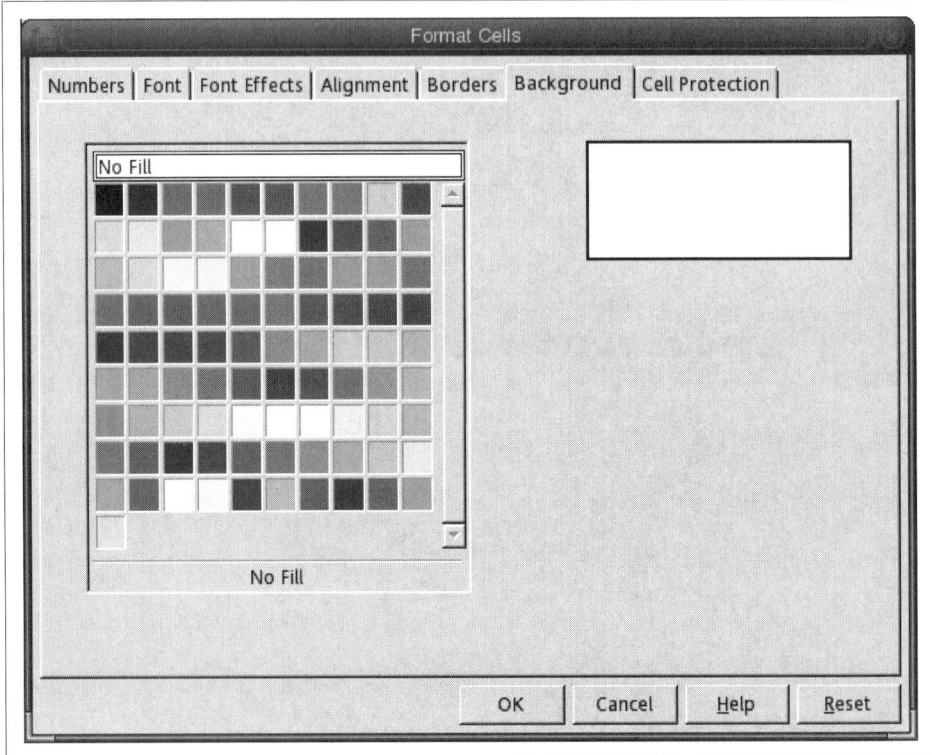

Figure 8-10. Format Cells dialog; Background tab selected

Figure 8-12 shows our table fully dressed with cell backgrounds, set according to our taste. (Sorry you have to see it in gray, in the printed book, instead of in riotous color.)

Formatting numbers

When you first enter numbers in a cell, they have no formatting. To indicate a unit such as dollars ($12), or dollars and cents ($12.43), you need to apply currency formatting or another type of number formatting. You can also conform to various local standards such as formatting data with commas to separate thousands.

To format some of the data in thousands, first highlight the desired range to format, then from the Main menu, select Format → Cells.... This opens the Format Cells dialog, where you should select the Numbers tab by clicking on it. Figure 8-11 shows the variety of formatting options available to you.

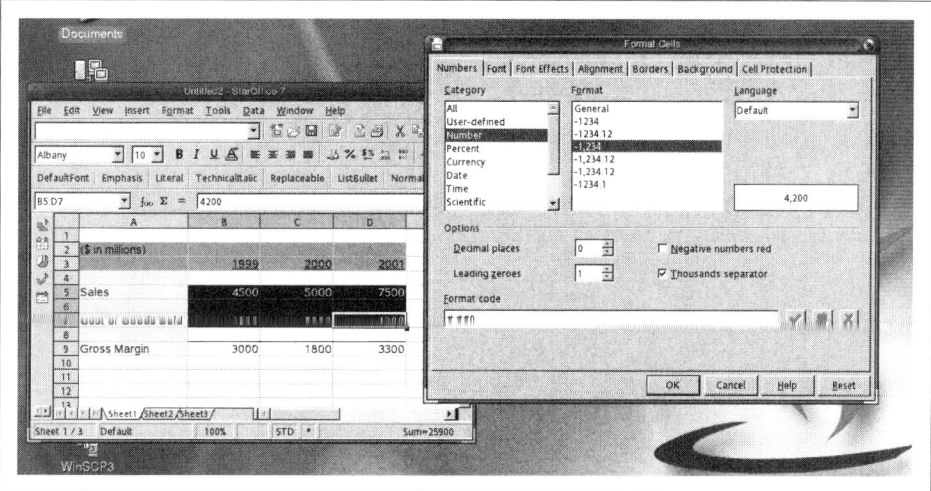

Figure 8-11. Number formatting

Select Number in the Category list at left, then choose your desired number format from the Format list in the center. For our purposes, we want -1,234. That done, click the OK button, and the numbers in your designated range appear with the new formatting.

Note that in Figure 8-12 we chose to vary the number formatting only in the Gross Margin row. Using currency formatting sparingly can make the table easier to read by removing clutter.

You can see by browsing through the Format Cells dialog box that there are many facilities for applying custom formatting to cells and characters in them. The dialog box offers the following tabs, which are also visible in Figures 8-10 and 8-11:

- Numbers
- Fonts
- Font Effects
- Alignment
- Borders
- Background
- Cell Protection

Freezing and Splitting Windows

It's hard to navigate through larger spreadsheets because the column and row headings disappear out of view. The Window → Freeze and Window → Split commands

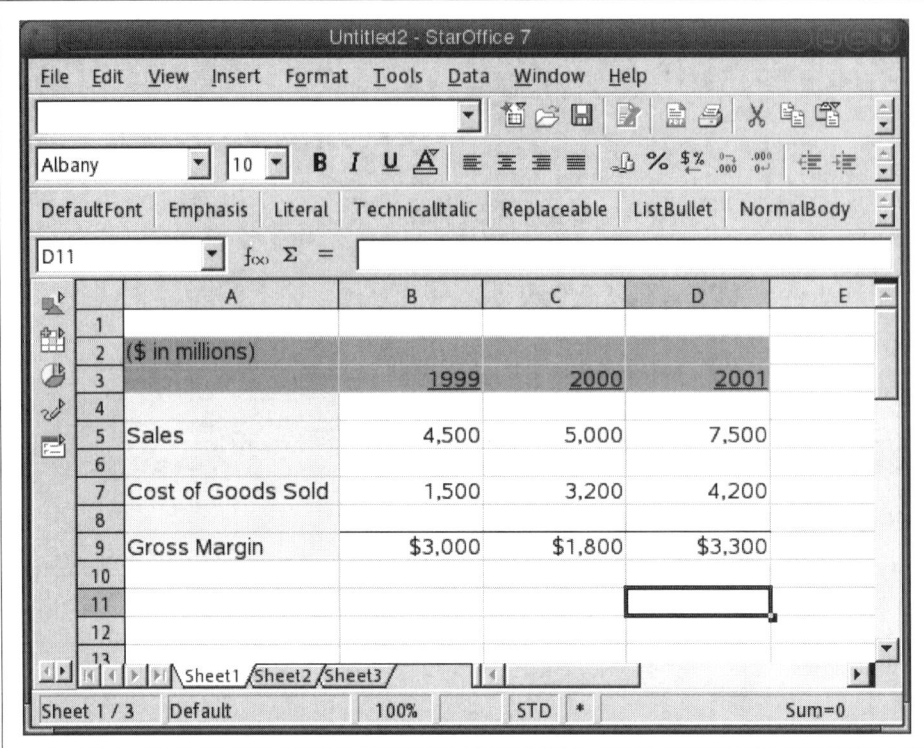

Figure 8-12. Varying number formats is communicative

permit you to lock column and row headings into place, while scrolling to view other sections of the spreadsheet.

To lock down your column and row headings, click on the cell where you want the freeze to take effect and select Window → Freeze from the Main menu. This will put a check mark on the Freeze item on the drop-down menu and lock the columns to the left of the highlighted cell, as well as the rows above the cell. The spreadsheet initially shows just lines to outline the frozen cells, as can be seen in Figure 8-13.

Now you can move down and to the right. Note in Figure 8-14 how Row 1, with all column headings, stays fixed and visible as you move down the spreadsheet. A similar effect takes place with the Column B row headings at the left if you scroll through the spreadsheet at the right.

Another interesting way to leave parts of your spreadsheet visible is to choose Windows → Split, instead of Window → Freeze. Now you can click on any pane and scroll it. The pane you clicked on moves, along with one of the panes next to it, depending on whether you scroll up and down, or right and left. The other two panes stay still.

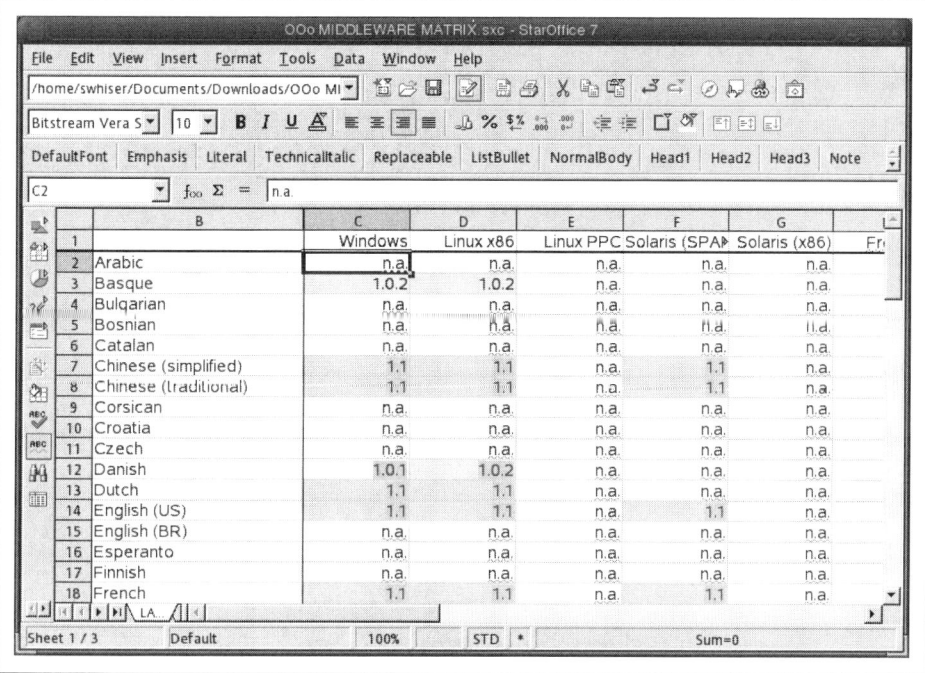

Figure 8-13. Freezing the column and row headings

To remove the Freeze or Split settings, simply click the checked selection on the drop-down menu, and the freeze or split lines go away.

Page Break View

Page Break View offers a detailed view of the current spreadsheet's page breaks for printing. To turn on Page Break View, select View from the Main menu and click on Page Break View in the drop-down menu. This sets a check mark at the selection. To turn off Page Break View, uncheck this selection on the drop-down menu.

Figure 8-15 shows a spreadsheet in normal view, just as Page Break View is about to be checked. Figure 8-16 shows the same spreadsheet with Page Break View turned on. Each page's number appears as a light gray watermark at the center of each page as it comes out of the printer.

You can quickly set or adjust page breaks by dragging the outside blue lines to cover the desired range, and just as easily move the page-dividing lines to include the desired columns and rows on the proper printed page. Page Break View also offers a way to view and navigate larger spreadsheets from a higher perspective.

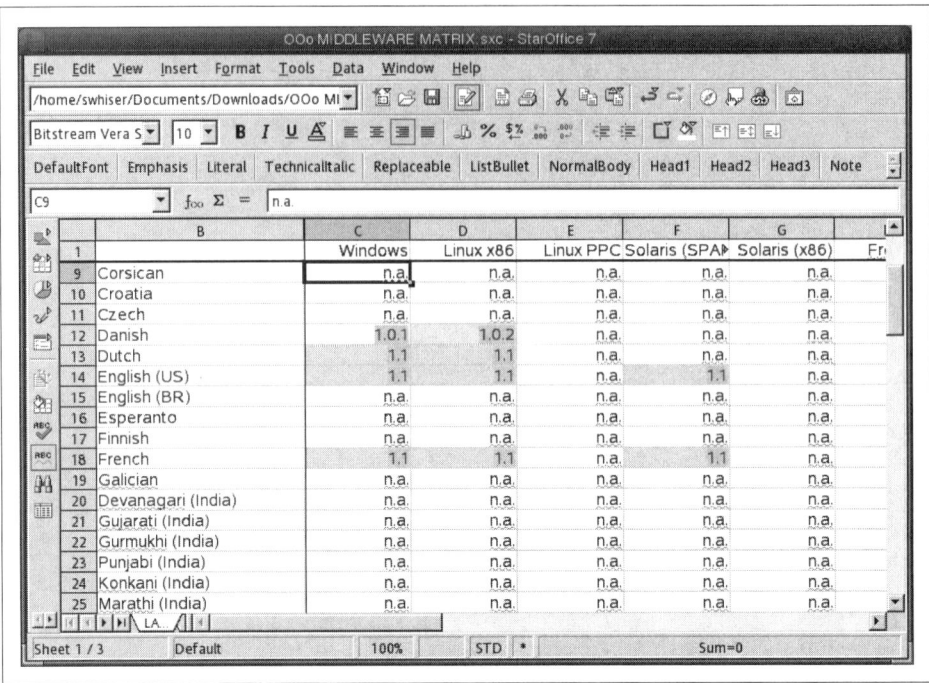

Figure 8-14. Row 1 is frozen

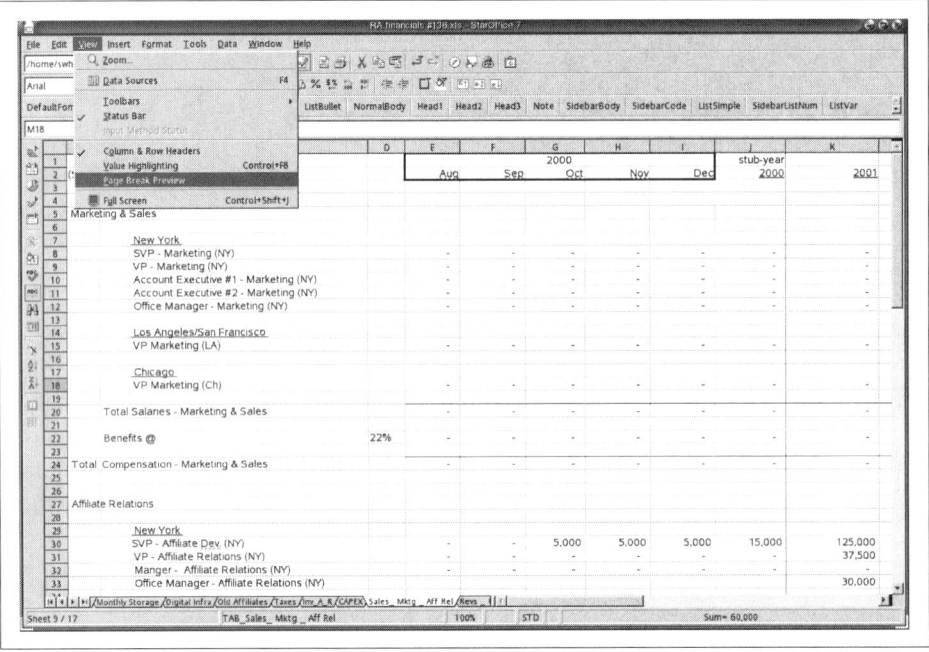

Figure 8-15. Spreadsheet in normal view

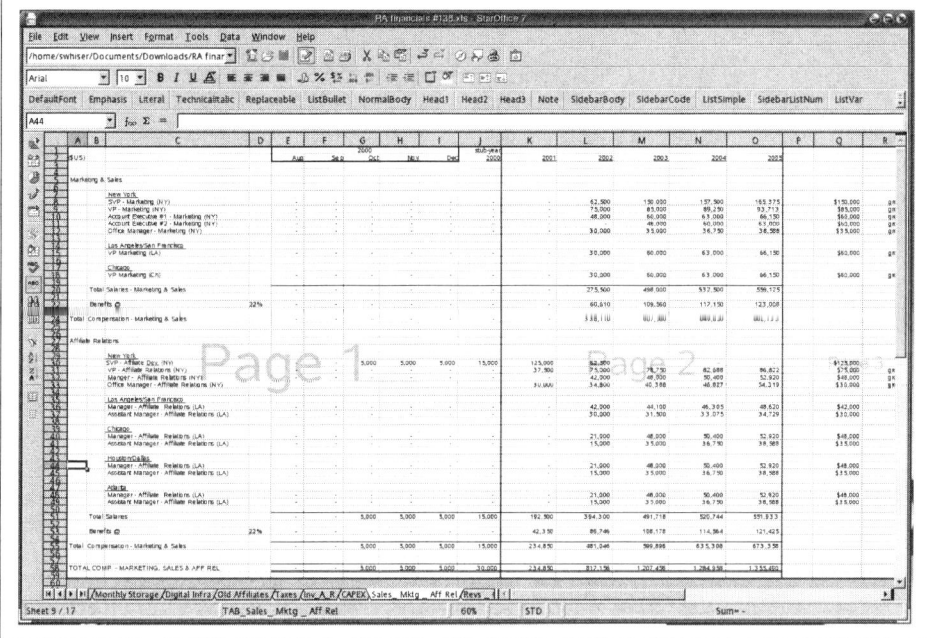

Figure 8-16. Spreadsheet in page break view

Setting the Print Range

When you create a new spreadsheet from scratch, it has no print range set. Such a spreadsheet appears gray when in Page Break View. To set a print range for your spreadsheet, make sure Page Break View is turned on, then highlight the full area you want to print by clicking on the cell in one corner and dragging the mouse pointer across the entire range. Finally, select Format → Print Ranges → Define. Any spreadsheet content that's outside the range you set this way is not printed.

If there is a print range already defined and you need to adjust it, simply grab the corner of the blue outline (or just grab a side) with the mouse and stretch it to include all the desired cells of your new print range.

To "grab," first move the mouse pointer over the blue outline of the print range and you see the mouse pointer turn to a bidirectional arrow. The arrow permits you to drag the print range blue outline to a different place, simply by clicking and dragging the line to the desired location.

Functions

StarCalc has a full array of function types, including:

- Financial
- Database

- Temporal (Date & Time)
- Array
- Statistical
- Informational
- Logical
- Mathematical
- Textual

StarCalc's functions, their syntax, and their required formats are well documented in the Help drop-down menu off the Main menu. Select Help → Contents and the Help window opens up. Then, in the Index tab at the "Search term" field, type **functions**, and press the Enter key. Here, you can double-click on the name of a function in the left pane to view the information about that function. Figure 8-17 illustrates the Help Index and information on the financial function called PV, which calculates the present value of a stream of regular payments or cash flows. PV is a spreadsheet function that's understandably popular with MBAs and bankers.

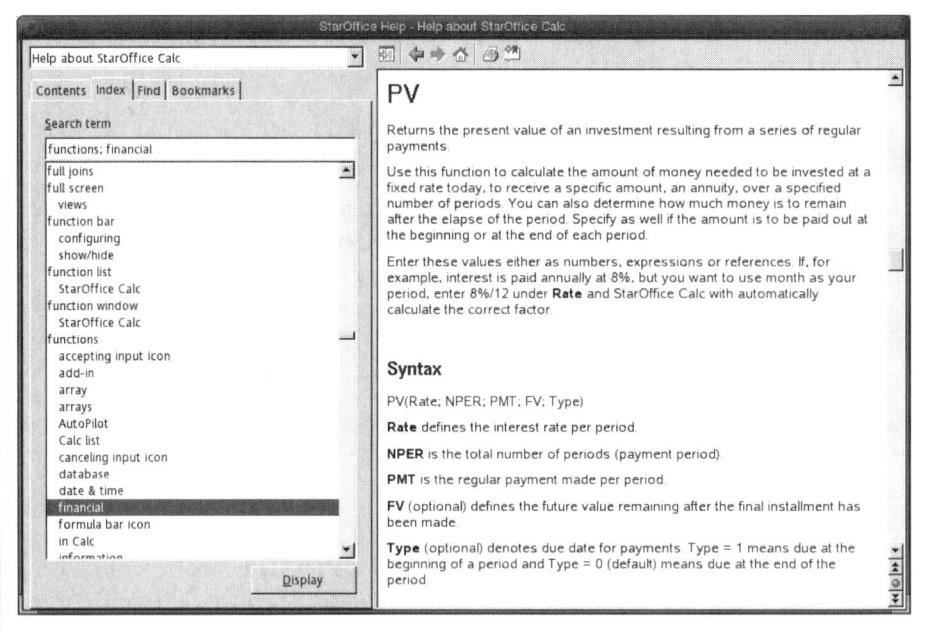

Figure 8-17. The PV (present value) Function

When entering a function into a cell, always remember to precede the entry with an equal sign (=). The example, offered in Figure 8-18, indicates in the formula field what the PV function formula looks like when it is correctly typed into a cell, and the necessary information for the function is properly cell-referenced:

```
=PV(B1;B2;B3)
```

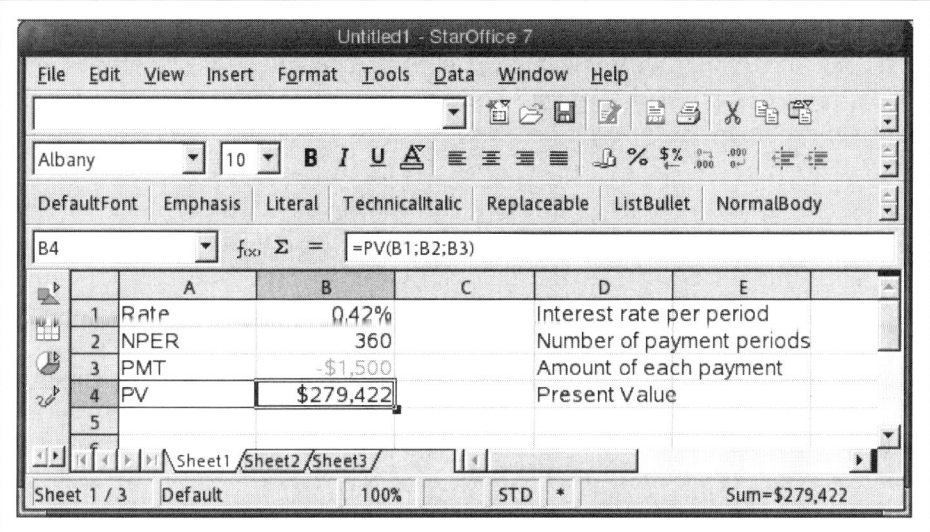

Figure 8-18. A common mortgage problem, solved

PV Function for the Real World

The function in Figure 8-18 is a common mortgage problem. If you are guaranteed terms by your bank on a 30-year loan at 5 percent interest per annum, and you know that you have exactly $1,500 per month to spend on your new house, the question to answer is, "What is the purchase price that corresponds with my maximum monthly payment of $1,500?"

The PV Function is perfect for solving such a problem. (MBAs will fondly recall that mortgage payments made by you to the bank are outgoing and, therefore, negative. Make your payment input negative, or the resulting present value is negative.) The number of periods is 30 years times 12 months (360 periods), and the periodic interest rate is 5 percent per year, divided by 12 months (0.42 percent per month), as indicated in Figure 8-18.

You could just as readily use the PMT (Payment) function to determine what the monthly payment is on your 10-million Euro dream home.

It is possible also to enter numbers as well as cell references into the body of a function. In the Formula Field, this looks like:

```
=PV(.0042;360;-1500)
```

However, using cell references leaves room for easily trying alternative inputs or for generating a sensitivity analysis, using a range of choices for one variable.

Creating Graphs

In overall quality, StarCalc's ability to create and render graphs needs improvement, but its functionality is adequate for the simplest types of graphs. The example, shown in Figures 8-19 through 8-23, demonstrates the creation of a simple bar graph from a table of numbers.

In Figure 8-19, we create a graph based on a simple table with a column of labels (the different operating systems employed by users of OpenOffice.org) and a column of numbers (the number of responses indicating use of the respective operating system). We want to show the relative scale of responses for each category, so it's clear that a bar graph is suitable for this purpose. Generally, the graph type you select is dictated by the kind and amount of data you are portraying and by the most important point(s) you need to communicate. We exclude the totals line, in this case, because its inclusion distorts the scale and interferes with the graph's main purpose of the comparison of category responses. Totals information, if relevant to an audience, may be included in a textual footnote to such a graph.

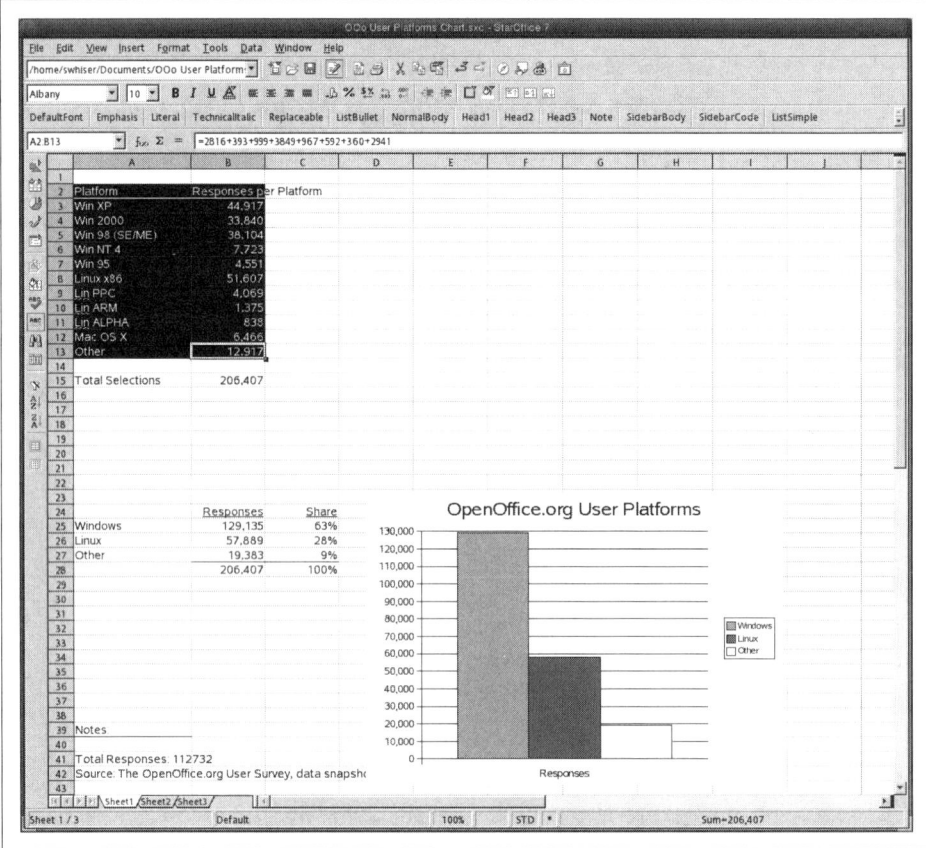

Figure 8-19. Creating a graph from a table of numbers

First, highlight the range of data to be included in the table. Figure 8-19 illustrates the desired data range already highlighted. For this particular graph, it's necessary to include the column headings as labels but exclude the totals row at bottom of the table. We are excluding the totals line for this type of graph because its inclusion interferes with the primary message of comparison of responses for each category. It also changes the scale of the graph and seriously disarranges the presentation of information.

Next, from the Main menu, select Insert → Chart. This opens the AutoFormat Chart wizard. (See Figure 8-20.)

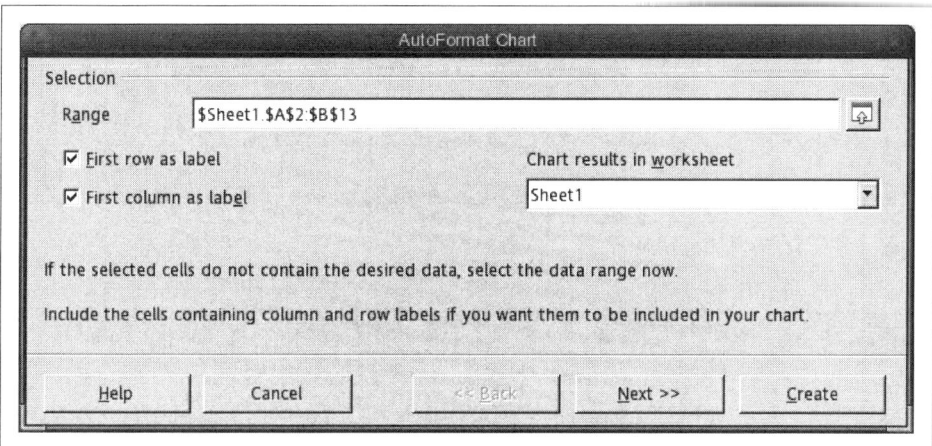

Figure 8-20. The AutoFormat Chart wizard

In this particular case, it's necessary to check the two check boxes, labeled "First row as label" and "First column as label" to enable the wizard to reference the proper axis labels automatically. Note that in the Range field of the AutoFormat Chart wizard, your predefined range has been picked up by the wizard, so you don't need to enter or adjust it. Click the Next button.

Here, make a few additional settings to allow the AutoFormat Chart wizard to create an accurate and informative chart. This particular table offers data series in rows (it's a series of *one*, so don't be confused), so the proper setting, in this case, is to click the radio button for "Data series in: Rows," as shown in Figure 8-21. Also notice in Figure 8-21 that we have checked the box for "Show text elements in preview." This provides a WYSIWYG (What-You-See-Is-What-You-Get) view of the bar graph in progress, visible over on the left side of the AutoFormat Chart dialog in Figure 8-21. If the graph or text looks incorrect at this juncture, click the back button to adjust some settings or pick a different chart type, if necessary. Click the Next button.

This takes you to the dialog for labeling the main chart title and the axes, and provides a check box to include or exclude the legend. (See Figure 8-22.)

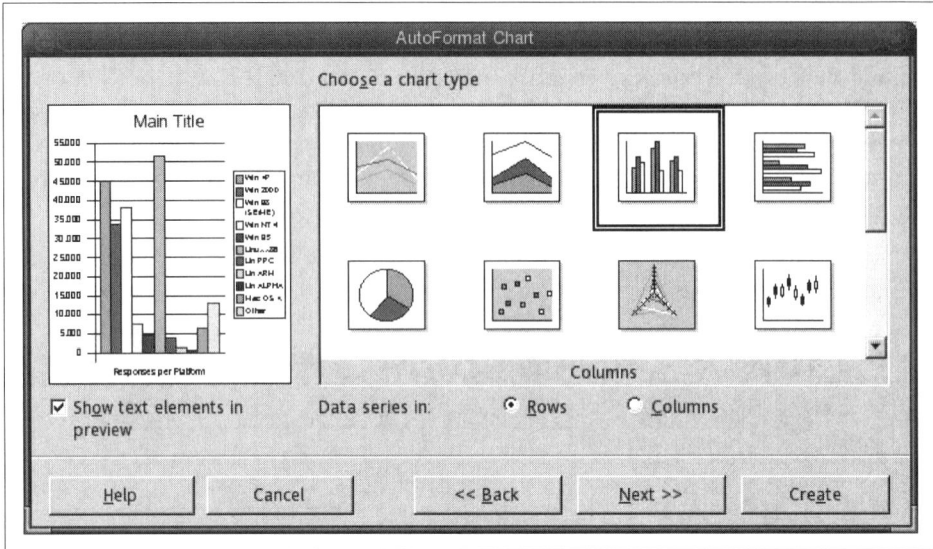

Figure 8-21. Additional chart settings

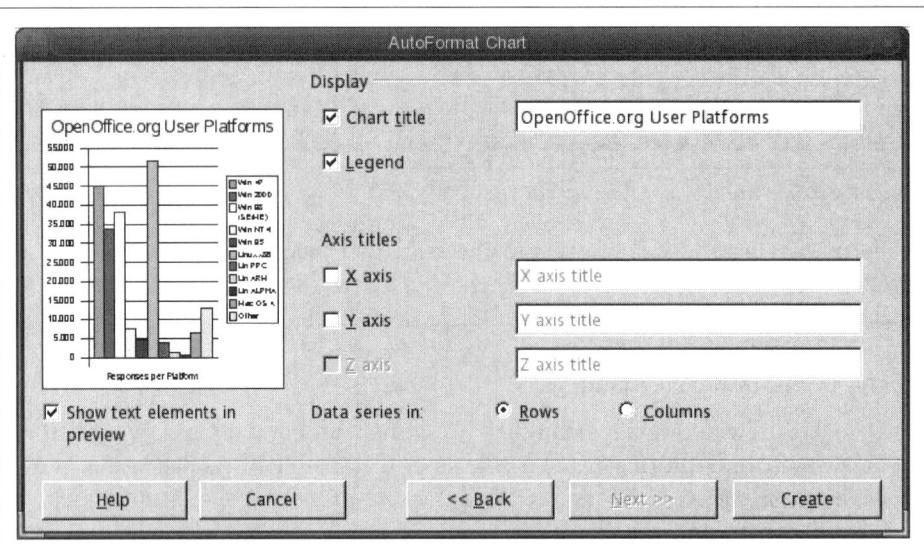

Figure 8-22. Entering the chart title and labels

In this case, we chose to show the legend (the Legend box is checked) because the colors in the legend indicate which platform is represented by each bar in the graph. Figure 8-22 shows the dialog after the main title, "OpenOffice.org User Platforms," has been written into the Main Title field. (See Figure 8-23.)

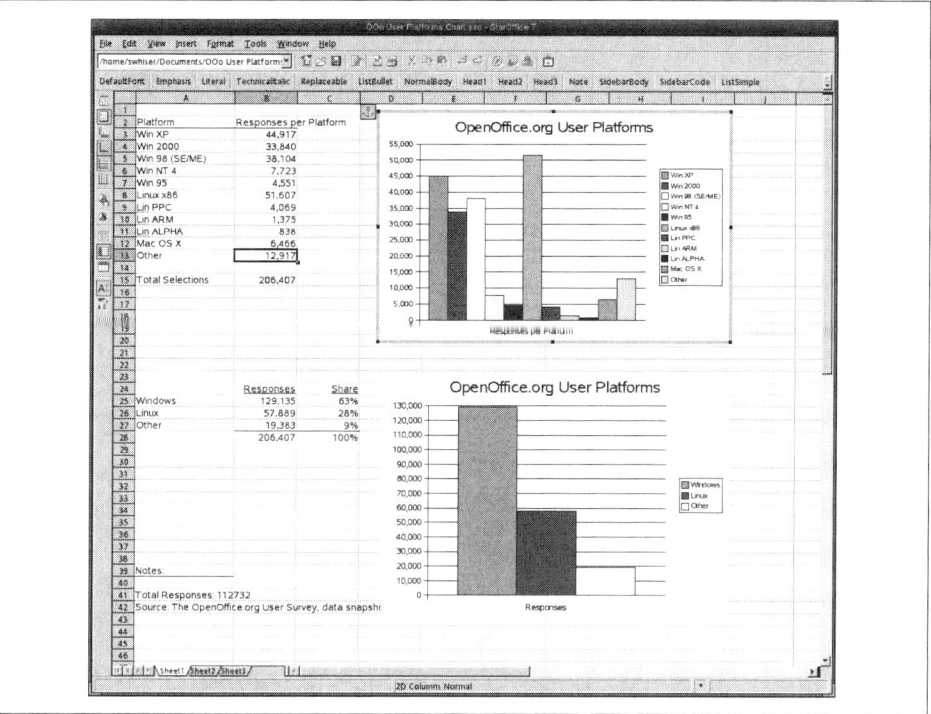

Figure 8-23. The bar graph is complete

Finally, click the Create button at the bottom right corner of the dialog, and the graph appears in the live worksheet. You can now adjust the size or placement of the graph by grabbing one of the gray edges to move one of the black squares .

Worksheets, or Sheets

One StarCalc spreadsheet file (sometimes called a "Workbook") contains three sheets by default but can hold up to 256 sheets in total.

Figure 8-24 shows the three sheets of a standard, default spreadsheet file. In the figure, note from the white coloration of the sheet tab that sheet 1 is live, or current. The gray coloration of sheets 2 and 3 indicate they are present but not visible.

To move among sheets, simply click on a sheet tab, and it becomes the live sheet.

Adding a new sheet

To add a new sheet, right-click on the sheet area, or any one of the sheet tabs, to call up the menu, shown in Figure 8-25.

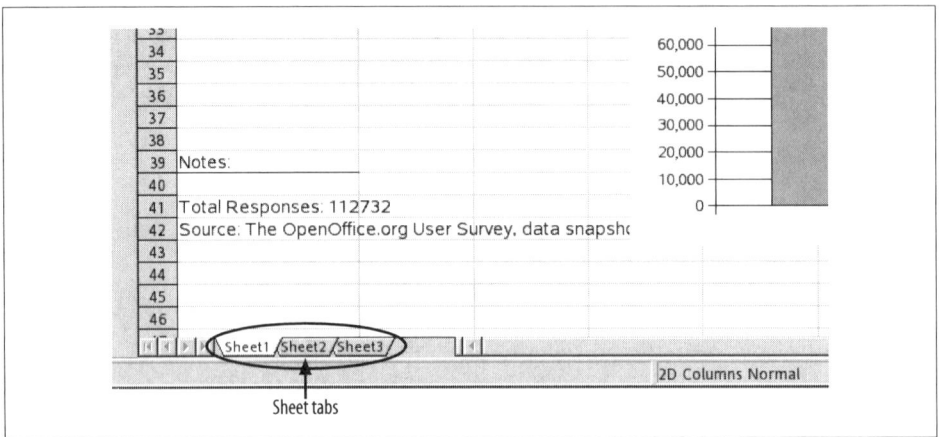

Figure 8-24. Three sheets to the wind

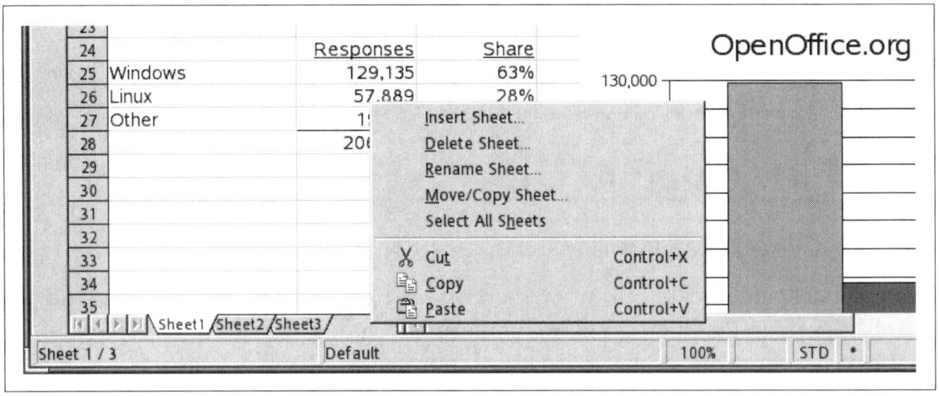

Figure 8-25. The menu for manipulating sheets

Then select Insert Sheet… from the menu, and the Insert Sheet dialog box appears. Here, you can designate the names, positions, and number of the new sheets. Note that you can add multiple sheets. You can also bring in sheets from another file; after you browse and select a file, the names of its sheets are displayed for you to choose from.

Deleting a sheet

To delete a sheet from a workbook, use the same menu, shown in Figure 8-25. First select the sheet you want to delete. Then right-click the sheet bar or live sheet tab and select Delete Sheet…. This activates a confirmation dialog asking if you are certain you want to delete this sheet. To delete the sheet, answer by clicking on the Yes button. Answering No leaves the live sheet in place.

Renaming a sheet

To rename a live sheet, right-click the target sheet's tab and select Rename Sheet… from the menu that appears. This activates the Rename Sheet dialog, where you can enter the new name for the sheet in the Name field.

Selecting a group of sheets

To select more than one sheet at a time, hold down the Ctrl key, while clicking on each sheet tab you want to select.

Selecting concurrent sheets is useful when entering content, such as column headings or labels, that you want to have on many sheets. It saves the repetition of setting up multiple sheets with the same information.

If you have a workbook with many sheets and want to select a long range of contiguous sheets, click on the tab of the left-most sheet in your target range. Then, while holding down the Shift key, click on the right-most sheet tab of your target range. This selects all sheets included in that range.

To deselect that same group, hold down the Shift key, while clicking on the tab of the first sheet (the left-most sheet, in this case) that you selected in that range.

To deselect a selected sheet (other than the live sheet, which always remains selected), hold down the Ctrl key, while clicking on its sheet tab.

Navigating among many sheets

If you have a spreadsheet with many sheets, like the one illustrated in Figure 8-26, not all the tabs are visible at the bottom. To make a tab visible so you can select its sheet, you need to use the sheet navigation arrow buttons at left of the sheet tabs.

By clicking the arrow buttons, you can move the sheet tabs over one by one. The buttons that have arrows and thin vertical bars allow you to jump all the way to the first or last tab. The arrow buttons change according to context: when you are on the left-most tab, the arrows to move right are highlighted and available. The converse is true when you are on a sheet toward the right extreme.

Sorting Data

To sort a list or chart of numerical or textual information, first highlight the full range to be sorted (including labels, but excluding unwanted data such as totals) and then select Data → Sort from the Main menu. This launches the Sort dialog box, where you can designate the sorting order among other parameters.

In the case, as illustrated in Figure 8-27, we want to reorder the data to put the largest responses at the top. Therefore, in the Sort dialog, we select to sort by the "Responses per Platform" column (where the numbers are) and set the radio button

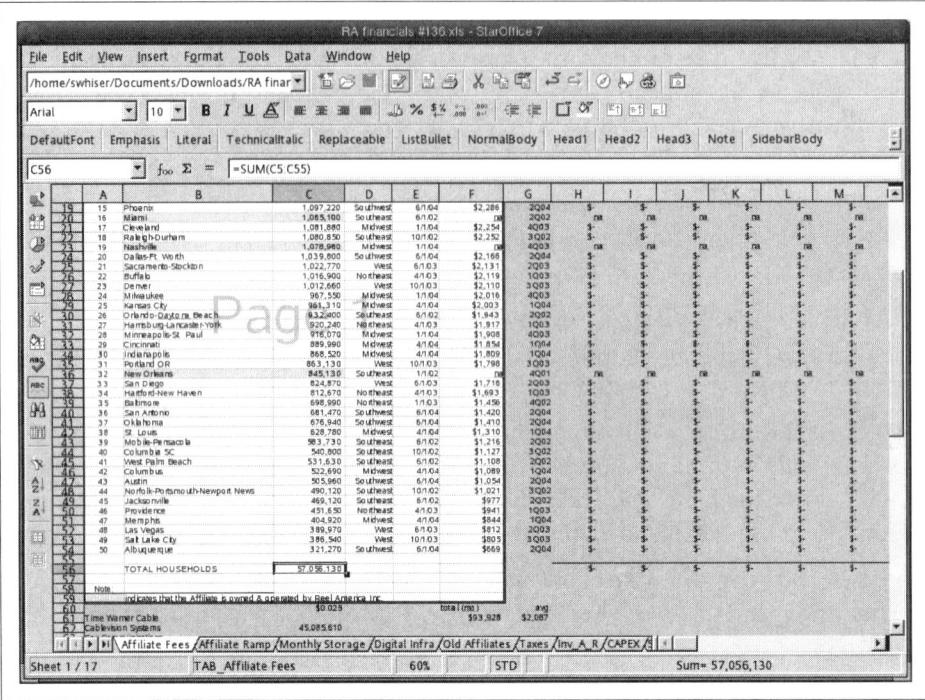

Figure 8-26. A file with 17 sheets

at the right to Descending. Then we press the OK button. Notice how rearranging the order of the source chart automatically registers the new order in the bar graph that was previously generated. (See Figure 8-28.)

Data Sources

Instead of having its own database format, StarCalc is designed to interact with many different varieties of external databases. Data Sources is the name for StarCalc's powerful feature set for interacting with databases and for linking forms and reports to information contained in databases. StarCalc offers a variety of ways to link to a MySQL or Adabas D database, for example, or many other data sources—including MS Outlook, Outlook Express, Mozilla, and your JDS address book in the Email and Calendar program.

In StarCalc, call up the Data Source View by choosing Tools → Data Sources… from the Main menu, or simply by pressing the function key, F4. Press F4 again to close the Data Source View.

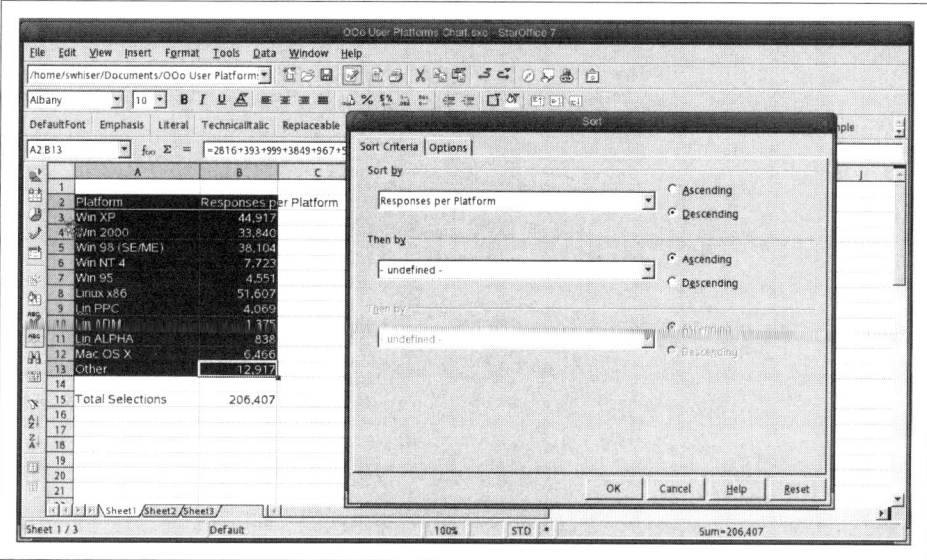

Figure 8-27. Sorting a simple table

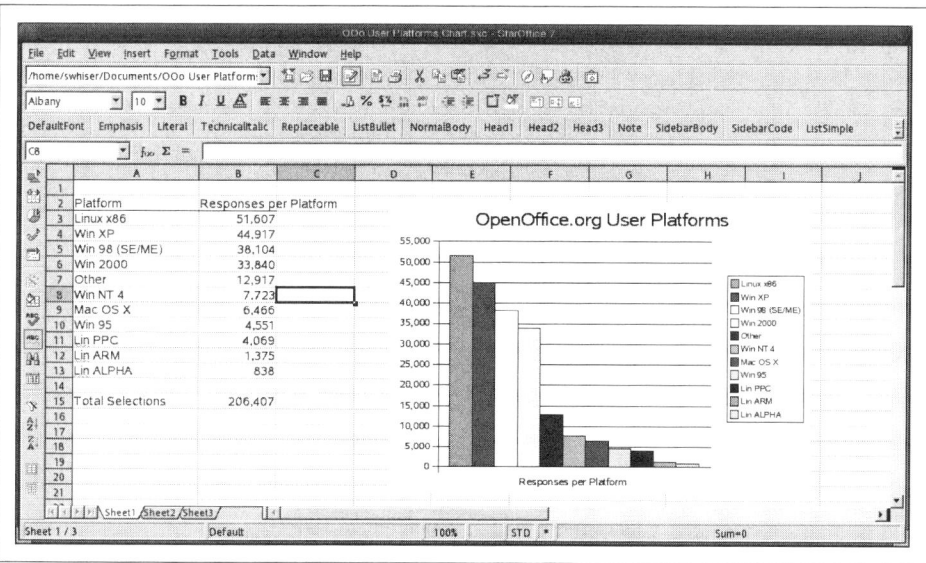

Figure 8-28. Table (and graph) successfully sorted

Having made such a promising introduction, it's regrettable to say that Data Sources is outside the scope of this book. It's unfortunate because interacting with databases is becoming more relevant to the web-enabled desktop user. Furthermore, StarOffice's database interactivity is a hot focus of development activity and promises to get stronger as well as easier for the average user to handle, with each progressive release of the StarOffice software.

To learn more about Data Sources in StarCalc and across all modules of StarOffice, look here: *http://docs-pdf.sun.com/816-5405/816-5405.pdf*.

Macros

Creating or handling macros in StarCalc is not within the scope of this book. However, we can offer some general information that may be useful to macro users. Macros could come into play for all the different modules of StarOffice (and MS Office), but here we deal strictly with their relevance to StarCalc (and MS Excel).

StarCalc uses its own macro-scripting language called StarOffice Basic (or "StarBasic"). This is a different macro language from the one used by Microsoft in MS Office, which is called Visual Basic (or "VBA").

VBA macros are not able to run in StarCalc, creating a significant barrier for migration from MS Excel to StarCalc for users who have many large or significant VBA macros within their spreadsheets. VBA macros that come with MS Excel files currently must be rewritten in StarBasic for these files to be fully useful in StarCalc.

Sometime "early next year [2005]," Sun Microsystems promises to release a new Visual Basic-to-Star Basic macro conversion tool to facilitate the automatic conversion of VBA macros to StarBasic macros.

Meanwhile, StarCalc is set by default to save VBA macros to be available and written back, whenever a StarCalc spreadsheet file is saved again in the MS Excel file format. This offers three options:

1. You can reimport a spreadsheet to Excel to run the stored VBA macros.

2. You can store the VBA macros to manually rewrite them in StarBasic.

3. You can preserve them unused in StarCalc, to be converted later to StarBasic when Sun's macro conversion tool becomes available.

Because VBA macros do not run in StarCalc, the viruses associated with them pose no threat, as long as you use StarCalc. If you want to leave off the macros (for security reasons or because you just don't want them) when importing Excel files, turn off the default in Tools → Options → Load/Save → VBA Properties.

If you are interested in macros, feel free to consult the StarOffice Basic Programmer's Guide at *http://docs.sun.com/db/doc/817-1826?q=star+basic*.

StarImpress

StarOffice Impress (also known as "StarImpress") is the presentation module included in the StarOffice suite. Users who are familiar with most recent versions of Microsoft PowerPoint can feel at home in StarImpress.

In this section, we cover the basic features of StarImpress.

StarImpress Basics

Experienced PowerPoint users can get quite far on their existing knowledge. If you are new to presentation software, the basics covered below should be enough to get you started.

Tips for Presentation

These elementary principles should help you make a clear, strong impression:

- Public speaking, even in small informal settings, is an art that (like writing) takes years to master. With presentation software handy, it's tempting to let the computer do the talking. However, if we merely read from cluttered slides or compete with the dense, projected content on the screen, we may never get our key points across.
- Don't abuse the pulpit. Stick to the fundamentals to win an audience and make a strong impression.
- Keep slides simple and uncluttered: one to three items per slide. Organize your thoughts carefully and group sub-topics under larger topics.
- Use the information on the screen to complement the physical presentation. *You're* the information!
- Use color-coding or symbols sparingly, for cognitive efficiency.
- A crisp background theme in subtle hues projects your brand, with feeling.

Remember, the audience wants you to succeed—at first.

Creating a Presentation from Scratch with Autopilot

To launch StarImpress, click on StarOffice 7 in the Launch menu. If you are creating a new presentation, you don't have to suffer the panic that normally arises from staring at a blank screen. In the Templates and Documents dialog box, click on the New Document icon in the left pane. Then, in the Title pane, double-click on Presentation (third from the bottom). This launches the AutoPilot Presentation wizard, shown in Figure 8-29.

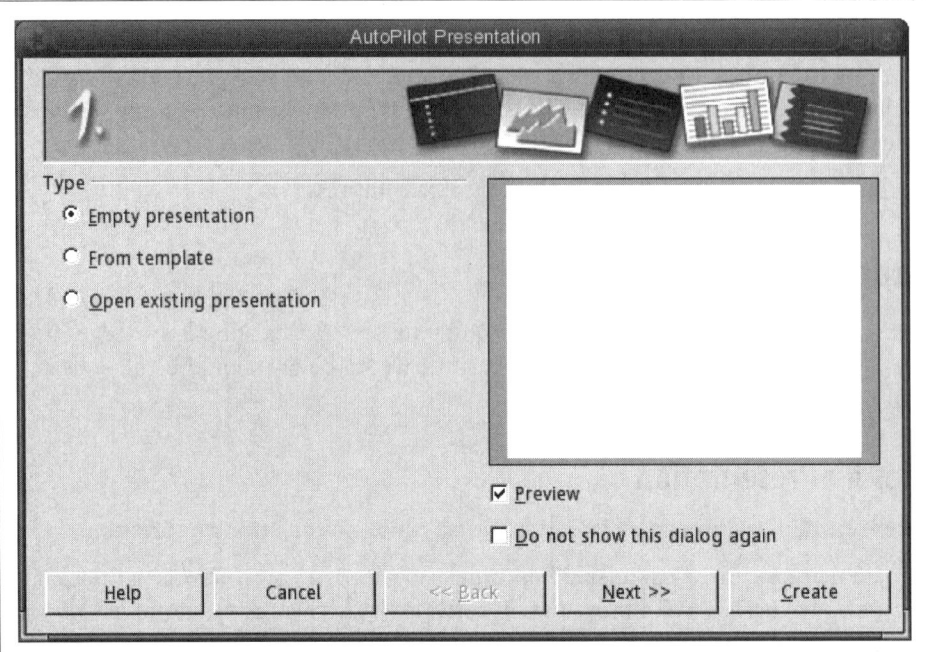

Figure 8-29. Step 1: AutoPilot Presentation wizard

In Figures 8-29 through 8-34, we take you through the beginning steps of a minimalist presentation, with the fewest possible changes entered into the dialogs. For the simplest and quickest result, we encourage you to proceed through the Autopilot dialogs by simply pressing the Next button. Along the way, we point out some of the opportunities for embellishment, but for this example, you may ignore them.

Although you have the opportunity in Step 1 to start work from an existing presentation template, we're using the default setting to create an empty presentation in this example.

Click the Next button, which reveals Step 2 in Figure 8-30.

 Here, you could skip Step 2 (Figure 8-30) and Step 3 (Figure 8-31) by pressing the Create button instead of Next. This lands you directly on the Modify Slide dialog. (See Figure 8-32.)

Now you can select formatting design characteristics and output formats (screen, paper, overhead sheet, or slide), but the default of "screen" suffices.

Click the Next button. Figure 8-31 shows Step 3.

In Step 3, you can select slide transition effects and transition speeds for the whole presentation, but for this simplest of examples, change nothing. Later, we show you how to edit transitions and other features into your complete presentation.

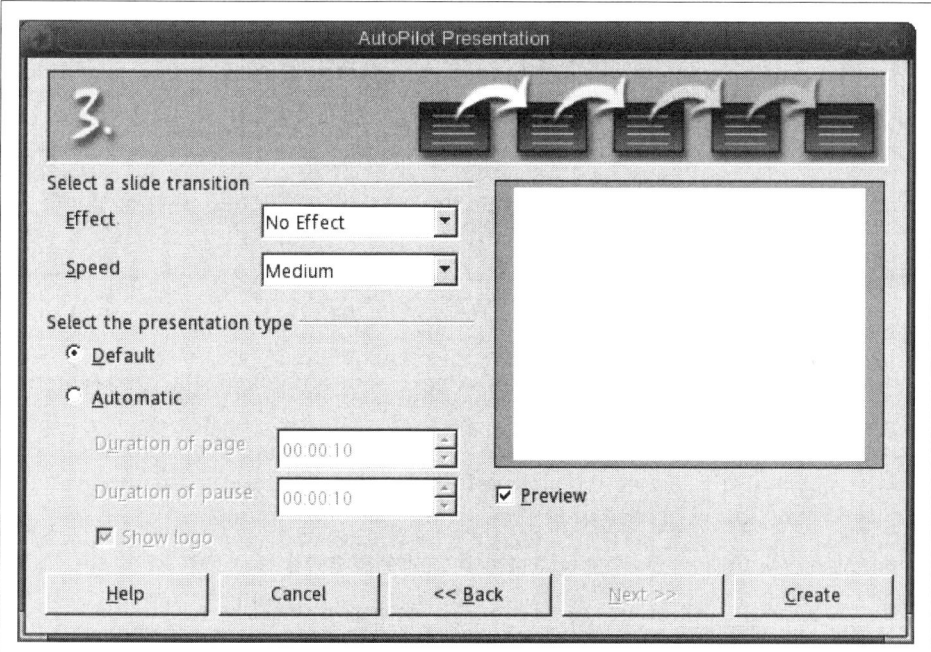

Figure 8-30. Step 2: select a design and output medium

Figure 8-31. Step 3: select slide transitions

Click the Create button, which takes you to the Modify Slide dialog, shown in Figure 8-32.

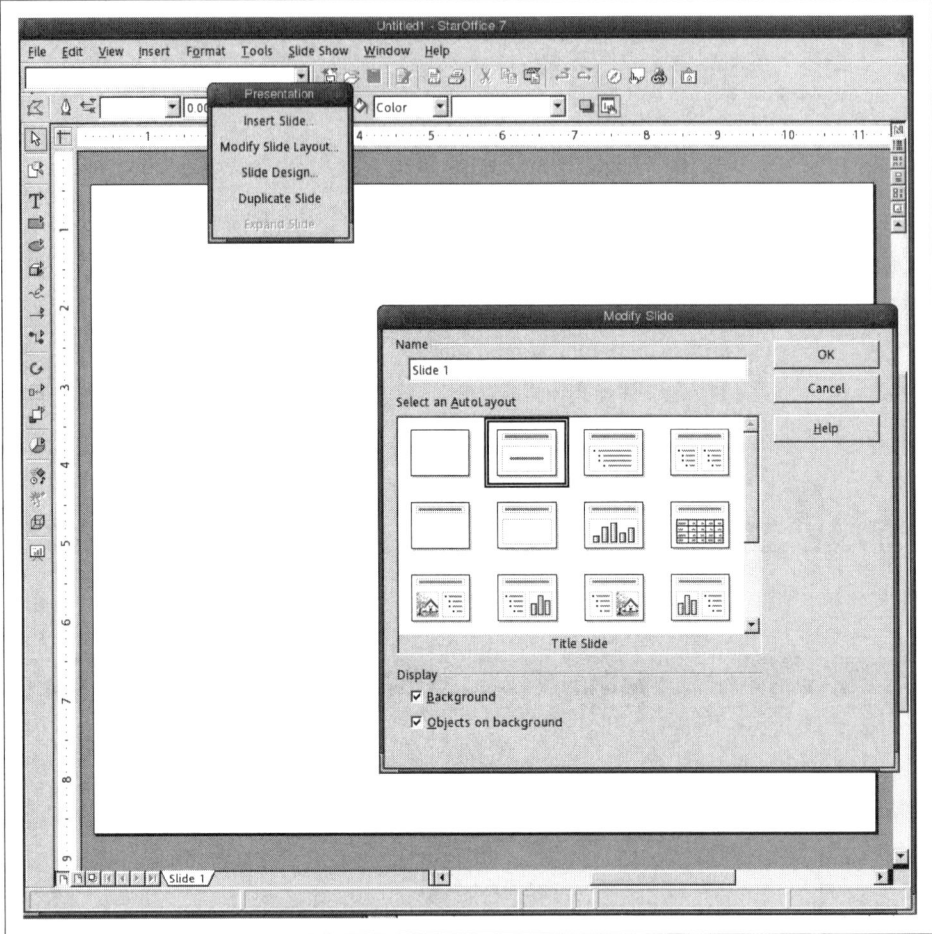

Figure 8-32. The Modify Slide dialog in context

In the Modify Slide dialog, you can choose the layout of the first slide from among a host of stock layouts offered. (See Figures 8-32 and 8-33 for greater detail.) Choose your preferred layout by highlighting it with a single click and then press the OK button. Here, you can also enter an alternative name for Slide 1 in the name field. We show you later how to change slide names during the edit process.

This presents your first slide, such as the one shown in Figure 8-34, ready for you to enter text, copy in a graphical object, or do any other operation necessary to complete your presentation.

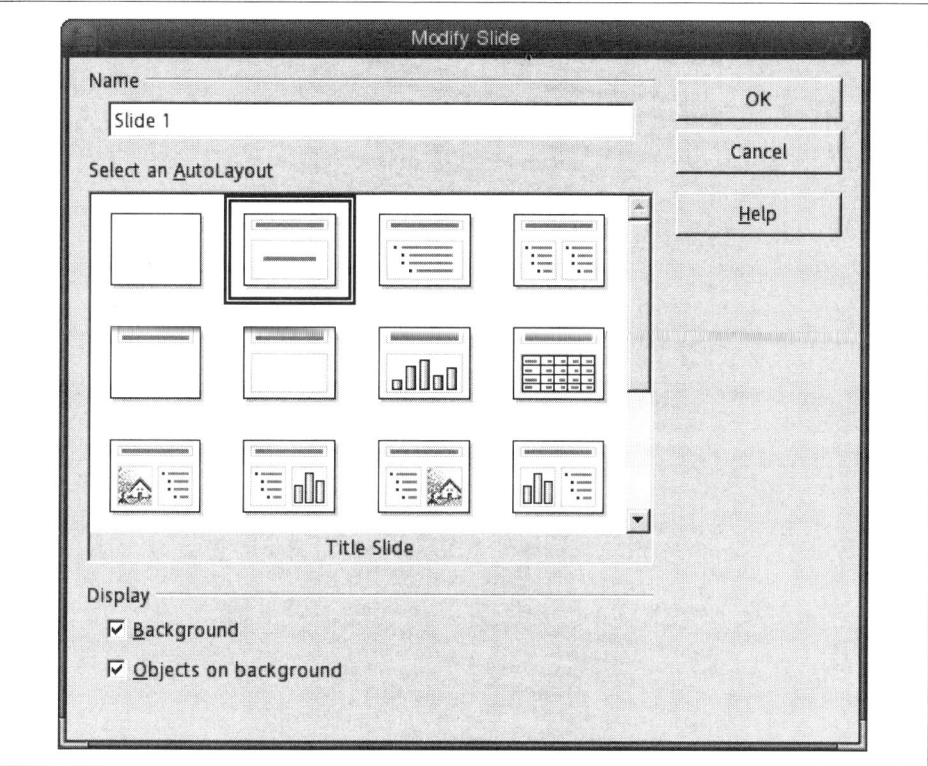

Figure 8-33. The Modify Slide dialog

From here, continue to add slides by clicking Insert → Duplicate Slide or Insert → Slide. See the "Adding slides" and "The Presentation Palette" sections for further ideas on how to insert new slides into a presentation.

Opening an Existing Presentation

To open a presentation you have created earlier or received from someone else, simply click once on a presentation file's icon in its folder. JDS is set up to seamlessly open MS PowerPoint files (which have a *.ppt* file suffix). By default, each file is saved in the same format it had when you opened it (PowerPoint, StarImpress, etc.).

Alternatively, you can select File → Open from the Main menu and browse your file system to find the existing file with which you want to work. This is consistent with all other StarOffice modules.

Saving a Presentation

To save your current presentation in its existing location and format, click the Save icon (the little floppy disk image) on the Function bar and the file is saved into its

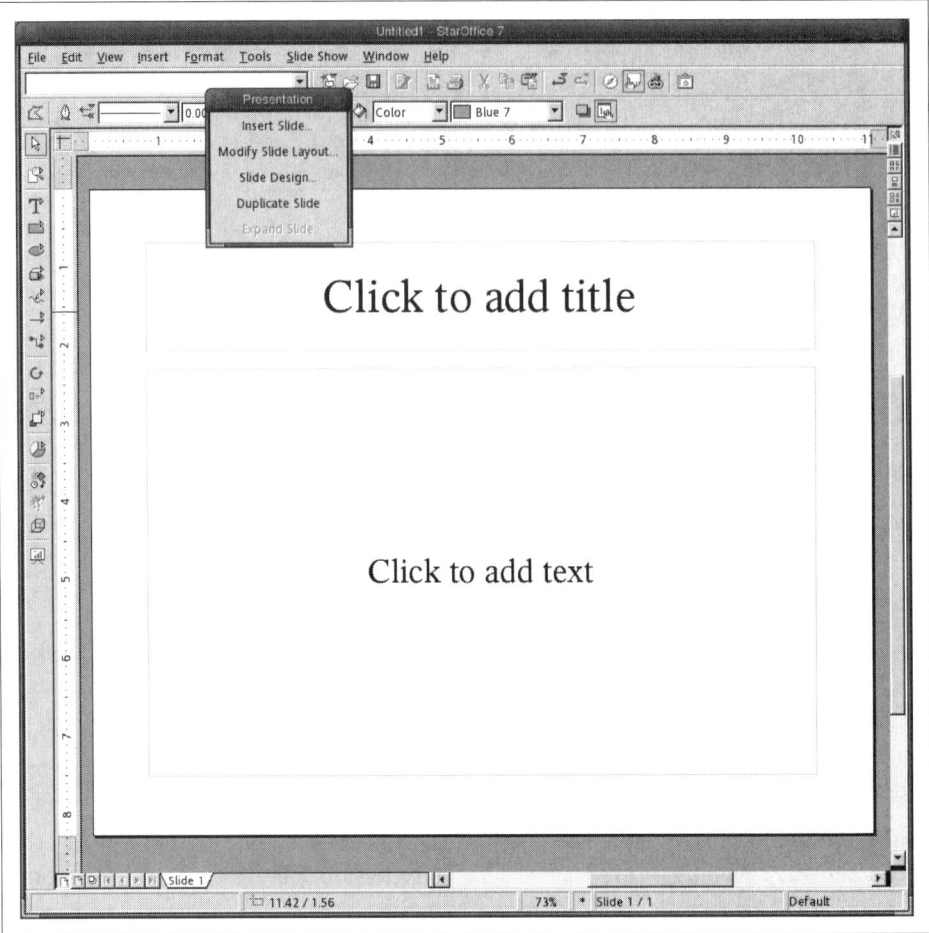

Figure 8-34. First slide, awaiting input

present location in your filesystem. The same result occurs if you select File → Save from the Main menu.

If you are saving the presentation for the first time, the Save dialog window opens to allow you to select a folder and fill in the file name field. Do this, then click the Save button. By default, the Save dialog window opens to the Documents directory (folder) in your filesystem. That is, user *swhiser* by default saves documents to */home/swhiser/Documents*. This default also is consistent with other StarOffice modules.

If you need to change the filename, folder, or format of the presentation file you are saving, save by selecting File → Save As and fill out the Save As dialog, accordingly.

Export Formats

One of the principal strengths of StarImpress is the sheer number of file formats to which you may export your presentation. Table 8-1 lists the various export file formats available.

Table 8-1. StarImpress file formats for export

Format	Name	File extension
BMP	Windows Bitmap	.bmp
EMF	Enhanced Metafile	.emf
EPS	Encapsulated Postscript	.eps
GIF	Graphics Interchange Format	.gif
HTML	Hypertext Markup Language	.html, .htm
JPEG	Joint Photographic Experts Group	.jpg, .jpeg, .jfif, .jif, .jpe
MET	OS/2 Metafile	.met
PBM	Portable Bitmap	.pbm
PCT	Mac Pict	.pct
PDF	Printable Document Format	.pdf
PGM	Portable Greymap	.pgm
PNG	Portable Network Graphic	.png
PPM	Portable Pixel Map	.ppm
PWP	Placeware	.pwp
RAS	Sun Raster Image	.ras
SVG	Scalable Vector Graphics	.svg
SVM	StarView Metafile	.svm
SWF	Macromedia Flash	.swf
SXI	StarImpress native file format	.sxi
TIFF	Tagged Image File Format	.tif, .tiff
WMF	Windows Metafile	.wmf
XPM	X PixMap	.xpm

Export to HTML

Among the most useful facilities here is the ability to export a presentation to the HTML or web page format. This feature allows us to painlessly convert any presentation we've given to the Web so the audience, as well as those who were unable to attend, can visit the material from any Internet-enabled location on the planet, at their own convenience.

Figures 8-35 to 8-42 guide you through the steps to export to HTML, while altering the fewest settings possible, and while pointing out some of the optional settings along the way.

Start by selecting File → Export... from StarImpress's Main menu. This launches the Save As window. Here, change the File format drop-down box to HTML Document and designate the filename and directory of the resulting HTML files. Then click the Export button to kick off the HTML Export dialog series.

First, select a design. (See Figure 8-35.) If it's your first time, leaving the default, as is, and clicking the Next button is fine.

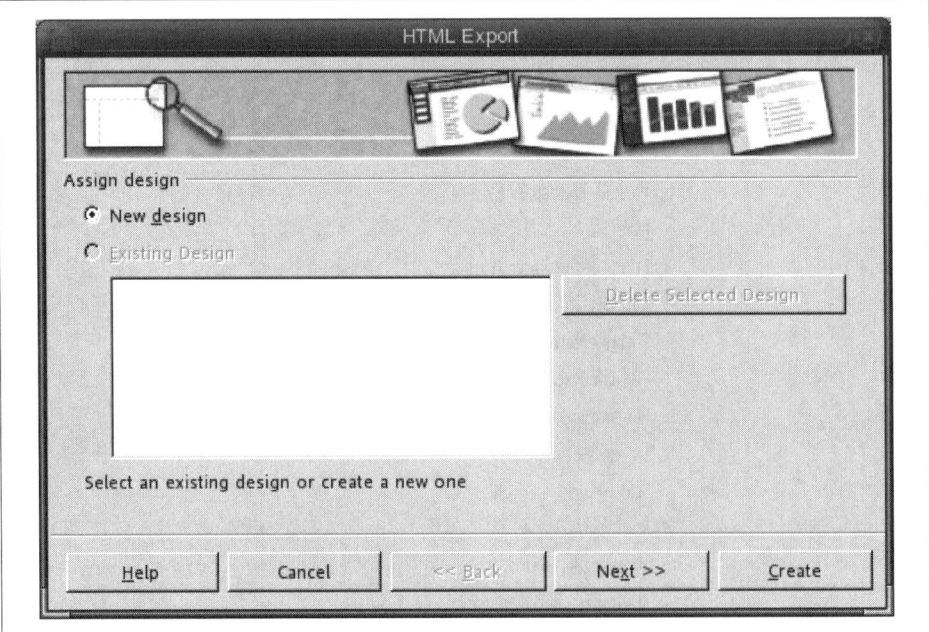

Figure 8-35. Choose a design to export

Figure 8-36 offers a number of options, known as *Publication types*, that affect how the presentation appears and can be manipulated. Among these types are:

Standard HTML format
A simple HTML or web page with navigational buttons or links for each page of the presentation.

Standard HTML with frames
Similar to Standard HTML format but with a navigational index of links along the left edge of the page.

Automatic

A dynamic web presentation that advances automatically, according to certain timings and settings that you can establish here or leave at defaults.

WebCast

Code in the form of either Active Server Pages or Perl scripts, according to your selection, that permits you to orchestrate a real-time webcast. In the webcast, you can change slides, while members of the audience view what you are doing in their browsers. Files exported in either WebCast mode require the use and configuration of a server.

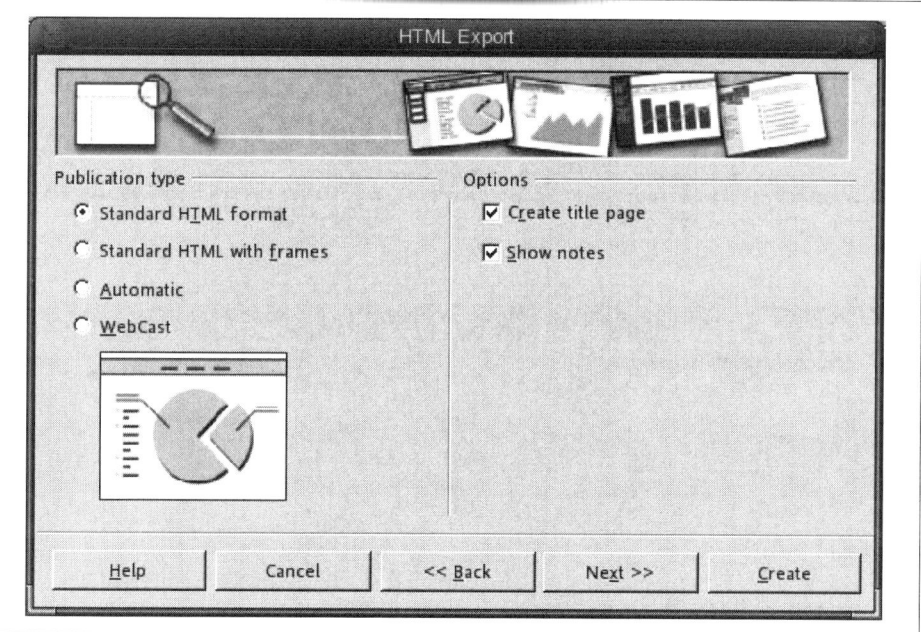

Figure 8-36. Publication types and options

Here, we accept the default and click Next. This shows Figure 8-37, which offers various choices for graphics.

Here, you can alter the format of graphics in the output and the resolution of output, and turn sound effects on or off. Leaving the settings at their defaults works fine.

Click Next to show the dialog in Figure 8-38.

This screen permits you to enter information that appears on the title page of the new web presentation. Enter the desired information and click Next for Figure 8-39.

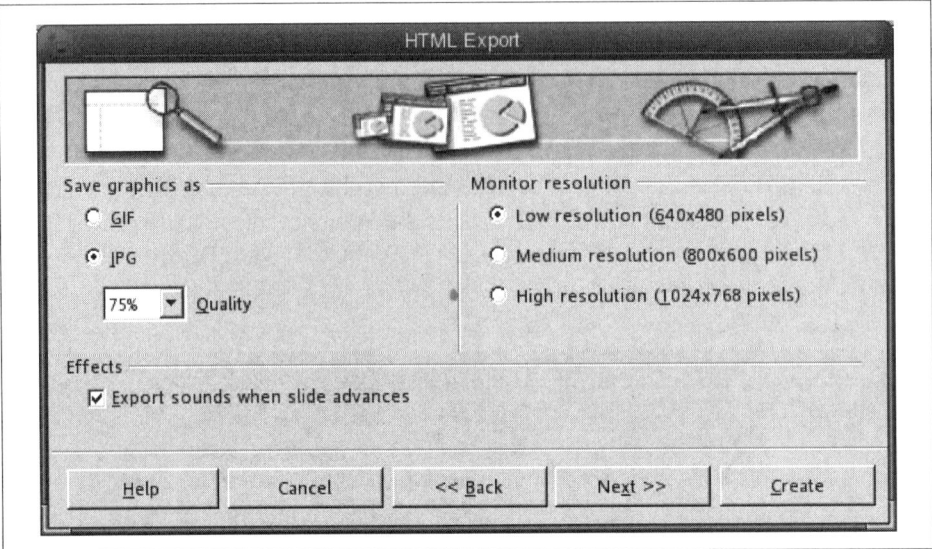

Figure 8-37. Graphics, resolution, and effects settings

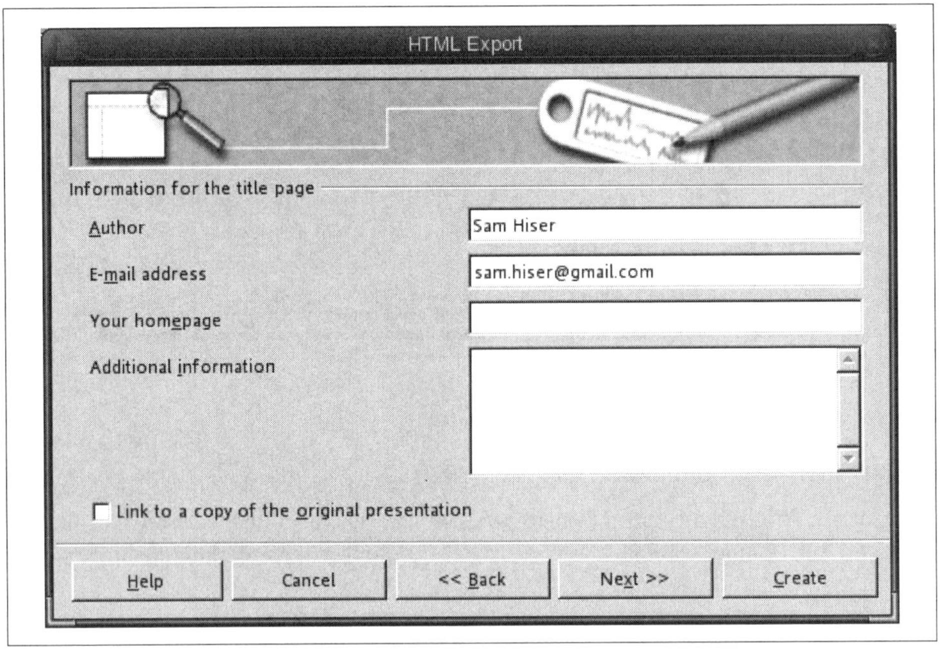

Figure 8-38. Add title page information

Here, you can set the look of the navigational elements you like, such as forward and backward arrows. Leaving the "Text only" box checked (the default setting) produces text links, but you also have a choice of four styles of colorful buttons.

Click Next for Figure 8-40.

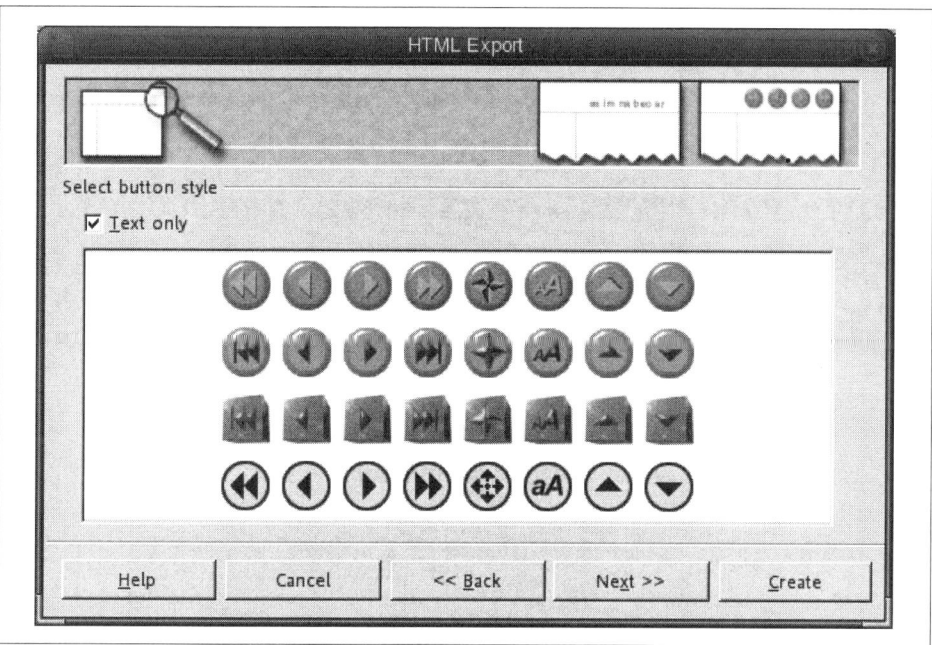

Figure 8-39. Choose navigational buttons

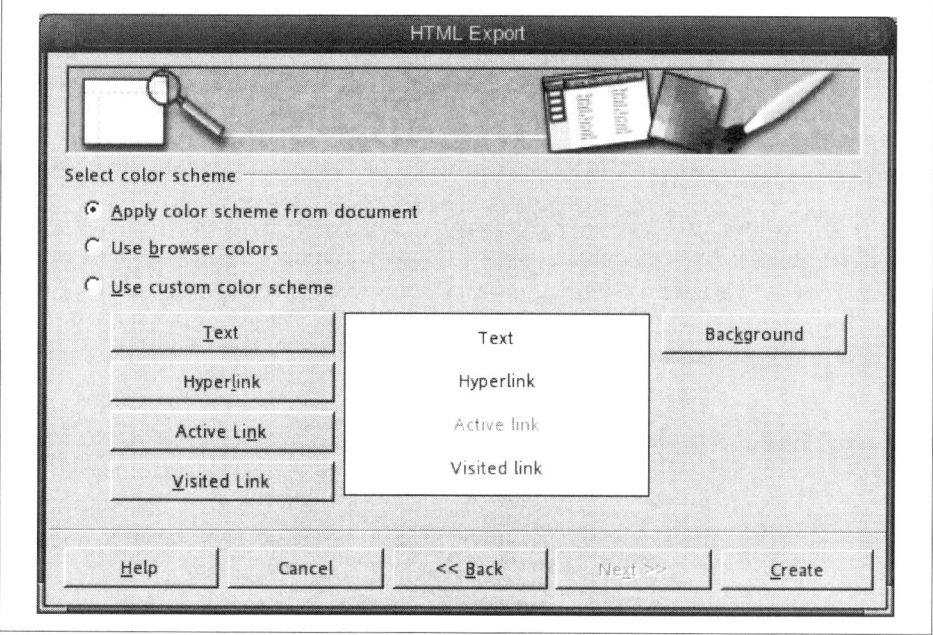

Figure 8-40. Select a text color scheme

In this final screen of the export process, you can alter the default color scheme of the text. Leaving settings alone works fine for first-timers.

Finally, click the Create button. Figure 8-41 illustrates a page of the final web presentation that we have just created.

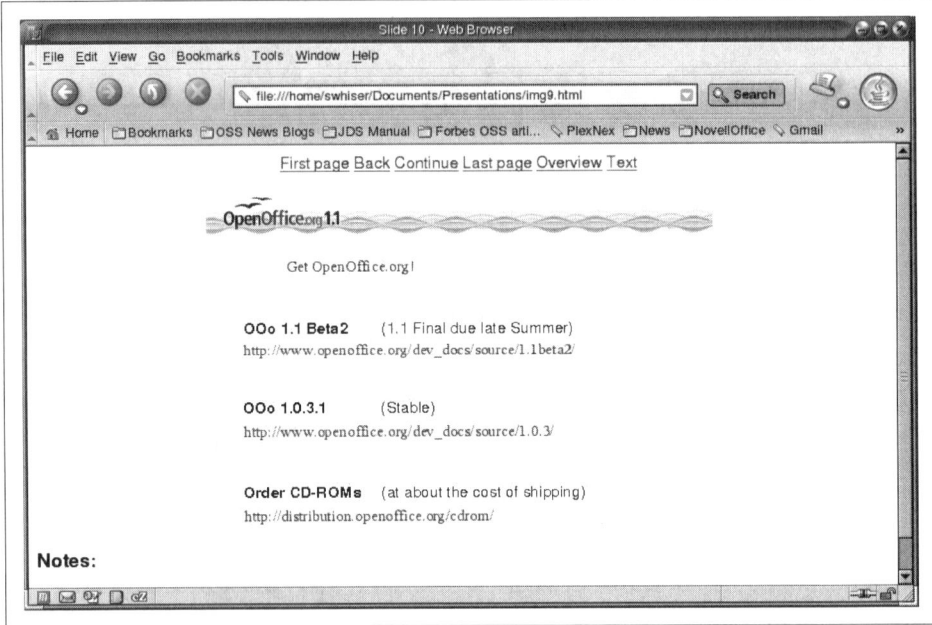

Figure 8-41. The final result

Export to Macromedia Flash

Not to be overshadowed, among the many output formats, is Macromedia Flash. This is yet another universally acceptable file format (along with PDF and HTML, in particular), which guarantees that anyone with a web browser (that is, everyone with a desktop computer) can view your presentation. Many of the same benefits of converting a presentation to HTML web pages (described above) hold, too, for the Flash format.

To export your presentation to Flash, proceed to the Main menu and select File → Export.... This opens the Export dialog box where you should go to the File Format: drop-down field and select "Macromedia Flash (SWF)(*.swf*)." In the Export dialog box, if you do not alter the folder or save path, the new Flash version of your presentation is automatically placed in the same folder as the original *.sxi* presentation file. Now, click the Export... button, and the Flash version of your presentation is created.

A Limitation of JDS's Flash Player

JDS is bundled with Macromedia Flash Player 6 for Linux. This transparent browser plug-in enables you to view Flash files via the web browser. Clicking on a Flash presentation's file icon (file extension is *.sxf*) in a desktop folder launches a Flash presentation in the web browser. To advance through the presentation, simply click on the face of each slide. Going backward is disabled, so you must keep advancing forward through the presentation to loop around to the desired slide again. This limitation is based on a deficiency of integration, which we expect to be corrected in later versions of JDS.

StarImpress Workspace Views

You can select from several different orientations or views to make it easier to work with your presentations. These have no effect on the final presentation, as seen by your audience, but they simply give you different ways to look at and navigate among your slides, while creating and editing them.

You can change the view setting from the Main menu by selecting View → Workspace and checking the desired view setting in the drop-down menu. The five Workspace Views include:

- Drawing View
- Outline View
- Slides View
- Notes View
- Handout View

Drawing View is the most common view. It makes one slide visible at a time. Because the slide fills the available window, it is easy to edit and is the view used most often by most people, while building a presentation. See Figure 8-42 for an example.

Figures 8-43 through 8-46 illustrate the additional views.

The Workspace Views are easiest to change with a single click of the small icons arrayed vertically along the right edge of the StarImpress window, toward the top, as shown in Figure 8-47.

StarImpress Modes

Modes are states in which only certain editing functions can be performed or orientations/views can be elicited.

The three modes are accessed and altered from the Main menu under View → Slide, View → Master or View → Layers, where the active mode is evidenced by the checkmark.

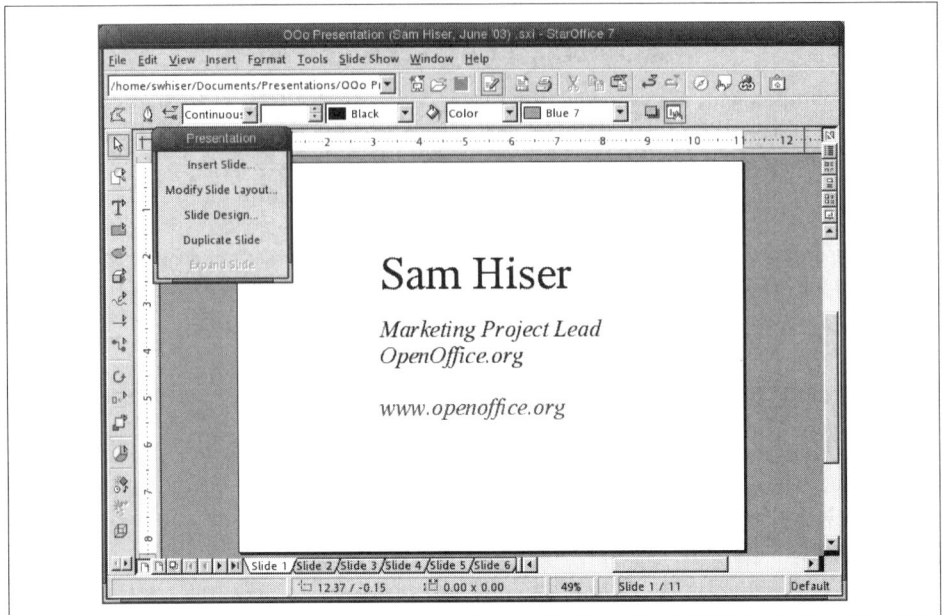

Figure 8-42. Drawing View

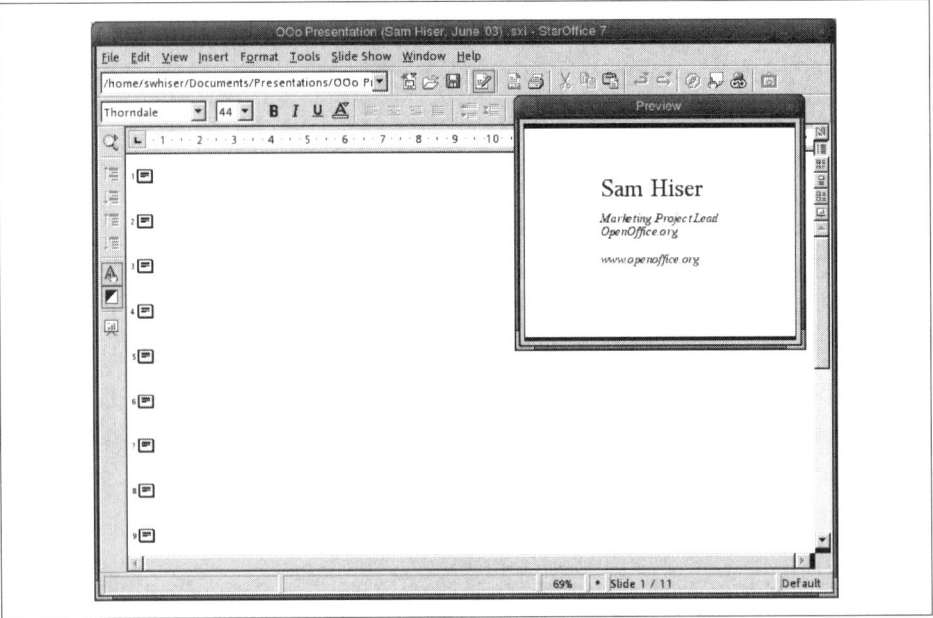

Figure 8-43. Outline View

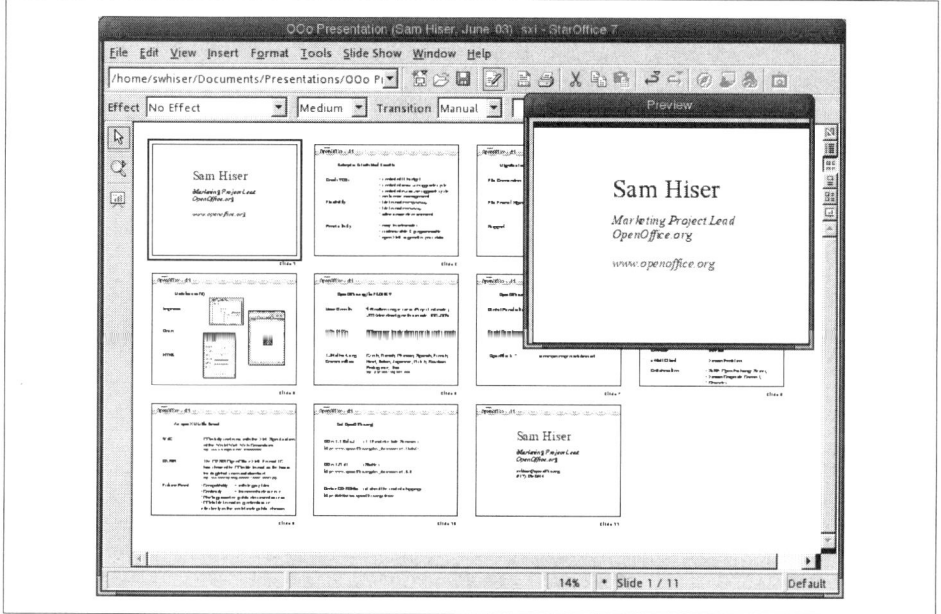

Figure 8-44. Slides View

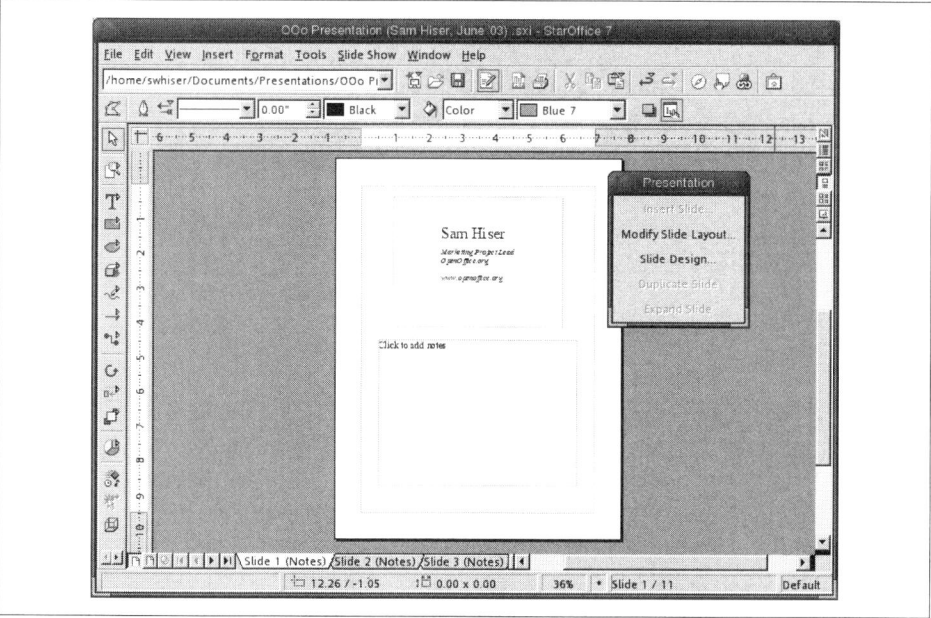

Figure 8-45. Notes View

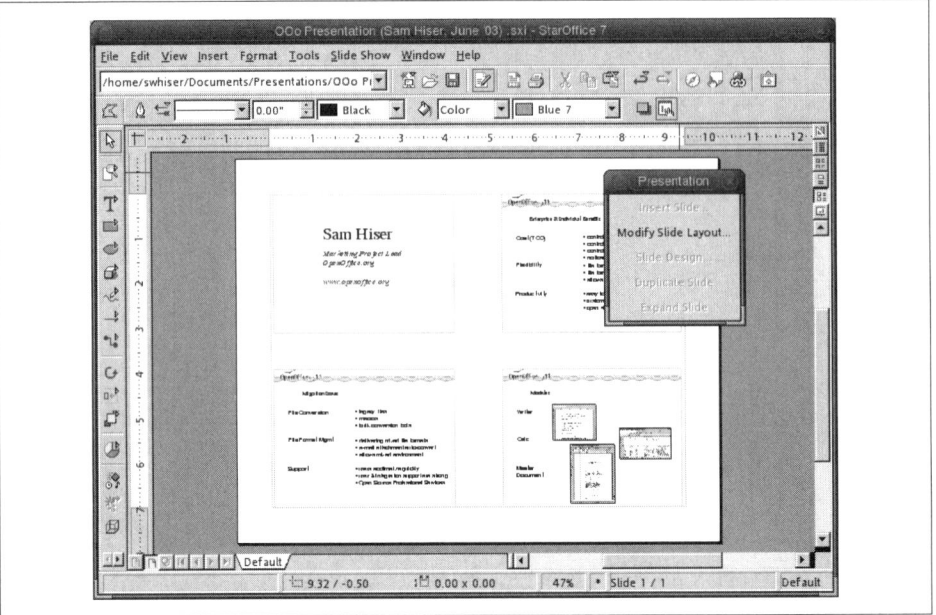

Figure 8-46. Handout View

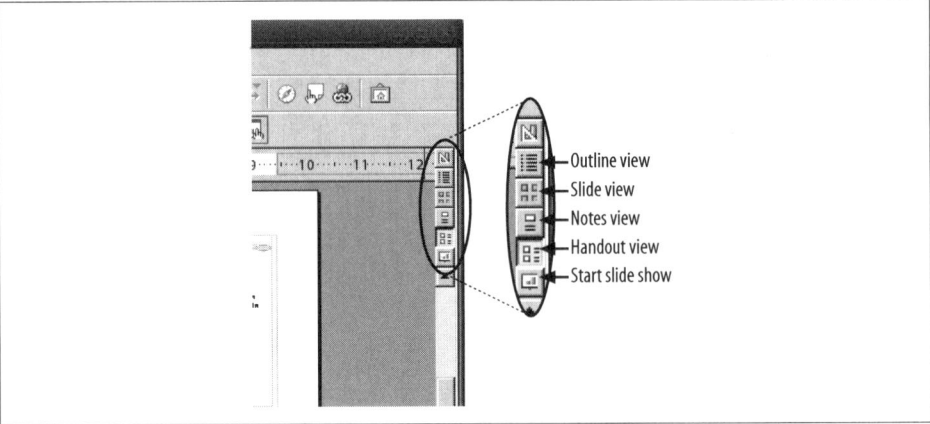

Figure 8-47. Workspace View icons

 It's a recurring point of confusion for StarOffice users that Modes are accessed and changed under Views from the Main menu. It makes it worse that StarImpress changes the View settings based on Mode settings. And, unforgivably, the Mode icons at the bottom left corner of the workspace. (See Figure 8-48.) have been mislabeled: the mouse rollover labels for the three Mode icons read "Slide View," "Master View," and "Layer View." These labels should read, "Slide Mode," "Master Mode" and "Layer Mode."

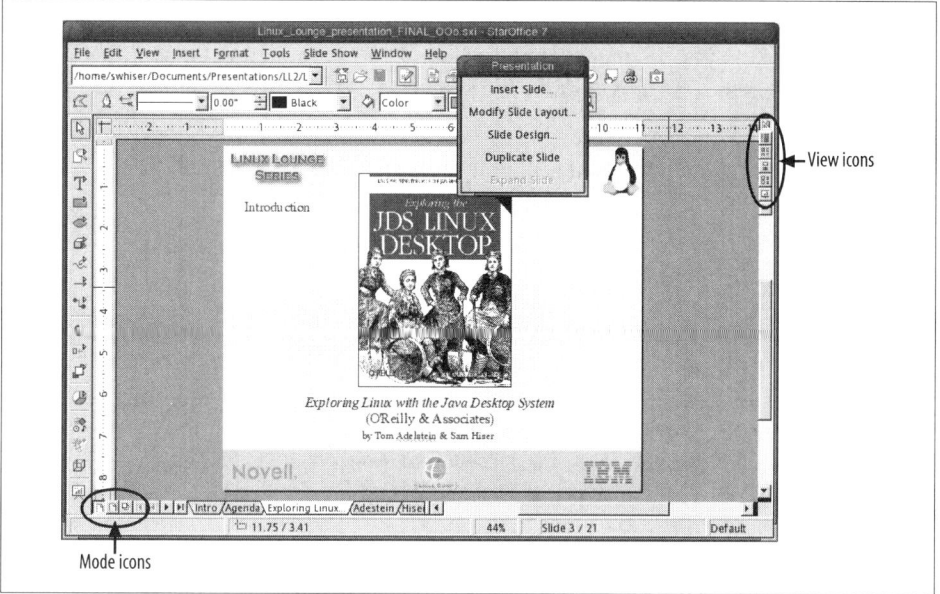

Figure 8-48. Control your modes and views

Due to the complexity of changing Views and Modes from the Main menu, we recommend using the Mode icons (at the bottom left edge of the workspace) and View icons (along the upper-right edge of the workspace) to change and visually confirm the current View/Mode. Passing the mouse pointer over each icon and pausing reveals its roll-over label, if you need to know which icon is which. Figure 8-47 introduces the View icons, and Figure 8-48 shows where both sets of View and Mode icons are located on the workspace.

Slide Mode

This is the common working mode for creating a presentation. Only Drawing View and Notes View are available to Slide Mode.

Master Mode

Master Mode is where you set global formats such as fonts, and add elements, such as logos, backgrounds, or themes that you may wish to carry across every slide.

To enter Master Mode, select View → Master from the Main menu.

Layers Mode

Layers Mode helps you segregate three different kinds of elements, so you can edit each kind of element (via tabs), without conflict:

Layout
> Includes only the normal text and graphical elements

Controls
> Includes only the buttons, the navigational elements you've inserted

Dimension Lines
> Includes dimensional lines that you create (and then usually hide) to measure objects in a slide

Layers may be locked, hidden, added, or deleted to help you organize elements within your presentation. The complexity of layers puts its functionality outside the scope of this book. However, the power of layers for aiding the organization of a presentation makes it worth mentioning for users who are inclined to pursue further knowledge on their own.

Editing a Presentation

Altering an existing presentation is quite straightforward.

Entering text

To enter or edit a sequence of text, click once on the text. You see a shaded block appear around the text with green squares at intervals around the box, as illustrated in Figure 8-49. Move the cursor to the appropriate place and enter changes. Clicking elsewhere in the slide makes the shaded block go away, and you can move on.

Using bullets

To introduce a bullet to a line of text, click once on the targeted text, then click the bullets icon, centrally located on the Object bar. If you're not sure what to press, let the mouse hover over the icons and choose the one where the Bullets On/Off balloon appears.

If you are sophisticated about the formatting of your bullets, click the alternative Bullets icon, at the extreme right of the Object bar. This brings up a dialog box with a selection of bullet and numbering styles, and other formatting options.

Importing graphics, tables, and charts

To import a graphic, table, or chart from another program, web page, or module of StarOffice, simply copy the element from its native source and paste it into your slide.

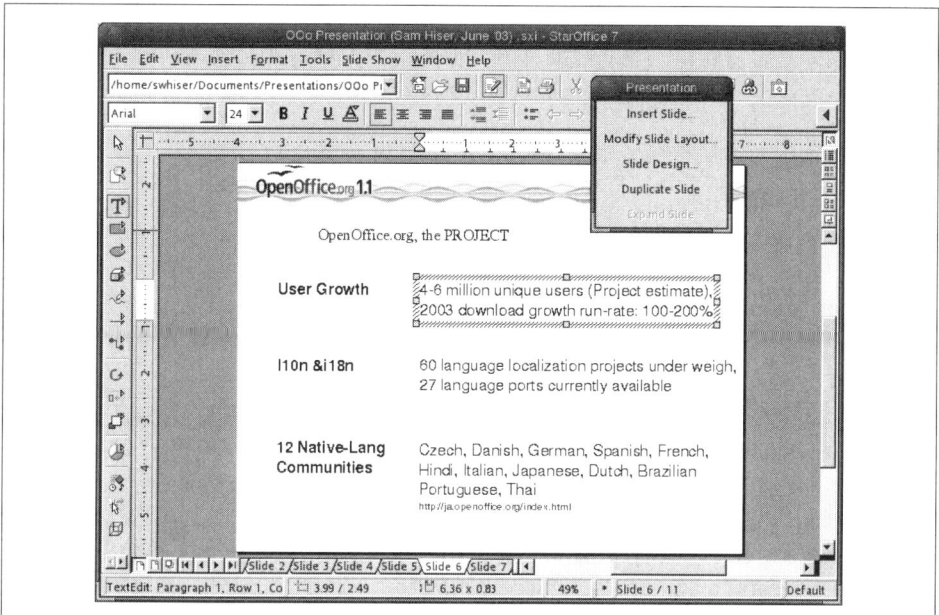

Figure 8-49. Editing textual elements

This, for example, may involve highlighting the item in its original application with a single click and pressing Ctrl-C to copy it (actually placing the element onto the desktop's clipboard). Then click in your slide once and press Ctrl-V to paste in the element.

The landing spot may not be perfect, so adjust the position of the imported object by clicking on it and holding the mouse button, while shifting the position of the mouse pointer, a simple drag-and-drop.

Adding slides

To add or insert a slide into your presentation, simply select Insert → Slide from the Main menu, choose the desired AutoLayout format in the Insert Slide dialog that appears, and press the OK button. You can name the new slide in the Name field of the Insert Slide dialog. The name you enter there appears on the slide's tab, toward the bottom of the window. The Insert → Slide procedure produces a blank slide, inserted just to the right of the current slide, which you can then fill in, as desired.

Quite often it's quicker to duplicate a nearby slide by selecting Insert → Duplicate Slide and then making a few adjustments.

Deleting slides

You can quickly delete a slide by right-clicking on its tab and selecting Delete… from the contextual menu. Alternatively, from the Main menu, select Edit → Delete Slide.

Moving slides around

In the view/mode, in which most people normally edit or build a presentation (i.e., Drawing View, Slide Mode—see Figure 8-48 to locate the View and Mode icons and check the current setting), the easiest way to move slides around is to simply click, drag and drop the tab of any slide to insert it into a new sequence among the tabs.

While this method is speedy, it offers poor visibility of the surrounding slides' contents. The best way to move slides around is to change the view to Slide View by clicking the Slide View icon at the upper-right edge of the workspace. (See Figures 8-47 and 8-48.) Now, with many slides in full view (although they are small), it is easy to click, then drag and drop a given slide from its current location to another location with a clear view of the slides. Note in Figure 8-50 how a helpful vertical black bar appears to emphasize a new destination, when you drag a slide over other slides. Also note how the dragged slide appears in outlined form as you move it.

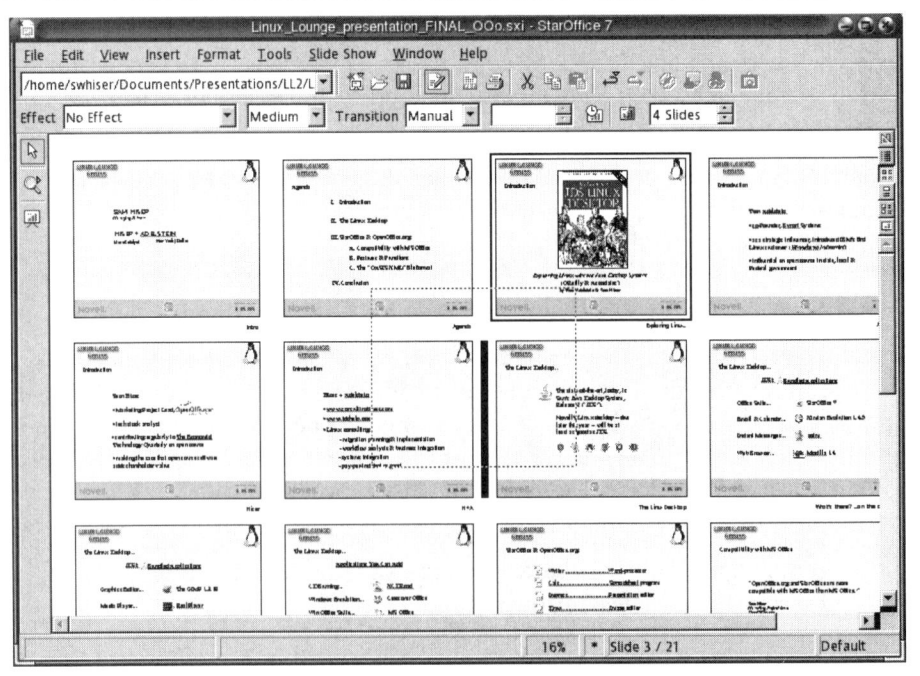

Figure 8-50. Moving a slide in Slide View

Changing the background (color, fill, or gradient)

A simple change of background fill for a color, gradient, or hatching pattern, for either a single slide or the entire presentation, is easy to effect. To change the background for a single slide, enter Slide Mode (if you are not already there) by clicking the Slide Mode button at the extreme left of the tab bar, along the bottom edge of your workspace. (See Figure 8-48.) Then, select Format → Page from the Main menu and, in the Page Setup window, click on the Background tab. In the Fill area, now select one of the Color, Gradient, or Hatching radio buttons. Then select the appropriate choice and press OK.

To change the background for every slide in your presentation, simply repeat the above procedure, after clicking on the Master Mode button that is second from the left on the tab bar, along the bottom edge of your workspace. (See Figure 8-48.)

Changing the background (bitmap image)

Most presentations have a logo or unique image that is imbedded as part of the background of each slide. Companies typically provide a high-quality image that employers can use; if you're in a smaller organization or working alone you may need to find or build a background image of your own. There are many different kinds of digital image formats around, but StarImpress uses the bitmap image format for introducing custom backgrounds to a slide presentation.

To insert a bitmap image as a background, first import a bitmap image you've stored somewhere on your filesystems and then make the background change, as further described below. To import a bitmap file, select Format → Area from the Main menu and, in the Area window, select the Bitmaps tab. Here, click on the Import… button at the right, find the bitmap file on your system, and click the Open button. This brings you back to the Background tab, where you notice that the bitmap file has been added to the Bitmap list.

 You can use The GIMP, JDS's image manipulation program, to save most *.png, .jpg, .gif,* or other compression-formatted image files as bitmap files to use as a background to a slide presentation. Download a desirable image file from its source on the Web or email it to yourself and save it in a known folder on your filesystem. Typically, */home/ YOUR_HOME/Documents/* is a fine example of a path or folder for this purpose. Then, open the image file in The GIMP and save it in the bitmap (*.bmp*) format or file type. When it's time to import it into your StarImpress Bitmap list, go and fetch it from that */home/YOUR_ HOME/Documents/* folder to which you earlier saved it.

To change the background of a single slide to a bitmap image, enter Slide Mode (click the Slide Mode button at the extreme left, along the bottom edge of the workspace) and then select Format → Page from the Main menu. Then, click on the Background tab, click the Bitmap radio button there, and select your image from the Bitmap list. To display the entire image as the background, which is customary for an uncluttered appearance, clear the Tile check box (in the Position area of the Background tab window) and make sure that the AutoFit check box is checked. (If you want a tiled look, leave the Tile box checked.) Then, click the OK button. Now you are prompted by a small Page Settings window, which asks you, "Background Settings for all pages?" with a Yes and a No button. Click the No button if you want this bitmap image as the background for only the current page of your presentation, and your image is then set as the background to that current page.

To change the background for all the slides in your presentation to a bitmap image, enter Master Mode (click the Master Mode button that is second from the left, along the bottom edge of the workspace) and then select Format → Page from the Main menu. Click on the Background tab, click the Bitmap radio button there, and then select your image from the Bitmap list. Finally, click the OK button.

Changing the bitmap image background for all slides in a presentation can be tricky, especially if you've inherited the presentation from someone else in your organization and it already has a bitmap background that you want to change. If you have difficulty changing the background from one bitmap image to another in Master Mode, you can return to Slide Mode and delete the background bitmap image for each individual slide. Then go back and set the background for the whole presentation in Master Mode.

To delete each individual slide's background while in Slide Mode, click somewhere on the background's surface (avoiding any content elements in the slide, such as text or graphics). You will see eight small green squares appear around the extreme edges of the slide. Press the Delete key to make the bitmap image background. Repeat the procedure for each slide individually.

The Presentation Palette

Notice the floating Presentation palette in Figure 8-34. This device allows you to perform several rapid functions when building or editing your presentation. They include:

- Insert Slide…
- Modify Slide Layout…
- Slide Design…
- Duplicate Slide
- Expand Slide

To turn off the Presentation Palette, click the icon at the extreme right of the presentation toolbar, just below the Function bar.

Putting on a Slideshow

Once you have created a presentation, putting on a slideshow is a trivial undertaking.

Starting a slideshow

To start a slideshow of a presentation that is open and live on your desktop, simply press the function key, F9. This starts a full-screen slideshow at the current slide.

If you want to start at a particular slide, just click on that slide, then press F9.

Ending a slideshow

To end a slideshow and return to the mode you had for editing the presentation, press the Esc key.

Slideshow transitions

To set the transition for a single slide, select Slide Show → Slide Transition from the Main menu. The illustration in Figure 8-51 shows the transition options available.

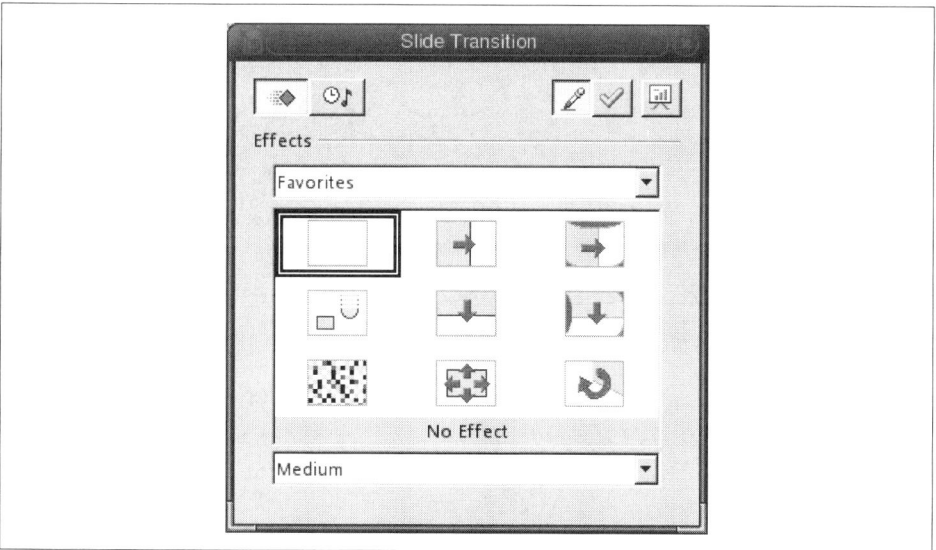

Figure 8-51. The Slide Transition window

You can choose a slow, medium, or fast transition speed in the drop-down menu at the bottom of the Slide Transition window.

If you favor using a single kind of slide transition throughout your whole presentation, it's most efficient to set this up for all slides at the same time, using AutoPilot, when you first start building a presentation. See "Creating a Presentation from Scratch with Autopilot" and refer to Figure 8-31.

Custom slideshows

You can set up many different versions of the same presentation, using only chosen slides and different settings. This is convenient for adapting different parts of one large presentation to specific audiences. You can also use it to preconfigure versions of a presentation that offer greater detail, and thus, you can switch to these spontaneously during a presentation to cover the intricate points that you might otherwise spare a general audience.

To define a new Custom Slide Show, from the Main menu of your live source presentation, select Slide Show → Custom Slide Show..., which opens the Custom Slide Shows dialog (Figure 8-52), and press the New button.

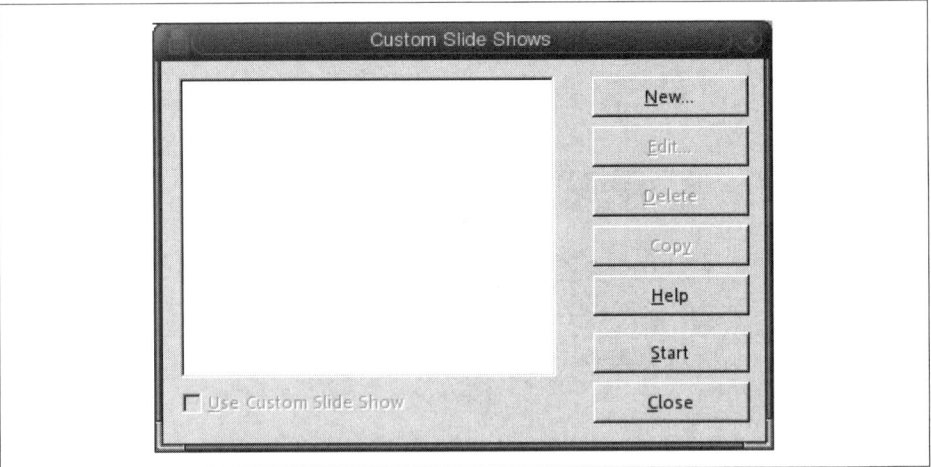

Figure 8-52. The Custom Slide Show dialog

This opens the Define Custom Slide Show dialog (Figure 8-53), where you can name the new version of your slide show and select which slides are to be included. To select a given slide for inclusion, highlight that slide in the Existing slides pane at the lefthand side of the dialog. Then, click the uppermost of the two arrow buttons, and your chosen slide is entered into the Selected slides pane at the righthand side of the dialog.

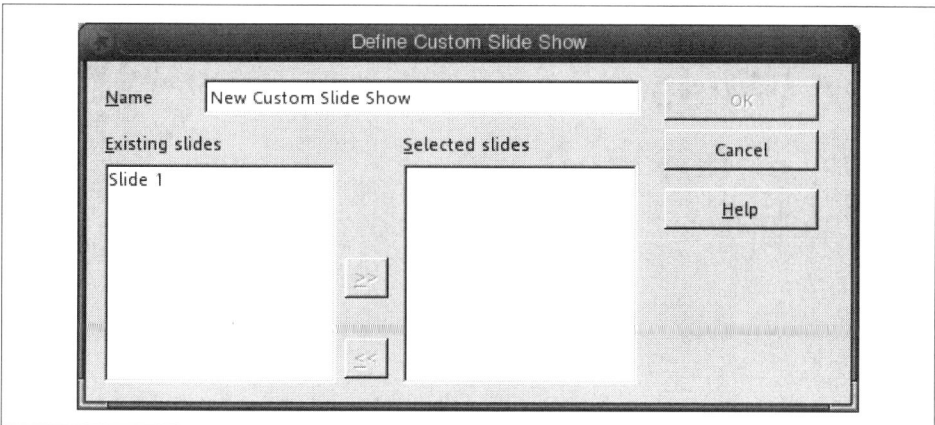

Figure 8-53. The Define Custom Slide Show dialog

CHAPTER 9

Using Windows Applications with JDS

You have now become conversant with the core programs of the Java Desktop System. Although you can see the power of the many Linux applications available on JDS, you may still have a need for software used on Windows computers. JDS can run Windows programs by using:

- Remote Desktop Protocol (RDP) clients, which connect to a Windows Terminal Server
- Native Linux Windows emulators
- Virtual servers, which run on the GNOME desktop

We examine each of these, with the greatest focus on the use of native Linux Windows emulators.

In the past, people who had conflicts between software and operating systems would partition their hard drives and dual boot. If they needed to use Visio for drawing flow charts, they would boot into Windows, but if they ran a suite of Enterprise Applications, they would boot back into Linux. People consider dual booting tedious and unproductive.

Several solutions assist people to use Windows and Linux software together; most of these are found on the Linux side. In this chapter, we introduce you to the major solutions and offer installation details for a promising and popular solution: CodeWeavers' CrossOver Office.

 We define emulation as a process of imitation (simulation) of one computer system by another. The imitating program, or device (emulator), accepts the same data, executes the same programs, and achieves the same results as the system it imitates.

Remote Desktop Protocol

JDS comes with a built-in client that can connect to a Microsoft server to run Windows applications. Known as the RDP, the protocol was developed to provide remote display, keyboard, and mouse connections and print streams over a network for Windows-based applications running on a Windows server. The print streams, keyboard input, and mouse clicks transmit over the network between the server and the terminal emulation software. Each user logs on and sees only his or her individual session, which the server manages transparently, independent of any other client session.

The JDS client runs with the X Window System and the GNOME desktop. Microsoft Terminal Services delivers the Windows desktop and the Windows-based applications to a wide variety of desktops, including those that normally do not run Windows. Through emulation, this allows the same set of applications to run on diverse types of desktop hardware.

Figure 9-1 shows the native JDS client, which connects to a Windows Terminal Server (WTS). This allows you to run your Linux desktop and Windows programs without having to dual boot. Figure 9-2 depicts the architecture that allows JDS to run WTS applications.

WTS is used in large organizations, as its costs run very high. Aside from the cost of the hardware Windows Server licenses and Client Access Licenses (CALS), each user requires a WTS license, and each application requires licenses for people wanting to run the application. The value proposition of RDA sits with the user who uses a thin client solution.

Other solutions we discuss in this chapter provide access to Windows applications for far less money for individual users and provide and perform just as well.

WINE

WINE is the most used open source solution to run Windows software with JDS. WINE is an open source implementation of the Windows Application Program Interface (API). Windows applications run on WINE (the interface), which in turn runs on Linux. This produces an environment in which JDS and other Linux systems can run Windows applications side by side with native Linux applications.

For example, WINE allows you to share your desktop space between MS Word and Evolution, overlapping their windows, launching them, and minimizing them utilizing the desktop and window management features you've been using. The cutting and pasting tools, for instance, move text between the two applications in the same manner as they do between two JDS applications.

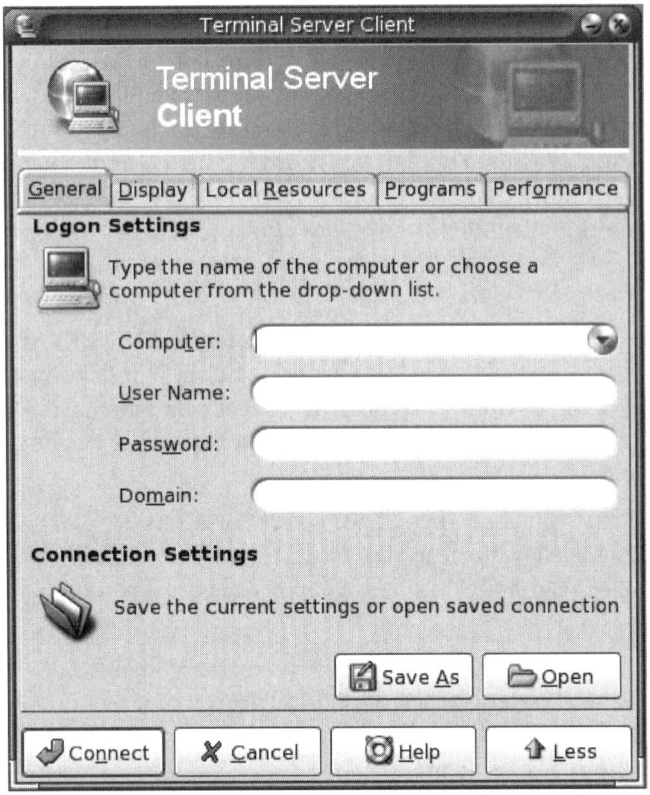

![Terminal Server Client window screenshot]

Figure 9-1. Built-in remote desktop client for Windows

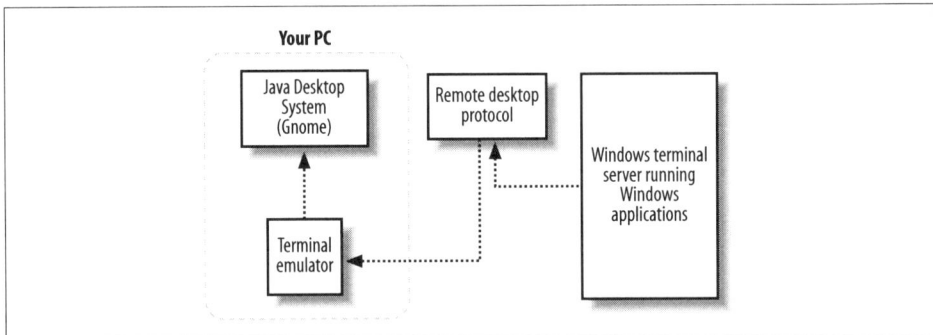

Figure 9-2. Interaction between JDS and Windows Terminal Server using RDP

Since WINE is written in Linux code, it runs natively in JDS; therefore it consumes little memory, and it doesn't require a major investment. Windows' software performance is not diminished. In fact, some people report that a Windows application, running over WINE, offers a more responsive experience than the same application running on the Windows operating system, because Linux is such an efficient multi-tasking operating system.

WINE does not come bundled with JDS. If you want to use it, you have to add it. You can install it from its source code and run it from the command line (open a Terminal window, as shown in Chapter 5) or through one of the available commercial implementations.

Not all applications that run on Windows run on WINE. Many applications need special support, and WINE is being upgraded over time to support more and more of them. Currently, the most popular applications that can run on JDS, while utilizing WINE, are MS Office applications, Lotus Notes, Photoshop, Quicken, and Visio.

WINE does not require Microsoft Windows to operate, as it is an alternative implementation consisting of 100 percent Microsoft-free code that operates through the Linux kernel. WINE provides both a development toolkit (Winelib) for porting Windows source code to JDS and a program loader, allowing many unmodified Windows programs to run on JDS. However, running proprietary Windows applications does require a license from the software vendor—it's illegal to take an unlicensed copy of the software and install it on your system, whether you're using WINE or anything else.

WINE provides:

- Support for running many of the most popular Win 95/98, NT/2000/XP, Windows 3.1 and DOS programs
- X11-based graphics display, including remote display to other systems running X
- DirectX support for games
- Support for sound and alternative input devices
- Printing through a PostScript interface driver to standard Unix/Linux PostScript print services
- Support for serial modem devices
- TCP/IP networking
- Support for scanners, CD writers, and more

Now, let's look at the commercial implementations of WINE and other solutions that, like WINE, do not require dual booting.

VMWare

EMC Corporation owns and distributes this software package, which emulates a virtual machine on Linux. Information can be found at *http://www.vmware.com/*.

VMWare runs an Intel x86 compatible operating system in parallel to your currently running operating system. You could use JDS and simultaneously run Windows XP, Windows 2000, or Windows NT in a virtual machine on the same screen. In fact, you can run many different operating systems at once, all on top of the native one. This can be useful for intensive testing of software on different operating systems.

VMWare requires a commercial license, which costs approximately $200. You also need a licensed copy of the version of Windows you want to run. You may also suffer a performance hit, because VMWare creates a virtual computer on your operating system.

Win4Lin

NeTraverse, of Austin, TX, owns and markets the product called Win4Lin. NeTraverse products come from a technology developed primarily by the original SCO Group called MergeTM. NeTraverse allows you to run a version of Windows 95/98/ME in Linux. Compared to VMWare, this has a performance advantage. The cost of Win4Lin runs to approximately $100, and you also need a license for the version of Windows you want to run. More information can be found at *http://netraverse.com/*.

WINEX

TransGaming provides a branch of WINE that enables gaming solutions. The company's objectives are to work with the most successful game developers toward multiplatform releases of the most popular games, and to enrich the gaming experience for end-users by providing games on those platforms on which they wish to play. Those platforms include Linux and JDS. WINEX supports such games as Marble Blast Gold, the SIMS, and Kohan. Although JDS users want to have games available, the topic requires a broader coverage than we can provide here. More information can be found at *http://www.transgaming.com*.

CodeWeavers Crossover Office

CrossOver Office uses WINE for its implementation of the Windows APIs (application program interfaces). APIs let a platform offer hooks that applications (such as Microsoft Office) understand and can run on.

The advantages of CodeWeavers CrossOver Office include:

- Low cost ($39.95 for home users)
- Native Linux code
- Added functionality in Linux web browsers
- Ease of installation for Windows Applications
- The ability to launch applications from the main JDS menu
- Integration: applications open in JDS Windows and appear native to Linux
- Ease of use

The product can be downloaded from the Internet or purchased on a CD-ROM. In Figure 9-3, you can see how simple installation of CrossOver Office is. To install it, we opened a Terminal window, and then typed:

    ls

to show the name of the *.rpm* package that contains CrossOver Office (in our case, it's *cxoffice-2.1.0-1.i386.rpm*):

    su

    Password: *(root password typed here)*
    rpm -i cx

followed by pressing Tab, so we are reminded of the full name again.

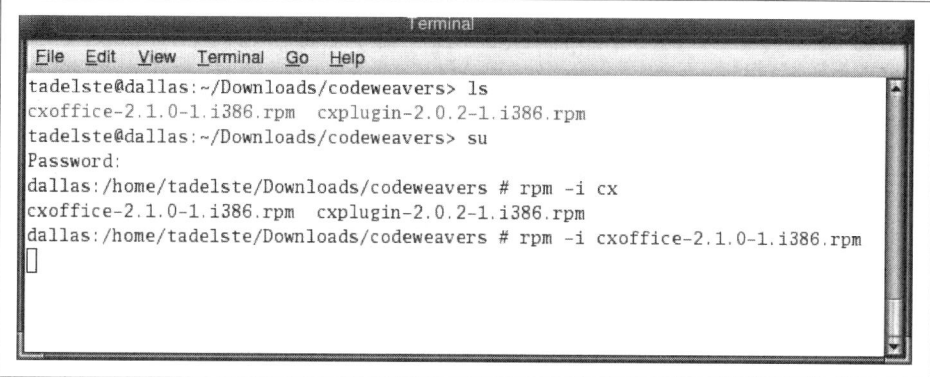

Figure 9-3. Installation sequence of CrossOver Office

We finished by typing the full name and pressed the Return key to start installation.

Once CrossOver Office is installed, Windows applications integrate directly with the desktop on JDS. In Figure 9-4, you can see the CrossOver menu, which we selected from the Launch menu with Applications → CrossOver. You may now install further Windows applications by choosing Applications → CrossOver → Office Setup.

Also notice that your Windows applications launch from the main menu. For example, in Figure 9-4, the Windows Applications menu item is shown at the bottom of the center menu.

CrossOver Office provides Windows plug-ins for Linux browsers. The plug-ins work on JDS and integrate with Mozilla. You can also add Microsoft Office viewers to compare (for example) the looks of a StarOffice document with a Microsoft document before you send it out.

The CrossOver plug-ins also integrate with the desktop to let you open Word, Excel, or PowerPoint, using any viewers or applications from Microsoft Office that you

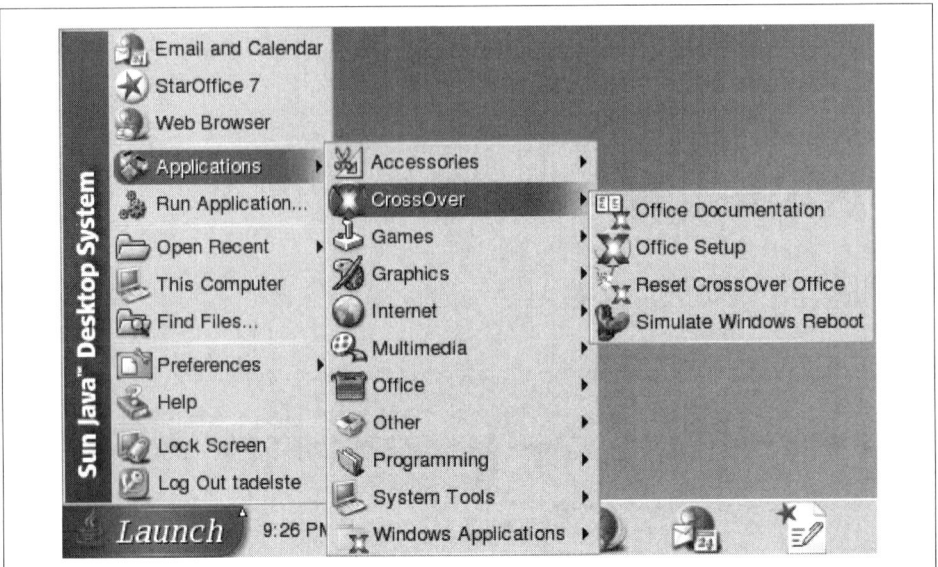

Figure 9-4. CrossOver Office menu

installed. You can open attachments directly from your mail client. CrossOver Office uses native Windows plug-ins.

For example, Apple makes a native Linux plug-in for QuickTime, but it does not support a movie format used by many web sites. That format is called the Sorenson movie format. With CrossOver Office plug-ins, you can view material, using all the QuickTime movie formats.

Starting CrossOver Office the first time

After you install CrossOver Office, notice that the installation script adds menus to the Gnome applications menu. At that point, select Office Setup to run the first time configuration script. After the initial configuration completes, you see a screen similar to the one in Figure 9-5.

When you select the Install button under "New software," you see a screen similar to the one in Figure 9-6, which lists many Windows programs from which to choose.

If you don't see a program listed, you can select "Install unsupported software." For example, you can try downloading a program called WinSCP from *http://winscp. sourceforge.net/eng/*. Developed under the Windows format, it works perfectly with CodeWeavers on JDS and allows you to have visual Secure FTP and Secure Copy on our JDS distribution.

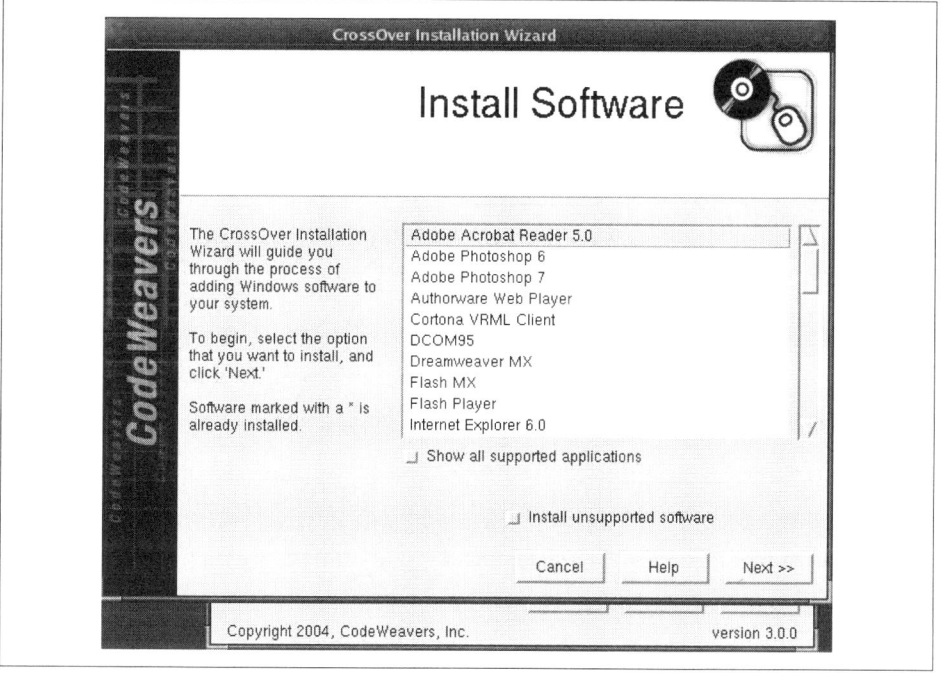

Figure 9-5. Preparing to install a Windows application

Figure 9-6. Windows software list

After we selected Internet Explorer 6 and clicked Next, CodeWeavers Office downloaded and opened DCOM 95 for installation. We accepted the option, and a license agreement opened for us to accept or decline. Figure 9-7 shows the results after we selected Internet Explorer 6 to install. The figure presents a screenshot of the agreement you would see if you decided to follow this example.

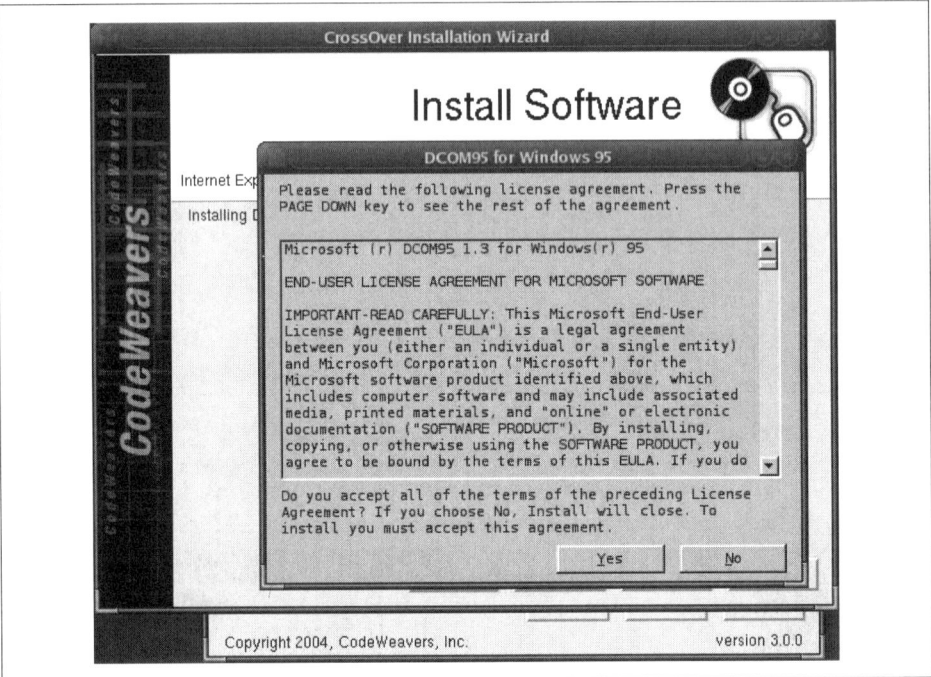

Figure 9-7. First license agreement for installing Internet Explorer

CrossOver Office installed DOM95 and downloaded the setup program for the Browser and Internet Tools. In Figure 9-8, you can see the End User License Agreement (EULA) for Microsoft's IE browser. The CodeWeavers program downloaded and stepped through the installation process without user intervention.

The installation program used by CodeWeavers incorporates non-Microsoft code. The retrieval of Internet Explorer and the various Internet tools, Outlook Express, and the various components occurs similarly to the way it would during a Windows installation.

Once we accepted the Microsoft EULA, CrossOver Office presented us with the screen, shown in Figure 9-9. We chose the Typical set of components and the installation process continued.

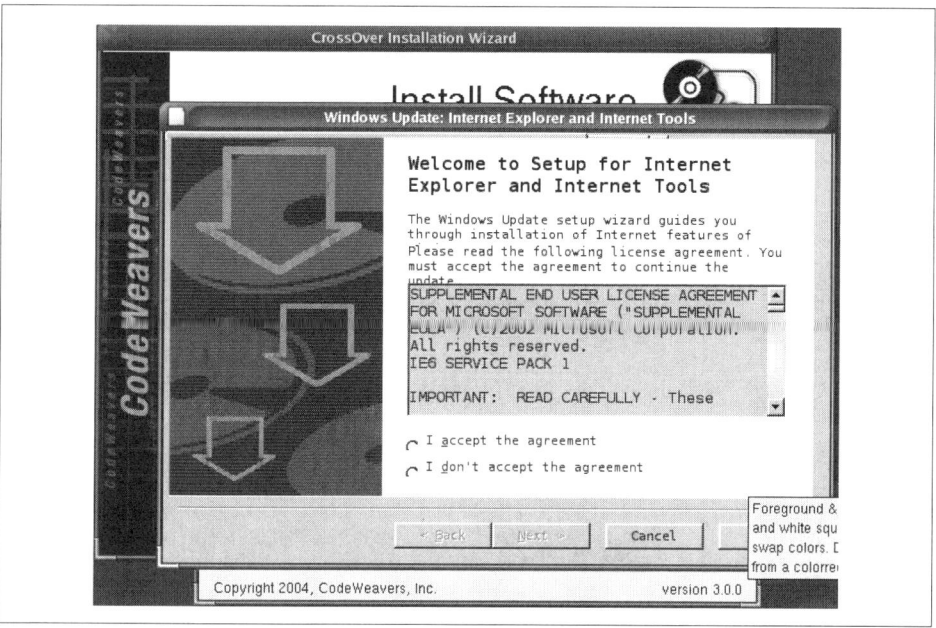

Figure 9-8. End user license for Internet Explorer

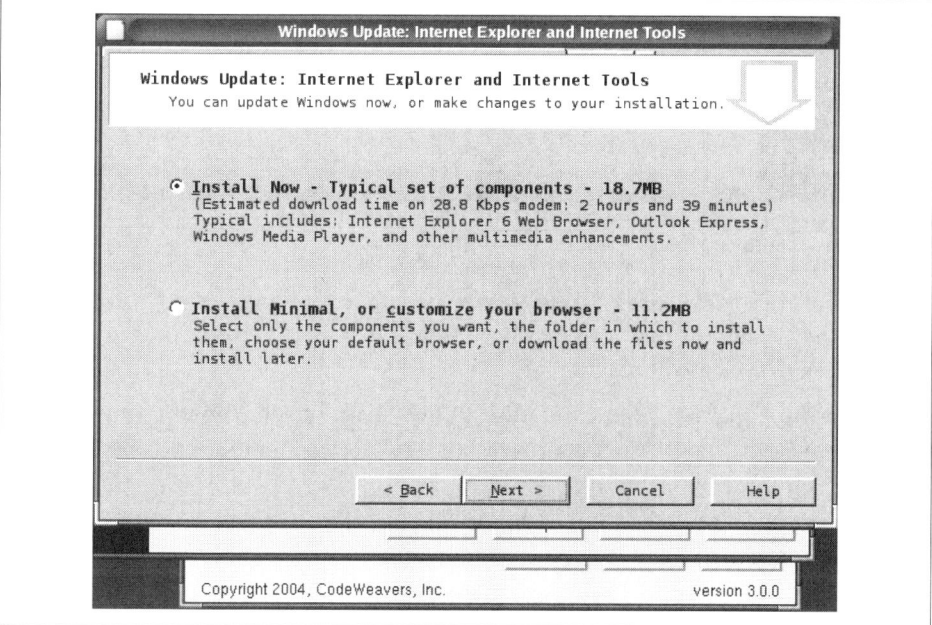

Figure 9-9. The selection screen of options for Internet Explorer

Interestingly, the CodeWeavers Office installation seems familiar to Microsoft Windows users. If you purchase Off-the-shelf Windows applications, notice that the installation follows the same steps it would in Windows, even though it's happening in native Linux code.

Once all the Internet Explorer code downloads, CrossOver Office begins installing each component, which includes only native Windows code. (See Figure 9-10.)

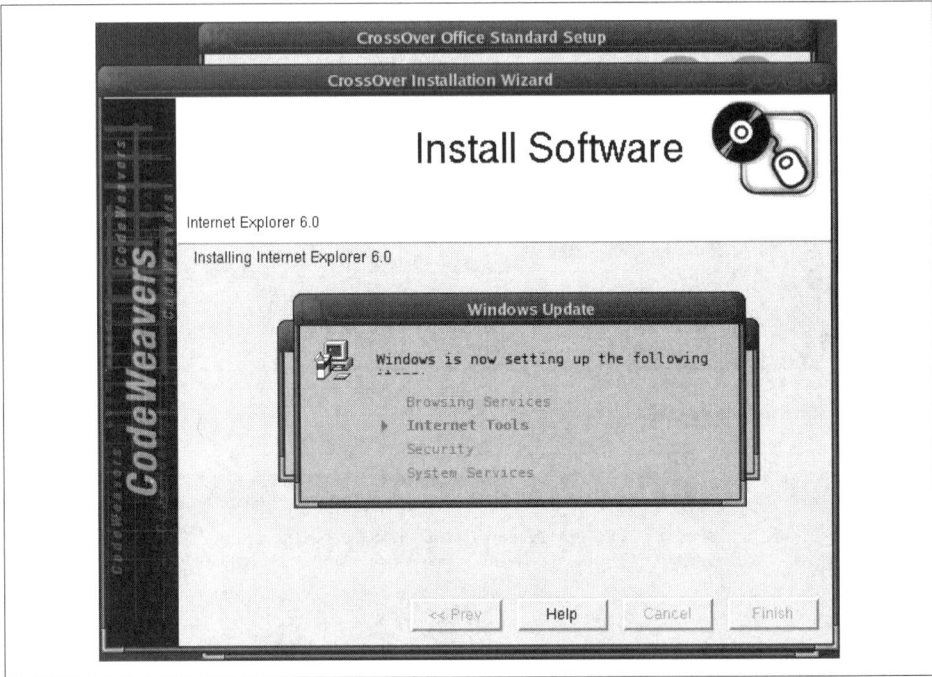

Figure 9-10. Simulated Windows reboot

After completing installation, CodeWeavers simulates a Windows reboot, as shown in Figure 9-11. We do not have to shut down JDS; CrossOver Office continues the installation, as indicated in Figure 9-9.

In contrast to Figure 9-5, the CrossOver Office Setup screen, shown in Figure 9-12, now indicates that four programs have been installed. The first entry is Microsoft Internet Explorer 6 SP1 and Internet Tools.

After installation, we can select Internet Explorer from the desktop and run Google, for instance. Results appear in Figure 9-13.

In Figure 9-14, you can see that Internet Explorer runs in native Linux code. The real test, however, remains. Can Internet Explorer display a complex web site such as Fox News and provide both video and audio context with Windows Media Player?

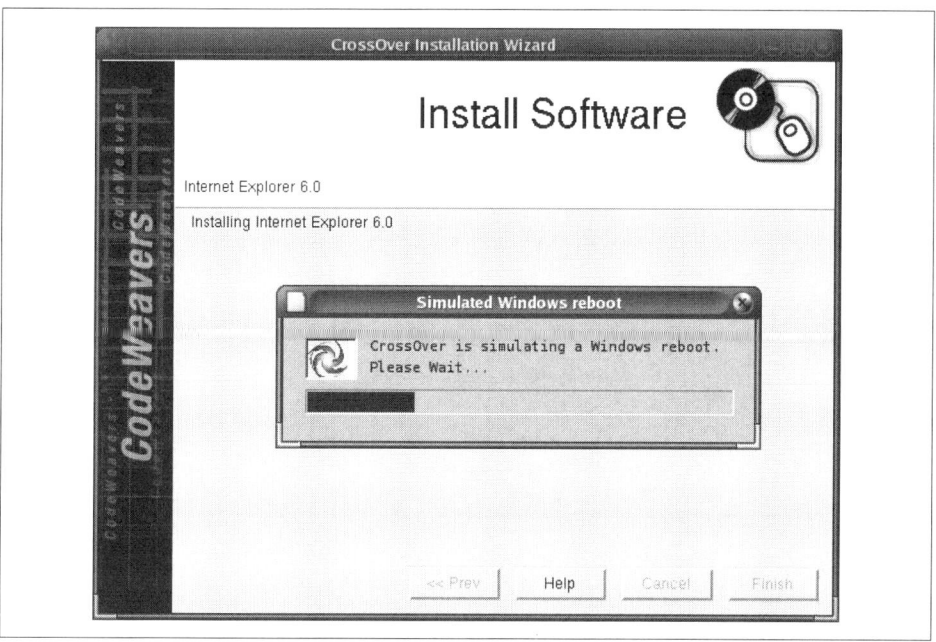

Figure 9-11. Post-reboot installation screen

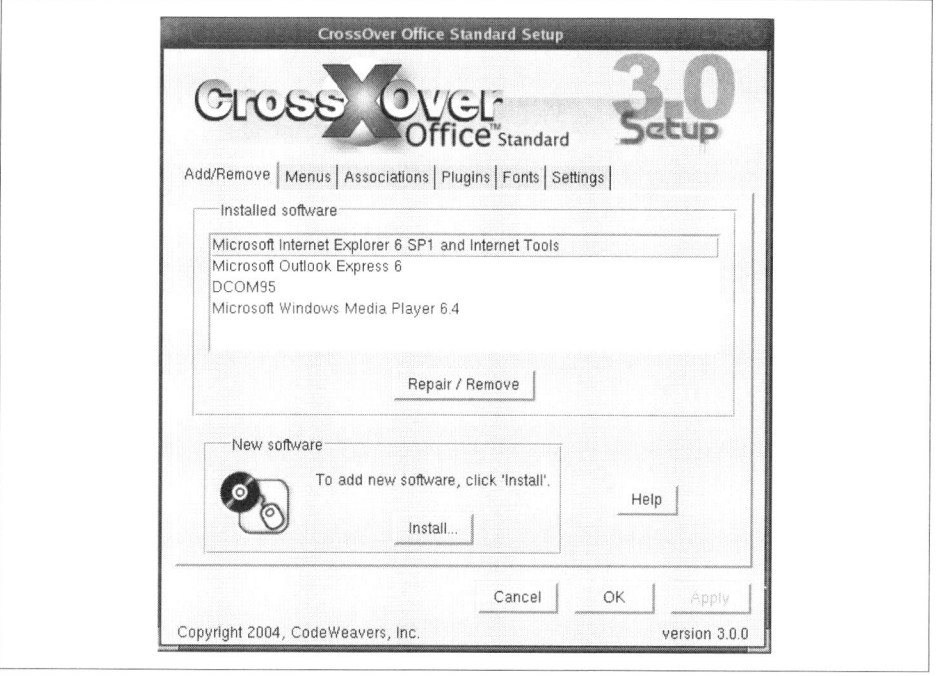

Figure 9-12. CrossOver Office setup status

Figure 9-13. Internet Explorer running in WINE

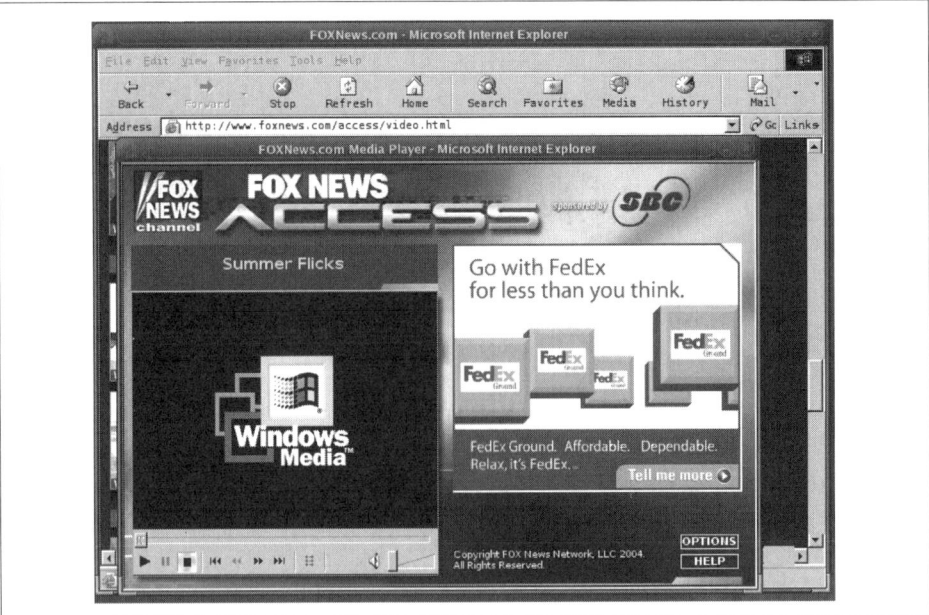

Figure 9-14. Internet Explorer running Windows Media Player 7.0

We navigated to the Fox News web site and chose Windows Media Player to view a video. The web site popped up a screen asking us to download Macromedia Flash and Windows Media Player, Version 7. We obliged and Internet Explorer installed each plug-in on the fly, after which it began playing the video. Figure 9-14 shows the screen after we installed the plug-ins and watched the video. We selected the stop button to take the screenshot.

Using Windows Applications with JDS

In this chapter, we discussed using software written for Microsoft Windows platforms on JDS. In the past, people have had difficulty bridging gaps between the Linux and Windows platforms. Several solutions exist, which allow you to run Windows applications on Linux without rebooting.

In Chapter 10, we discuss JDS applications such a Acrobat Reader, Real Player, and the GNU Image Manipulation Program (GIMP). These applications add additional functionality to JDS for working with Portable Document Files (PDFs), audio and video formats, and image editing in native Linux, without emulation.

CHAPTER 10

Using Other JDS Software

The Java Desktop System provides a number of applications familiar to long-time users of non-Linux operating systems. In this chapter, we'll cover these and discuss some enhancements to an existing Linux product. In this chapter, you will learn about:

- Adobe Acrobat Reader
- RealPlayer plug-ins
- Image Editor

Adobe Acrobat Reader and StarOffice PDF Creator

If you surf the Internet, you know the popularity of Portable Document Format (PDF) files. Uses for PDF files were also described in Chapter 7. Adobe Acrobat Reader allows you to view and print these files. On JDS, Acrobat Reader is provided through the package named acroread. Whenever you click on an icon for a PDF file, it is displayed by Acrobat Reader. You can also start the reader by invoking Applications → Graphics → PDF Document Viewer, as shown in Figure 10-1 (an unusual menu to place a PDF viewer). It works as a plug-in to Mozilla's web browser when you choose a PDF file as a link from a web page. A typical PDF display looks like Figure 10-2.

> With Acrobat Reader, you cannot create PDF Documents, only view them. In StarOffice, you can create PDF Documents with the PDF Export Utility, as shown in Figure 10-3. More information is available in Chapter 7.

With Acrobat Reader integrated into Mozilla, when you select a link that contains a PDF document it will automatically open. You can also save the file to your system, using the appropriate icon in the Acrobat Reader toolbar, or print the file.

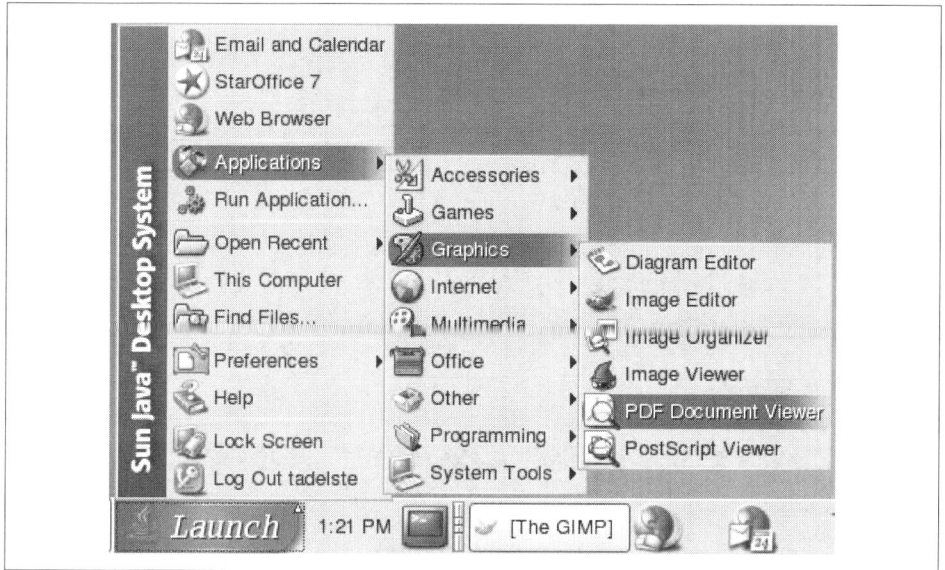

Figure 10-1. Launching Acrobat Reader

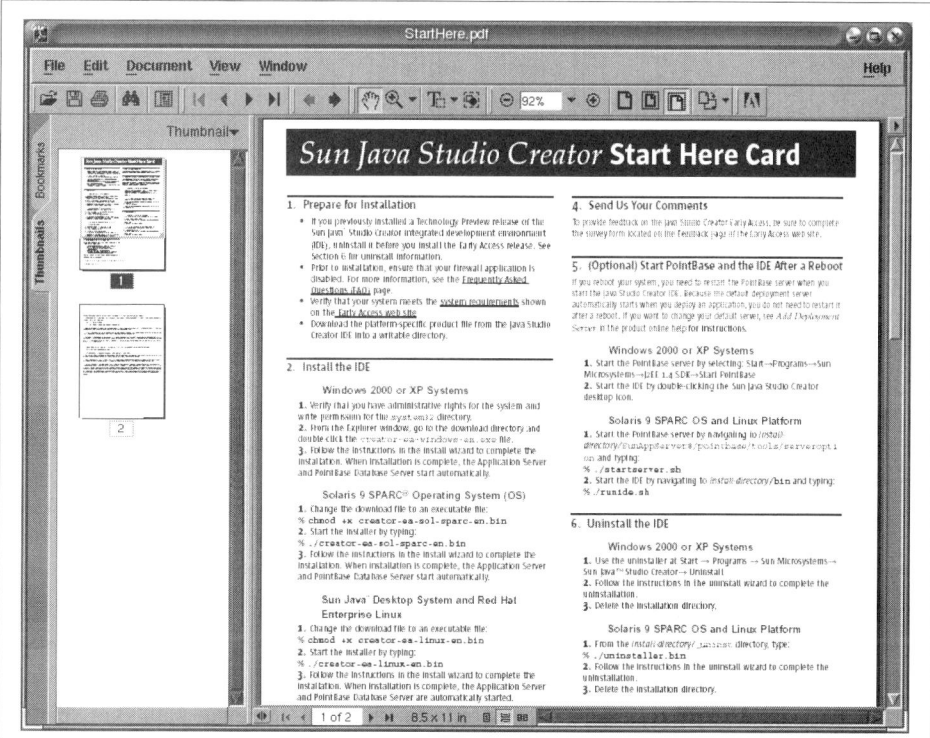

Figure 10-2. Acrobat Reader in JDS

Figure 10-3. Export Utility from StarOffice

PDF documents often contain links and bookmarks pointing to other areas of a document or to other documents, such as the underlined text, shown in Figure 10-4. Selecting a link in the text opens the associated page. You can also see these links in the bookmark tab by selecting the sidebar view icon, which is the fifth icon from the left on the main toolbar.

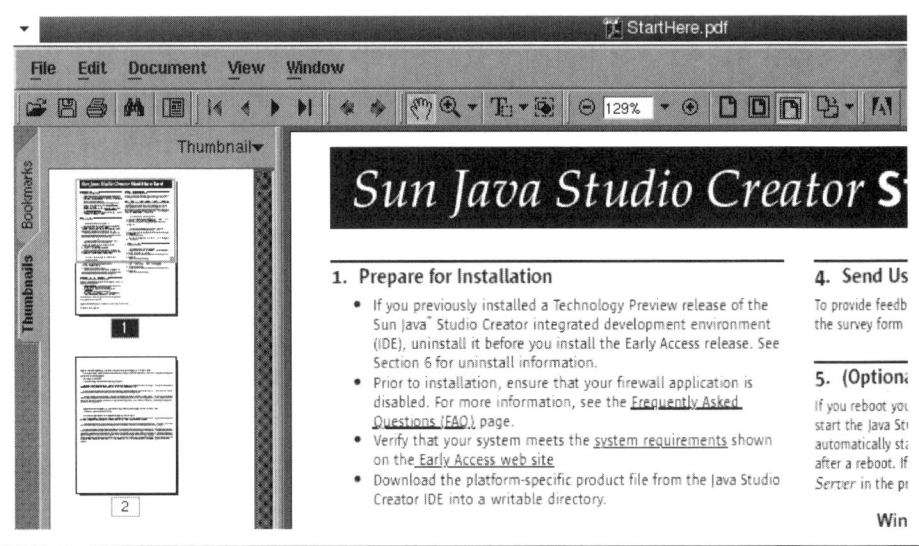

Figure 10-4. The menu and toolbar of Acrobat Reader

In Figure 10-4, you can see some of the important icons at the top of Acrobat Reader. We cover the ones you may not recognize here.

As stated above, the fifth icon from the left, with the small arrow, allows you to view or conceal the left pane of the application. In that pane, you see two tabs: Thumbnails and Bookmarks. We discussed Bookmarks already. Thumbnails are useful for navigating a large document.

You can copy text and graphics from a PDF file, using two buttons in the middle of the task bar: one showing a large T and the other showing a small dotted box with pictures inside. After pressing the T button, select some text using your mouse. This text is now available to be pasted into a StarOffice document or other application. The graphics icon works similarly for graphics.

As of this writing, Adobe has not provided applications for the Linux platform. In the past, independent developers wrote free PDF readers such as Ghostview and xPDF for Unix and Linux systems. In JDS, we have the good fortune of having Acrobat Reader available and pre-configured.

RealPlayer 8 Plug-in

RealPlayer provides audio playback and video presentations. It runs automatically when you select an audio or video file in JDS's Web Browser or on your local system in Nautilus. RealPlayer can also be found on the Launch menu. With the RealPlayer plug-in, you can watch streaming video and listen to audio from Internet radio stations and news organizations.

The JDS version of RealPlayer is the one provided for Linux by Real Networks, without official support. However, the company has provided a support forum for Linux and has an open source project called HelixCommunity (*http://helixcommunity.org*). The JDS version is RealPlayer 8, but the Helix project provides a G2 Player compatable with RealVideo 10. Sun works with RealNetworks and the Helix community on development of the Helix Player and their streaming G2 Video Server.

Figure 10-5 shows a screenshot of the Fox News web site, which offers considerable video content. When you select a story from the web site for the first time, you have the option to choose a viewing format. The choices include RealPlayer and Windows Media Player. RealPlayer does not support the format used by Microsoft Windows Media Player. By choosing RealPlayer, you can receive the video stream and watch the broadcast.

In Figure 10-6, we captured a frame of one broadcast while in play. The RealPlayer application renders the screen with high-quality resolution and provides audio of similar quality.

Sun is collaborating with RealNetworks to develop open source tools and products that allow content providers to develop the most advanced online content, without being locked in to Microsoft products. High-Defintion Television (HDTV) is likely to be offered over open source server software developed by the Helix Community. This is made possible with the support of Sun and RealNetworks, combined with Sun server hardware.

GNU Image Manipulation Program (GIMP)

Anyone familiar with photo and graphic manipulation software such as Photoshop, Corel Draw, or PaintshopPro recognizes the power of GIMP for modifying graphic images. GIMP represents one of the most popular and useful applications in the open-source pantheon. Applications with the functionality of GIMP tend to cost upwards of $1,200 when you include their plug-ins and add-ons.

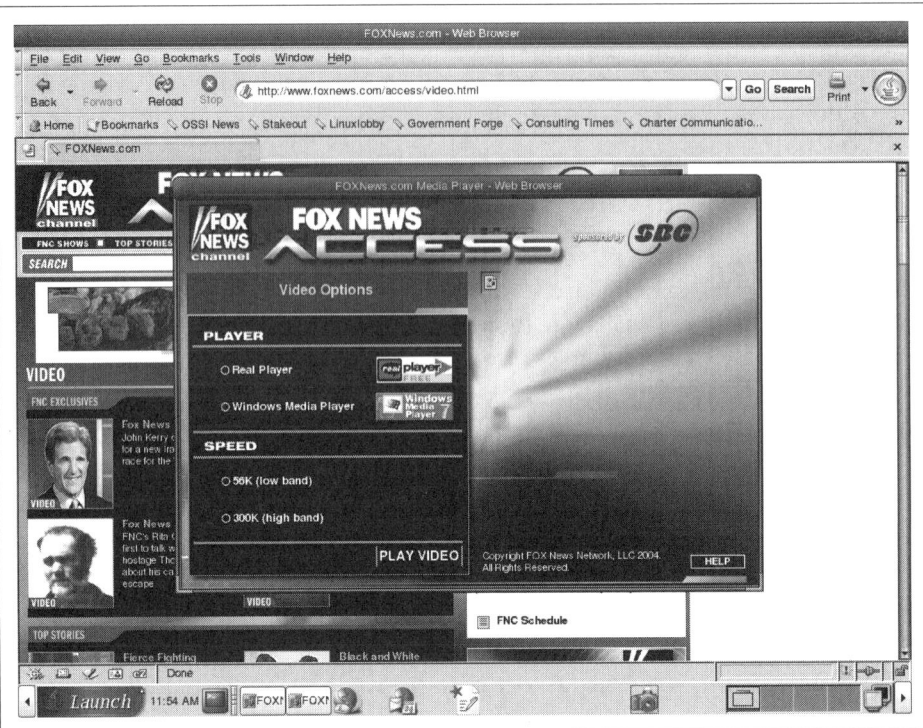

Figure 10-5. Configuring your Media Player

Our treatment in this chapter does not include a GIMP tutorial. If you want to learn to use GIMP, you can find ample documentation in bookstores and on the Web. The GIMP manual, which includes approximately one thousand pages, exists at *http://manual.gimp.org*. Here we focus on the engineering improvements in GIMP, provided by Sun for the JDS.

One of the first things users of GIMP notice is the opening screen that pops up when you select it from the Launch menu through Launch → Applications → Graphics → Image Editor. Figure 10-7 represents a new face to GIMP, provided by the Sun development team.

Before Sun enhanced GIMP, users typically had difficulties adjusting to the project's interface and style of navigation, which resembled PhotoShop 3.0. Sun has added features to allow for drop-down menus and increased productivity, by adding common criteria to the usability design.

In Figure 10-8, you can see the ease with which one can find an image file. By using a spatial browser, you can start with a directory in the left pane, choose a file from a directory in the middle frame, and see a reasonably recognizable thumbnail of the image in the right pane.

Figure 10-6. RealPlayer video playing newscast

Figure 10-7. Sun's Splash screen for GIMP

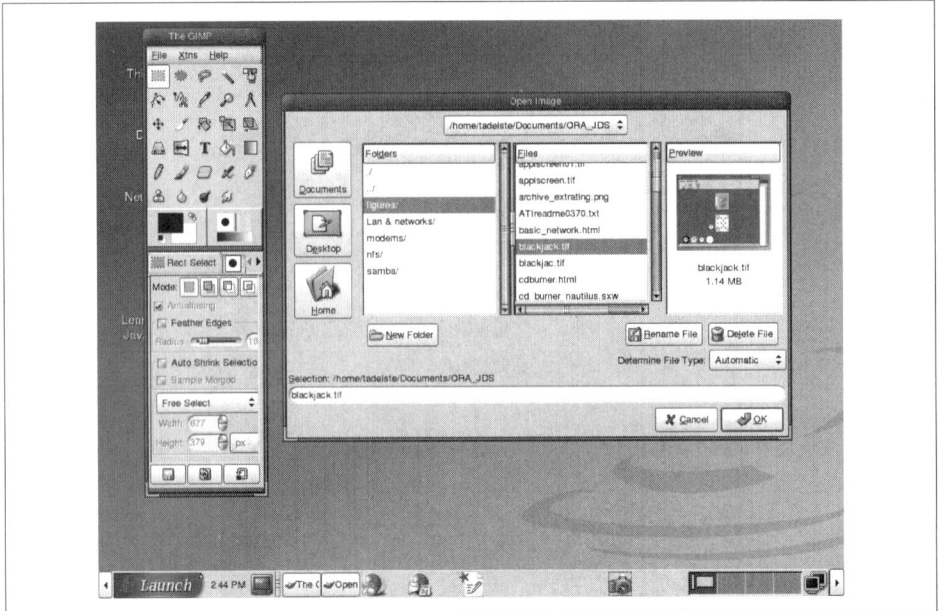

Figure 10-8. Sun's Spatial Image Browser for opening GIMP files

Another enhancement of GIMP in JDS allows you to capture an image, select a portion of the image, and use a drop-down menu from the horizontal tool bar above to create a new canvas containing the portion. Since the size of the new canvas matches the selected area of the image, you can paste the selection into the new workspace. (See Figures 10-9 and 10-10.)

Prior to Sun adding toolbars to the top panel of GIMP, one had to right-click the mouse in the image field to see the standard menu selections. Figure 10-11 shows the former usability menu, which was a thin vertical listing of features. Sun did not eliminate the vertical menu system in its new design, but added to its top-level, horizontal menus to create more ease of use. (See Figures 10-10 through 10-12.)

If you have used GIMP in the past, you recognize that the new usability features incorporated by Sun have great value. If you are changing over from another graphics application, you may feel pleasantly surprised by the industrial strength of GIMP on JDS. If you want to learn to use a powerful image manipulation program, you will find GIMP easy to learn and friendly.

Using Other JDS Software

In this chapter, we have explored the use of the Acrobat Reader, which allows us to view Portable Document Files, which we can download from the Internet or make using StarOffice7. We also covered the use of RealPlayer for audio and video formats and the use of Gimp, as modified by Sun for JDS.

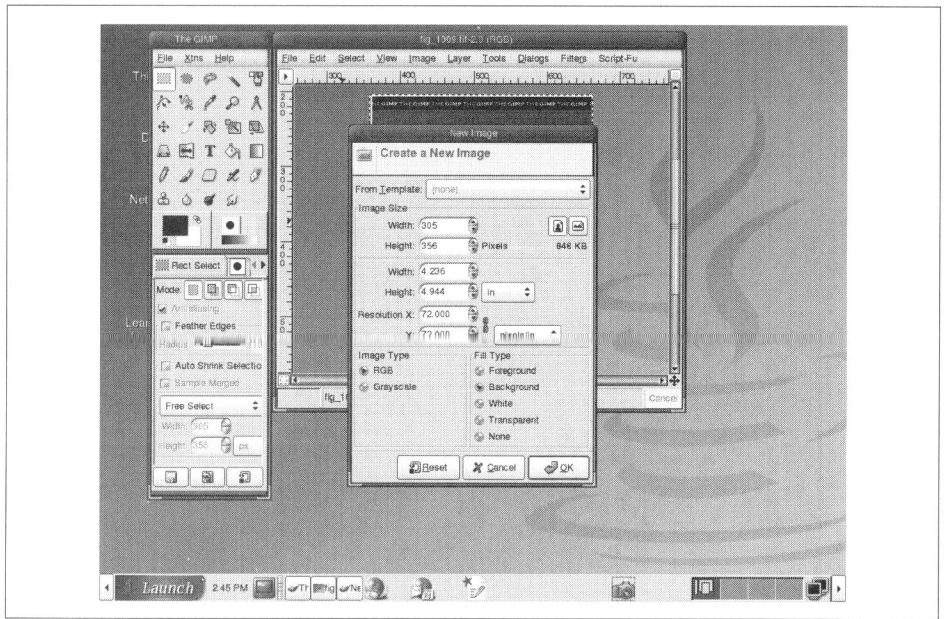

Figure 10-9. New image screen with automatic sizing of a selection within an image

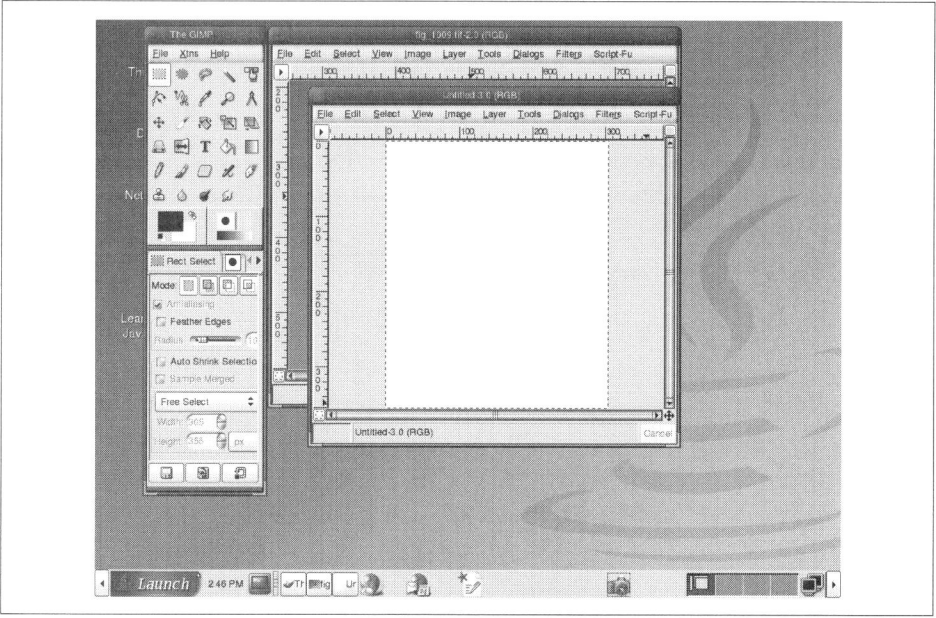

Figure 10-10. New canvas resulting from a drop-down menu

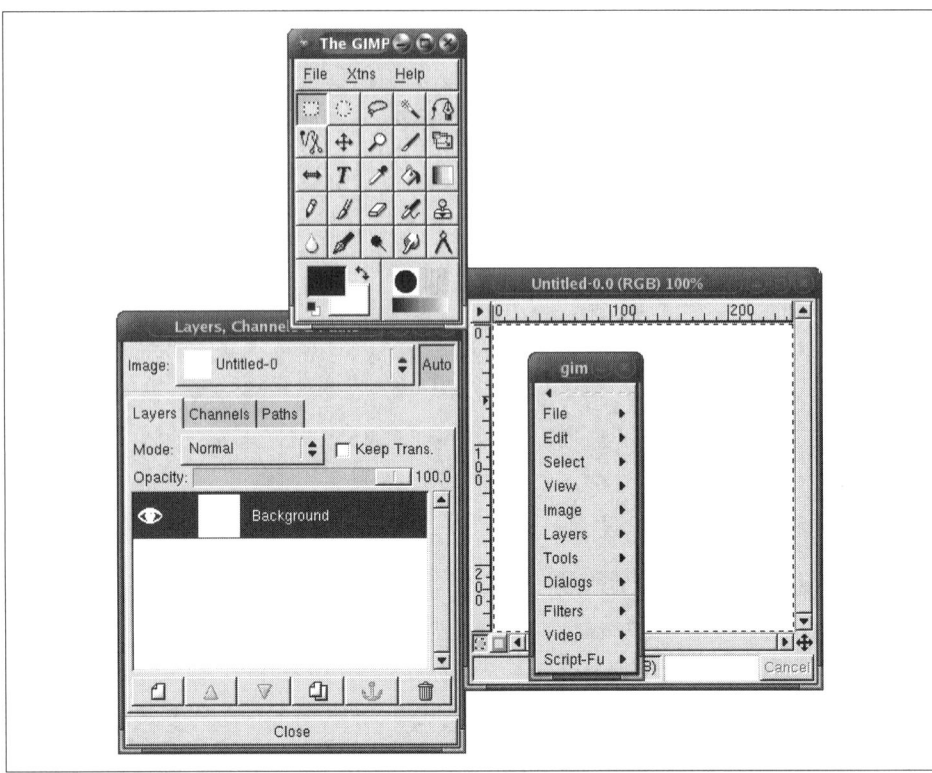

Figure 10-11. Previous navigation system of GIMP used before the release of JDS

Following this chapter are appendices, which cover several technical subjects, including the JDS installation processes, Linux text commands, and using the RPM package management system, to mention a few.

We hope that you enjoy exploring Linux through your JDS.

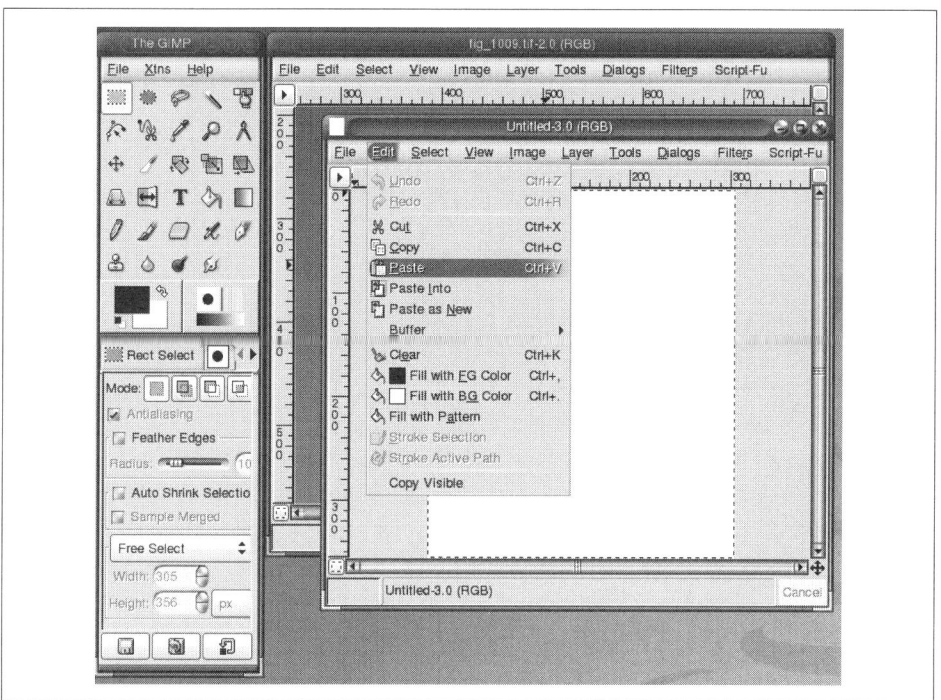

Figure 10-12. JDS navigation adds horizontal menus

Linux Commands

alias
> Creates a command that runs other commands. Aliases are a handy way to customize your system and to provide shortcuts for common activities. For example, the following alias creates an easy-to-remember name for unpacking a compressed archive:
>
> ```
> alias extract='tar zxovf'
> ```
>
> Put an alias into the file */etc/bashrc* if you would like the alias to be always accessible to all users on the system. Type alias alone to see the list of aliases for your account. Use unalias to remove an alias.

alias ls="ls --color=tty"
> Creates an alias for the command ls to enhance its format with color. In this example, the alias is also called ls and the color option is evoked only when the output is done to a terminal (not to files).

apropos *topic*
> Shows which man (documentation) pages cover the *topic* specified.

bash *filename*
> Runs a script, or file containing bash shell commands.

bunzip2 *filename*.bz2
> bunzip2 stands for big unzip. The command decompresses files with the extension *.bz2*. Such files have been zipped with bzip2 compression utility, which is usually reserved for large files and/or directories.

cat *filenames*
> Combines all listed files in order and displays them on the screen. Useful for showing plain text files; if they are long, they should be displayed with *less* or *more*. Also often used to combine files into a single file specified after a > character, as in:
>
> ```
> cat a1 a2 a3 > complete_file
> ```

cd *directory*

cd stands for change directory. For example, if you want to change to a sub-directory in your home directory, you could issue the command cd Documents. Using cd without the directory name takes you to your home directory. Using cd with the slash (cd /) takes you to the root of the system directory.

cd .

Takes you to your previous directory; a convenient way to toggle between two directories.

cd ..

The two periods take you one directory up—for instance, from */home/tadelste/subdir* to */home/tadelste*.

CTRL-c, CTRL-z, CTRL-s, *and* CTRL-q

Invoked by pressing the CTRL key. Respectively, these stand for stop the current command, suspend current command, stop the data transfer, and resume the data transfer.

cp *source destination*

Copies files. For example:

    cp /home/sam/*filename*.

copies a file to the current working directory (denoted by the final period). Use the -R option to copy the contents of whole directory trees. Thus:

    cp -R my_existing_dir/ ~

copies a subdirectory under the current working directory to the home directory.

chmod *perm filename*

chmod stands for change mode. Changes the file access permission for the files you own (unless you are root, in which case you can change any file). You can make a file accessible in three modes—read (r), write (w), and execute (x)—to three classes of users: owner (u), members of the group that owns the file (g), and others on the system (o). The letter a refers to all modes or all users.

chmod g+w *filename*

Makes the file available for writing to members of the group that owns it.

chmod a-x *filename*

Removes the permission from all users to execute the file *filename*.

chmod o-x *filename*

Adds permissions to just the owner to execute the file *filename*.

chown *new_ownername filename*

chown stands for change owner. Changes the ownership of a file or directories. A recommended practice is to use chown *username:usergroup filename*, which sets a new owner and group at the same time.

date

> Shows current date and time. The root user can use this command to reset the date and time.

dd if=/dev/fd0H1440 of=floppy_image

dd if=floppy_image of=/dev/fd0H1440

> dd stands for data duplicator. Create an image of a floppy (*/dev/fd0H1440*) to the file called *floppy_image* in the current directory. Then (presumably after removing the floppy disk and inserting another) copy the file to the floppy disk.

dmesg | less

> Prints kernel messages seen at boot time. Use less /var/log/dmesg to see what dmesg put into this file after the most recent system bootup.

eject

> Ejects the CD-ROM tray. This command defaults to the CD-ROM, but could be used to eject other removable media by specifying the mount point or device—for instance: eject /dev/floppy.

fg %job

> Puts a job in the foreground after it has been placed in the background (usually by issuing it with a trailing & character). Jobs are numbered, starting from 1.

find / -name *filename*

> Finds the file called *filename* on your filesystem, starting the search at the very top from the root directory. The *filename* may contain wildcards (*,?). For example, *docu_*.txt* refers to any file that begins with *docu_* and ends with *.txt*.

find ~ -name *filename*

> Searches for *filename* starting from your home directory and searching all subdirectories under it.

gunzip *filename*.gz

> Decompresses a file that was compressed with gzip. The command is pronounced "gee unzip."

halt *or* reboot

> Issued as root. Halt or reboot the machine.

history

> Shows a list of previously issued commands.

ifconfig

> Issued as root. Displays information on the currently active network interfaces. The first Ethernet card displays as eth0, the second as eth1, etc. The interface lo stands for the loopback interface, which should be always active.

init 6

> Reboots the machine into single-user mode. Used to perform system administration or other tasks that require all users to be logged out.

jobs

Shows jobs that have been placed in the background by issuing them with a trailing & character.

kill *PID*

Forces a process shutdown. First, determine the PID of the process to kill using ps -aux.

less *filename*

Scrolls the content of a text file. Press q when done. less is roughly equivalent to the more command but has extra options.

ln -s *source destination*

Creates a symbolic or soft link called destination to the file *source*. The symbolic link just specifies a path where to look for the real file.

ls *directory*

Lists the contents of the specified directory. Can also be used to list specific files, or issued without arguments to show the contents of the current directory.

ls -al |more

Lists the contents of the current directory in a long format that shows extra information, such as who owns the file and the access permissions.

If a file is accessible to all users in all modes, the leftmost columns of the output shows:

```
-rwxrwxrwx
```

The initial hyphen can sometimes be another character, such as CW for directory. The next triplet shows the file permissions for the owner of the file, the next triplet for the group that owns the file, and the final triplet for others (or the rest of the world). When permission is denied, the *ls* command shows a hyphen.

mkdir *directory*

Makes a new directory. You can use this in your home directory to create a subdirectory. As root, you can make a directory regardless of permissions.

more *filename*

Similar to less. Terminates when you reach the end of the file or files.

mount -t auto /dev/fd0 /mnt/floppy

Issued as root. Mount a floppy disk. The directory */mnt/floppy* must exist and must *not* be your current directory. The type of the filesystem will be automatically detected. Before trying to remove the disk, issue the *amount* command.

mount -t auto /dev/cdrom /mnt/cdrom

Issued as root. Mount the CD. The directory */mnt/cdrom* must exist and must *not* be your current directory. Before trying to remove the disk, issue the *amount* command.

```
umount /mnt/floppy
umount /dev/cdrom
```
> Unmounts the floppy or CD-ROM. Note that the umount command is missing an n. Depending on your setup, you may not be able to unmount a drive that was mounted by somebody else.

`mv source destination`
> Moves or renames files. The same command is used for moving and renaming files and directories.

`passwd`
> Changes your password. You are prompted for it twice, to make sure you enter the password correctly as you meant to enter it.

`passwd user_name`
> Issued as root. Creates or changes a password for an existing user.

`ping machine`
> Checks if you can contact another machine (through the machine's name or IP address). If the network is operating and you can reach the machine, a series of messages are sent and the results are printed. Press CTRL-C to terminate the command.

`ps`
> Stands for print status or process status. Displays the list of currently running processes with their process ID numbers. Issued without arguments it shows only those commands started from the current shell.

`ps aux | less`
> Lists all the processes currently running on the system, together with the name of the user who owns each process. Using *less* allows you to scroll up and down in the process list.

`pwd`
> Displays the name of your current directory. This allows you to see your position in the directory tree.

`rm filenames`
> Removes or deletes files. You must own the file (or be root) in order to remove it. Warning: there is no reasonable way to recover removed files. Use the -i option if you would like to be prompted before each file is removed.

`rm -r directory`
> Removes a directory and all its contents. Can be dangerous because you don't see exactly what is being removed unless you add the -i option.

`rmdir directory`
> Removes an empty directory. Use rm -r (after careful thought!) to remove a directory that has files or subdirectories in it.

`shutdown -h` *time*

Issued as root. Bring the system down to a halt. The preferable way to shutdown the system using the command line. The *time* specifies a delay so that users can wrap up their work and log off; if you are the only user, you can specify now for the time.

`su` *user_name*

Stands for substitute user ID. You need to enter the user's password. When issued without arguments, it allows you to become root (if you have the privileges to do so). Type exit to return you to your previous login. Don't habitually work on your machine as root. The root account is for administration and the `su` command is to ease your access to the administration account when you require it.

`tar zxvf` *filename*`.tar.gz`

Stands for tape archiver. Useful to unpack a tarred and compressed tarball (a file with a *.tar.gz* or *.tgz* extension) that you download from the Internet.

`tar xvf` *filename*`.tar`

Unpack a tarred but uncompressed tarball (a file).

`unzip` *filename*`.zip`

Decompress a file (a *.zip* file) zipped with the ZIP compression utility, usually from a Windows computer.

`useradd` *user_name*

Issued as root. Creates an account for a user.

`useradd -m -g authors sam`

Issued as root. Creates an account called `sam`. The -m option creates a home directory, and the -g option assigns `sam` to the `authors` group.

`userdel` *user_name*

Issued as root. Removes an account. The user's home directory and the undelivered mail must be removed manually.

`which` *executable_name*

Shows the full path to the executable that would run if you typed its name on the command line.

`whereis` *command*

Prints the locations for the binary, source, and manpage files of the command *command*.

`whoami`

Prints your login name. Often used when several windows are open, and one may be a root account or an account on a remote system.

zcat *filename*.gz | more

Stands for zip cat. Displays the contents of a compressed file. Other utilities for operating on compressed files without an extra decompression step are also available: zless, zmore, zgrep, etc.

zip *filename*.zip *filename1 filename2*

Compresses the two files *filename1* and *filename2* to a zip archive called *filename*.zip. To zip a whole directory, add the -r option.

Online Documentation

In addition to the documentation included with the JDS installation CD set, there is a host of useful information online about how to use and administer the JDS software and its most important applications. If the links provided below are not relevant to your immediate needs, a web search of your own is likely to turn up a surprising amount of useful information.

The Linux Documentation Project

This is the focal point of open source contributions to the documentation of the GNU/Linux operating system. The web site offers guides, HOWTO's, manpages, and answers to frequently asked questions.

> *http://www.tldp.org*

JDS Community Support

- The Sun JDS community Forum (*http://supportforum.sun.com/sjds/*)
- A community-supported web site offering support to the JDS user community with HOWTOs, RPM's, JDS news, and errata for this book (*http://jdshelp.org*)

Java Desktop System (Release2)

Sun's JDS User Documentation (*http://docs.sun.com/db/coll/1107.1*):

- GNOME 2.2 Desktop Accessibility Guide (PDF)
- GNOME 2.2 Desktop on Linux System Administration Guide (PDF)
- GNOME 2.2 Desktop on Linux User Guide (PDF)
- Java Desktop System Release 2 Installation Guide (PDF)
- Java Desktop System Release 2 Quick Start User Guide (PDF)

- Java Desktop System Release 2 Release Notes (PDF)
- Java Desktop System Release 2 Troubleshooting Guide (PDF)
- Java System Update Service User's Guide (PDF)
- Ximian Evolution 1.4 Sun Microsystems Edition User Guide (PDF)

Web Browser (Mozilla)

http://www.mozilla.org/catalog/end-user/:

- Mozilla Installation and Getting Started Guide (PDF)
- Introduction to Mozilla—A Manual for First Time Users (PDF)
- Mozilla User Guide (PDF)
- Other documentation

Instant Messenger (gaim)

- Documentation for gaim 0.78 (*http://gaim.sourceforge.net/downloads.php*)

StarOffice 7

Sun's StarOffice 7 Collection (*http://docs.sun.com/db/coll/so7en*):

- StarOffice 7 Office Suite—Administration Guide, English (PDF, $)
- StarOffice 7 Office Suite—Basic Programmer's Guide, English (PDF, $)
- StarOffice 7 Office Suite—Setup Guide, English (PDF, $)
- StarOffice 7 Office Suite—User's Guide, English (PDF, $)
- StarOffice Configuration Manager Version 1—Installation and Usage (PDF, $)

"PDF" indicates a free download in Adobe PDF format; "$" indicates printed matter for purchase.

StarOffice Tutorials for Kids

- *http://www.sun.com/products-n-solutions/edu/commofinterest/staroffice/star_tutorial/index.htm*
- StarOffice Educational Template Collection (*http://www.sun.com/products-n-solutions/edu/solutions/staroffice.html*)

OpenOffice.org Documentation (FAQs)

- OpenOffice.org's Unofficial FAQ ("uFAQ") (*http://opensource.mimos.my/fosscon2003cd/extras/ooo_ufaq.html*)
- OpenOffice.org's FAQ Page (*http://www.openoffice.org/faq.html*)
- Sun's OpenOffice.org FAQ (*http://wwws.sun.com/software/star/openoffice/faq.html*)

Tutorials (Digital Distribution's Flash Demos)

- An Introduction to OpenOffice.org 1.1 (*http://www.digitaldistribution.com/samples/openofficeintro/*)
- First Steps with OpenOffice.org 1.1 Writer (*http://www.digitaldistribution.com/samples/writerfirststeps/*)
- First Steps with OpenOffice.org 1.1 Calc (*http://www.digitaldistribution.com/samples/calcfirststeps/*)
- First Steps to OpenOffice.org 1.1 Impress (*http://www.digitaldistribution.com/samples/impressfirststeps/*)
- First Steps with StarOffice 7 Data Sources (*http://www.digitaldistribution.com/samples/so7createdatasource/*)

Help, HOWTOs, Templates, and Other Items

- Online Help Forum (*http://www.oooforum.org*)
- OOoDocs (*http://www.ooodocs.org/*)
- OOoDocs' HOWTO Repository (*http://www.ooodocs.org/modules.php?name=Content&pa=showpage&pid=3*)
- The OOo Dictionary Installer (*http://www.ooodocs.org/dictinstall/*)
- OOoExtras (*http://ooextras.sourceforge.net/*)
- OOoMacros (*http://www.ooomacros.org/*)
- Andrew Brown's Word Count Macro (*http://www.ooomacros.org/user.php#98079*)
- OpenOffice.org's Online File Converter (in 14 languages) (*http://www.oooconv.de/engine/OOOconv.php?lang=en*)

Informational Mailing Lists

- OpenOffice.org's Users' Mailing List (*subscribe-users@openoffice.org*)
- OpenOffice.org's Discuss Mailing List (*subscribe-discuss@openoffice.org*)

Secure Connections Through SSH

Developers built SSH (Secure Shell) so they could log in to another computer over a network with the protections of encryption (scrambling data) and authentication (making sure a person or system is really what is claimed). Using SSH, a person can execute commands and send passwords securely. Earlier protocols such as FTP and Telnet transmitted their information in plain text, allowing people snooping on the Internet to get the passwords and use them to gain access to others' accounts and data. SSH also replaces older Unix commands such as rlogin, rsh, and rcp (remote logon, remote shell, and remote copy).

SSH allows you to:

- Run a single command on a remote system (ssh followed by the desired command)
- Start a shell on a remote system where one can enter a series of commands (ssh without specifying a command)
- Copy a file from one system to another (scp)
- Download a file from an FTP site (sftp)

Additionally, SSH provides secure X connections and secure forwarding of arbitrary TCP connections.

The traditional remote command protocols are vulnerable to different kinds of attacks. Somebody who has root access to machines on the network, or physical access to the wire, can gain unauthorized access to systems in a variety of ways. It is also possible for such a person to log all the traffic to and from your system, including passwords (which SSH never sends in the clear).

The X Window System also has a number of severe vulnerabilities. With SSH, you can create secure remote X sessions that the user can access as if the session was running on his local machine. As a side effect, using remote X clients with SSH is more convenient for users.

Encryption keys, by default, are exchanged using a data encryption format called RSA, and data used in the key exchange is destroyed every hour (keys are not saved anywhere). Every host has an RSA key that is used to authenticate the host when RSA host authentication is used. Encryption is used to protect against IP-spoofing; public key authentication is used to protect against DNS and routing spoofing.

Examples

SSH is a program for logging in to a remote machine and for executing commands on a remote machine.

When you first log on to a remote machine with SSH, you see something similar to the following message:

```
The authenticity of host 'memphis.org (memphis.org)' can't be established.
RSA key fingerprint is 8c:e2:4b:4d:9b:79:cd:e9:84:36:72:32:2b:3b:7e:48.
Are you sure you want to continue connecting (yes/no)?
```

This is perfectly normal; as long as you have no reason to think someone is trying to spoof the real system, you should press the Enter key to answer yes. Another message is displayed and you are logged in:

```
Warning: Permanently added 'memphis.org,memphis.org' (RSA) to the
list of known hosts.
```

After your first logon, your session looks more like this:

```
willtonj@rome:~> ssh willtonj@memphis.org
=======================================================
        SSH port 22 access restricted to authorized users only
=======================================================
willtonj@memphis.org's password:************
Last login: Thu May 13 12:05:54 2004 from 65.123.111.109
=======================================================
linux@memphis.org is on 222.102.131.176
grizzly:~>
Connection to memphis.org closed.
willtonj@rome:~> sftp willtonj@memphis.org
Connecting to memphis.org...
=======================================================
        SSH port 22 access restricted to authorized users only
=======================================================
tilltonj@memphis.org's password:
5332: Permission denied, please try again.
tilltonj@memphis.org's password:************
willtonj@rome:~> sftp willtonj@memphis.org
Connecting to ...memphis.org
willtonj@memphis.org's password:************
sftp>
```

At this point, you have connected to the remote host and can use any Linux/FTP commands. The following commands are unique to SFTP:

---

cd *path*
    Change remote directory to *path*.

lcd *path*
    Change local directory to *path*.

chgrp *grp path*
    Change group of file *path* to *grp*.

chmod *mode path*
    Change permissions of file *path* to *mode*.

chown *own path*
    Change owner of file *path* to *own*.

help
    Display this help text.

get remote-path [*local-path*]
    Download file.

lls [ls-*options* [*path*]]
    Display local directory listing.

ln *oldpath newpath*
    Symlink remote file.

lmkdir *path*
    Create local directory.

lpwd
    Print local working directory.

ls [*path*]
    Display remote directory listing.

lumask *umask*
    Set local umask to *umask*.

mkdir *path*
    Create remote directory.

put *local-path* [*remote-path*]
    Upload file.

pwd
    Display remote working directory.

exit, quit
    Quit SFTP.

rename *oldpath newpath*
    Rename remote file.

rmdir *path*
    Remove remote directory.

rm *path*
> Delete remote file.

symlink *oldpath newpath*
> Symlink remote file.

version
> Show SFTP version.

!*command*
> Execute *command* in local shell.

! Escape to local shell.

? Synonym for help.

scp copies files between hosts on a network. It uses SSH for data transfer, uses the same authentication, and provides the same security as SSH.

To copy local file *filename* to *filename* on remote machine memphis.org, enter:

```
grizzly:~>scp -p filename :memphis.org: filename
```

-p preserves modification time, access time, and mode from the original.

Copy *filename* from remote machine memphis.org to local file *filename*:

```
grizzly:~>scp -p memphis.org: filename filename
```

Finally, you can use SSH with the -X option and generate an X session. For example, Run this command:

```
grizzly:~>ssh -X willtonj@memphis.org
tilltonj@memphis.org's password:********
cf11 grizzly:~>gnomine
```

and in a short time, a window appears as if it was on your system, and you are playing GNOME mines.

Using RPM Manager

This section describes the RPM package management system. You'll use a package whenever you install an application on JDS. We introduced packages in Chapter 5, along with basic information on how to install them. This appendix, based on material from *Linux in a Nutshell* (O'Reilly), tells you in detail how to install, upgrade, delete, and check for packages on your JDS system. JDS has some significant differences from other versions of Linux. A package is a compressed file containing the files necessary to install an application or another piece of software, such as a library. Many applications require the presence of other files or packages, such as particular libraries (and even specific versions of the libraries). Such requirements are known as *dependencies*. No package can be installed until all the packages it depends on are installed. When you attempt to install a package, error messages tell you whether other packages are needed.

Package management systems offer many benefits. As a user, you may want to query the package database to find out what packages are installed on the system and what their versions are. If you are a developer, you need to know how to build a package for distribution.

Among other things, package managers do the following:

- Provide tools for installing, updating, removing, and managing the software on your system
- Allow you to install new or upgraded software directly across a network
- Tell you what software package a particular file belongs to or what files a package contains
- Maintain a database of packages on the system and their state, so you can find out which packages or versions are installed on your system
- Provide dependency checking, so you don't mess up your system with incompatible software
- Provide PGP, MD5, or other signature-verification tools

- Provide tools for building packages

Any user can list or query packages, however, installing, upgrading, or removing packages generally requires superuser privileges. This is because the packages are normally installed in systemwide directories that are writable only by root. Sometimes you can specify an alternate directory to install a package into your home directory or into a project directory where you have write permission.

RPM Package Manager backs up old files before installing an updated package. Not only does this let you go back if there is a problem, but it also ensures that you don't lose your changes (to configuration files, for example).

The RPM Manager

Using RPM is straightforward. A single command, *rpm*, has options to perform all package management functions except building packages.* For example, to find out if the Emacs editor is installed on your system, you could say:

```
% rpm -q emacs
emacs-21.2-18
```

The rpmbuild command is used to build both binary and source packages.

The rpm Command

RPM packages are built, installed, and queried with the *rpm* command. RPM package names usually end with an *.rpm* extension. rpm has a set of modes, each with its own options. The format of the rpm command is:

rpm [*options*] [*packages*]

With a few exceptions, as noted in the lists of options that follow, the first option specifies the rpm mode (install, query, update, etc.), and any remaining options affect that mode.

Options that refer to packages are sometimes specified as *package-name* and sometimes as *package-file*. The package name is the name of the program or application, such as *gif2png*. The package file is the name of the RPM file, such as *gif2png-2.4.6-1.i386.rpm*.

RPM provides a configuration file for specifying frequently used options. The default global configuration is usually */usr/lib/rpm/rpmrc*, the local system configuration file is */etc/rpmrc*, and users can set up their own *$HOME/.rpmrc* files. You can use the --showrc option to show the values RPM will use for all the options that may be set in an *rpmrc* file:

rpm --showrc

---

* In older versions of RPM, the build options were part of the rpm command.

The *rpm* command includes FTP and HTTP clients, so you can specify an *ftp://* or *http://* URL to install or query a package across the Internet. You can use an FTP or HTTP URL wherever *package-file* is specified in the commands presented here.

Any user can query the RPM database. Most of the other functions require superuser privileges.

General options

The following options can be used with all modes:

`--dbpath` *path*
> Use *path* as the path to the RPM database instead of the default */var/lib/rpm*.

`-?`
`--help`
> Print a long usage message (running rpm with no options gives a shorter usage message).

`--pipe` *command*
> Pipe the rpm output to *command*.

`--quiet`
> Display only error messages.

`--rcfile` *filelist*
> Get configuration from the files in the colon-separated *filelist*. If --rcfile is specified, there must be at least one file in the list and the file must exist.

`--root` *dir*
> Perform all operations within the directory tree rooted at *dir*.

`-v`
> Verbose. Print progress messages.

`--version`
> Print the version number of rpm.

`-vv`
> Print debugging information.

Install, upgrade, and freshen options

Use the install command to install or upgrade an RPM package. The install syntax is:

```
rpm -i [install-options] package_file ...
rpm --install [install-options] package_file ...
```

To install a new version of a package and remove an existing version at the same time, use the upgrade command instead:

```
rpm -U [install-options] package_file ...
rpm --upgrade [install-options] package_file ...
```

If the package doesn't already exist on the system, -U acts like -i and installs it. To prevent that behavior, you can freshen a package instead; in that case, rpm upgrades the package only if an earlier version is already installed. The freshen syntax is:

```
rpm -F [install-options] package_file ...
rpm --freshen [install-options] package_file ...
```

package-file can be specified as an FTP or HTTP URL to download the file before installing it.

The installation and upgrade options are:

--aid

> If rpm suggests additional packages, add them to the list of package files.

--allfiles

> Install or upgrade all files.

--badreloc

> Used with --relocate to force relocation even if the package is not relocatable.

--excludedocs

> Don't install any documentation files.

--excludepath *path*

> Don't install any file whose filename begins with *path*.

--force

> Force the installation. Equivalent to using all of --replacepkgs, --replacefiles, and --oldpackage.

-h, --hash

> Print fifty hash marks as the package archive is unpacked. Use with -v or --verbose for a nicer display.

--ignorearch

> Install even if the binary package is intended for a different architecture.

--ignoreos

> Install binary package even if the operating systems don't match.

--ignoresize

> Don't check disk space availability before installing.

--includedocs

> Install documentation files. This is needed only if excludedocs: 1 is specified in an *rpmrc* file.

--justdb

> Update the database only; don't change any files.

--nodeps

> Don't check whether this package depends on the presence of other packages.

`--nodigest`
> Don't verify package or header digests.

`--noorder`
> Don't reorder packages to satisfy dependencies before installing.

`--nopost`
> Don't execute any post-install script.

`--nopostun`
> Don't execute any post-uninstall script.

`--nopre`
> Don't execute any pre-install script.

`--nopreun`
> Don't execute any pre-uninstall script.

`--noscripts`
> Don't execute any pre-install or post-install scripts. Equivalent to specifying all of `--nopre`, `--nopost`, `--nopreun`, and `--nopostun`.

`--nosignature`
> Don't verify package or header signatures.

`--nosuggest`
> Don't suggest packages that provide a missing dependency.

`--notriggerin`
> Don't execute any install trigger scriptlet.

`--notriggerun`
> Don't execute any uninstall trigger scriptlet.

`--notriggerpostun`
> Don't execute any post-uninstall trigger scriptlet.

`--notriggers`
> Don't execute any scripts triggered by package installation.

`--oldpackage`
> Allow an upgrade to replace a newer package with an older one.

`--percent`
> Print percent-completion messages as files are unpacked. Useful for running rpm from other tools.

`--prefix path`
> Set the installation prefix to *path* for relocatable binary packages.

`--relocate oldpath=newpath`
> For relocatable binary files, change all file paths from *oldpath* to *newpath*. Can be specified more than once to relocate multiple paths.

--repackage

Repackage the package files before erasing. Rename the package as specified by the macro %_repackage_name_fmt, and save it in the directory specified by the macro %_repackage_dir (by default, /var/tmp).

--replacefiles

Install the packages even if they replace files from other installed packages.

--replacepkgs

Install the packages even if some of them are already installed.

--test

Go through the installation to see what it would do, but don't actually install the package. This option lets you test for problems before doing the installation.

Query options

The syntax for the *query* command is:

```
rpm -q [package-options] [information-options]
rpm --query [package-options] [information-options]
```

There are two subsets of query options. *Package selection* options determine what packages to query, and *information selection* options determine what information to provide.

Package selection options

package_name

Query the installed package *package_name*.

-a, --all

Query all installed packages.

-f *file*, --file *file*

Find out which package owns *file*.

--fileid *md5*

Query package with the specified MD5 digest.

-g *group*, --group *group*

Find out which packages have group *group*.

--hdrid *sha1*

Query package with the specified SHA1 digest in the package header.

-p *package_file*, --package *package_file*

Query the uninstalled package *package_file*, which can be a URL. If *package_file* is not a binary package, it is treated as a text file containing a package manifest. Each line of the manifest contain a path or one or more whitespace-separated glob expressions to be expanded to paths. These paths are then used instead of *package_file* as the query arguments. The manifest can contain comments that begin with a hash mark (#).

`--pkgid` *md5*

> Query the package with a package identifier that is the given MD5 digest of the combined header and contents.

`--querybynumber` *num*

> Query the *num*th database entry. Useful for debugging.

`-qf, --queryformat` *num*

> Specify the format for displaying the query output, using tags to represent different types of data (e.g., NAME, FILENAME, DISTRIBUTION). The format specification is a variation of the standard *printf* formatting, with the type specifier omitted and replaced by the name of the header tag inclosed in braces ({ }). For example:

    %{NAME}

> The tag names are case-insensitive. Use `--querytags` to view a list of available tags. The tag can be followed by `:`*type* to get a different output format type. The possible types are:

`armor`

> Wrap a public key in ASCII armor.

`base64`

> Encode binary data as base64.

`date`

> Use strftime(3) "%c" format.

`day`

> Use strftime(3) "%a %b %d %Y" format.

`depflags`

> Format dependency flags.

`fflags`

> Format file flags.

`hex`

> Use hexadecimal format.

`octal`

> Use octal format.

`perms`

> Format file permissions.

`shescape`

> Escape single quotes for use in a script.

`triggertype`

> Display trigger suffix.

`--specfile` *`specfile`*

> Query *specfile* as if it were a package. Useful for extracting information from a spec file.

`--tid` *`tid`*

> List packages with the specified transaction identifier (*tid*). The tid is a Unix timestamp. All packages installed or erased in a single transaction have the same tid.

`--triggeredby` *`pkg`*

> List packages that are triggered by the installation of package *pkg*.

`--whatrequires` *`capability`*

> List packages that require the given capability to function.

`--whatprovides` *`capability`*

> List packages that provide the given capability.

Information selection options

`-c, --configfiles`

> List configuration files in the package. Implies -l.

`--changelog`

> Display the log of change information for the package.

`-d, --docfiles`

> List documentation files in the package. Implies -l.

`--dump`

> Dump information for each file in the package. This option must be used with at least one of the following: -l, -c, or -d. The output includes the following information in this order:
>
> ```
> path size mtime md5sum mode owner group isconfig isdoc rdev symlink
> ```

`--filesbypkg`

> List all files in each package.

`-i, --info`

> Display package information, including the name, version, and description. Formats the results according to --queryformat if specified.

`-l, --list`

> List all files in the package.

`--last`

> List packages by install time, with the latest packages listed first.

`--provides`

> List the capabilities this package provides.

`-R, --requires`

> List any packages this package depends on.

-s, --state

> List each file in the package and its state. The possible states are normal, not installed, or replaced. Implies -l.

--scripts

> List any package-specific shell scripts used during installation and uninstallation of the package.

--triggers, --triggerscript

> Display any trigger scripts in the package.

Uninstall options

The syntax for erase, the uninstall command, is:

```
rpm -e package_name ...
rpm --erase package_name ...
```

The uninstall options are:

--allmatches

> Remove all versions of the package. Only one package should be specified; otherwise, an error results.

--nodeps

> Don't check dependencies before uninstalling the package.

--nopostun

> Don't run any post-uninstall scripts.

--nopreun

> Don't run any pre-uninstall scripts.

--noscripts

> Don't execute any pre-uninstall or post-uninstall scripts. Equivalent to --nopreun --nopostun.

--notriggerpostun

> Don't execute any post-uninstall scripts triggered by the removal of this package.

--notriggers

> Don't execute any scripts triggered by the removal of this package. Equivalent to --notriggerun --notriggerpostun.

--notriggerun

> Don't execute any uninstall scripts triggered by the removal of this package.

--repackage

> Repackage the files before uninstalling them. Rename the package as specified by the macro %_repackage_name_fmt and save it in the directory specified by the macro %_repackage_dir (by default, /var/tmp).

--test

> Don't really uninstall anything; just go through the motions. Use with -vv for debugging.

Verify options

The syntax for the verify command is:

```
rpm -V|-y|--verify [package-selection-options] [verify-options]
```

Verify mode compares information about the installed files in a package with information about the files that came in the original package, and displays any discrepancies. The information compared includes the size, MD5 sum, permissions, type, owner, and group of each file. Uninstalled files are ignored.

The package selection options include those available for query mode. In addition, the following verify options are available:

--nodeps
 Ignore package dependencies.

--nodigest
 Ignore package or header digests.

--nofiles
 Ignore attributes of package files.

--nogroup
 Ignore group ownership errors.

--nolinkto
 Ignore symbolic link errors.

--nomd5
 Ignore MD5 checksum errors.

--nomode
 Ignore file mode (permissions) errors.

--nordev
 Ignore major and minor device number errors.

--nomtime
 Ignore modification time errors.

--noscripts
 Ignore any verify script.

--nosignature
 Ignore package or header signatures.

--nosize
 Ignore file size errors.

--nouser
 Ignore user ownership errors.

The output is formatted as an eight-character string, possibly followed by an attribute marker, and then the filename. The possible attribute markers are:

c   Configuration file

d   Documentation file

g   Ghost file (contents not included in package)

l   License file

r   Readme file

Each of the eight characters in the string represents the result of comparing one file attribute to the value of that attribute from the RPM database. A period (.) indicates that the file passed that test. The following characters indicate failure of the corresponding test:

5   MD5 sum

D   Device

G   Group

L   Symlink

M   Mode (includes permissions and file type)

S   File size

T   Mtime

U   User

Database rebuild options

The syntax of the command to rebuild the RPM database is:

```
rpm --rebuilddb [options]
```

You also can build a new database:

```
rpm --initdb [options]
```

The options available with the database rebuild mode are the --dbpath, --root, and -v options described earlier.

Signature check options

RPM packages may have a PGP signature built into them. PGP configuration information is read from the *rpmrc* file. There are three types of digital signature options: you can check signatures, add signatures to packages, and import signatures.

The syntax of the signature check mode is:

```
rpm --checksig package_file...
rpm -K package_file...
```

The signature checking options -K and --checksig check the digests and signatures contained in the specified packages to insure the integrity and origin of the packages. Note that RPM now automatically checks the signature of any package when it is read; this option is still useful, however, for checking all headers and signatures associated with a package.

The following options are available for use with signature check mode:

--nogpg
> Don't check any GPG signatures.

--nomd5
> Don't check any MD5 signatures.

--nopgp
> Don't check any PGP signatures.

The syntax for adding signatures to binary packages is:

```
rpm --addsign binary-pkgfile...
rpm --resign binary-pkgfile...
```

Both --addsign and --resign generate and insert new signatures, replacing any that already exist in the specified binary packages.*

The syntax for importing signatures is:

```
rpm --import public-key
```

The --import option is used to import an ASCII public key to the RPM database so that digital signatures for packages using that key can be verified. Imported public keys are carried in headers, and keys are kept in a ring, which can be queried and managed like any package file.

Miscellaneous options

Several additional rpm options are available:

--querytags
> Print the tags available for use with the --queryformat option in query mode.

--setperms *packages*
> Set file permissions of the specified packages to those in the database.

--setugids *packages*
> Set file owner and group of the specified packages to those in the database.

--showrc
> Show the values rpm will use for all options that can be set in an *rpmrc* file.

---

* In older versions of RPM, --addsign was used to add new signatures without replacing existing ones, but currently both options work the same way and replace any existing signatures.

FTP/HTTP options

The following options are available for use with FTP and HTTP URLs in install, update, and query modes:

--ftpport *port*

> Use *port* for making an FTP connection on the proxy FTP server instead of the default port. Same as specifying the macro %_ftpport.

--ftpproxy *host*

> Use *host* as the proxy server for FTP transfers through a firewall that uses a proxy. Same as specifying the macro % ftpproxy.

--httpport *port*

> Use *port* for making an HTTP connection on the proxy HTTP server instead of the default port. Same as specifying the macro %_httpport.

--httpproxy *host*

> Use *host* as the proxy server for HTTP transfers. Same as specifying the macro %_httpproxy.

The rpmbuild Command

The rpmbuild command is used to build RPM packages. The syntax for rpmbuild is:

> **rpmbuild** -[**b**|**t**]*step* [*build-options*] *spec-file* ...

Specify -b to build a package directly from a spec file, or -t to open a tarred, gzipped file and use its spec file.

Both forms take the following single-character step arguments, listed in the order they would be performed:

p   Perform the prep stage, unpacking source files and applying patches.

l   Do a list check, expanding macros in the files section of the spec file and verifying that each file exists.

c   Perform the build stage. Done after the prep stage; generally equivalent to doing a make.

i   Perform the install stage. Done after the prep and build stages; generally equivalent to doing a make install.

b   Build a binary package. Done after prep, build, and install.

s   Build a source package. Done after prep, build, and install.

a   Build both binary and source packages. Done after prep, build, and install.

The general rpm options described earlier can be used with rpmbuild.

The following additional options can also be used when building an rpm file with rpmbuild.

`--buildroot` *dir*

> Override the `BuildRoot` tag with *dir* when building the package.

`--clean`

> Clean up (remove) the build files after the package has been made.

`--nobuild`

> Go through the motions, but don't execute any build stages. Used for testing spec files.

`--rmsource`

> Remove the source files when the build is done. Can be used as a standalone option with rpm to clean up files separately from creating the packages.

`--rmspec`

> Remove the spec file when the build is done. Like `--rmsource`, `--rmspec` can be used as a standalone option with `rpmbuild`.

`--short-circuit`

> Can be used with `-bc` and `-bi` to skip previous stages.

`--sign`

> Add a GPG signature to the package for verifying its identity and origin.

`--target` *platform*

> When building the package, set the macros `%_target`, `%_target_arch`, and `%_target_os` to the value indicated by *platform*.

Two other options can be used standalone with `rpmbuild` to recompile or rebuild a package:

`--rebuild` *source-pkgfile*…

> Like `--recompile`, but also build a new binary package. Remove the build directory, the source files, and the spec file once the build is complete.

`--recompile` *source-pkgfile*…

> Install the named source package, and prep, compile, and install the package.

Finally, the `--showrc` option is used to show the current `rpmbuild` configuration:

```
rpmbuild --showrc
```

This option shows the values that will be used for all options that can be set in an *rpmrc* file.

RPM Examples

Query the RPM database to find Emacs-related packages:

```
% rpm -q -a | grep emacs
```

Query an uninstalled package, printing information about the package and listing the files it contains:

```
% rpm -qpil ~/downloads/bash2-doc-2.03-8.i386.rpm
```

Install a package (assumes superuser privileges):

```
% rpm -i sudo-1.5.3-6.i386.rpm
```

Known Problems and Solutions

The following describe known issues and workarounds for the Java Desktop System.

Problem: Panel Crashes

When you log in to the Java Desktop System after rebooting your system, your panel may crash and restart immediately in Release I.

Solution

Use On-line Update to acquire the necessary patch.

Problem: Connecting by Modem

When you are using a modem for your network connection and require a dial-up PPP connection.

Solution

Use the Linux PPP dialer command line utility *wvdial*, discussed in the section "Modem sessions" in Chapter 4.

Problem: Can't Run File from Remote Directories

When you try to open a document from an NFS or Samba mounted directory, the File Manager displays an error if the application owning the document cannot handle a filename argument passed as a URL.

For example, StarOffice, OpenOffice, vi, acroread, and ggv applications cannot handle URLs, therefore the File Manager encounters errors when opening NFS files with these applications.

The same problem arises for files on Samba (SMB) mounted directories.

Solution

To open such files, first copy them to a local directory—not a Samba or NF directory.

Problem: Sound Recorder Slide Bar

The slide bar and time counter do not work when recording a new *.wav* file in Release I. No indication exists that a recording is taking place.

Solution

Upgrade to Release II.

Problem: Sound Recorder Stops

You can't play a *.wav* file more than once in an instance of sound recorder.

Solution

Open another instance of Sound Recorder and play the *.wav* file as a workaround.

Problem: Backspace Is Inserted

When you log in to a Java Desktop System from a Sun Ray™ client or Solaris machine, a backspace is inserted each time you press the L key on your keyboard.

Solution

Two possible workarounds exist:

- After you log in to the Java Desktop System, use the xmodmap command to redefine the L key.
- Log in to the Java Desktop System as root and remove the */etc/X11/Xmodmap* file.

Problem: RPMs Don't Recognize the Linux Release on Your Machine

When you attempt to install these RPM files on your system, the installation may fail. RPMs require a specific Linux version in */etc/SuSE-release* for the installation to succeed on your system.

Solution

Two possible workarounds exist:

- Use RPMs from a version of Linux that the RPM recognizes—for example: SuSE Linux 8.1 (i386) Version=8.1.
- Build RPMs from source. For example, use an rpm with the *src.rpm* extention.

Problem: Clock Settings

The Clock applet takes the time from the system clock, which in turn, takes the time from the hardware clock. Sometimes the hardware clock does not reflect accurate time.

Solution

You can change the time for the hardware clock in the following ways:

- Enter the BIOS setup and change the time directly.
- Use the ntpdate command to set the time zone and synchronize the clock, as in the following example:

      ntpdate -b clock.fmt.he.net.

- Synchronize the hardware clock to the Unix clock, using the following command:

      hwclock --systohc

You can obtain a list of Internet time servers from *http://www.boulder.nist.gov/timefreq/service/time-servers.html*.

Problem: VMWare Failure

VMWare 4.0.x has trouble running on your JDS system.

Solution

Install kernel sources using Launch → Applications → System Tools → Administration → software install. Then reinstall Vmware.

Problem: Help

Releases I & II of the Java Desktop System includes applications that have Help manuals taken from the GNOME free software community. These are incomplete.

Solution

Find or purchase SuSE Linux 8.1-9.1 User Guide and/or the Administrative Guide. Utilize Internet documentation. Purchase this O'Reilly book.

Problem: Sun Java Desktop Doesn't Support DVD Playback

The Movie Player (called Totem) supports on gstreamer for DVD playback and the current version of gstreamer lacks the plugins for DVD playback.To play DVDs on JDS, you will need a workaround. DVD playback can be enabled by installing another movie player, e.g. Xine or MPlayer. A procedure for installing Xine includes downloading rpms from *http://cambuca.ldhs.cetuc.pub-rio.br/xine/*.

Solution

You will need the following rpm libraries:

- curl-
- libdvdcss
- w32codec
- xinw-ui
- linbxine

Install the termcap package by clicking on the Launch → Applications → System Tools → Administration → software install. Next, upgrade the installed curl version on JDS using:

```
rpm -Uhv curl-7.10.3-1.i386.rpm
```

Install the other packages as root using:

```
rpm -i libdvdcss-1.2.8-1.network.i386.rpm libxine1-1_cvs-040109.i586.rpm
w32codec-0.52-1.i386.rpm
xine-ui-0.9.23cvs-031230.i586.rpm
```

To play a DVD, start xine by opening a terminal window and typing:

```
xine
```

Click the DVD button in the xine toolbar, to start playing a DVD.

To burn a CD, double click the This Computer icon on the JDS desktop, then go to the Go menu and select CD Recorder. Drag and drop any files to this window, then click the Write To CD button. Note that only the root user can burn CDs.

```
ln -s /dev/cdrom /dev/dvd
```

Problem: ATI Video Cards

ATI DVI video cards won't start X.

Solution

ATI distributes ATI Proprietary Linux Driver 3.7.6, which you can find on the company's web site. Go to *http://ati.com/support/driver.html* to select the driver. Follow the instructions at *http://ati.com/support/infobase/linuxhowto-ati.html*.

Installation Guide

Normally, installing the JDS is easy using the CDs included with your original JDS installation media. We assume that you have the media and plan to use this method. Essentially, you can use the same steps to upgrade JDS to a later version from CD-ROM images that you can download or purchase from Sun.

If you plan on installing JDS from a server set up by your organization, the material in this appendix probably does not pertain to you.

The Java Desktop System comes with documentation that can help you install the system. This information is on the Documentation CD that accompanies your JDS Media. At the time of this writing, you can find the installation guide under the path *cdrom/en/Java-Desktop-System-R2/java-desktop-system-r2-documentation.html*. This appendix contains information similar to what you can find in Sun's Documentation. In the event you do not have the ability to access the documentation, you can use the information contained here to install your system—but it is subject to change.

We also provide some explanations of the installation process not found on the Sun Documentation CD and some suggestions about what to do if you run into problems. Let's begin by looking at the requirements for using JDS.

System Requirements

To successfully install JDS, you are required to have a personal computer (PC) that meets certain modest hardware resources. Sun Microsystems provides both a minimum supported configuration and a recommended one. The minimum supported configuration requires an Intel Pentium II 266 MHz compatible processor, a 4 GB hard disk, 128 MB of RAM, and a color monitor with at least an 800×600 screen resolution.

Ideally, Sun recommends a Pentium III compatible processor, 600 MHz or faster, at least 4 GB of hard disk space, at least 256 MB of RAM, and 1024×768 screen resolution or better. However, we have found the system runs best with a Pentium IV processor and 512 MB of memory. The system can also achieve excellent performance with a DRI monitor and Video card if the manufacturer provides a configuration utility for the DRI driver.

Your PC should boot from an installation CD. Intel systems have different ways of booting from the CD- or DVD-ROM. For example, some Laptops allow you to boot from the CD-ROM only if you press a specific button. Sometimes it is not enough to reboot a system with the CD-ROM installed; you may have to insert the CD-ROM, power down the system, and power it up again.

If you try inserting the CD-ROM and powering up the system, but it insists on booting from the hard disk as usual, you may need to enter the BIOS utility and select the order in which your CD-ROM boots. The exact procedure varies from system to system; one example of a BIOS display is shown in Figure F-1.

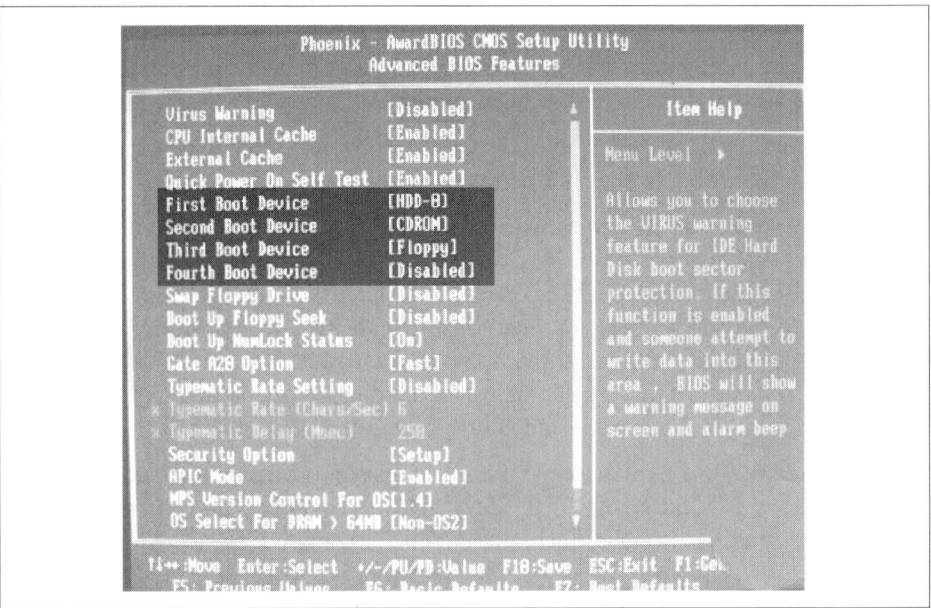

Figure F-1. BIOS utiltiy

The screen in the BIOS utility shows the order of booting. In this situation, the first boot device listed is the hard drive (HDD-0).

You need to change this order so that the CD-ROM becomes the first boot device. In the example screen, you select the First Boot Device by using the arrow keys on your keyboard. You then press the Enter key and another screen appears offering you different device options, such as the hard drive, CD-ROM or Floppy. If you choose the CD-ROM, you may or may not have to reset the remaining devices, depending on the type of computer you have.

Figure F-2 shows an example of a different computer manufacturer's BIOS. Although Phoenix made both systems, notice the difference in the type of page displayed. In this figure, we selected the Boot Menu, which contains only four entries, each devoted to selecting the boot sequence.

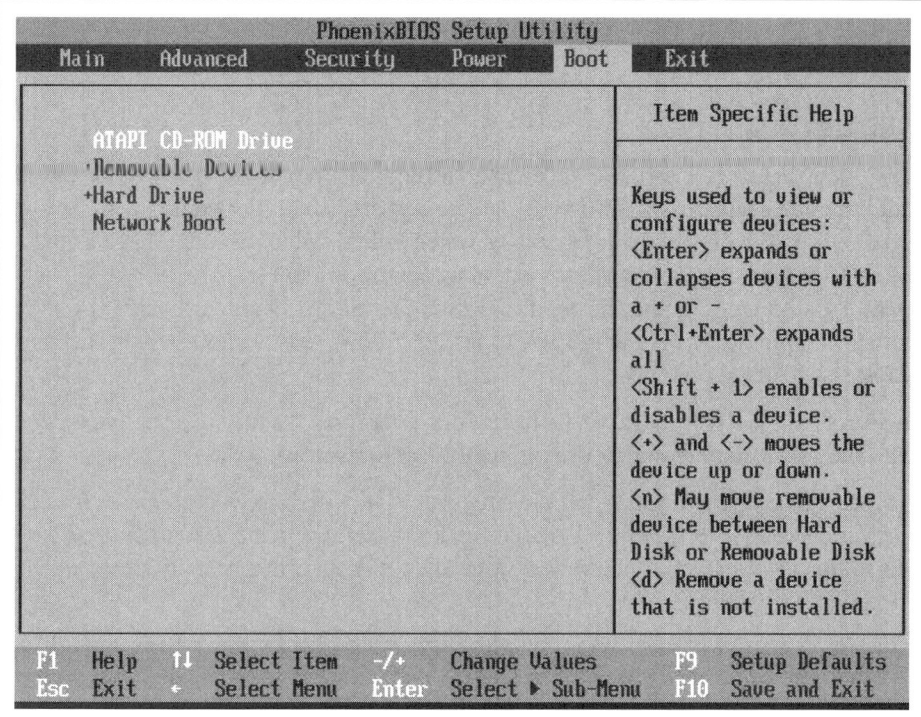

Figure F-2. BIOS utility on a different computer

On the righthand side of the screen, you can see the instructions for selecting the device you want to begin the boot process. If the system doesn't find a CD-ROM in the drive tray, it will seek a system disk in the next device, and so on.

We recommend that you look at your computer's documentation to determine how to boot from the CD-ROM. Unfortunately, so many different systems exist that methods vary not only from manufacturer to manufacturer but from model to model. If you like, of course, you can go back in the BIOS and restore the previous order of booting once you have successfully installed JDS and don't anticipate the need to reinstall it.

You need to have certain information ready before you begin your installation. For example, you will need to know:

- The username and password you wish to use
- The root password you wish to use

- Network configuration information, such as how your system will determine its IP address (DHCP or Static), the gateway address, and netmask (See Chapter 4)
- The status of any existing operating systems if you plan to dual boot (as described in the following section)
- How you will partition your disk (partitions are explained in the sidebar below)
- ISP configuration information (See Chapter 4)

Dual Booting

Many people like to have two operating systems to boot from. This is not like the simultaneous use of multiple operating systems described in Chapter 9. Dual booting allows you to choose your operating system when you boot, but you can't switch back and forth between them during system operation; you have to reboot to change operating systems. Despite the rigidity of this practice, it is very convenient for people with ample disk space who need to run Windows, for example, for some activities and JDS for others.

To install Linux on a machine with another operating system in place, you need a dual-boot environment and approximately 5 GB of free disk space.

Typically, Windows installations use an entire hard disk, leaving no space for other operating systems. Sun's JDS Installation Program can create a partition allowing you to install the Linux operating system, even if the disk is already taken up by a Windows formatted partition.

What Are Partitions?

A partition is a physical section of a drive that can be treated as a separate disk. Each partition contains its own file system. Some partitions can be subdivided further into partitions, a bit of complexity that is needed to overcome restrictions in the Intel x86 chip architecture.

Three types of partitions exist: *primary*, *extended*, and *logical*. Four primary partitions can exist on a single drive. Generally, one primary partition is used for the files that boot the system and another for the files that the operating system and its users access when it is running, but there is great flexibility in the choice of what to partition.

An extended partition takes up the slot of a primary partition but can be broken down into logical partitions, which allows a drive to have more than four logical divisions. You can format each logical partition to support Linux or another operating system.

The Boot Process

When a computer powers up, the CPU runs startup code from a system's read-only BIOS (Basic Input Output System). This procedures is called a POST (Power-on Self Test). During POST, the system sets up the hardware for use. Prior to starting the operating system, the system loads and runs a program stored on the first sector of the first drive called the master boot record (MBR). JDS uses a program called GRUB to look for the primary partitions and to see which one is tagged as the active partition. The active partition has its own boot record, which starts the operating system located on that partition.

If you have less than 5 GB available, consider installing an additional drive or carve the space out of your existing drive using a free utility such as FIPS or a commercial product such as PartitionMagic. (The JDS utility does not work with NTFS-formatted drives.)

Repartitioning a drive involves some risk, so be sure to back up your data before repartitioning.

Because Windows cannot resize existing partitions, the JDS Installation Program checks your hard disk to find out how it's laid out and proposes an appropriate partition setup to permit JDS to run.

 If your existing Windows takes up the entire disk with an NTFS file system, the JDS installation program does not enable you to resize your partition, but proposes instead replacing your existing partition. In order to keep your Windows partition and permit dual booting, use third-party partition applications such as PartitionMagic to resize your partitions and create special partitions for JDS.

Installing JDS

As described earlier, installing JDS involves inserting the first CD-ROM from the JDS distribution into your CD-ROM drive and powering up the computer again so it boots from this CD-ROM. At that point, the installation procedure displays a list of options:

- Boot from hard disk
- Installation
- Installation—ACPI Disabled
- Installation—Safe Settings
- Manual Installation
- Rescue System
- Memory Test

The first option is provided in case you left your installation CD in your CD-ROM drive by mistake but don't want to start an installation. If so, choose the first option. Otherwise, choose the installation option that pertains to you, and press the Enter key.

The installation program then displays Sun's Binary Code License Agreement. If you accept the agreement, click on Accept and the installation will continue. If you do not accept the agreement, the installation will not continue and you will have to abort the installation. For Linux users who have installed free distributions, accepting the Binary Code License Agreement may be a new twist for you. JDS contains proprietary components that require the agreement. Installation is not an irreversible decision, however. If you decide later that you do not want to continue using JDS because of the license or for any other reason, you can wipe the drive clean and change to a free Linux distribution.

Now, you should be in the installation program. You will notice several sections of dialog boxes. Follow the procedure as they appear.

1. In the Language Selection, choose the language you want to use and then click on Accept. (See Figure F-3.)

2. The JDS installation program browses your hardware and displays its findings.

   If the JDS installation program finds an existing Linux system on your hard drive, a variety of options will be displayed. Because this appendix is primarily written for first-time installers, we assume that you choose the first option and offer instruction for this option throughout the rest of the appendix.

   • New installation. Choose this if no Linux system exists on your machine or if you want to replace an existing Linux system completely.

   • Update an existing system. Select this option if you want to upgrade a JDS already installed on your machine. This option preserves configuration settings from your existing system. Use this option only if you have an earlier release of JDS on your system.

   • Boot installed system. Use this option to fix the problem manually if you have a Linux system on your hard disk that you cannot boot.

   • Abort installation.

 If you have another Linux distribution on your system, such as RedHat, SuSE or Debian, you can replace the existing distribution. If you want to keep your home directory, back it up and choose this option, *otherwise, you will lose your data and the distribution.* Letting both systems remain on your hard drive goes beyond the scope of this appendix; consult other documentation to explain how to use your bootloader to allow for multiple Linux systems.

Select your language:

Čeština
Dansk
Deutsch
English (UK)
English (US)
Español
Français
Ελληνικά
Italiano
日本語
한글
Lietuvių
Magyar
Nederlands
Norsk
Português brasileiro
Romanian
Русский
简体中文
Slovenčina

Abort

Accept

Figure F-3. Installation program language selection

3. Next, you are presented with the Installation settings for your system. These are shown in Figure F-4. They include the partitions that will be created and a brief listing of the main software to be installed.

Many of the items shown on the Installation Setting screen are actually links or bookmarks that you can click, just like links on a web page, to alter the default settings. You can visit the links to make last-minute changes to your partitions or other choices. For example, if you place your mouse an underlined section such as Mode or Keyboard layout and click, a new page will open dedicated to that section.

To illustrate, if you click Partitioning to modify the default settings, the JDS Installation Program checks your hard disk and displays the following options:

- Accept proposal as is.
- Base the partition setup on this proposal.
- Create a custom partition setup.

Figure F-4. Installation settings

If you have special reason to change the defaults, read the sections "Resizing Your Partition" and "Creating a Custom Partitions Table" for instructions you can follow at this point.

As another example, if you click on Software, you'll get a new screen and have the opportunity to change the default setup. First you'll see a screen offering you two options:

- Default system with StarSuite—for Japan, China, Korea and Taiwan only
- Default system with StarOffice—for all other countries

You will also have the option to change the defaults by using the selections available in Figure F-5. In this situation, we suggest you select Development Tools.

You can also select special configuration options for a modem and for a Laptop computer. After you select the appropriate options, click Accept.

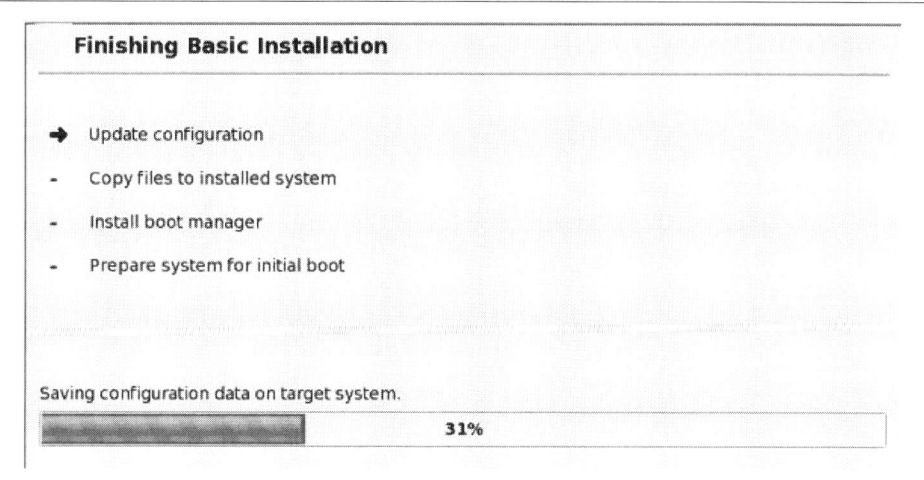

Finishing Basic Installation

➡   Update configuration

–   Copy files to installed system

–   Install boot manager

–   Prepare system for initial boot

Saving configuration data on target system.

31%

Figure F-5. Changing the software options

Once you have configured the system the way you want, you'll once again see a screen similar to Figure F-4. Make sure the changes took effect. You can now continue with the installation by clicking Accept.

4. The JDS Installation Program displays a message informing you that the installation will be performed according to the settings made in the previous dialogs. Click Yes to commit the installation and all the choices made so far.

5. A message is displayed informing you that the JDS Installation Program is preparing your hard disk. When the installation begins, a screen is displayed containing the following window panes:

Current Package

Displays the name, description, and size of the installation package and a status bar showing how much of the installation of that package is complete.

Installation

Displays the status of the percentage of installation completed from that CD, as well as the estimated time remaining to complete the download.

Installation Log (extract)

Displays a log of activity for all the packages currently being installed on your system.

When the download of the packages from CD 1 is complete, the JDS Installation Program displays a screen informing you that the basic installation is finished and the system automatically reboots.

6. After the system reboots, a dialog requests you to insert CD 2. Insert CD 2 and click OK.

7. When the packages you need from CD 2 are installed, a dialog requests you to insert CD 3. Insert CD 3 and click OK.

8. When all the packages you need from CD 3 are successfully installed, the JDS Installation Program prompts you to enter a password for *root*, the system administrator. Choose a hard-to-guess password for the root user and enter it twice in the boxes, shown in Figure F-6. Click Next.

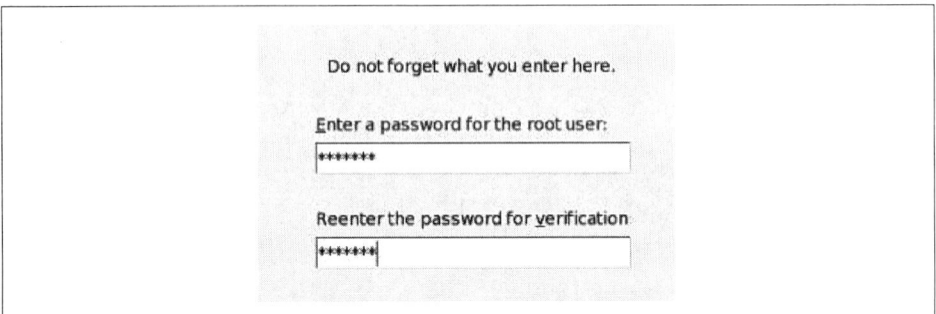

Figure F-6. Root password screen

 Make a note of the root password in case you forget it. You will need it in the future.

9. The JDS Installation Program prompts you to add a new user. Enter the first name, last name, user login, and password for the user you want to add and click Next. A new user account is created with the details you enter. This will be the user you normally use to access the system; the *root* account should be used only for critical system administration tasks.

10. The JDS Installation Program starts to initialize the Desktop settings as follows:

    • Text mode only—no graphical desktop
    • Graphical desktop environment

    Select Graphical desktop environment and click Accept.

11. For a standalone, non-networked installation, the JDS Installation Program tries to detect local printers only. Click Yes if you have a local printer attached to your system. Otherwise, click "Skip detection."

12. The JDS Installation Program writes the system configuration and displays the Installation Settings for the following hardware devices:

    • Network interfaces
    • Printers
    • Modems

- ISDN adapters
- Sound

To change any of the Installation Settings, click Change. Click Next to accept the settings as displayed on the Installation Page. JDS displays a message that the configuration is saved successfully, and the system automatically reboots.

13. Eject CD 3.
14. At the login screen, log in with the username and password that you set up for the new user.

You are now ready to use the JDS.

Resizing Your Partition

The JDS installation program chooses a layout for your partitions that it believes makes sense for your disk. If you have reasons to change the partitions, you can do so before installation. (Once installation is complete, you can't change the partitions safely without wiping out your data.)

The following procedure outlines how to resize the partitions:

1. From the Installation Settings dialog, select Partitioning, select "Base partition setup on this proposal" option, and click Next.
2. Highlight the partition that you want to resize and click Resize.
3. Use the slider to set how much space you want to allocate to your Windows partition and your Linux partition and click OK.

   Click Next to save the partition table and return to the Installation Settings screen.

 The minimum allocation of space for Linux is 3024 MB.

Creating a Custom Partitions Table

If the partition table recommended by the JDS Installation Program is unsuitable for the JDS installation requirements, you may need to create a custom partition table. This should include at least one partition for your data and one swap partition, which the operating system needs to support multiprocessing. In this section, as an example, we create:

- A 5 GB partition mounted at the root (the / directory) for system files
- A 512 MB swap file
- A partition containing the rest of the available disk space, mounted at /usr, for user directories

The following procedure outlines how to create a custom partition table. This procedure overwrites your existing Windows partition. Before proceeding, back up any files you want to keep.

1. From the Installation Settings dialog, select Partitioning, select "Create custom partition option," and click Next.

2. Select "Custom partitioning, for experts option," then click Next to launch the Expert Partitioner dialog.

3. Select the device that refers to the disk where you want to install the application, for example /dev/hda, then click Delete to erase all partitions on that disk.

4. Click Create to create a new partition and select the Primary option.

5. In the pop-up window, set the size and location for the partition. For instance, to create a single 5 GB partition that holds all the files for JDS, set the Start Cylinder to 0, set the End Cylinder to + 5 GB, and set the Mount Point to / .

6. Click Create to create a new partition and select the Extended option.

   Make sure all the choices you make in the pop-up window are consistent and valid. For example, the Start Cylinder value must be one more than the End Cylinder of the previous partition hda1, and the End Cylinder can be the same as the End Cylinder for the entire disk /dev/hda.

   If you want multiple partitions for various directories, you are likely to exceed the limit of four partitions that the x86 imposes using only primary partitions. Luckily, you can bypass the restriction by using one or more extended partitions. Typically, you create one extended partition that covers the remainder of the disk, and then create all the logical partitions you need inside that extended partition.

7. Click Create to create a new partition.

8. Select Swap from the pull-down menu beneath the Format option.

9. Specify the size of the swap partition using the + syntax in the End field. For example, if your system has 256 MB RAM, you probably need 512 MB of swap memory, which is expressed as + 512 MB.

10. Click Create to create a new partition. A new partition to occupy the remainder of the disk is configured. Set the Mount Point to /usr.

11. Click Next to save the partition table and return to the Installation Settings screen.

Checking for and Installing System Updates

The Java System Update Service enables you to:

- Install software updates for JDS.
- Choose which updates to install from a list of available updates.
- Specify which server to check for available updates.

To launch the Java System Update Service application, choose Launch → Applications → System Tools → Online Update.

Some Common Troubleshooting

In this section we list a few common problems and how you can handle them. Sun's customer service is available to JDS users to get them started.

Monitor Out of Range

Monitor Video Out of Range problems occur primarily with LCD Monitors. A monitor able to handle a 1280×1024 at 75 Hz will fail because it will be preset to an 85 Hz refresh rate/vertical frequency that that the monitor cannot manage. Similarly, a 15-inch monitor able to handle 1024×768 at 70 Hz will fail because the preset resolution is 1280×1024 at 75 Hz.

To prevent these problems, during installation, select 1024×768 or 800×600 temporarily, depending on the capacity of your monitor, by pressing F2. You will then see a menu of different resolutions to use. Use your arrow keys on your keyboard to select the resolution you want.

After the software packages are installed, the automatic (SaX2) hardware configuration will set your monitor to VESA 1280×1024 at 75 or 85 Hz, depending on whether the monitor is 19, 17, or 15 inches. You will want to change resolution at this stage, or the monitor will run out of range when rebooting to the graphical login screen.

On reboot, if the monitor encounters the out-of-range problem, it shows a black screen. But you can solve this without a cumbersome re-installation.

After rebooting Linux, at the point when the display goes black and gray just before the graphical login screen is supposed to start up, select Alt-F1 from the keyboard, followed by the Enter key. This breaks the startup of the graphical login screen, and presents a text-based command line login instead. Log in as root with root password.

Next, enter the following command

```
init 3
```

followed by the Enter key. At the # prompt that again appears, enter:

```
sax2 -l
```

to start the SaX2 graphical configuration tool in a low resolution mode.

Now it is possible in SaX2 to change the monitor and resolution settings. Test it and customize the size and position before saving the configuration.

Reboot the system. The graphical login screen should now be displayed properly.

Sony VAIO Laptop with a ATI Radeon IGP 345M Video Card Does Not Work

The ATI Radeon IGP 345M requires Xfree86 Version 4.3.

Run X-version from the command line. You will see the following information:

```
XFree86 Version 4.3.0
Release Date: 27 February 2003
X Protocol Version 11, Revision 0, Release 6.6
Build Date: 25 March 2004
Module Loader present
To resolve the problem, add these sections to your /etc/X11/XF86Config-4 file:
Section "Device"
Identifier "ATI"
Driver "radeon"
VendorName "ATI"
BoardName "Mobility U1"
EndSection
Section "Screen"
Identifier "Screen0"
Device "ATI"
Monitor "Monitor0"
DefaultDepth 24
SubSection "Display"
Depth 24
Modes "1024x768" "800x600" "640x480"
EndSubSection
EndSection
```

Install Fails on Disk 2

Run the following command as root:

```
dd if=/dev/cdrom of=/dev/null
```

If the media is fine, you should get a result such as the following:

```
linux:~ # dd if=/dev/cdrom of=/dev/null
1316996+0 records in
1316996+0 records out
```

If a physical defect on the media prevents the data from being successfully read, you will get an error message.

If you do not receive an error, your system may be slowed down by the capacity of the CPU. Wait a little longer—on some machines the decompress and timeouts are excessively long on this package install.

Having Trouble with Wireless LAN Card

Wireless LAN cards may or may not work in JDS. Unfortunately, this is a general Linux problem, not isolated to JDS. Several projects exist to help resolve the problems depending on the type of LAN card you own.

A commercial solution comes from Linuxant which you can find at *http://www. linuxant.com/driverloader/*.

Linuxant supports chipsets from the following manufacturers:

- Atheros
- Broadcom (AirForce)
- Cisco (Aironet)
- INPROCOMM
- Intel (PRO/Wireless 2100, 2100A, 2200BG - Centrino)
- Intersil (Prism GT/Duette/Indigo)
- Marvell (Libertas)
- Realtek (RTL8180L)
- Texas Instruments (ACX100, ACX111/TNETW1130)

Free solutions may be found at:

- *http://www.linux-wlan.org/*
- *http://tuxmobil.org/pcmcia_ci10028.html/*

Glossary

access permissions

The operations a person or group can perform on a file or other resource; a security feature also known as access rights. Permissions traditionally can be read, write, or execute.

address book

The software component of JDS's Email and Calendar program that organizes names, addresses, phone numbers, email addresses, and other details associated with the user's personal and business contacts.

application

A software program sometimes distributed separately from the operating system and sometimes included and integrated with the operating system to share the same windowing, control features, and look and feel with other applications and system tools. An application offers a user an interface with controls for manipulating data—in the case of the StarOffice, the control of formatted text, text files, and many other file formats; in the case of Web Browser, the control of access to Web pages on the Internet. A few other examples of applications included with JDS are Email and Calendar, Instant Messenger, GIMP and File Roller. See *operating system*.

archive

A single file containing multiple files, often compressed. Facilitates transfer of files between computers. Archival formats include TAR, ZIP, and GZ and are usually reflected in the trailing extension (*.tar*, *.zip*, *.gz*, etc.) of the filename.

background process

A program that runs while users do other things. Some processes known as *daemons* are started in the background and remain there. Other processes run in the background temporarily.

backup

A duplicate of data, which one can use to restore data that has been lost, damaged, or erroneously changed.

bandwidth

The capacity of a communications channel. For example, analog bandwidth is measured in cycles per second, while digital bandwidth is a volume of data that may be sent through a channel, measured in bits per second. Bandwidth impacts transmission speed. A large amount of data flowing through a narrow channel takes longer than the same amount of data flowing through a broader channel.

binary

Code compiled into an executable program, as opposed to source code that is human-readable but usually not executable. Some Linux software is distributed as source code, some as both source and binaries, and some only in binary format.

BIOS

Basic Input Output System. A hardware component that initializes important hardware processes on Intel x86 systems. Linux takes over management of the hardware from the BIOS when the bootloader appears on the screen.

bookmarks

The list you create within your web browser of stored web pages to which you would like to return. Also known as "favorites" in the Windows lexicon.

booting

A sequence of computer operations that extend from powering up the system until the system becomes ready to use.

browser

A program that searches and displays content. Often applied to programs that offer graphical displays of content on the World Wide Web, a browser can also refer to a program that looks for files on a desktop or in directories. In networking terms, a browser can look for hosts or computers in a network and broadcast information on the network about the addresses and names of other computers.

buddy

A person with whom you chat via the Internet using an Instant Messenger program.

buddy list

A list of Instant Messenger account names of friends or colleagues with whom you engage in chat. This list is stored by your Instant Messenger program to make it easy to manage chat sessions and see when colleagues are online and available for chat.

bzip2

See *gzip*.

calendar

The component of JDS's Email and Calendar program that tracks appointments and tasks.

client

A workstation in a computer network in which central resources are controlled by a different computer that is a server. Also, a program or computer that makes requests of a server on a local area network or over the Internet.

command line

A text-based mode of operating a computer in which a user enters commands at a prompt. Also called a CLI, or command-line interface.

compile

To turn the source code of a program into an executable (binary) program.

console

A terminal or a dedicated window on the screen that offers a character-based interface to the operating system.

contacts

The people and their associated information in the address book component of the JDS Email and Calendar program. See *address book*.

cursor

The block or vertical-line character that marks the input location on a computer screen. Also, the symbol representing the location of the mouse or other graphical interface device.

daemon

A background process, normally not associated with any real, human user. A daemon usually offers a service such as sending web pages, and sleeps in the background until an event such as the request for a web page triggers it into activity.

desktop

The operating system user interface, typically designed to represent an office desk with objects on it. The operating system desktop uses program and data icons, windows, and taskbars to launch and manage programs and files. GNOME is the name of the desktop interface in JDS.

device driver

The code that serves as an agent between the operating system and a device such as a hard drive, monitor, printer, flash memory, etc. The driver tells the operating system what capabilities the device has and translates system commands into instructions the device understands.

dialog

A window that opens up on the desktop to assist you in performing one of many possible commands or in carrying out functions. Used often in directions such as "Select Format → Character from the Main menu, and in the Character dialog, press the OK button."

directories

The equivalent of computer system folders in which users and systems place files, programs, and subdirectories for storage. Linux uses a standard set of directories to store files common to all Linux systems.

DNS

Domain Name Service. A database of Internet names and addresses that translates alphabetic domain names into numeric IP addresses. DNS is almost always consulted by web browsers, mail servers, and other programs that accept domain names such as *sun.com*.

driver

See *device driver*

email

Electronic mail.

environment

A collection of options set by the system or the user in a command shell, such as the paths (directories) in which to find programs, the username, the current path, and the appearance of the prompt. Each piece of information is stored in an environment variable. These variables can be assigned by the shell's configuration files.

Ethernet

Popular standard for connecting systems near each other into a network. A LAN architecture developed by Xerox Corporation, DEC, and Intel in 1976. Ethernet uses a star or bus typology. The Ethernet specification serves a standard, which specifies the physical and low-level software levels of a networking stacks.

Evolution

The brand name of JDS's Email and Calendar program.

export

To send data out of an application, typically into a file or a format you designate.

EXT2

The native filesystem used by Linux prior to the 2.4 kernel. It offers high throughput, long filenames, permissions, and error tolerance.

EXT3

A journaling filesystem used by Linux. It has a significant advantage over other journaling filesystems in that users can upgrade from the popular EXT2 filesystem without having to back up and restore data, and can manage EXT3 with EXT2 tools. The journal prevents the filesystem from being corrupted in case of a hardware or system crash. Other journaling filesystems for Linux include JFS, XFS, and ReiserFS.

favorites

See *bookmarks*.

file content sniffer

Specifies a pattern to search for in a file. A file content sniffer associates the pattern with a MIME type; for instance, a *.doc* extension refers to a Microsoft Word file. If a match for the pattern is found, the MIME type associated with the pattern helps the system decide which program to invoke to handle the file.

file extension

Also known as a *file suffix*. The last part of a filename, which follows the last period in the file. Many applications use the file extension to determine what to do with a file. For instance, if you use Nautilus or StarOffice to open a file with the extension *.ppt*, they treat it as a PowerPoint file and open it with its presentation software, StarImpress.

file format

The data format of a file or document. For example, StarWriter is programmed to interpret MS Word's proprietary file format just as effectively as the XML file format of its own documents. A format is often indicated in a file's extension; a few examples include *.doc* (Word file), *.sxw*

(StarWriter file), *.txt* (plain text file), *.pdf* (PDF file), and *.ppt* (PowerPoint file).

filesystem

A way of organizing files on the disk or other storage medium. Also refers to the software that tells the operating system how to access and decipher the contents of the medium.

filter

A program that reads data, processes it according to a set of predefined conditions, and outputs the processed data in a different order. Examples include filtering out spam from email or translating PostScript to plain text.

firewall

A system designed to protect a computer network from unauthorized access, especially via the Internet. Also refers to software performing that functions on a general-purpose computer. JDS offers this type of firewalling software, but it is an advanced feature that requires a knowledgeable system administrator to configure. Cable modems and DSL connections, because they are usually "always on" when the computer is powered on, are especially vulnerable to assault from the outside, but anyone who connects to a network is subject to malicious intrusion. A firewall helps prevent this.

free software

Software with source code that is available to everyone. The software is not only universally available for use, but can be altered by anyone for personal use or redistribution. Similar to *open source* software, though there are subtle differences. While free software is theoretically also free of charge, the difficulty of downloading and building the software gives many organizations an opportunity to perform these tasks for the user and charge a fee for the software. Much of the software discussed in this book is free software.

FTP

File Transfer Protocol. A method for transferring files to and from other computers, often used to access software repositories in order to download programs or documents.

function bar

The StarOffice toolbar that provides icons for the user to perform common file and edit functions in one click, such as file save, file open, export to PDF, print, cut, copy, and paste.

gaim

GNU AOL Instant Messenger, JDS's instant-messaging program.

GIMP

GNU Image Manipulation Program, a popular image editor/paint program for Linux. GIMP is included with JDS.

GNOME

The desktop software that provides the graphical environment on top of Linux for JDS. Everything the user does to open, close, or move windows; manipulate the mouse and use keystrokes within those windows; or navigate the system with Nautilus is handled by GNOME.

GUI

Graphical User Interface. The collection of icons, windows, and other onscreen graphical images that allow the user to interact with the operating system. *GNOME* is an example of the GUI for JDS. GNOME and Linux together comprise the JDS operating system.

gzip

GNU zip. A file compression program for Linux. Compression compacts files to save storage space and reduce transfer time. A similar utility using a different format is bzip2; its output can be recognized by the *.bz2* file extension.

history

A facility of the JDS Web Browser for keeping track of the web pages the user has recently visited. The history feature allows you to retrieve a web page by pulling down the location bar in the browser or typing just a few characters into the bar. You can also manage your browser's "historical memory," or list of previously visited web pages.

---

home directory

The directory—also known as a folder—into which JDS places a user after he logs on, and where the user generally stores the files on which he works. An example of a home directory would be */home/swhiser*.

host name

Name of a machine in JDS, usually the name by which the computer can be reached on the network.

IM

Refers both to a program called Instant Messenger and the activity of instant messaging, or chatting over the Internet using the Instant Messenger program. See also *gaim* and *Instant Messenger*.

IMAP

See *POP*.

incoming mail server

The computer—usually located remotely at your Internet service provider's facility—responsible for fielding and forwarding email addressed to you. You need to enter the name of your incoming mail server into the setup wizard of your JDS Email and Calendar program in order to receive and view your email from within the Email and Calendar program.

Instant Messenger

The name of the program for Internet chat. There are many such programs offered by various Internet providers (America Online, MSN, Yahoo!, and so on). Because these chat networks tend to use different protocols, some instant-messenger client programs support only one of these protocols, while others—including the JDS Instant Messenger, *gaim*—support almost all of them.

IP

See *TCP*.

ISP

Internet Service Provider. A company that provides your connection to the Internet, usually for a monthly fee.

Java

The object-oriented programming language developed by Sun Microsystems, intended to be operating system–independent. Java provides a trademarked set of technologies for creating and safely running programs in both standalone and networked environments.

JDS

The Java Desktop System.

kernel

The core of the operating system, on which the other components depend. The kernel manages such tasks as low-level hardware interaction, sharing resources, memory allocation, input/output, security, and user access. It provides and controls the way any other software component can access resources. The kernel runs with a higher privilege than other programs (user-mode programs). The power and robustness of the kernel play a major role in shaping overall system design and reliability.

LAN

Local Area Network. A way to provide communication between computers within a building or across a small campus. Many technologies, such as NFS or Samba file sharing, are intended to be used on a LAN as opposed to the wider Internet. See *WAN*.

link

A pointer to a file, similar to a shortcut on Windows. Also, a specification in a web page or other source that refers to a document somewhere else. In Linux, a distinction exists between "hard" and "soft" (or "symbolic") links. Hard links, which are more limited and are now rarely used, refer to positions in a single filesystem, while symbolic links point to names of files and can easily cross boundaries between disks and systems.

Linux

The computer operating system that is the foundation for the Java Desktop System. Linux is an open source variant of the Unix operating system that was originally developed by Bell Labs in the early 1970s. "Linux" is a trademark of Linux Torvalds, the lead developer of the Linux kernel.

login

The entering of a computer system by typing one's account name (username or user ID) and password. Also refers to the account name used to gain access to a computer system.

logout

The exiting of a user from the computer system. The Linux system continues to run for other users and processes.

mail server

See *incoming mail server* and *outgoing mail server*.

main toolbar

The StarOffice toolbar located along the left edge of an open document window, which provides one-click access to certain common facilities, including spellchecking, inserting objects, inserting tables, find and replace, document layout, and others.

manpages

Traditional documentation for Linux systems, which one can read using the *man* command and other utilities. For instance, entering *man mkdir* at the command line reveals documentation for the *mkdir* command.

MBR

Master Boot Record. Occupies the first physical sector of a hard disk. During system startup, content is loaded from the MBR to main memory and executed by the BIOS. This code then loads the operating system or a bootloader.

MIME

Multipurpose Internet Mail Extension. A standard for representing different types of data, varying as widely as web pages, MP3 music files, and spreadsheets. Originally developed for electronic mail, it is now used on the Web, on local graphical desktops, and elsewhere.

MIME information file

A text file that associates MIME types with filename extensions and filename patterns. MIME information files have a *.mime* file extension.

MIME keys file

Provides information about a MIME type that is used in the user interface. For example, an icon that applications can display to represent files of that MIME type. MIME keys files have a *.keys* file extension.

MIME type

Identifies the format of a file. The MIME type enables applications to read the file. For example, an email application can use the image/jpeg MIME type to detect that a JPEG image is attached to an email.

module

Used in the context of the StarOffice office suite, as in "spreadsheet module," this term refers to one of the six software components of the office suite that share a similar menu layout and functionality. The six modules of StarOffice are StarWriter, StarCalc, StarImpress, StarDraw, StarHTML, and StarMath.

mount

To make a filesystem that is stored on a local or remote disk accessible from a directory on your workstation. When a system contains many disks or partitions of disks, each must be mounted. A mount point is the directory where a mounted filesystem appears.

MP3

A compression procedure and format for audio files, which reduces the size by a factor of 10.

multitasking

The ability of an operating system to run more than one program, or task, at a time. A preemptive multitasking operating system, such as Linux, frees up resources when ordered to by the operating system, on a priority basis, so that one application is unable to hog resources when they are needed by another program.

multithreading

Concurrently running programs divided into subcomponents, or threads. Multithreading offers efficient utilization of processors and other system resources. Multithreaded programming requires a multitasking operating system, such as Linux, capable of running many programs concurrently. A word processor can make good use of multithreading, such as printing in the background while spellchecking in the foreground. See also *process*.

Nautilus
The file manager used by JDS. Nautilus is a window that displays folders and files and lets you move around the system, view information about files, and move or open files.

network
A group of computers and/or associated devices connected by hardware and software communications facilities to share data and peripheral devices, such as printers and modems.

newbie
Someone who has just started to use and learn about a system or community of people (for instance, a "Linux newbie").

NFS
Network File System. A filesystem that allows the sharing of files across a network or (less often) the Internet, making files appear as if they were on local disks. NFS allows different makes of computers running different operating systems to share files and disk storage. See also *Samba*.

NIS
Network Information Service. Networking software that lets a system administrator control network information and services from a central server called the NIS master.

object bar
The StarOffice toolbar that provides icons for one-click access to common formatting changes, including bold and italic fonts, underline, justification, and other characteristics of text and graphics.

OMF file
Open Source Metadata Framework file. This is a file that is associated with the XML file for a technical manual. The

OMF file contains information about the manual that is used by the Help browser. OMF files have a *.omf* extension.

open source
See *free software*.

operating system
Performs tasks such as recognizing input from the keyboard, sending output to the display screen, keeping track of files and directories on the disk, and controlling peripheral devices such as disk drives and printers. The operating system is centered on the kernel, but contains other software as well. GNU/Linux, also known as Linux, is the name of the operating system used by JDS.

outgoing mail server
The computer—usually located remotely at a corporate center or Internet service provider's facility—responsible for fielding and forwarding email that a user sends to others. You need to enter the name of your outgoing mail server into the setup wizard of your JDS Email and Calendar program in order to send out email from within the Email and Calendar program.

owner
The user who has access to a file, usually the one who created the file.

PAM
Pluggable Authentication Modules. A replaceable module for system security that allows programs to be written without knowing the authentication scheme deployed. A module can be replaced later without rewriting the programs that require the security provided by the module.

partition
A logically independent section of a hard drive, or a contiguous section that is treated by the operating system as a physical drive. Linux treats partitions as if they were separate physical entities.

path
Denotes the location of a file or directory. The path is an absolute path if it begins with the root directory (that is, starts with

a slash) and includes every subdirectory—for example, */home/tadelste/Documents*. Otherwise, the path is a relative path—for example, *tadelste/Documents*. Also, a list of such locations where the computer will look for commands if the full path is not given.

permission

See *access permissions*.

PIM

A Personal Information Management software program. JDS's Email and Calendar is a PIM, performing many of the same functions as, for example, MS Outlook.

PKI

Public Key Infrastructure. An encryption apparatus for enhancing privacy and authenticating electronic communications such as email. (See also *Public key encryption*).

POP

An email protocol used to deliver mail from an incoming mail server to end users. Another such protocol is IMAP.

process

An executing program. More precisely, a collection of code, data, and other system resources, including at least one thread of execution, that performs a data-processing task. Processes can consist of multiple threads that share files, memory, and other resources, although threads on Linux are called "lightweight processes," which makes the terminology confusing. Each process executes with a different ID and different access rights.

prompt

A symbol that appears in a terminal to indicate that the computer is ready to receive a command. With Linux, the two most common prompts are the user prompt ($) and the root prompt (#).

protocol

An agreed-upon method of communications used by computers. Usually describes the messages exchanged and the rules one should follow to perform activities on a network, such as transmitting

data. Low-level protocols define the physical standards such as bit- and byte-ordering and the transmission and error detection and correction of a bit stream. High-level protocols deal with data formatting, including the syntax of messages, character sets, and sequencing of data.

proxy

An intermediary program that makes requests on behalf of clients. Proxies are often used as trusted agents to access the Internet on the client's behalf through a network firewall, and for handling requests through protocols not implemented by the user agent.

Public key encryption

A particular type of data encryption that requires every participant in a communication chain to have two separate keys: a public key and a private key. When a targeted message is being secured for transmission, data is encrypted with the recipient's public key and can be decrypted only when her private key is applied to the message. To authenticate a message—or prove that the sender is who he claims to be—the sender's private key is first used to sign data, and then the sender's public key is applied by the recipient to the message to guarantee its provenance. See also *PKI*.

ReiserFS

A general-purpose filesystem designed and implemented by a team led by Hans Reiser. It is currently supported by Linux. With Linux Version 2.4.1, it was the first journaling filesystem to be included in the standard kernel. Now it is a strong alternative to EXT3, and JDS uses ReiserFS automatically for some partitions.

root

The user account with authority to perform all system-level tasks. Also called *superuser*. A system administrator must become the root user to perform certain functions, such as creating new user accounts, changing passwords, installing most kinds of software, and carrying out other tasks ordinary users are not allowed to perform for security reasons.

RPM

A packaging and installation tool for Internet downloads, included with JDS distributions. The initials originally stood for Red Hat Package Manager. The tool produces files with a *.rpm* extension. Some RPMs contain prebuilt binaries, while some, known as source RPMs, provide all the source code required to build binaries.

Samba

A set of programs that allows JDS and other Unix or Linux systems to share files and printers with Microsoft Windows systems. Similar to NFS. Named after the protocol used for Windows file and printer sharing, SMB (now enhanced and called CIFS).

screensaver

An application that replaces the image on a screen when the screen is not in use. The screensaver application for the GNOME Desktop is XScreenSaver. A screensaver display shows images of the user on the screen when the screen is not in use.

script

A series of commands in an executable file in human-readable text format. Used to automate the repetitive execution of commands.

server

A computer on a network that is dedicated to a particular purpose and that stores all information and performs the critical functions for that purpose. For example, a web server stores all files related to a web site and performs all work necessary for hosting the web site. The systems that make use of server offerings are called *clients*.

shell

A series of text prompts offering a command-line interface to the operating system. The shell interprets the commands typed at a terminal and can also run scripts containing commands. By default, JDS offers the shell called *bash*.

signature

In the context of email, a signature is a text sequence that you set up in the Email and Calendar program and is appended to outgoing email. You can have a signature appended automatically or store multiple signatures and manually select the appropriate one for each outgoing email message.

slash (/)

The symbol used in file pathnames to separate directory and filenames.

SMTP

Simple Mail Transport Protocol. An email protocol used to send mail from end-user computers to mail servers, and exchange it among mail servers.

source code

The human-readable programming statements from which executable programs can be built.

SSH

Secure Shell. Sometimes known as Secure Socket Shell,. this is a Linux command interface and protocol for securely gaining access to a remote computer. It allows you to log in without revealing your password to potential snoopers, and encrypt all data traveling from your computer to another computer using different types of encryption algorithms.

StarCalc

The spreadsheet module of StarOffice. Functionally equivalent to MS Excel.

StarImpress

The presentation module of StarOffice. Functionally equivalent to MS PowerPoint.

StarOffice 7

The office suite included with JDS.

StarWriter

The word-processing program included with StarOffice. Functionally equivalent to MS Word.

superuser

See *root*.

symbolic link

See *link*.

tar

Tape Archive. A file-packaging tool included with Linux for combining several files into one for archiving. Tar was originally designed for tape backup and then used with other storage media. When run by itself, it produces files with a *.tar* extension. When combined with *gzip* for data compression, the resulting file extension may be *.tgz* or *.tar.gz*.

tarball

A file created with the tar utility, containing one or more other archived and possibly compressed files.

TCP

Transmission Control Protocol. Like UDP, a protocol used by some applications over the Internet or local networks using Internet software. Because TCP is the most common protocol used on top of the basic Internet protocol (IP), the whole suite of Internet protocols is sometimes casually referred to as TCP/IP.

terminal

In the past, a physical device with a keyboard and monitor connected to a central computer. The term also describes programs that emulate actual terminals. In JDS, a terminal emulation of that sort exists under System Tools and provides users with a command-line interface.

thread

See *multithreading* and *process*.

TrueType fonts

A variety of fonts designed to be printer-independent. Used in JDS systemwide to provide a high-quality look and feel.

UDP

User Datagram Protocol. Like TCP, a protocol used by some applications over the Internet or local networks using Internet software.

URI

Uniform Resource Identifier, or Universal Resource Identifier. A string that identifies a particular location in a filesystem or on the Web. This is a more general term than the more familiar URL.

URL

Uniform Resource Locator, or Universal Resource Locator. A string that identifies a resource on the Web and can be used by a web server and web browser to retrieve content over the Web. A typical URL is *http://www.sun.com/software/looking_ glass/*, which contains the protocol used to retrieve the resource (*http://*), the domain name of the system hosting the resource (*www.sun.com*), and a directory or filename that represents the actual resource fetched (*software/looking_glass/*).

user account

A set of resources for an individual logging in to a system. Generally, each person using a system has a single user account, and a special user account is set aside for the root user. However, people could have multiple accounts. Furthermore, some system services run under their own user accounts, which are never used for anyone to log in.

VESA

Video Electronic Standards Association. The consortium that defines video standards. In JDS, the term VESA appears when monitors are configured. One can choose the VESA standard and enter the horizontal and vertical frequencies as well as color depth when it is necessary to manually configure a specific monitor.

vfolder

A virtual representation of items that reside in a physical location or locations on your system. For example, a vfolder might represent the contents of several directories. In terms of menus, a vfolder is a representation in a menu of items that might be physically located in several directories.

WAN

Wide Area Network. In contrast to LAN (local area network), a WAN is a dedicated company, school, or agency network that's distributed among offices or buildings that are located many miles apart, even across countries or continents. A WAN typically uses the standard Internet communication protocols, just like a LAN or the Internet itself, but requires special equipment and configuration.

web browser

See *browser*.

Web-mail service provider

A company that provides hosting services for downloading, viewing, and distributing email. Yahoo!, Hotmail, and Gmail are among the free web mail service providers. Many, if not most, Internet service providers also provide a web-based interface for handling email.

web-safe color palette

A general-purpose palette of 216 colors. The web-safe color palette is designed to optimize the use of color on systems that support 8-bit color. The web-safe color palette is also called the Netscape color palette and the Netscape color cube.

window

A graphical frame—-with a blue name band and control buttons on top in JDS—through which you view and interact with programs and system tools on the desktop.

window manager

The layer between the user and the X Window System. It provides the desktop display and handles activities that affect a whole window, such as moving, resizing, or closing it.

wizard

A software utility that helps you perform certain computer functions by taking you through a series of interactive steps. People use wizards to set up a program for installation. Some wizards provide templates that allow a user to enter information to create documents such as web pages, letters, and spreadsheets. In JDS, some wizards are called assistants.

X Window System

The graphical windowing environment for JDS. It provides the underlying programming required by the GNOME user interface.

X11

Version 11 of the X Window System. This version that has been in use ever since the X Window System achieved widespread use and commercial viability.

XDM

The X Display Manager. A user-friendly frontend for logging in to the X Window System. It provides a graphical login screen and enables remote use of an X server.

XFree86

A free software version of the X Window System commonly used on Linux.

XML

eXtensible Markup Language. This is a powerful markup language encompassing the rules for standard document layout. It is used for for formatting documents and designing Web Services. GNOME uses XML to define schemas in the desktop, menu, icons, and configurations. XML is a standard governed by the World Wide Web Consortium (*http://www.w3.org*). The implementation of XML specifically for office software file formats—the same one found in StarOffice and OpenOffice.org—is developed and governed by the Organization for the Advancement of Structured Information Standards, or OASIS (*http://www.oasis-open.org*).

Index

We'd like to hear your suggestions for improving our indexes. Send email to *index@oreilly.com*.

About the Authors

Tom Adelstein works as a Linux consultant helping companies develop open source business strategies and running a diversified practice dedicated to providing support, maintenance, and service to Linux enterprises.

He has written professionally since 1985. Perhaps he is best known for creating a Linux replacement for Microsoft Exchange and helping get Linux moving on the IBM Mainframe. Tom also wrote the first comprehensive business accounting program for microprocessor-based systems prior to the PC revolution. His program CAS (Client Accounting System) has been ported to every known software platform since. Even as the founder of six startup companies, Tom has managed to share his experiences as a journalist and author for 20 years.

Tom's interest in the Java Desktop System stems from his background as a system specialist, which began when he became one of the first CPA IT consultants in the industry. Before CPAs were qualified to audit computer systems, Tom began developing programs to do just that. Tom became one of the first users of JDS. Working with his wife, Yvonne—a novice computer user—he dedicated his effort to making her a proficient Linux user without having to dive deep into the conceptual framework of the operating system. Today, Yvonne is an avid user of JDS.

Sam Hiser is a GNU/Linux consultant based in New York. He was a consultant to Sun Microsystems and marketing project lead of the OpenOffice.org development project through its 20 millionth download. Sam now contributes to JDShelp.org, a community site that provides support and resources to users of the Java Desktop System. He is a contributing editor for *LinuxWorld Magazine* and writes about information technology for *The Economist* and other publications. He holds an M.B.A. from The Fuqua School of Business at Duke University and lives with his wife and daughter in New York City.

Colophon

Our look is the result of reader comments, our own experimentation, and feedback from distribution channels. Distinctive covers complement our distinctive approach to technical topics, breathing personality and life into potentially dry subjects.

The image on the cover of *Exploring the JDS Linux Desktop* portrays women miners. While the traditional role of women in the Old American West was to maintain the homestead, quite a number of women flouted gender conventions to work as prospectors and miners. Undaunted by long hours spent underground shoveling earth and setting dangerous explosives, women miners dedicated their lives to financially supporting their families in times of poverty and hardship. During the California Gold Rush, women eager to "strike it rich" prospected for gold right alongside men. Female miners were also instrumental in supporting America's war effort during World War II by mining tungsten, much in demand for its wear-resistant properties.

Through their courage and toil, these miners left behind a legacy of empowerment and choice for future generations of women.

Matt Hutchinson was the production editor for *Exploring the JDS Linux Desktop*. Darren Kelly, Emily Quill, and Mary Anne Mayo provided quality control. GEX, Inc. provided production services.

Emma Colby designed the cover of this book, based on a series design by Hanna Dyer and Edie Freedman. The cover image is a 19th-century engraving from the Dover Pictorial Archive. Clay Fernald produced the cover layout with QuarkXPress 4.1 using Adobe's ITC Garamond font. David Futato designed the CD label.

David Futato designed the interior layout. The chapter opening images are from the Dover Pictorial Archive, *Marvels of the New West: A Vivid Portrayal of the Stupendous Marvels in the Vast Wonderland West of the Missouri River*, by William Thayer (The Henry Bill Publishing Co., 1888), and *The Pioneer History of America: A Popular Account of the Heroes and Adventures*, by Augustus Lynch Mason, A.M. (The Jones Brothers Publishing Company, 1884). This book was converted by Joe Wizda to FrameMaker 5.5.6 with a format conversion tool created by Erik Ray, Jason McIntosh, Neil Walls, and Mike Sierra that uses Perl and XML technologies. The text font is Linotype Birka; the heading font is Adobe Myriad Condensed; and the code font is LucasFont's TheSans Mono Condensed. The illustrations that appear in the book were produced by Robert Romano and Jessamyn Read using Macromedia FreeHand 9 and Adobe Photoshop 6. The tip and warning icons were drawn by Christopher Bing. This colophon was written by Sanders Kleinfeld.

Better than e-books

Search
inside electronic versions of thousands of books

Browse
books by category. With Safari researching any topic is a snap

Find
answers in an instant

Read books from cover to cover. Or, simply click to the page you need.

Search Safari! The premier electronic reference library for programmers and IT professionals

O'REILLY NETWORK
Safari Bookshelf

 Addison Wesley

 Sun microsystems
 O'REILLY

 ALPHA
 AdobePress

 Java
 SAMS

 Microsoft Press
 que
 New Riders

 Peachpit Press
macromedia PRESS
Cisco Press
PRENTICE HALL PTR

Related Titles Available from O'Reilly

Linux

Building Embedded Linux Systems

Building Secure Servers with Linux

The Complete FreeBSD, *4th Edition*

Even Grues Get Full

Exploring the JDS Linux Desktop

Extreme Programming Pocket Guide

Knoppix Hacks

Learning Red Hat Enterprise Linux and Fedora, *4th Edition*

Linux Cookbook

Linux Device Drivers, *3rd Edition*

Linux in a Nutshell, *4th Edition*

Linux iptables Pocket Reference

Linux Network Administrator's Guide, *3rd Edition*

Linux Pocket Guide

Linux Security Cookbook

Linux Server Hacks

Linux Unwired

Linux Web Server CD Bookshelf, *Version 2.0*

LPI Linux Certification in a Nutshell, *2nd Edition*

Managing RAID on Linux

OpenOffice.org Writer

Programming with Qt, *2nd Edition*

Root of all Evil

Running Linux, *4th Edition*

Samba Pocket Reference, *2nd Edition*

Test Driving Linux

Understanding the Linux Kernel, *2nd Edition*

Understanding Open Source & Free Software Licensing

User Friendly

Using Samba, *3rd Edition*

O'REILLY®

Our books are available at most retail and online bookstores.
To order direct: 1-800-998-9938 • *order@oreilly.com* • *www.oreilly.com*
Online editions of most O'Reilly titles are available by subscription at *safari.oreilly.com*

Keep in touch with O'Reilly

1. Download examples from our books

To find example files for a book, go to:

www.oreilly.com/catalog

select the book, and follow the "Examples" link.

2. Register your O'Reilly books

Register your book at *register.oreilly.com*

Why register your books?

Once you've registered your O'Reilly books you can:

- Win O'Reilly books, T-shirts or discount coupons in our monthly drawing.
- Get special offers available only to registered O'Reilly customers.
- Get catalogs announcing new books (US and UK only).
- Get email notification of new editions of the O'Reilly books you own.

3. Join our email lists

Sign up to get topic-specific email announcements of new books and conferences, special offers, and O'Reilly Network technology newsletters at:

elists.oreilly.com

It's easy to customize your free elists subscription so you'll get exactly the O'Reilly news you want.

4. Get the latest news, tips, and tools

www.oreilly.com

- "Top 100 Sites on the Web"—PC Magazine
- CIO Magazine's Web Business 50 Awards

Our web site contains a library of comprehensive product information (including book excerpts and tables of contents), downloadable software, background articles, interviews with technology leaders, links to relevant sites, book cover art, and more.

5. Work for O'Reilly

Check out our web site for current employment opportunities:

jobs.oreilly.com

6. Contact us

O'Reilly & Associates
1005 Gravenstein Hwy North
Sebastopol, CA 95472 USA

TEL: 707-827-7000 or 800-998-9938
(6am to 5pm PST)

FAX: 707-829-0104

order@oreilly.com
For answers to problems regarding your order or our products. To place a book order online, visit:

www.oreilly.com/order_new

catalog@oreilly.com
To request a copy of our latest catalog.

booktech@oreilly.com
For book content technical questions or corrections.

corporate@oreilly.com
For educational, library, government, and corporate sales.

proposals@oreilly.com
To submit new book proposals to our editors and product managers.

international@oreilly.com
For information about our international distributors or translation queries. For a list of our distributors outside of North America check out:

international.oreilly.com/distributors.html

adoption@oreilly.com
For information about academic use of O'Reilly books, visit:

academic.oreilly.com